MuleSoft Platform Architect's Guide

A practical guide to using Anypoint Platform's
capabilities to architect, deliver, and operate APIs

Jitendra Bafna

Jim Andrews

MuleSoft Platform Architect's Guide

Copyright © 2024 Packt Publishing

All rights reserved. No part of this book may be reproduced, stored in a retrieval system, or transmitted in any form or by any means, without the prior written permission of the publisher, except in the case of brief quotations embedded in critical articles or reviews.

Every effort has been made in the preparation of this book to ensure the accuracy of the information presented. However, the information contained in this book is sold without warranty, either express or implied. Neither the authors, nor Packt Publishing or its dealers and distributors, will be held liable for any damages caused or alleged to have been caused directly or indirectly by this book.

Packt Publishing has endeavored to provide trademark information about all of the companies and products mentioned in this book by the appropriate use of capitals. However, Packt Publishing cannot guarantee the accuracy of this information.

Group Product Manager: Aaron Tanna
Publishing Product Manager: Uzma Sheerin
Senior Editor: Nisha Cleetus
Technical Editor: Vidhisha Patidar
Copy Editor: Safis Editing
Language Support Editor: Safis Editing
Project Coordinator: K Thoshith Vignesh
Proofreader: Nisha Cleetus
Indexer: Hemangini Bari
Production Designer: Prafulla Nikalje
Marketing Coordinator: Deepak Kumar and Mayank Singh

First published: July 2024
Production reference: 1190724

Published by Packt Publishing Ltd.
Grosvenor House
11 St Paul's Square
Birmingham
B3 1RB, UK

ISBN 978-1-80512-618-8
www.packtpub.com

This book has been in progress for a long time and I want to thank my parents, who have raised me, and planted the seed of knowledge in me, and nurtured it. To my loving wife, you have always been a source of profound inspiration and relentless support. To my kids, the lifeline and the light of my life.

– Jitendra Bafna

To my wife Debra, you are a constant source of encouragement, support and love. The world is so much more fun with you and your smile in it. To my daughters Elizabeth and Grace, who are already out there being super-heros in the world, you have inspired me to be a better version of myself and always remind me to "Be Awesome". To my parents and brother for all the life steerage. And to my best friend Gil, for teaching me the fine arts of design along with the science of good architecture.

- Jim Andrews

Contributors

About the authors

Jitendra Bafna is a Senior Solution Architect and expert with vast experience in designing and solutioning the integrations and APIs solutions. He is a TOGAF 9.2 Level 1 and Level 2 certified and has expertise in various integration platforms. Jitendra has expertise in architecting and setting up MuleSoft Platform including CloudHub, CloudHub 2.0, Runtime Fabric, Hybrid, Flex Gateway, and Customer Hosted Platform. He completed his Bachelor of Engineering in Computer Science from Mumbai University and a Certificate Programme in Digital Transformation and Innovation from Indian Institute of Management Indore (IIM-I) in 2023.

I would like to first and foremost thank my parents, loving wife, and kids for their continued support, patience, and encouragement throughout the long process of writing this book. Thanks to all MuleSoft Community Managers, leaders, and members for continued support, inspiration and encouragement that I get from the MuleSoft Community.

Jim Andrews is an Integration Architecture Specialist, a MuleSoft evangelist, and a life-long learner: He has been designing and building integration solutions for dozens of clients for over 30 years in an ever-evolving technical landscape. A student of architectural methods, he holds TOGAF 9 Level 1 & 2 certifications. As a volunteer for the MuleSoft certification team, Jim helped develop exams for MuleSoft Developer L2, Integration Associate, Integration and Platform Architecture. A member of the MuleSoft Developer Community and Houston Meetup Leader, Jim presents at Meetups, Dreamforce, and Salesforce TDX. In his spare time, he co-hosts the podcast *Bits That Bind*. Jim holds BSc degree in a Computer Information Systems from Tarleton State University.

I want to thank my wife for setting the example by plowing through all the writing you've had to do for your MBA. I also want to thank my co-author Jitendra for stepping up and helping when life started throwing me curveballs. And thank you Prajakta. Every week you found a way to encourage me and make writing this book easier. Thank you Mariana Lemus for encouraging me to step up in the MuleSoft Community many years ago, and to the other community managers, Sabrina Hockett, Sabrina Marechal, Isabella Navarro - I truly believe you run the very best developer community in the world. Thanks Packt for believing in me and Jitendra and giving us the space, time, patience, and resources to get this book completed.

About the reviewers

Jose Ramon Huerga began his journey as a self-taught programmer at just 14 years old in the 80s, mastering C++. He earned a degree in Computer Engineering from the Universidad Autonoma of Madrid and has worked in the UK, Germany, Switzerland, Argentina, and Spain, leading projects in content management, integration, and API management. Jose is a MuleSoft Ambassador and leads the MuleSoft Meetup group of Barcelona. He coauthored the book "Kong: Becoming a King of API Gateways" and is a frequent speaker on APIs and integration. Married to Margarita, he is the proud father of two, Carlos and Victor. Jose loves learning new technologies and staying updated.

D. Rajesh Kumar is an Enterprise Architect with over 18 years of extensive experience in the IT industry. For the past 10+ years, he has specialized in the MuleSoft platform, working across various domains on end-to-end platform setups, architecture, design, and **Center For Enablement** (C4E) setups. He has written multiple technical blogs and has been a speaker and meetup leader, sharing his insights on advanced MuleSoft topics, integration strategies, and architectural patterns. He is a certified MuleSoft Architect and a MuleSoft Ambassador, recognized by MuleSoft for his expertise and contributions to the community. Currently, he is working as an Enterprise Architect at TCS, driving large-scale digital integration initiatives.

Table of Contents

3

Leveraging Catalyst and the MuleSoft Knowledge Hub   49

4

An Introduction to Application Networks   69

5

Speeding with Accelerators   85

6

Aligning Desired Business Outcomes to Functional Requirements   99

7

Microservices, Application Networks, EDA, and API-led Design   117

8

Non-Functional Requirements Influence in Shaping the API Architecture   143

9

Hassle-free Deployment with Anypoint iPaaS (CloudHub 1.0)   157

10

Hassle-Free Deployment with Anypoint iPaaS (CloudHub 2.0)   197

11

Containerizing the Runtime Plane with Runtime Fabric   229

12

Deploying to Your Own Data Center   269

15

Controlling API Sprawl with Universal API Management   351

18

Tackling Tricky Topics   425

Index   451

Other Books You May Enjoy   468

Preface

We are living in the era of Digital Transformation, where organizations rely on APIs to enable innovation within the business and across business partners. A robust, secure, and flexible enterprise platform is key to driving successful business outcomes which enable this innovation to thrive.

This book is a comprehensive guide exploring the capabilities and architecture of the Anypoint Platform. Beginning with an overview we will look at how business outcomes and functional requirements can be addressed in MuleSoft with out of the box Platform capabilities. This book will then walk you through best practices and the usage of core components including API Manager, Anypoint Monitoring, hosting options including CloudHub, CloudHub 2.0, Runtime Fabric Manager, and customer hosted. The book will also explore how Catalyst and Accelerators can be leveraged successfully from the start of a project through go-live and support, enabling faster, more efficient development cycles so you can release your APIs and get started innovating with the business.

By the end of this book, you will be able to master the Anypoint Platform capabilities and architect solutions that will not only enable but empower the Digital Transformation of your company.

Who this book is for

Technical Architects with knowledge of Integration and APIs looking to understand how to implement these solutions with the MuleSoft Anypoint Platform

MuleSoft Senior Developers who want to take on MuleSoft Platform Architect roles, are planning to take the MuleSoft Platform Architect certification exam and want to understand the platform capabilities in-depth.

Infrastructure Architects who need to understand and define MuleSoft hosting options and who are responsible for their organizations Anypoint Platform strategy.

What this book covers

Chapter 1: What is the MuleSoft Platform? In this chapter we will examine MuleSoft and the Anypoint Platform. We'll identify the components and how they relate to each other. And we will describe the platform's role in an organization and high level capabilities it provides as an integration Platform as a Service. We'll also review a history of traditional integration approaches and how MuleSoft solves the need for a modern integration approach.

Chapter 2: Platform foundation components and the underlying architecture, The Anypoint platform is made up of many different services, components, and capabilities. This chapter examines at a high level the major components of the platform, why they are important to integration, if and how they interact. Essentially, this chapter begins to explore the properties and characteristics of the platform including Exchange, Runtime Manager, API Manager, Monitoring. This chapter will also point to later chapters where a more detailed exploration of certain services (such as CloudHub 2.0) and design an architecture to make the best use of them.

Chapter 3: Leveraging Catalyst and the Mulesoft KnowledgeHub, MuleSoft provides customers and partners access to a framework and methodology for delivery enterprise integration. This chapter will describe the methodology and how it combines business outcomes with technology and organization enablement using a library of artifacts, templates, and examples gathered from the field across numerous MuleSoft projects and deployments.

Chapter 4: Introduction to Application Networks, The structure produced through API-led connectivity is a network of nodes and applications. In this chapter we will discuss the logical concept of the application network, the physical manifestation, the benefits and the challenges of the network. This chapter will show how designing an application network not only enables the creation of a composable enterprise but also how it impacts the different platform deployment approaches.

Chapter 5: Speeding with Accelerators, MuleSoft has developed and made available 8 accelerators accessible through Anypoint Exchange. In this chapter, the reader will learn how these accelerators can save time across the various stages of the API lifecycle. The reader will gain a perspective on how the building blocks in each accelerator can be used and customized and what different assets, patterns, mappings, and endpoints have been included. Following a use case of a retail music store, the reader will walk through setting up and customizing the Retail Accelerator.

Chapter 6: Aligning desired business outcomes to functional requirements, A critical step in getting the most out of the MuleSoft platform is to understand the desired business outcomes and turn those outcomes into functional requirements. This chapter looks at how functional requirements line up with the platform capabilities. The reader will look at how these functional requirements can influence architecture decisions and design patterns such as data models, granularity, concurrency, and HTTP methods. The chapter will include examples of using bounded context data models vs. enterprise data models, using asynchronous APIs with polling and callbacks.

Chapter 7: Microservices, Application Networks, and API led design, The MuleSoft Platform is very flexible and is able to accommodate multiple approaches to architecture design. This chapter will address popular architecture design approaches and how these will look when deployed to (or managed by) the Anypoint Platform. The chapter will also compare and contrast the architecture approaches, examine pros and cons of each, and suggest best practices for designing solutions.

Chapter 8: Non-Functional Requirements influence in shaping the Architecture, Every architect must manage a set of non-functional requirements. These non-functional requirements describe the technical constraints of the solution and document how the solution should behave. What kind of performance is expected? What about availability? What happens when disaster strikes? Who can access and when? Is security critical or not? What kind of encryption is needed? The reader will see in this chapter how the answers to these questions influence the architecture design and how the design should use MuleSoft Platform.

Chapter 9: Hassle-free deployment with Anypoint iPaaS (CloudHub), In this chapter the reader will learn approaches to deployment using MuleSoft CloudHub. This chapter will look at what are the differences and how are the two cloud iPaaS environments similar. This chapter will also look at the different ways to deploy your solution to the Anypoint CloudHub offerings and the pros and cons of each of these methods. It will also examine licensing implications of your design and architecture approach.

Chapter 10: Hassle-free deployment with Anypoint iPaaS (CloudHub 2.0), In this chapter the reader will learn approaches to deployment using MuleSoft CloudHub 2.0. This chapter will look at what are the differences and how are the two cloud iPaaS environments similar. This chapter will also look at the different ways to deploy your solution to the Anypoint CloudHub 2.0 offerings and the pros and cons of each of these methods. It will also examine licensing implications of your design and architecture approach.

Chapter 11: Containerizing the Runtime Plane with Runtime Fabric, This chapter will introduce the Anypoint Runtime Fabric (RTF). The chapter will look at the basic concepts of containerization using some of the industry standards such as EKS and AKS. It will then look at how RTF aligns with these container concepts and platforms. The chapter will also examine the different approaches MuleSoft supports with RTF, including self-managed containers and Anypoint managed containers.

Chapter 12: Deploying to your own Data Center, As a hybrid integration platform as a service, MuleSoft can run anywhere including inside a businesses data center on the businesses own iron. This chapter takes a look at how to set up the server to run the MuleSoft engine and how to connect it to the control panel so it can be managed. The chapter will also take a brief look at Private Cloud Edition (PCE) and how it allows an organization to run both the control plane as well as the runtime plane from their own hardware and servers from within their own development center.

Chapter 13: Government Cloud and EU Control Plane: Special considerations, This chapter will show the reader some important differences when working with the Government Cloud as well as the EU Control Plane. The chapter will give a brief introduction to FEDRAMp compliance. The reader will learn the government cloud is deployed in a special AWS region which is FEDRamp compliment.

Chapter 14: Functional Monitoring, Alerts, and Operation Monitors: Advanced monitoring techniques, This chapter will show the reader what are the capabilities provided by Anypoint Monitoring and what are the different alerts that can be configured on APIs and Servers. The reader will learn about Functional Monitoring and some of the advanced features of Anypoint Monitoring.

Chapter 15: Controlling API Sprawl in one Platform with Universal API Management, This chapter will show the reader how to manage MuleSoft APIs and Non MuleSoft APIs lifecycle using API Manager. The reader will learn Mule Gateway, Flex Gateway, Service Mesh, API Proxies, Analytics, Alerts etc.

Chapter 16: Addressing non-functional requirements from thought to operate, This chapter will show the reader about implementing Non-Functional requirements like HA, Fault Tolerance, Resilience and allocating and optimizing the vCores to enhance the application performance.

Chapter 17: Prepare for exam success, This chapter will show the reader how to prepare for the MuleSoft Certified Platform Architecture Exam - Level 1 and eligibility criteria for the exam. It will tell what are the important topics for the MCPA exam and recommendations and guidelines for the exam.

Chapter 18: Tackling Tricky Topics, The MuleSoft Exams are not meant to be tricky. They have been designed and developed to set the bar at just the right level to ensure the exam takers know the material. Occasionally some of the topics covered in the Platform Architecture exam are a bit more difficult and can seem tricky. This chapter will look at the topics that may be more difficult.

To get the most out of this book

Software/hardware covered in the book	Operating system requirements
Java 8 or Java 17	Windows, macOS, or Linux
Maven	
Anypoint Studio IDE and Anypoint Platform	

Download the color images

We also provide a PDF file that has color images of the screenshots and diagrams used in this book. You can download it here: `https://packt.link/gbp/9781805126188`.

> **Disclaimer on images**
>
> Some images in this title are presented for contextual purposes, and the readability of the graphic is not crucial to the discussion. Please refer to our free graphic bundle to download the images. You can download the images from `https://packt.link/gbp/9781805126188`

Conventions used

There are number of text conventions used throughout this book.

`Code in text`: Indicates code words in text, database table names, folder names, filenames, file extensions, pathnames, dummy URLs, user input, and Twitter handles. Here is an example: "The backup and restore process is simple via `rtfctl`."

A block of code is set as follows:

```
<plugin>
  <groupId>org.mule.tools.maven</groupId>
  <artifactId>mule-maven-plugin</artifactId>
  <version>3.8.6</version>
  <extensions>true</extensions>
  <configuration>
    <standaloneDeployment>
      <muleHome>${mule.home }</muleHome>
      <muleVersion>${app.runtime}</muleVersion>
    </standaloneDeployment>
  </configuration>
</plugin>
```

Any command-line input or output is written as follows:

```
./rtfctl backup <path_to_store_backup>
```

Bold: Indicates a new term, an important word, or words that you see onscreen. For instance, words in menus or dialog boxes appear in **bold**. Here is an example: "Checking specifically for **Design Architecture & Implementation**, as shown in *Figure 3.1*, we find a playbook step that may be helpful.

> **Tips or important notes**
> Appear like this.

Get in touch

Feedback from our readers is always welcome.

General feedback: If you have questions about any aspect of this book, email us at customercare@packtpub.com and mention the book title in the subject of your message.

Errata: Although we have taken every care to ensure the accuracy of our content, mistakes do happen. If you have found a mistake in this book, we would be grateful if you would report this to us. Please visit www.packtpub.com/support/errata and fill in the form.

Piracy: If you come across any illegal copies of our works in any form on the internet, we would be grateful if you would provide us with the location address or website name. Please contact us at copyright@packt.com with a link to the material.

If you are interested in becoming an author: If there is a topic that you have expertise in and you are interested in either writing or contributing to a book, please visit authors.packtpub.com.

Share Your Thoughts

Once you've read *MuleSoft Platform Architect's Guide*, we'd love to hear your thoughts! Scan the QR code below to go straight to the Amazon review page for this book and share your feedback.

https://packt.link/r/1805126180

Your review is important to us and the tech community and will help us make sure we're delivering excellent quality content.

Download a free PDF copy of this book

Thanks for purchasing this book!

Do you like to read on the go but are unable to carry your print books everywhere?

Is your eBook purchase not compatible with the device of your choice?

Don't worry, now with every Packt book you get a DRM-free PDF version of that book at no cost.

Read anywhere, any place, on any device. Search, copy, and paste code from your favorite technical books directly into your application.

The perks don't stop there, you can get exclusive access to discounts, newsletters, and great free content in your inbox daily

Follow these simple steps to get the benefits:

1. Scan the QR code or visit the link below

https://packt.link/free-ebook/9781805126188

2. Submit your proof of purchase

3. That's it! We'll send your free PDF and other benefits to your email directly

1

What is the MuleSoft Platform?

In this chapter, we start by taking a high-level view of the MuleSoft Anypoint Platform. We will then look back at the evolution of different integration approaches and how the current modern integration approach fits within the MuleSoft platform. We will look at the different components that form the core building blocks of MuleSoft and how they relate to each other. These components form the basis of the architectural capabilities available in this platform. Next, the chapter will describe where this technology fits within any organization and in particular those looking to seize the future through modernization, digital innovation, and business transformation. We will also look at what MuleSoft is capable of as an **integration Platform as a Service (iPaaS)** and why MuleSoft is important in the modern integration approach.

In this chapter we're going to cover the following main topics:

- What is MuleSoft and iPaaS?
- How have integration approaches evolved?
- The architectural capabilities of MuleSoft
- Solving the modern challenge to integration
- How the MuleSoft architecture delivers modern integrations

Technical requirements

Many of the MuleSoft components and services discussed in this chapter are available by signing up for a free trial MuleSoft account and by downloading the MuleSoft Anypoint Studio. Also, you will find a GitHub repository for the chapter here as well.

- Download MuleSoft Anypoint Studio, (visit `https://www.mulesoft.com/lp/dl/anypoint-mule-studio`.

- Fill out the form providing:

  - email address

  - operating system

- Check your email to get the download link to the latest Anypoint Studio version. (Note this link will only be valid for 24 hours.)

- Sign up for a free 30-Day MuleSoft account, visit `Anypoint.MuleSoft.com/login/signup`

What is MuleSoft and iPaaS?

Trying to define the MuleSoft platform requires us to look at it through several different lenses. There is much ground to cover when examining the Anypoint Platform because it addresses so many aspects of API Integration but at its heart is a Mule carrying the load and doing a great deal of heavy lifting.

Through a developer lens, MuleSoft is:

- A comprehensive directory of services,

- A pre-built connector,

- A building block, and

- A powerful developer portal.

It boasts a customizable, searchable public and private API directory called **Anypoint Exchange**. The integrated tooling with **Anypoint Design Center** makes the platform capable of designing, developing, and versioning API specifications using all the industry standard languages and presents them for testing using mocking services and publishing these API specifications through Exchange so other developers can find and use these building blocks.

Through an architect lens, the MuleSoft runtime engine is a platform providing deployment solutions capable of:

- microservice style API and application isolation,
- horizontal and vertical scaling,
- zero downtime deployment,
- container-based runtimes,
- on-premises and managed cloud based runtimes.

These capabilities are augmented with **Anypoint API Monitoring** and analytics features which share an operations lens.

Through operations lens, MuleSoft can be seen as:

- an **API Security** and
- **API Management** platform.

The platform has comprehensive management tools and universal API management capabilities to manage **Service Level Agreements (SLAs)**, versioning, and security, and to apply policies to MuleSoft developed APIs as well as non-Mule APIs developed with other tooling running in remote environments.

The Anypoint platform is all of these things. Its performance in these areas is one of the reasons it regularly lands as a Leader in Gartner's magic quadrant for Enterprise iPaaS solution as well as for Full Life Cycle API Management Solution.

Gartner was first to describe the term iPaaS defining it as "*a suite of cloud services enabling development, execution and governance of integration flows connecting any combination of premises and cloud-based processes, services, applications, and data within individual or across multiple organizations*". Garner glossary) As this definition suggests (cloud services), the MuleSoft Anypoint platform has been developed using an API first design approach, making all of the services highlighted above (and detailed throughout the rest of this book) available as APIs themselves.

MuleSoft is a sophisticated, powerful, dynamic, and feature rich integration platform solution providing technical architects with the tools and capabilities needed to design and deliver solutions for complex integration requirements.

This book is intended for those who need to see this platform through the architects' lens. The MuleSoft Platform Architect's job is to keep all these viewpoints of the platform in mind and understand how the combination and interaction of these different platform building blocks work with each other. Doing this will enable the organization to create flexible, scalable, and reusable solutions capable of driving the business vision forward through innovation and digital transformation.

How have integration approaches evolved?

An iPaaS is the latest generation in a long line of Integration solutions which have evolved over the years. The need to integrate applications has been around practically since the second computer system was developed and architects realized the first system offered data and functionality that would add value to the second system. Let's take a quick look at how integration approaches have evolved across major innovations leading to this newest generation of iPaaS. To help us visualize the different approaches, consider the following simplified use case.

J&J Music Store Use Case

J&J Music is a business founded in 1970 that sells records direct from the publishers. They regularly receive large shipments from the publishers and these records must be added to the inventory available for sale. The company developed an inventory system allowing them to keep up with the number of records they are carrying in their store. Using this system, they were able to increase the quantity on hand when new shipments of a record arrive. As records leave the shelves of the store, they can update the system to reflect the new quantity. This was all done manually by the inventory management team. A different team handles the sales.

The sales clerks in the store eventually realize they also need a system to help keep up with all the orders being placed, so they build a Sales System to track the orders and invoices. As the store grew, the sales clerks realized they were often unsure if a product was available for purchase. They needed to login to the Inventory system and check the quantity before completing the sales transaction. However, because they are not part of the inventory management team, they do not update the inventory quantity.

This worked for a while but with multiple clerks serving multiple customers, the quantity in the inventory system became unreliable. The business then decided to integrate these two systems so each of the clerks would see the same inventory totals. Moreover, the sales system would automatically decrease the inventory system total for a product whenever a purchase was made. This would allow the inventory management team to reduce staff as they would now only need to update the system when new product shipments arrived.

Point to Point

We learned in our geometry classes the shortest distance between two points is a straight line. In the early days of systems development, the architectural straight line between systems was the most direct approach to integrating them. And despite advances in technology, many if not most organizations still have systems connected with **point-to-point** integration.

Thinking about the use case described previously, an architect designed a point-to-point solution, seen here in Figure 1.1, to integrate the inventory system and the sales system. The design diagram as seen in *Figure 1.1* shows the relationship between the Inventory System and the Sales System.

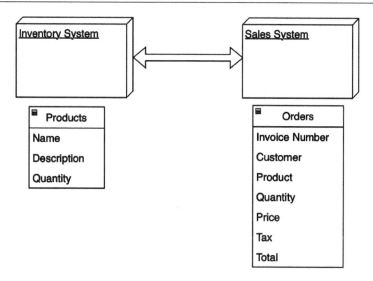

Figure 1.1 - Inventory and Sales Systems with example tables

As you can see in this figure, the connection from the inventory system to the sales system is a direct connection. Developers for J&J Music wrote new code in the Sales system to connect directly to the Inventory system database. The developers needed the exact details of the inventory system's connection requirements and protocols as well as the specifics of how and where the product information was stored. You can see in the diagram the table and fields were captured as well.

This integration approach begins simple enough but begins to break down as more and more systems are added to the system landscape with each system requiring data from the other systems. Even without additional systems this approach is fragile as it requires each system to know the details about every other system it will connect with. If the inventory system changed any of those details, the integration would cease to work.

Let's say the Inventory system decided to normalize their database and now they have a product master table, and a product inventory table. Now, with the quantity moved to the product inventory table, every integration must update code for this one integration point to continue to work. In *Figure 1.1* this doesn't seem like a big problem to the J&J Music architect because only 1 other system is affected. However, in a point-to-point integration approach, we must confront the **N(N-1) rule**. This formula, where N is the number of systems being integrated, identifies the number of connections needed in total for the integration. In *Figure 1.1* this number is *2(2-1) = 2*. Now let's refer to *Figure 1.2* which introduces a third system, the Accounting System.

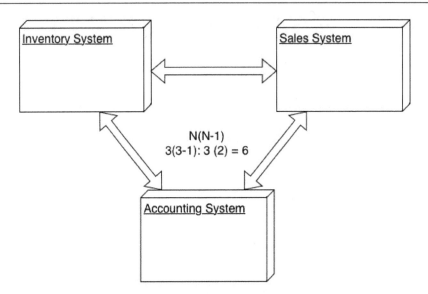

Figure 1.2 - Addition of Accounting System and Connections Formula

As you can see in this new architecture diagram, adding an accounting system and integrating it with both the Inventory and Sales systems means we have 6 connections to consider: *3(3-1) = 6*. Adding a 4th system would take the total to 12 and so on and so forth. The complexity associated with making changes to systems integrated with a point-to-point strategy now becomes exponential with each new system added to the landscape. If we consider an organization with hundreds of applications, all integrated using this pattern, it's easy to understand why the architecture term *"Big Ball of Mud"* was coined. *Figure 1.3* shows a not unreasonable 14 system connected point to point.

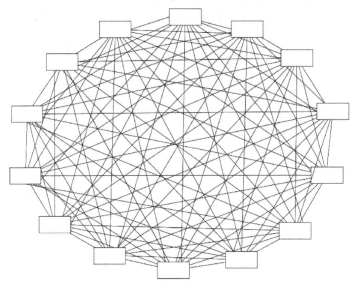

Figure 1.3 - Big Ball of Mud Architecture

With 14 systems in *Figure 1.3*, the number of connections to manage is 182!

The limitations to point-to-point integration include:

- **Tight Coupling**: Each system must be aware of the other systems and any change made to one potentially impacts all the other systems it communicates with.

- **Scalability**: Adding new systems and components to this kind of integration causes the management and maintenance of these systems to increase in complexity. At a certain point this architecture becomes known as the big ball of mud.

- **Interoperability**: Each system will likely have its own unique technology footprint with unique protocols and connectivity requirements. These differences make it increasingly difficult to make point-to-point connections and integrations.

Middleware and Remote Procedure Calls

The limitations and issues with point-to-point integration became more pronounced as large enterprises and business continued to expand their software footprint. Systems began moving off of mainframes and onto midrange systems such as IBM's AS/400 and even onto desktop applications developed using a client-server architecture.

During this time, **Remote Procedure Call (RPC)** was developed to improve the communication detail dependency when calling a remote computer system over the network. For the client initiating the call, the RPC appears to be a local function call. RPC using some middleware on the network would handle the requests coming from a client. The RPC Framework provides standards for protocols and data encoding and handles the network communications.

Standards were developed to handle the different data encoding requirements of different systems. **Common Object Request Broker Architecture (CORBA)** and the more modern protocol **gRPC** are two examples of of these standards. CORBA (as the name implies) used an Object Request Broker (ORB) to manage and standardize calls between systems and was released by the Object Management Group in the early 1990's.

Around the same time frame, Microsoft and Java had similar protocols release. Java RMI allows objects in one Java virtual machine (VM) to invoke methods on objects in another VM. It is specific to the Java programming language and is primarily used for building distributed applications in Java. DCOM is a proprietary technology developed by Microsoft for building distributed applications on Windows platforms. It is an extension of the **Component Object Model (COM)** and allows objects to communicate across a network. DCOM is specific to the Windows operating system.

gRPC is a modern RPC framework released by Google in 2016 using HTTP/2 as the communication protocol and is also language agnostic, a trait it shares with CORBA.

Enterprise Service Bus

While RPC is a communication method, the **Enterprise Service Bus (ESB)** is an architectural pattern and software infrastructure enabling and facilitating the communication of applications across a common **middleware** layer. The concept and first ESB products began to show up in early 2000. Unlike the RPC approach which relied on a request-response interaction, the ESB introduced a broad range of integration functionality based on messaging patterns supporting many different communication approaches including **request-response**, **publish-subscribe**, and yes even point-to-point. In many cases, products included message transformation, service orchestration, and message routing.

The ESB also enabled enterprises to begin considering ways to connect many of their legacy systems which had stood as data silo's previously along with external partners.

Gregor Hohpe and Bobby Woolf's seminal book *Enterprise Integration Patterns* was published in 2003 and described these message-based integration design patterns. This was a major influence on many products and ESBs but perhaps none so much as MuleSoft. In 2007, Ross Mason and Dave Rosenberg introduced MuleSoft as a lightweight ESB platform. From very early on, this platform included a framework implementation of the patterns described by Hohpe and Woolf.

Let's go back now to the J&J Music store. Some 35 years after opening the store has become a global success. Ownership successfully transitioned to cassette tapes, and CD's and have been investigating a joint venture with a device manufacture that allows users to carry digital music in their pocket. The integration requirements over the years have grown significantly. Now the CIO has decided to purchase an ESB platform to support an aggressive plan to integrate a new accounting system. Refer to Figure 1.4 which shows an ESB architecture for J&J Music Store.

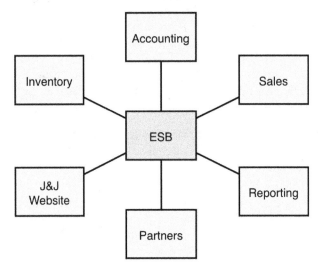

Figure 1.4 - ESB Hub & Spoke Architecture

In *Figure 1.4* we can see the ESB performing as a message broker. Each system can produce messages which are routed to the message broker. The broker then determines which system to forward the message to.

At one point, ESBs were widely adopted in enterprise IT for their potential to simplify integration and communication between diverse systems. However, several factors contributed to the decline in popularity of traditional ESBs:

- **Complex Configurations**: Setting up and configuring an ESB could be complex. The configuration and maintenance of ESBs often required specialized skills, making it challenging for some organizations to manage.

- **Performance Overhead**: ESBs introduced additional layers and processing steps, potentially leading to performance overhead. In situations where high-performance, low-latency communication was crucial, the overhead of an ESB became a concern.

- **Monolithic Architecture**: Traditional ESBs often followed a monolithic architecture, making them less suitable for the modern trend toward microservices and more lightweight, modular architectures. Microservices and containerization became popular for their flexibility and scalability, and traditional ESBs struggled to adapt to these trends.

- **Need for Agility**: Modern businesses require agility to quickly adapt to changing market conditions. Traditional ESBs, with their heavyweight and centralized nature, could hinder the agility of development and deployment processes.

- **Service Mesh and API Gateways**: Newer approaches, like service meshes and API gateways, emerged as alternatives that were more focused on specific aspects of communication and often provided a more flexible and decentralized architecture.

- **Evolution of Integration Patterns**: Event-driven architectures and messaging systems gained popularity as alternative approaches to integration. These architectures often focused on lightweight communication between services and embraced more decentralized and scalable patterns.

- **Rise of Cloud-Native Technologies**: The rise of cloud-native technologies, containerization, and serverless computing shifted the focus toward more modular and scalable solutions. ESBs were designed in an era before these technologies, faced challenges in adapting to the new paradigm.

- **API-Centric Approaches**: Organizations increasingly adopted API-centric approaches to integration. Technologies like RESTful APIs and lightweight messaging became more prevalent for connecting applications and services.

While traditional ESBs have lost some of their popularity, the concept of integration remains crucial. Organizations have just transitioned to a more modern and agile integration approach allowing them to align with the evolving landscape of technology and business requirements.

Service Oriented Architecture

About the same time ESB platforms were being introduced to the enterprise IT discussions, **Service-oriented Architecture (SOA)** began to gain popularity. In the late 1990s and early 2000s, enterprise applications were being built at web applications using n-tier designs and leveraging patterns such as Model-View-Controller. Browser, Java, and Microsoft based front ends were handling thin client UX functionality, and business logic was developed and run on Java and Microsoft applications running on a web server and using database connectors to run SQL queries and stored procedures on a normalized relational database management system (RDBMS) running on a different server.

Enterprises had just made it past the Y2K crises and businesses began a serious movement away from monolithic mainframe-based systems. SOA was a brand-new approach requiring a major paradigm shift which focused on developing applications from multiple distinct services.

Like ESB, SOA was presented as an architectural pattern and did not come with generally agreed upon protocols or industry standards. SOA is often mistakenly exclusively associated with **SOAP Web Services**. However, SOAP Web Services is a messaging protocol defining how to describe interacting with an object in another system. SOA can be implemented using SOAP-based services and well-structured XML or using RESTful web services or both. SOAP uses the **Web Services Definition Language (WSDL)** as the standard for describing the functionality offered by the web service.

SOA is generally defined as having 4 main components:

- Service Provider
- Service Broker
- Service Registry
- Service Consumer

Given that an Enterprise Service Bus (ESB) is implemented as a platform enabling and facilitating services across a common middleware layer, SOA is often implemented using an ESB platform. Also, it is worth mentioning that **Universal Description, Discovery, and Integration (UDDI)**, the Service Registry mentioned above, is in one sense, the grandfather of API Portals. It's adoption however was limited in comparison to other directories which followed.

Representational State Transfer (REST Services)

Representational State Transfer (REST) is an architectural approach to building network-based systems defined by Dr. Roy Fielding primarily in *Chapter 5* of his dissertation "*Architectural Styles and the Design of Network-based Software Architectures*", published in 2000. It is often abused as simply a protocol based on JSON message structure and HTTP verbs and in fact, in many cases seems to have taken on a life of its own.

The most common imagery used to describe Fielding's vision of RESTful Web Services is, appropriately enough, a web site. Each page represents a particular state of the system, responding to parameters and requests. And each page contains knowledge of where the consumer may wish to navigate next. For example, an invoice page may be requested for a specific customer. The resulting page may be a list of products on an invoice. Navigation here may be to a specific product on the invoice. From there the consumer may be able to navigate to the quantity of the product in the inventory. And from the quantity, navigation to a backorder page where additional product could be purchased. The message payload should include hyper-links indicating valid navigation the API consumer may wish to take.

This network-based approach provided the foundation for an integration approach which MuleSoft refers to as the Application Network. REST provides a common mechanism, and indeed a language, with which to interact and integrate with the data and processes of an organization's systems and applications, and to do so in a reusable way. This Application network is discussed in more detail in *Chapter 4* of this book.

Whereas SOAP can be used over any transport layer, RESTful Web Services operate over HTTP and typically use the verbs defined by the protocol: GET, POST, PUT, PATCH, DELETE. Like SOAP, RESTful web services initially used Swagger as the standard for describing the functionality of these services. Swagger eventually became **Open API Specification (OAS)**; you can think of this as Swagger 2.0. RAML was also introduced as a standard for describing REST functionality as well.

iPaaS

Whether an organization has point-to-point, or the latest ESB technology, or some combination, one thing they all had in common was the need to acquire compute resources, deploy servers to the data center, install and maintain software, and upgrade to newer versions of the software while trying to avoid as much down time as possible. Enter the iPaaS. With the iPaaS, organizations can fast track the implementation of RESTful APIs and create re-usable building blocks. These building blocks can operate on different compute resources running on-premise as well as in the cloud.

In 2002 Jeff Bezos issued his now famous *"API Mandate"* memo and the race to the cloud was on. As described earlier in the section on SOA, enterprises were moving away from the monolithic system. They were also beginning to move away from their data centers and into the cloud.

This move to the cloud was a gradual move for some organizations. One major energy organization, for example, began by moving away from allocating specific, individual servers to individual projects and towards virtual computing to cut down on dock-to-rack time. The virtual computing was still running on servers and hardware, operating inside the company's data center and still required operations and maintenance teams to manage the compute, memory, and storage allocations. This also meant the operations team had to stay ahead of new hardware requests and production system growth. And when development or testing environments were idle, they couldn't easily reallocate the resources for other purposes.

For other companies, the ability to acquire compute services without the costs of building out a data center provided a huge economic advantage. A major solar energy company was born in the cloud on **Salesforce** and never had to develop their own "on-premises" data center. If additional databases or file space or web apps were needed, the company simply added those services in the cloud space they occupied. About the only on-premises information computing done took the form of spreadsheets on company laptops.

Eventually Cloud Computing, such as Amazon's **AWS**, meant that every aspect of the data center could be allocated and provisioned as a service. Many companies have now moved their data center entirely to the cloud and other newer companies were born in the cloud and never had their own data center. Need a CPU? It's a service. More memory? A service. Private Network? Also a service. Message queue? Web Server? IP address? Database? Service, service, service, and service. Need a system to help manage your customers (CRM)? A service. Eventually, every aspect of the on-premises data center was made available as a service, on a Cloud Computing platform.

MuleSoft leveraged cloud computing early on, and the platform's architectural approach to integration enabled companies all along the spectrum of cloud computing to develop solutions to help enable their digital transformation. The iPaaS offers companies the ability to buy a subscription for compute, storage, memory, runtime, monitoring, security, messaging, logging, as well as scheduling, alerting, cataloging, and management of integration components. All these services provided almost immediately upon request and for the most part, outside of any data center acquisition requirements.

Earlier, we outlined some of the reasons ESBs began to lose popularity as an integration solution. Let's take a quick look at some of the reasons iPaaS took over some of that popularity and why it is considered a more modern and flexible solution compared to plain ESBs.

- **Cloud-native architecture**: iPaaS solutions are typically well suited for cloud based environments. Traditional ESBs require adaptation to get them to work with cloud services

- **Low-code/no-code**: the iPaaS platforms such as MuleSoft provide ways to deliver integrations with clicks not code. Most ESBs require specialized skills and complex configuration.

- **Scalability**: Being born in the cloud and cloud-native, iPaaS solutions have been built with scalability in mind whereas ESBs were not initially designed to dynamically scale across a distributed platform and cloud environment.

- **Modularity and Microservices**: iPaaS solutions are designed with a great deal of flexibility when it comes to integration design patterns and even protocols.

- **Focused on an API-Centric approach**: the iPaaS platform places an emphasis on using an API integration approach enabling the "network-based", or application network concept mentioned earlier. ESBs used a more traditional service based, often pub/sub based, approach to integration and was not as easily aligned to the API approach.

Understanding the historical context and the approach to integration taken over the years we've just looked at, we can begin to look at the MuleSoft Platform through the architecture lens. This lens will help us identify where gaps exist in the current organization, the problems they may be causing, and how to replace them with new capabilities. But before we take a high-level look at the services and capabilities that make up the MuleSoft Anypoint platform, let's consider the challenges organizations continue to face when it comes to integration.

What is the modern challenge to integration?

Organizations have experienced challenges to integration for decades. Integration of applications across an enterprise has always been a complex task often made the more difficult because of early architectural design decisions. For example, point-to-point integration of two systems as described earlier in this chapter seemed like a good idea with lots of pros until the number of systems increased beyond two.

Truthfully though, increasing beyond two applications wasn't the real problem. In many organizations, the real issue is either not prioritizing architecture as a discipline or employing "*it's just*" architecture. As in, "*it's just one extra system, go ahead and have it connect to the database and read this table*". Because integrating three systems doesn't seem like that much more than integrating two. And four systems don't seem like that much more than three. Of course, the problem here is before long there are hundreds of critical systems in your organization, and you have ended up with the "*big ball of mud*" architecture shown earlier, unable to maneuver as quickly as the business wants to. IT is then left holding the bag trying to just keep the wheels on with no capacity to take on new projects or engage with the business to understand their ever-growing list of value-added ideas and innovation and desired business outcomes.

Fortunately, volumes have been written about integration across the enterprise because of all the challenges inherent to the effort. With all this history and with all these patterns, solutions, technologies, dissertations, architecture, methodologies, and platforms, we can now assert that the challenge of integration is resolved! Right?

Sadly, this is not the case. Let's look at two primary reasons the industry has yet to find total enlightenment when it comes to integration.

Breaking the law is harder than you think

For many organizations, the law Melvin Conway introduced in 1967 has proven as difficult to overcome as Newton's law of gravity from 1687. Conway's law states the design of systems reflect the communication structure of the organization. In many of the organizations I have spoken with about integration, the *chair-to-keyboard* or *swivel-chair* integration approach to integration is the *pattern* used to connect applications because the applications exist in the same silos as the organization operating the application. The best they can hope for is an email, ideally with a spreadsheet attached so they can capture the parts they need in their own system. This is one of the same challenges observed by Hohpe and Woolf in their *Enterprise Integration Patterns* published in 2004. What they suggested was that the departments and the IT teams in an organization must change how they interact with each other if enterprise integration is to be successful.

Changing these policies takes an extraordinary effort. At one company, the CIO dictated a three-word strategy: *best of breed*. This was repeated all the way down through the ranks of the business and the IT organizations. The strategy described a policy which encouraged bringing in the very best system available for the corporate function needed. And if it couldn't be found off the shelf, then build the best system. The strategy also established a policy to develop a central architecture team and an **enterprise application integration (EAI)** information bus platform capable of integrating these best of breed applications using asynchronous messaging with an enterprise **canonical** model.

The result was impressive. The mission critical applications in the organization were able to publish and subscribe to broadly agreed upon data structures. And the data from one system was made available to other systems in near real-time. However, this was not without significant costs and drawbacks. Maintenance and upgrade costs of the EAI platform, in addition to cost overruns of bespoke applications built when the marketplace couldn't yield the called for *best of breed* application, eventually forced the organization to abandon the strategy. A new CIO called for a new strategy, *fit for purpose*, recommending the business look for COTS (commercial off-the-shelf) solutions bundling more functions together at the expense of any one of them being perhaps not quite the best you could build or buy.

While each CIO had their own reasons and their own strategy, the key to the success for each one was how well they were able to promote the new policy and gain buy in from all of the relevant stakeholders in the business and in IT.

Business innovation at the speed of technical debt

If the silos of business isn't challenging enough, the speed at which businesses must innovate just to keep up may give an integration architect whiplash. Bundled with a load of technical debt however, can significantly slow the speed of innovation.

In his seminal work, The Innovators Dilemma, Clayton Christensen described how leading companies in businesses as diverse as computer manufacturers, hard drive manufacturers, and excavators were disrupted by innovative changes in technology. None of these great businesses were prepared for or able to move quickly when these new companies with new technology began to shift from idea to market leader. As Christensen describes it, the legacy firms are victims of their own success. And, in many of these cases, the new company or division also doesn't have the technical debt held by the incumbent technology or company.

Today, innovation is being driven across most industries through digital transformation. Digital transformation of the companies culture. Digital transformation of the supply chain. Digital transformation of the sales and marketing. Digital transformation of the relationship with the customer. Now more than ever, having the right data at the right time from the right place is important, perhaps even critical, to the operations and long term success of a business.

At the same time many companies are asking their IT departments to do more with less. IT is asked to work faster and harder (often stated as "*work hard play hard*" to soften the blow). They're asked to set up better automated deployment or change the project methodology to something leaner. But IT is very often just trying to keep the basic operations of all the systems under their remit running. So, the business finds a way which may involve spreadsheets, loading files, extracting files, or even standing up a simple web portal. Almost all of this technical debt which only adds to IT's workload.

I observed a payroll process involving a spreadsheet of pay, extracted from a mainframe system and manually modified before attempting to load it into PeopleSoft. And the source for the paychecks going out? The spreadsheet itself, after loading it to PeopleSoft, was sent to the payroll company. Possibly after a few more "*adjustments*". This makes digital transformation of payroll difficult if not impossible and is a daunting challenge for integration to tackle.

In some cases, IT has tried to get ahead of the curve by starting a cloud migration journey. Shifting assets and resources to a cloud provider has helped eliminate some of the overhead associated with maintaining all the servers and databases in the data center. The cloud can also help IT projects provision, start up, and shut down servers in minutes or hours. This sounds and works great until the request comes in to integrate this new system in the cloud with the systems still in the data center.

What can be done if complex, siloed organizations and siloed data and technical debt have stymied innovation in the IT department and the business leadership just showed up with a new idea to transform lagging sales and underperforming quarterly reports with digital innovation? Let's look next at the capabilities and services in the MuleSoft platform which help address these issues and then why APIs are so important in the modern approach to integrating systems across the business.

The Architectural capabilities of MuleSoft

The MuleSoft Anypoint platform can be used to deliver integration solutions architected on premises, in the cloud, or a combination of on premise and cloud. The latter is referred to as **hybrid IPaaS**. Note the individual services and capabilities available in the Anypoint platform depend on the subscription purchased.

In this section, we will look at how the Anypoint Platform is organized. We will look at the options available in the platform on where to run integration applications and where to manage the platform. We will take a brief look into some of the reasons why organizations will choose one option over another.

Planes of operations

There are two logical "planes", **Control Plane** and **Runtime Plane**, within which the components and services of the MuleSoft Anypoint Platform exist and operate. In the Anypoint Platform high level diagram shown in *Figure 1.5* we can see the services included in the Control plane in the top half and the Runtime plane in the lower half.

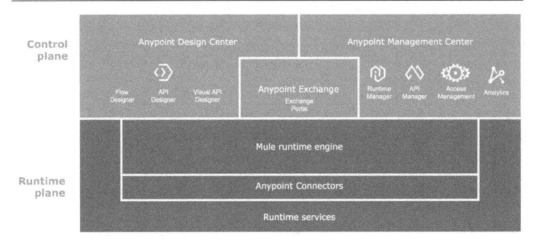

Figure 1.5 - Anypoint Platform High Level view

The control plane refers to all the components used to:

- Manage the platform

- Develop code

- Design and publish API specifications

- Collaborate with other developers

- Configure and manage runtime settings

- View logs

- Manage APIs

Essentially the control plane is where the platform itself is managed along with every API or Mule application you developed and are running somewhere. The "running somewhere" is the domain of the runtime plane.

The runtime plane is made of many components or services responsible for running the MuleSoft applications but at its heart is a **Java Virtual Machine (JVM)**. This includes the Mule runtime engine, but it also includes the services where the runtime engine can be hosted including Runtime Fabric and CloudHub. The runtime plane also includes services used by a MuleSoft application while it is running. This includes:

- **Virtual Private Cloud (VPC)**

- **Virtual Private Network (VPN)**

- **Object Store V2**

- **Anypoint MQ**

- **Connectors** and any associated drivers

- **DataGraph**

- **Dedicated Load Balancers (DLB)**

When you open the Design Center in Anypoint, you are operating within the control plane. When you deploy and start your MuleSoft application either through the Runtime Manager interface in Anypoint or using an Anypoint CLI command, you are operating components in the control plane. The running applications and all the services they can use, along with the runtime engine are part of the runtime plane.

The screen shown in *Figure 1.6* is running in the control plane and hosts all the services seen here. When you log in to your trial Anypoint platform you may see a few components are missing. Components such as Anypoint MQ and Partner Manager are items requiring additional licensing.

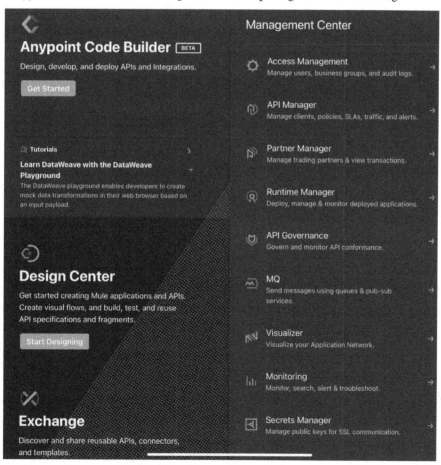

Figure 1.6 - Anypoint Control Plane and available components and services

The figure shows many of the services available in MuleSoft including:

- **Anypoint Code Builder (ACB)** – A new developer IDE offering based on Visual Code, able to operate fully in the cloud without any installation required.

- **Design Center** – A cloud based development tool for building API specifications in **RAML** or **OAS** and **AsyncAPI**

- **Exchange** – A catalog of artifacts including API's, Connectors, Templates, Examples, Snippets, Dataweave, all of which can be shared with other consumers in order to support reuse.

- **Management Center** (and all the controls therein) – All of the controls and management capabilities of the platform including:

  - Access management

  - API Management

  - Runtime Management

  - Governance

  - Anypoint MQ management

  - Visualizer for creating views of APIs

  - Monitoring

  - Secrets management

We will learn more about these different services and more about the runtime plane options in the next chapter. But first let's consider the architectural advantages of having these two planes.

- **Fault tolerance**: When the control plane is down, whether because of an outage or upgrades, the runtime plane and all the running applications can continue to operate. Likewise, when the control plane identifies an application is not running for some reason, the control plane can restart the service or attempt to run it in a different availability zone.

- **Hosting flexibility and regulation compliance**: Organizations can choose to run the control plane in the cloud, with everything installed, hosted, and managed by MuleSoft. Some EU organizations may require all their assets, data, and metadata to be operated strictly within the EU. This is supported by with an EU hosted Control Plane. Organizations requiring FedRAMP compliance can run the Control Plan in the MuleSoft hosted AWS GovCloud. Some organizations may have requirements or regulations preventing them from having any assets, data, and/or metadata in the cloud. For these organizations, the Anypoint Platform supports running the control plane in your own data center.

- The Runtime Plane can be fully managed by MuleSoft on the AWS public cloud, on an AWS VPC, and on the AWS GovCloud. There are also options for run on Customer-hosted infrastructure running the Mule runtime engine either directly on servers specially provisioned for the Mule Runtime or as an appliance in container deployments. Depending on the deployment selection for the control panel and runtime panel, the availability of Anypoint service configurations may change.

In the next section we will explore where the Control plane can be hosted, where the Runtime plane can be hosted, and the impact the hosting decision on one plane impacts the options of the other plane.

Platform deployment options

One of the jobs of the architect is to examine and understand the current state of the organization's systems landscape. Has the organization embraced a cloud managed services approach. Does the organization have critical systems still in their own data center. These next sections will describe the options available for hosting the planes and how they relate to each other.

Control plane hosting

Currently, there are 2 deployment options available from MuleSoft for running the control plane, the first of which has 3 deployment locations:

- Hosted and managed by MuleSoft

  - US AWS cloud

  - EU AWS cloud

  - AWS GovCloud

- Running control plane functionality locally on the organizations own hardware, hosted and managed by the organization.

Running the Control Plane on the organization's own infrastructure uses a product called Anypoint Platform **Private Cloud Edition (PCE)**. Installing this product requires working with MuleSoft professional services during the installation.

Runtime plane

The runtime plane as described earlier, is where your programs run. This is where the HTTP connector you added to a flow, listens to the port you told it to listen to. It's where the Dataweave transformation logic sits waiting for a payload to reshape. It is also the domain of Anypoint Object Store V2 and Anypoint MQ.

In order to run these components, we must have compute resources, memory resources, storage and network resources. MuleSoft provides four options where the MuleSoft runtime engine can execute:

- **CloudHub**

- **CloudHub 2.0**

- **Runtime Fabric**

- **Standalone**

Later chapters will take a deeper look a each of these runtime hosting options. In *Chapters 9 and 10* we look at the MuleSoft hosted options, CloudHub and CloudHub 2.0. In *Chapter 11* we look at the nuances of containerizing the runtime plane with Runtime Fabric. And finally in *Chapter 12* we will look at the self-hosted standalone option of deploying the MuleSoft runtime engine on infrastructure obtained and managed by the organization.

But just because each of these can be a host for the runtime engine, does not mean all the other runtime plane components are supported in each of these environments. *Table 1.1* is a matrix showing the runtime components available for each hosting option for the runtime plane.

Anypoint Platform Component	CloudHub 2.0	CloudHub	Runtime Fabric	Standalone
Mule runtime engine	Y	Y	Y	Y
Anypoint MQ	Y	Y	Y	Y
Anypoint Object Store v2	Y	Y	N	N
Anypoint DataGraph	N	Y	N	N
Connectors	Y	Y	Y	Y

Table 1.1 - Hosting Options for Runtime Plane components

In this table we can see that DataGraph is not available in CloudHub 2.0, Runtime Fabric, or Standalone servers. We can also see that Object Store v2 is not available in Runtime Fabric or Standalone servers. We can also see the most flexible runtime hosting options is CloudHub and CloudHub 2.0.

In the next section we will see what combinations of these runtime hosting options can be used with the different control plane options.

Combining Control Plane hosts and Runtime Hosts

The control plane as we have said is responsible for managing all the things we have running in the runtime plane. Therefore, the deployment choices we make to host the control plane will impact where we can host the runtime plane.

Table 1.2 is a matrix showing the relationship between the Control Plane hosting option and the Runtime hosting option.

Runtime Plane	US control plane	EU control plane	MuleSoft Government Cloud	Anypoint Platform PCE
CloudHub 2.0	Y	Y	N	N
CloudHub	Y	Y	Y	N
Standalone runtimes	Y	Y	Y	Y
Runtime Fabric	Y	Y	N	N

Table 1.2 - Control Plane deployments and runtime hosting options matrix

We can see in the table If we are hosting our control plane in the US or EU, we can host the runtime plane in any of the 4 hosting options identified earlier. However, if you are hosting the control plane in the GovCloud the only hosting options are CloudHub and Standalone servers. CloudHub 2.0 and Runtime Fabric are not available in GovCloud. If you must host the control plane on your own servers and infrastructure (PCE) then you can only host the runtime plane on your own servers and infrastructure.

Sometimes an organization has to make difficult choices in deciding where to deploy both the control plane and the runtime plane. Federal and State governments often need to follow regulations and may require software solutions to be **FedRAMP** compliant. MuleSoft has a solution for this called Government Cloud but it also comes with other limiting factors and can be more expensive. When using Government Cloud the Runtime plane must be CloudHub, standalone MuleSoft Runtimes, or a combination of the two (Hybrid).

Likewise, European organizations may need to keep all software entirely within EU datacenters. MuleSoft provides an option to use an EU hosted control plane. This control plane will also limit CloudHub deployments to be in the EU region and in EU Availability Zones.

For organizations with a mandate to retain all IT infrastructure and systems under their direct control and within their data center, there is the option to install Private Cloud Edition and run both the control plane and runtime plane on your own hardware.

The architect's job in these situations is to understand how to navigate the differences. If the runtime host does not support Anypoint DataGraph, or Object Store v2, what options do we have instead? Do we even need DataGraph or Object Store v2? Moreover, if an organization is operating from the US or EU control plane and have every option open to them, what business criteria or IT policies or organizational resourcing constraints or any other of a host of environmental variables would prompt an architect to choose CloudHub over Runtime Framework. What would drive the architect to recommend combining CloudHub 2.0 with a standalone instance of the runtime engine.

To answer these questions, we need to understand each of these MuleSoft delivery approaches in a little more detail and see what they can do and what they can not. Where our applications will execute and what runtime plane capabilities are available is important. *Part 3* of this book will examine these details so we as architects can be equipped to answer these questions and make our recommendations. In the next section we will take a first look at the specific capabilities and components availabel in the platform.

MuleSoft capabilities and components

As we have seen already, the Anypoint platform provides the components to design, deploy, and manage the APIs we build. The platform also provides the components, and in many cases, the infrastructure to run or execute these applications. Let's review the different components that support each of these phases in the lifecycle of **API first development**.

Discover Capability

Anypoint Exchange can be thought of as a catalog or registry of all the different reusable components, or assets, available to use in your solution. This catalog can be searched for specific phrases or filtered based on pre-defined asset types or asset categories. You can list assets from your own organization or assets developed by MuleSoft. You can even filter based on the lifecycle stage the asset is in.

In *Figure 1.7*, We can see Exchange searching for all the assets provided by MuleSoft.

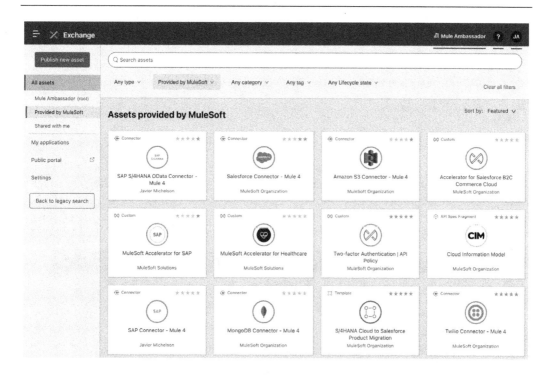

Figure 1.7 - Anypoint Exchange assets from MuleSoft

Looking at the different assets in this figure we can see the types of assets that can be registered or published to Anypoint Exchange has grown dramatically over the past 4 years. Initially Exchange was limited to Connectors and APIs. Anypoint Exchange is now home to 11 different types as of the time of this writing:

- **Connectors**: components, developed with the Mule SDK, which developers can use in MuleSoft flows to connect and interact natively with different systems.

- **Dataweave Libraries**: Developers can build Dataweave transformations which can be reused in other integrations.

- **Examples**: assets which provide an example application such as "How to Batch ETL with Snowflake"

- **Policies**: policies which govern the security of APIs, typically running in service mesh

- **API Spec Fragments**: reusable segments of RAML or OAS to be reused in the development of new API specifications.

- **REST APIs**: API specifciations for implementations which can used or consumed by other approved applications

- **RPA Activity Templates**: templates for the MuleSoft **Robotic Process Automation (RPA)** capability

- **Rule sets**: rules for API governance
- **SOAP APIs**: APIs which can used or consumed by other approved applications
- **Templates**: templates which can be copied and configured for your environment
- Custom (e.g. accelerators)

Design capability

API design begins with the API Specification. Whether the organization has standardized on the the **Open API Specification (OAS, formerly known as Swagger)** or **RESTful API Modeling Language (RAML)**, the specification can be created in Anypoint Platform Design Center. Design Center allows you to design specifications, fragments, and **AsyncAPI** specs as shown in Figure 1.8 Design Center API Specification.

Figure 1.8 - Design Center API specification

In this screen, MuleSoft can provide a guide or "*scaffolding*", making the development of the specification "*low-code/no-code*". This capability is also on the cloud so designers can get started without needing to install anything on their laptop or desktop.

API design specifications can also be created inside the two primary development tools, Anypoint Studio and ACB. Both tools allow you to synchronize your API specification with Design Center. Likewise, for any API specifications started in Design Center, you can open and work on these in Studio or ACB.

Management capability

The Anypoint Management Center provides several Anypoint capabilities focused on the operations and administration of the platform as well as the API applications running.

The screen in *Figure 1.9* shows the options in the Management Center.

Figure 1.9 - Anypoint Management Center

The list of management capabilities in *Figure 1.9* are defined here.

- **Access Management**: provides the capability to create Anypoint Platform users or set up an external identity provider (IdP) to manage users of the platform and the permissions they have been granted to the platform. It also exposes the audit logs which capture anything done on the platform from deploying an application to publishing an API.

- **API Manager**: provides the capabilities of applying policies, setting up service level agreements (SLAs), and securing APIs. The API Manager is also used to manage two types of API alerts. Alerts for API request/response/policy and alerts for contract changes or violations. API Manager also manages and deploys any proxy API runtimes you need to associate with an API to manage it.

- **Runtime Manager**: provides capabilities for the management of Anypoint VPCs, Anypoint VPNs or Private Spaces, MuleSoft applications, load balancers, standalone servers, and flex gateways across different environments. Additionally, application deployment, setup, and management can all be controlled from the Runtime Manager.

- **API Governance**: gives architects the capability to define rule sets for API conformance and monitor compliance and send notifications to developers to resolve compliance issues.

- **The Visualizer**: provides a graphical view of the APIs deployed to a Runtime plane, as observed through three lenses: Architecture, Troubleshooting, and Policies. The application view shows the relationship of the applications, the nodes, in your application network. The troubleshooting view includes metrics information for all the nodes in the application network. The policy view allows you to see an overview of the policies applied to the MuleSoft applications in your network.

- **Monitoring**: provides the capability to view performance dashboards, review logs and cpu/memory/disk consumption, and look for trends across deployed APIs. Monitoring also allows operations to look for stability issues of any APIs based on performance and usage findings.

- **Secrets Manager**: provides a secure vault for keeping certificates, key stores and trust stores, and username/password key value pairs safe. Security Manager is part of a Security capability which supports edge policies and tokenization in the Runtime Framework runtime plane.

We have now looked at some of the primary capabilities of the Anypoint platform, many of which we will go into more detail later. With a historical backdrop of the different approaches to integration, and now with all these new iPaaS platform capabilities available, let's take a look at some of the difficulties, new and old, organizations are facing today.

Why are APIs so important in delivering modern integrations?

APIs fundamentally change the architecture discussion from asynchronous messaging to synchronous conversational integration. It shifts the paradigm from production of data to a consumption model.

Many newer **commercial off the shelf systems (COTS)** already ship with this in mind, offering customers some form of integration interface for accessing processes and data within their system. Cloud based SaaS systems such as Salesforce, Fiserv, and Workday also expose their processes and data through a robust API. Other SaaS systems built a SOAP web services interface to access their data.

EDI transactions continue to simplify B2B partner integration. And many business partners are enriching that partner experience by offering a dedicated API allowing their partners to develop their own solutions rather than forcing them to use their web portal.

Unfortunately, this list does not account for the hundreds of legacy systems across the enterprise. These were often developed as an island, with no consideration of integrating with other systems. Being able to build safe, secure, but effective APIs to unlock the data in these legacy systems is an important first step in delivering modern integration architecture to an enterprise.

The MuleSoft platform supports this approach to integration by providing the services and components needed to build a consistent way of accessing system data across all sources of truth be it Cloud based SaaS, B2B, COTS n-tier designed software, or even legacy mainframe software. Publication of these

APIs in turn increases its reusability across new and future development efforts. Fine grained control of the deployment of APIs including firewalls, port security, certificates, SSL, and policies, allows architects to share access to a systems data in a safe and secure way that complies with governance, protocols, policies, and in some cases even laws.

Being able to design and develop these APIs using Low-code, no-code tooling also helps IT be more efficient in delivering integration solutions to the business. Particularly if the business users and IT team lack the skills required to develop complex, fault tolerant, performant, scalable application solutions to integration.

The late, great, Tina Turner wrote a song entitled "*We don't need another hero*" and this comes to mind when I ask other architects, do we need another integration platform architecture? We are going to begin to answer this question throughout the rest of this book. We will look in more detail at the platform architecture of MuleSoft. We will dig into the MuleSoft resources, accelerators, design approach, and strategies for deployment. We will examine how operations and management of the platform are as much the responsibility of the architect as design diagrams and code reviews.

In short, the rest of this book will serve as your personal guide to MuleSoft platform architecture and an API approach to addressing the modern challenges of enterprise application integration.

Summary

The chapter started by providing an overview of the MuleSoft and looking at what makes an iPaaS.

The chapter continued by looking back in some detail at the history of integration and how architectural approaches have evolved from point to point to SOA and REST.

The chapter then took a look at the building blocks, capabilities, and services available in MuleSoft. A brief examination was made of the control plane and the runtime plane and the options that support different configurations and hosting options for each one.

The chapter then looked at the current challenges facing integration. It examined the issues businesses have with digital transformation and the constraints IT often faces when trying to keep systems operational while at the same time, evolve or transform systems to meet the growing demands of the business.

The chapter then ended by looking at how APIs in general and the MuleSoft platform in particular is important to delivering modern integration solutions, unlocking system data in secure ways while supporting reusability.

In the next chapter, we will examine in closer detail, the foundation components and the underlying architecture.

Questions

1. What are the two planes of operation on which the Anypoint Platform runs?

2. What are the four hosting options available in the runtime plane?

3. Can you name the two capabilities that are unavailable when using the Runtime Fabric for hosting the runtime plane?

4. How does iPaaS differ from other approaches to integration? From Point-to-Point? From RPC? From SOA?

5. What issues have you or your organization faced that makes integration a challenge?

Answers

1. Control Plane and Runtime plane are the two planes the Anypoint Platform operates on.

2. CloudHub, CloudHub 2.0, Runtime Fabric (RTF), Stand Alone servers are the current options for hosting the MuleSoft Runtime Plane.

3. Object Store v2 and Anypoint DataGraph are not available when running in RTF.

4. iPaaS is a comprehensive suite of cloud services enabling integration development and governance connecting on-premises applications and data with cloud-based processes, services, apps, and data. Point to point involves one application reaching into another application directly to collect data directly. RPC is a kind of point-to-point architecture that involves invoking remote calls in another application and getting data back. SOA is a service-oriented architecture without any globally agreed upon standards, which provides an approach to object interaction through predefined services.

5. Your answer should vary here depending on the experiences of your organization. I have seen organizations that had older mainframe systems with complex processing of overnight batch data. This of course impacts the ability to have a realtime view of data.

Further Reading

- Gartners glossary terms: `https://www.gartner.com/en/information-technology/glossary/information-platform-as-a-service-ipaas#:~:text=Integration%20Platform%20as%20a%20Service%20(iPaaS)%20is%20a%20suite%20of,individual%20or%20across-s%20multiple%20organizations`.

- *Architectural Styles and the Design of Network-based Software Architectures* by Thomas Fielding `https://www.ics.uci.edu/~fielding/pubs/dissertation/top.htm`

- Enterprise Integration Patterns, Addison-Wesley 2004, pg 3, Gegor Hohpe, Bobby Woolf

- Christensen, Clayton M. The Innovator's Dilemma: When New Technologies Cause Great Firms to Fail. Boston, MA: Harvard Business School Press, 1997

2

Platform Foundation Components and the Underlying Architecture

The MuleSoft platform has been expanding and evolving, providing architects and designers with more and more capabilities, features, and functionality. Some changes have been subtle while others have introduced entirely new capabilities. And that doesn't even count all of the new connectors at one's disposal.

For example, among the changes from just the past couple of years, we have the following:

- Containerized runtimes – **Kubernetes**-based runtime engines
- Composer flows – **no-code** integration and development capability driven from the Salesforce platform
- API Community Manager – a user interface-driven portal to manage internal and external developers working with an organization's APIs
- API Experience Hub – a next-generation Community manager that integrates Anypoint Exchange and Salesforce Experience Cloud
- DataWeave modules – libraries of additional functionality supporting development with arrays, binaries, dates, math, crypto, and more

- DataGraph – a low-code/no-code user interface tool and query capability for data across an **application network** that allows developers to consume multiple APIs from the data service in a GraphQL request
- ServiceMesh – A gateway providing the ability to manage and secure APIs across an extended **microservices** network of Mule and non-Mule applications
- Flex Gateway – a lightweight **API gateway** for managing and securing APIs running on any platform
- API Governance – an automated tool to ensure developers of API specifications are following the standards, best practices, and rules outlined by the architecture team
- **Robotic Process Automation (RPA)** – a low-code/no-code functionality enabling businesses to automate processes and tasks requiring human input using "bots"
- **Anypoint Code Builder (ACB)** – a next-generation **Integrated Development Environment (IDE)** for developers designing and building MuleSoft APIs

This list only represents a fraction of the newest functionalities and capabilities offered in the MuleSoft ecosystem.

Fundamentally, the organization of the platform has remained consistent. As mentioned in the previous chapter, the MuleSoft Anypoint Platform is defined by a control plane and a runtime plane. In this chapter, we are going to cover the following main topics and the Anypoint Core Services that accompany them:

- The control plane functionality
- The runtime plane overview

We will outline the considerations that you as the architect will need to review and understand to help the organization select the appropriate combination of control and runtime planes. We will also take a first look at some of the core services of the platform.

There is a lot of flexibility available across the platform. Architects of the integration platform will need to understand their organization's technology limitations, regulatory responsibilities, short-term and long-term goals and objectives, and the business requirements and technical non-functional requirements for specific projects. We will look at these factors in this chapter to see the influence they have on the Anypoint Platform architecture.

Technical requirements

In this chapter, we will use Anypoint Platform configured in *Chapter 1*

The Anypoint control plane

The Anypoint control plane is a collection of products, tools, and services that together function as the central hub for managing and governing MuleSoft application runtime deployments and APIs. This control plane is architected as a set of microservices, allowing this central hub to be scalable, highly available, and fault tolerant. Furthermore, the services were built with an API-first design. This means development teams and operations teams have APIs at their disposal that can be used to interact with Anypoint Platform. In fact, there are three ways to interact with the services and components in the Anypoint control plane:

- Standard web frontend
- Anypoint Platform APIs
- The Anypoint Platform **Command-Line Interface (CLI)**

These services can be incorporated into your CI/CD pipeline and provide insight into its processes and performance via alerts and audit logs. In this book, we will primarily use the user interface web frontend of the control plane. A thorough examination of the CLI tools and the Platform APIs is beyond the scope of this book.

As architects, there are three things about the control plane we need to consider when designing an Anypoint Platform architecture:

- Where will we host it?
- How will we secure access to it?
- How will we organize it?

These services and management tools must run somewhere, so in this next section, let's look at the hosting options for the control plane.

Control plane hosting options

One of the jobs of the architect is to examine and understand the current state of the organization's systems landscape. Has the organization embraced a cloud-based managed services approach? Does the organization still have critical systems in its own data center? How important is time-to-market? Are there regulatory issues to be aware of? Sometimes we like to think we know where the finish line is already. The business has told us that it wants to modernize and we know what a modern system is, so why not just go and build that? But if we try to take shortcuts in the architecture process; if we don't take time to discover how things are currently laid out; if we don't understand the starting line, we will not be able to identify the actual gaps separating us from the future state architecture. These gaps will help identify, for example, what data and metadata issues the MuleSoft control plane should address.

Currently, there are two deployment options available from MuleSoft for running the control plane. The first option has three deployment locations:

- Hosted and managed by MuleSoft:

  - US AWS cloud in the US East (North Virginia) region

  - EU AWS cloud in the EU (Frankfurt) region

  - AWS GovCloud (US only)

- Hosted and managed by the customer:

  - This involves running the control plane functionality locally on the organization's own hardware/infrastructure, hosted and managed by the organization.

  - Running the control plane on the organization's own infrastructure uses a product called Anypoint Platform **Private Cloud Edition (PCE)**. Installing this product requires working with MuleSoft professional services during the installation.

Let's consider some questions that could influence the decision of where to place the control plane:

- Has the organization embraced a cloud-based managed services approach? If so, this typically makes the choice to utilize MuleSoft-managed infrastructure straightforward. However, if the organization has not fully embraced a cloud-based managed services approach, this is an opportunity for it to begin to understand what this means to its staff, operations, and IT capabilities. By itself, it certainly doesn't automatically point to the PCE.

- Are there regulatory issues to be aware of? Europe's **General Data Protection Regulation (GDPR)** and the United States' **Federal Risk and Authorization Management Program (FedRAMP)** have had a profound impact on information technology security requirements. Furthermore, businesses are under the constant threat of data breaches and ransomware causing disruption to their operations as well as their reputations. If your organization requires FedRamp compliance, you will either need to look to Government Cloud or self-hosted options. The GDPR may require retaining all data in the EU, so likewise, EU-based control hosting may be required in certain contexts.

- How important is time-to-market? Certainly, no option beats the MuleSoft-hosted control plane when combined with the MuleSoft-hosted runtime plane for critical time-to-market scenarios.

- Does the organization have its own policies requiring all critical systems and data to remain in its own data center, isolated from contact with the outside world? The PCE can solve this requirement. Note that while installing the PCE on cloud infrastructure such as AWS, Azure, or Rackspace is possible, it doesn't meet the requirement of keeping the system within the organization's data center and under its direct control.

Some of these questions may result in conflicting answers (such as time-to-market being very important, but the organization requiring an internal data center solution). The architect must work with the business and IT teams to understand any competing priorities and confirm their assumptions before recommending a control plane approach. For example, it may be assumed a US government or state agency requires FedRAMP compliance. However, this is not always the case and a standard US control plane that allows an agency to use **Runtime Fabric (RTF)** or CloudHub 1.0/2.0 is the most optimal solution.

Having determined the hosting requirements for the control plane and completed the provisioning with entitlements and licensing, we next need to understand how to secure access to the platform. We will look at this in the next section.

Securing the Anypoint control plane

Anypoint security is managed in the Management Center within Access Management. Here, administrators can manage users, business groups, and audit logs. There are two ways to manage users of Anypoint Platform:

- Anypoint managed users (not available to GovCloud implementations)

- External **identity providers (IdP)** and **Single Sign-On (SSO)**

In Access Management, users can be invited to join Anypoint Platform. Anypoint manages user security when this approach is used. Note that while users can use the same email used to register with other Anypoint Platform instances, the username must be unique for each account. After an account invitation is accepted, it is a best practice for the user to enable **multi-factor authentication (MFA)**, and in fact this is required as of August 1, 2023.

> **Note**
>
> MFA is configured within the user's profile page and not within the **User** tab of Access Management.

Each user's access to all the assets, entitlements, features, and capabilities of the platform is controlled through teams and permissions which replaced the now deprecated roles feature.

We can create teams to align with the activities that members of a given team are responsible for. We can then grant permissions to each team to give access to different features and capabilities of the platform along with the environment(s) they are allowed to perform those activities in. We will look at both business groups and environments in the next section.

Figure 2.1 shows an example team called **API Developers**, which is a child of the API designers' team and has permissions for certain activities and resources in the JJ Music Back Office.

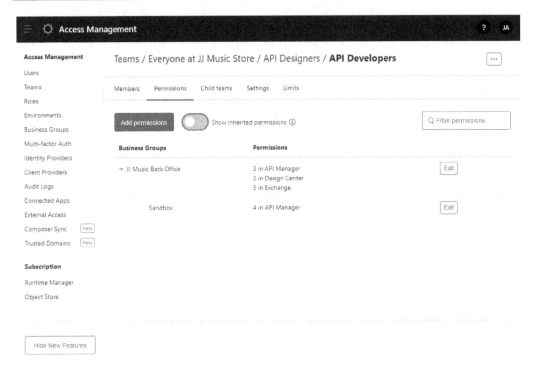

Figure 2.1 – Team permissions in Anypoint

You can also see in the preceding figure that permissions are inherited from the parents of the team.

> **Note**
> Team permissions are selected before identifying the business group against which to apply the permissions.

Users can also be managed using the organization's IdP. The settings to connect the organization's IdP to Anypoint Platform as a verifiable application are found in Access Management under the **Identity Providers** menu option. Anypoint supports OpenID Connect and SAML 2.0. The information required for each of these providers will vary slightly. Using an external provider such as Okta or Microsoft **Active Directory (AD)** shifts the burden of user management to a separate security platform responsible for authenticating users and validating their access to assets.

The following figure, from the MuleSoft Identity Providers documentation, shows the SAML flow that requires a user to authenticate their credentials with the IdP, which in turn provides an assertion to Anypoint Platform letting the platform know whether the user is authorized to access the requested resource.

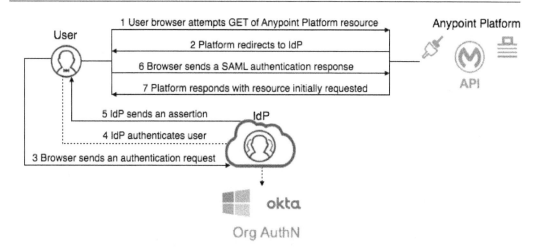

Figure 2.2 – SAML flow with Anypoint Platform

Setting up SSO to Anypoint requires coordination with the organization's security team. Getting hold of some of the information required by each side of the setup can resemble a chicken-and-egg scenario. Typically the IdP will need to complete the setup of its connection first and provide the required public key, metadata, sign-on and sign-off URLs, and issuer ID to the Anypoint administrator.

The IdP can also be used to map users to teams within Anypoint. The team must still be set up in Anypoint with the appropriate permissions. However, the business process for adding new users to Anypoint now includes what team, and thus what access, a person should be given.

> **Note**
>
> There are two similar-looking options in Access Management: **Identity Providers** and **Client Providers**. Client Providers allow an architect to set up an IdP using OpenAM, PingFederate, or OpenID Connect to authorize client applications that are accessing APIs. IdPs use OpenAM, PinFederate, or OpenID to authorize access to Anypoint Platform.

Now that the right people have access to Anypoint, let's look at the options we have for organizing and managing the Anypoint control plane.

Organizing the Anypoint control plane

There are two primary mechanisms for organizing Anypoint: business groups and environments. First, let's consider business groups.

Business groups

Business groups are a logical division of MuleSoft resources, allowing resources such as vCore and VPCs to be allocated at a departmental business-unit level. Furthermore, using teams, as identified in the previous section, business groups allow us to create groups of designers, developers, operators, and admins to manage the resources within a specific department.

Anypoint entitlements (the components and capabilities made available through licenses), however, are managed at the root business group level. Let's say an organization purchases 10 sandbox vCores and 5 production vCores. These vCores are allocated to the root organization created at the time Anypoint Platform was first provisioned. We can see in *Figure 2.3* the root business group created when the owners of the JJ Music Store provisioned MuleSoft as their integration platform.

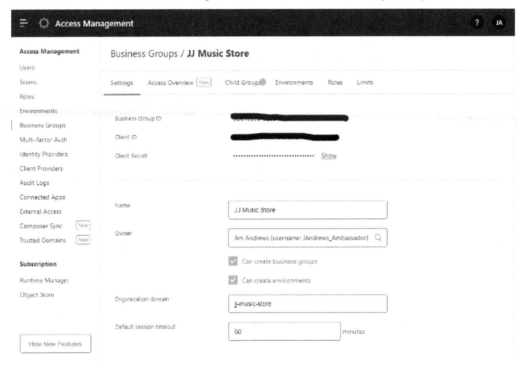

Figure 2.3 – Management Center control plane – Access Management

> **Note**
> Only users with the Organizational Administrator's permission (formerly role) can open the Business Units page.

We can also see in *Figure 2.3*, the business group ID, client ID, and client secret. The client ID and client secret of the organization are included only to support backward compatibility. The client ID and secret of each created environment should be used instead for access to assets of the organization by users who are not organizational administrators. Scrolling down, you will also see the default region for any CloudHub deployments.

> **Note**
>
> In trial accounts, this default will always be US-East (Ohio).

Organizationally, it is a good practice to establish at least one child business group and assign resources and entitlements to this group from the root business group. In *Figure 2.4*, we can see the details for the new group filled out and, in this example, all 1 vCore and 1 design vCore from the JJ Music Store group have been allocated to the child business group.

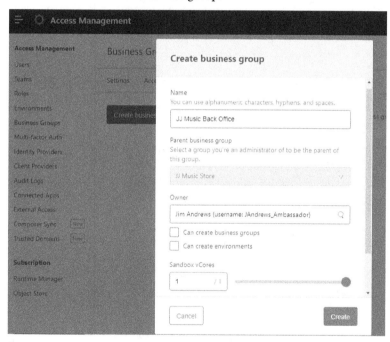

Figure 2.4 – Creating a child business group

At this point, the JJ Music Store business group will have 0 vCores available and thus will not be able to deploy any applications. Again, this is typically preferred as a best practice. Deployments should be associated with the child business group responsible for them. If more cores are needed and procured, the vCores will initially be allocated to the JJ Music Store business group by MuleSoft.

Now let's look at the role of environments in Anypoint Platform.

Environments

Environments are a logical grouping for separating deployments and applications and are created within the context of a business group. As mentioned in the preceding *Business groups* section, each environment has its own client ID and client secret. These can be used by CI/CD pipelines to direct deployments and can also be used by the developer in Anypoint Studio to identify the API Manager environment.

It is a best practice to define environments to line up with the organization's development and testing approach.

For example, one common methodology for testing uses four environments: Development, System Integration Testing, User Acceptance Testing or Staging, and Production. By setting up an environment to correspond with each of these testing phases, we can now develop environment property files in each application, allowing us to align data sources and system access. When all applications are subject to the testing methodology in the same way, we can also avoid any data-related errors caused when an integration shares data from one environment with another system connected to a different environment.

There are two types of environment types we can create:

- Production – used for deploying applications in a production live environment (uses production vCores)

- Sandbox – used for creating development and testing environments (uses sandbox vCores)

- In *Figure 2.5*, we can see a list of environments created to align with the testing approach of the JJ Music Back Office department. Note that the Design type of environment (along with design vCores) is for deploying applications from Design Center using Flow Designer, which has been marked as *End-of-Life*.

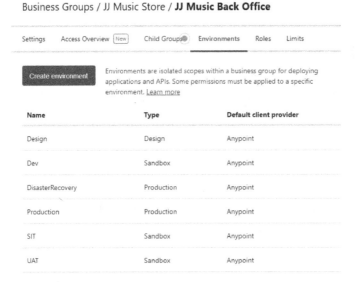

Figure 2.5 – Environments matching company testing approach

In this section, we looked at the different hosting options for the control plane, the options for securing the platform using the control plane, and the mechanisms that allow us to organize the platform across different departments and business units as well as across the different testing methodologies used in an organization. These environments also represent a bridge between the allocation of vCores, the grouping of applications for testing, and the actual deployment of these applications to a MuleSoft runtime engine. These runtime engines operate within a second plane called the runtime plane. The next section will look at some of the options we have for managing the runtime plane within Anypoint Platform.

The runtime plane overview

The runtime plane, as described earlier, is where your programs run. This is where the HTTP connectors you add to flows will listen to the port you told it to listen to. It's where the Dataweave transformation logic sits waiting for a payload to reshape. It is also the domain of Anypoint Object Store V2 and Anypoint MQ. In order to run these components, we must have compute, memory, storage, and network resources. In short, the runtime plane is the server or collection of servers used to run your applications.

> **Note**
> Anypoint Object Store V2 and Anypoint MQ settings are configured from the control plane.

The platform architect must consider several things when designing the runtime plane architecture. Let's first look at the runtime deployment options.

Runtime deployment options

MuleSoft provides four options for where to execute the MuleSoft runtime engine:

- **CloudHub** – MuleSoft-managed infrastructure running in a MuleSoft-owned AWS organization
- **CloudHub 2.0** – MuleSoft-managed containerized infrastructure
- **Runtime Fabric (RTF)** – A shared-responsibility Kubernetes cluster
- **Standalone MuleSoft runtime engine** – Customer-managed infrastructure

Later chapters will take a deeper look at the capabilities of each of these runtime hosting options. In *Chapters 9* and *10*, we look at the MuleSoft-hosted options, CloudHub and CloudHub 2.0. In *Chapter 11*, we look at the nuances of containerizing the runtime plane with Runtime Fabric. Finally, in *Chapter 12*, we will look at the self-hosted standalone option of deploying the MuleSoft runtime engine on infrastructure obtained and managed by the organization.

Next, let's consider the options we have on where to host the runtime plane.

Runtime plane hosting

As with the control plane, there are two options when it comes to where and how we can host the MuleSoft runtime engine:

- Hosted and managed by MuleSoft:

  - On MuleSoft's AWS cloud using CloudHub and CloudHub 2.0

  - On an AWS VPC

  - On AWS GovCloud

- Hosted and managed by the customer:

  - Manual setup of a MuleSoft runtime engine on the organization's bare-metal infrastructure, virtual machines, in their data center, or on their own cloud platform infrastructure (Azure, AWS, etc.)

  - Mule runtimes:

    - RTF on customer-managed Kubernetes

    - RTF as a MuleSoft appliance on VM/bare metal

When using a MuleSoft-hosted AWS option (CloudHub or CloudHub 2.0), the AWS region depends on where the control plane is hosted (as described earlier in this chapter):

- The US control plane allows the use of the following AWS regions (assuming global deployment is unchecked): US East and West, Canada, Asia/Pacific, EU, and South America, or standalone MuleSoft runtime engines including RTF

- The EU control plane restricts deployments to the EU (Frankfurt and Ireland) region or standalone MuleSoft Runtime engines including RTF

- The AWS GovCloud control plane restricts deployments to the AWS GovCloud region or standalone (not RTF) MuleSoft Runtime engines

- The PCE control plane requires standalone MuleSoft runtime engines and is not able to deploy to MuleSoft-managed runtime options

> **Note**
> The global deployment option is available within the US control plane. To enable it, you may need to contact your MuleSoft account manager.

Next, let's review how these runtime deployment options work with the core Anypoint components.

Core components in the runtime plane

There are several core components and capabilities that are part of MuleSoft and operate in the runtime plane:

- The Mule runtime engine
- Anypoint MQ (separately licensed messaging service)
- Object Store V2
- DataGraph
- Connectors

> **Note**
>
> While components such as MQ, DataGraph, and Object Store operate and run within the runtime plane, the management and configuration of these components occur in the control plane.

The availability of some of these core components depends on where the runtime is hosted. The following table is a matrix showing the runtime components available for each hosting option for the runtime plane.

Anypoint Platform Component	CloudHub 2.0	CloudHub	Runtime Fabric	Standalone
Mule runtime engine	Y	Y	Y	Y
Anypoint MQ	Y	Y	Y	Y
Anypoint Object Store v2	Y	Y	N	N
Anypoint DataGraph	N	Y	N	N
Connectors	Y	Y	Y	Y

Table 2.1 – Hosting options for runtime plane components

In the preceding table, we can see that DataGraph is not available on CloudHub 2.0, Runtime Fabric, or Standalone servers. We can also see that Object Store v2 is not available in Runtime Fabric or Standalone servers. We can also see the most flexible runtime hosting options are CloudHub and CloudHub 2.0.

In the next section, we will see what combinations of these runtime hosting options can be used with the different control plane options.

Combining control plane hosts and runtime hosts

The control plane, as stated earlier, is responsible for managing all the things we have running in the runtime plane. Therefore, the deployment choices we make to host the control plane will impact where we can host the runtime plane.

Table 2.2 is a matrix showing the relationship between the control plane hosting options and the runtime hosting options.

Runtime Plane	US control plane	EU control plane	MuleSoft Government Cloud	Anypoint Platform PCE
CloudHub 2.0	Y	Y	N	N
CloudHub	Y	Y	Y	N
Standalone runtimes	Y	Y	Y	Y
Runtime Fabric	Y	Y	N	N

Table 2.2 – Control plane deployments and runtime hosting options matrix

As we can see in the preceding table, if we host our control plane in the US or EU, we can host the runtime plane in any of the four hosting options identified earlier. However, if we host the control plane in GovCloud, the only hosting options are CloudHub or standalone servers. CloudHub 2.0 and Runtime Fabric are not available in GovCloud. If you must host the control plane on your own servers and infrastructure (PCE) then you can only host the runtime plane on your own servers and infrastructure.

Sometimes an organization must make difficult choices in deciding where to deploy both the control plane and the runtime plane. Federal and state governments often need to follow regulations and may require software solutions to be **FedRAMP** compliant. MuleSoft has a solution for this called Government Cloud, but it also comes with other limiting factors and can be more expensive. When using Government Cloud the runtime plane chosen must be CloudHub, standalone MuleSoft runtimes, or a combination of the two (hybrid).

Likewise, European organizations may need to keep all software entirely within EU data centers. MuleSoft provides an option to use an EU-hosted control plane. This control plane will also limit CloudHub deployments to those in the EU region and EU Availability Zones. Both GovCloud and EU control planes will be examined in more detail in a later chapter.

For organizations with a mandate to retain all IT infrastructure and systems under their direct control and within their own data center, there is the option to install PCE and run both the control plane and runtime plane on your own hardware.

The architect's job in these situations is to understand how to navigate the differences. If the runtime host does not support Anypoint DataGraph, or Object Store v2, what options do we have instead? Do we even need DataGraph or Object Store v2? Object Store v2 can be accessed via APIs, but will that be allowed given the requirements and regulations?

Moreover, if an organization is operating from the US or EU control plane and has every option open to them, what business criteria, IT policies, organizational resourcing constraints, or any other of a host of environmental variables would prompt an architect to choose CloudHub over RTF? What would drive the architect to recommend combining CloudHub 2.0 with a standalone instance of the runtime engine?

To answer these questions, we need to understand each of these MuleSoft delivery approaches in a little more detail and see what they can and cannot do. Where our applications will execute and what runtime plane capabilities will be available are important issues. *Later in* this book we willexamine these runtime deployment options in detail so we, as architects, can be equipped to answer these questions and make our recommendations.

In the next section, we will take a first look at the specific core capabilities and components available within the control plane.

Anypoint Core Services

As we have already seen, Anypoint Platform provides the components to design, deploy, and manage the APIs we build. The platform also provides the components, and in many cases the infrastructure, to run or execute these applications. Let's take a quick look at the different components that support each of these phases in the lifecycle of **API development**.

Management capability

Earlier, we identified the Anypoint Management Center, and specifically Access Management, as the core service for user management and platform organization. The Management Center is also where we can find the core services focused on the operations and administration of the platform as well as any running API applications.

The screen in *Figure 2.6* shows the options in the Management Center.

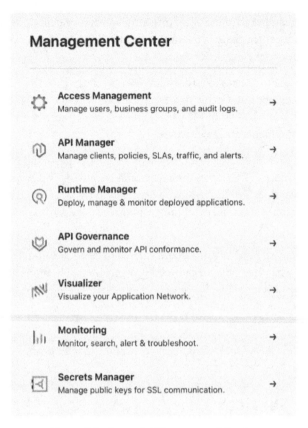

Figure 2.6 – Anypoint Management Center

The management capabilities in *Figure 2.6* are detailed as follows:

- **Access Management**: This was described earlier in the control plane section.

- **API Manager**: This provides the capabilities of applying policies, setting up **service-level agreements (SLAs)**, and securing APIs. The API Manager is also used to manage two types of API alerts: alerts for API request/response/policy, and alerts for contract changes or violations. API Manager also manages and deploys any proxy API runtimes you need to associate with an API in order to manage it.

- **Runtime Manager**: This provides capabilities for the management of Anypoint VPCs, Anypoint VPNs or Private Spaces, MuleSoft applications, load balancers, standalone servers, and Flex Gateways across different environments. Additionally, application deployment, setup, and management can all be controlled from Runtime Manager.

- **API Governance**: This gives architects the capability to define rule sets for API conformance, monitor compliance, and send notifications to developers to resolve compliance issues.

- **Visualizer**: This provides a graphical view of the APIs deployed to a runtime plane, as observed through three lenses: **Architecture**, **Troubleshooting**, and **Policies**. The application view shows the relationship between the applications (the nodes) in your application network. The Troubleshooting view includes metrics for all the nodes in the application network. The **Policy** view allows you to see an overview of the policies applied to the MuleSoft applications in your network.

- **Monitoring**: This provides the capability to view performance dashboards, review logs and CPU/memory/disk consumption, and look for trends across deployed APIs. Monitoring also allows operations to check for stability issues in any APIs based on performance and usage findings.

- **Secrets Manager**: This provides a secure vault for keeping certificates, key stores, and trust stores, and username/password key-value pairs safe. Security Manager is part of the security functionality that supports edge policies and tokenization in the Runtime Fabric runtime plane.

Design capability

API design begins with the API specification. Whether the organization uses the standardized **Open API Specification (OAS, formerly known as Swagger)** or **RESTful API Modeling Language (RAML)**, the specification can be created in Anypoint Platform Design Center. Design Center allows you to design specifications, fragments, and **AsyncAPI** specs as shown in *Figure 2.7*.

Figure 2.7 – Design Center API specification

In the preceding screenshot, MuleSoft provides a guide, or "scaffolding", allowing for low-code/no-code development of the specification. This capability is also on the cloud so designers can get started without needing to install anything on their laptop or desktop.

API design specifications can also be created inside the two primary development tools, Anypoint Studio and **Anypoint Code Builder (ACB)**. Both tools allow you to synchronize your API specification with Design Center. Likewise, for any API specifications started in Design Center, you can open and work on these in Studio or ACB.

You have put a lot of work into making sure the contract looks right, that the parameters are well defined and the payload examples are solid, and the mocking service appears to make the API work as expected. The APIs designed here now need to be shared so others can make use of these APIs to do bigger and better things, so they don't have to rebuild what you have already built!

The place to share your work is called **Anypoint Exchange** and we can publish from the Design Center directly to Exchange. In the next section, we will take a look at Exchange.

Discover Capability

Anypoint Exchange can be thought of as a catalog or registry of all the different reusable components, or assets, available to use in your solution. This catalog can be searched for specific phrases or filtered based on predefined asset types or asset categories. You can list assets from your own organization or assets developed by MuleSoft. You can even filter based on the lifecycle stage the asset is in.

In the following screenshot, we can see Exchange displaying a selection of the assets provided by MuleSoft.

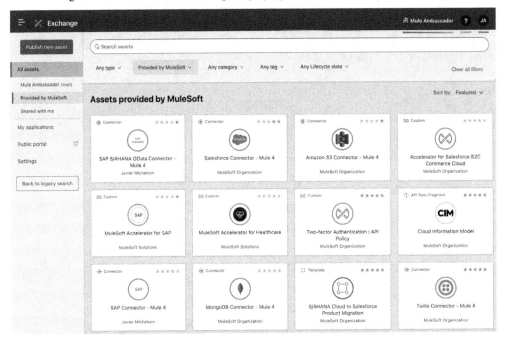

Figure 2.8 – Anypoint Exchange assets from MuleSoft

Looking at the different assets in the preceding screenshot, we can see that the types of assets that can be registered or published to Anypoint Exchange have grown dramatically over the past 4 years. Initially, Exchange was limited to Connectors and APIs. Anypoint Exchange is now home to 11 different types as of the time of this writing:

- **Connectors**: These are components developed with the Mule SDK that developers can use in MuleSoft flows to connect and interact natively with different systems

- **Dataweave libraries**: Developers can build Dataweave transformations that can be reused in other integrations

- **Examples**: assets that provide an example application, such as "How to Batch ETL with Snowflake"

- **Policies**: Policies that govern the security of APIs, typically running on a service mesh

- **API spec fragments**: Reusable segments of RAML or OAS to be reused in the development of new API specifications

- **REST APIs**: API specifications for implementations that can used or consumed by other approved applications

- **RPA activity templates**: Templates for the MuleSoft **Robotic Process Automation (RPA)** capability

- **Rule sets**: Rules for API governance

- **SOAP APIs**: APIs that can used or consumed by other approved applications

- **Templates**: Templates that can be copied and configured for your environment

- Custom (e.g., accelerators)

Once we have discovered an asset within Exchange that we want to use, we need to download it, import it, apply it, or request access to it, depending on the type of asset.

Summary

In this chapter, we looked in some detail at the control and runtime planes that make up Anypoint Platform. We considered some of the architectural decisions that need to be made and the business requirements that inform those decisions.

We looked at where the control plane and runtime plane can be hosted, and discovered two different ways to control access to the platform. We also considered the relationship between the control plane options and the influence those options have on the runtime plane.

We then took a quick look at the core services for designing, managing, and cataloging APIs within Anypoint Platform.

In the next chapter, we will look at Catalyst and the MuleSoft KnowledgeHub and see how we can leverage the Catalyst approach to increase the efficiency of our API projects.

Questions

1. What are the four hosting options available in the runtime plane?

2. Can you name the two capabilities that are unavailable when using Runtime Fabric for hosting the runtime plane?

3. What is Anypoint Exchange used for?

4. What are some of the considerations to keep in mind when determining where to host the control and runtime planes?

5. Describe the best practices for organizing resources in Anypoint Platform.

Further reading

MuleSoft business group documentation: `https://docs.mulesoft.com/access-management/business-groups`

Answers

1. CloudHub, CloudHub 2.0, RTF, and standalone servers are the current options for hosting the MuleSoft runtime plane.

2. Object Store v2 and Anypoint DataGraph are not available when using RTF.

3. Anypoint Exchange serves as a catalog of reusable assets comprising APIs, Connectors, Accelerators, Dataweave, RAML fragments, and more.

4. Data regulations, proximity to data, and cloud readiness.

5. Create child business groups and share resources with those groups. Create an environment for each testing phase included in your project and/or corresponding to your testing methodology.

3

Leveraging Catalyst and the MuleSoft Knowledge Hub

If your organization already has thousands of MuleSoft implementation projects from which you have studied the successes and failures, compiled what worked and what didn't, harvested hundreds of documents and documented dozens of best practices, and labeled, tagged, and organized it all into categories that align with product development, you might want chapter just to skip this chapter. If not, there are possibly some nuggets worth seeking out within the MuleSoft Catalyst Knowledge Hub that may make it easier for you and your company to deliver successful MuleSoft API projects.

MuleSoft customers and partners have access to an important MuleSoft resource that can help provide acceleration and lift to their integration and transformation initiatives and bring consistency to project development. This resource is Catalyst and the Catalyst Knowledge Hub. Catalyst is, simply put, MuleSoft's approach to delivering successful enterprise integration programs.

The approach Catalyst describes and the framework that goes with it is not intended to replace any project delivery methodology. Rather, it informs the kinds of activities and steps that should be included when planning different engagements. The Catalyst Knowledge Hub contains ready-to-use (and reuse) assets, best practices, and delivery approaches all collected from thousands of MuleSoft customers over years of implementations, and all centered around business objectives.

In this book, we have investigated some of the historical context around enterprise systems integration and how the MuleSoft platform itself developed out of this context. We have also looked at the core components and the structure of the platform itself. Much of the rest of this book focuses on the platform technology details and project design details. Catalyst helps to provide a structure and a framework around the architectural work, which is further described throughout the rest of this book.

In this chapter, we will cover the following topics:

- Catalyst, its core principles, and its engagements
- Leveraging the Catalyst Knowledge Hub
- Finding value in a **Center for Enablement (C4E)**

Exploring Catalyst, its core principles, and its engagements

We performed a very unscientific survey in which I asked a few different experienced MuleSoft professionals what Catalyst was and what benefit it provided organizations. Despite the small sample size, the results were interesting. Almost all saw the Catalyst as an important resource. Some considered it a project blueprint; others suggested it was a project methodology; a few I asked thought of it as a repository of templates and artifacts that could give them a good starting point. All had a different perspective on it.

Architects who take the **MuleSoft Certified Platform Architecture (MCPA)** course are introduced to Catalyst at a very high level, where it is described as a *framework* and an enterprise integration delivery *methodology* that adopts a big-picture view of delivering business outcomes, technology, and organizational enablement. It points to *playbooks* and the instructor will almost always point out the templates, documents, questionnaires, and other assets found in the Catalyst Knowledge Hub.

So, in a sense, all of those surveyed were on the right track. Each of them had made use of different parts of Catalyst and found value. In fact, as a delivery framework, Catalyst is intended to be pulled in and customized to fit the way any specific organization is organized.

But let's dig a little bit deeper into what Catalyst is, what makes up the foundation, how it is organized, and why it can be a useful tool for architects.

What is Catalyst?

Catalyst is, quite simply, MuleSoft's approach to delivery that takes a holistic view to achieving customer success, coupling outcomes-based technology delivery with organizational enablement. And what's in a name? Originally, Catalyst was called Outcome-Based Delivery, which was a mouthful. Catalyst evokes images of a substance that causes an acceleration or reaction without itself being affected. I like this image and name because this is exactly what an architect, and indeed an organization, should know about Catalyst. It is an accelerator for any MuleSoft program and, in truth, for any IT organization.

Catalyst includes playbooks for six different primary playbooks, all of which we'll review shortly. These playbooks include activities and steps to ensure the focus area is successful. Most of these steps include artifacts, best practices, templates, and documents as artifacts to support the execution of the steps.

But what does it mean when we talk about Catalyst as a methodology? Is this yet another project management approach for IT architecture work? There are already many different architecture frameworks and many project management methodologies currently in use by organizations. The **Open Group Architecture Framework** (**TOGAF**) and The Zachman Framework© are both popular approaches to enterprise architecture. The **Project Management Institute's** (**PMI's**) **Project Management Book of Knowledge** (**PMBOK**) is perhaps the leading example of a project methodology, along with Agile, Scrum, Waterfall, the critical path method, and extreme programming. Many others besides these have already been adopted by organizations to help manage their projects, identify risks, plan activities, provide stage gates for reviews, document current state architectures, ideate future state architectures, determine gaps, and build roadmaps to address all of the above.

Catalyst is not intended to replace these methodologies. Rather, it is meant to augment, accelerate, and enrich those methodologies. Ideally, organizations would utilize Catalyst to enrich their existing project methodologies and enterprise architectures. For example, Catalyst does not attempt to outline an approach for managing tasks. It does have steps, activities, and deliverables, all of which align well with an Agile project methodology or approach. However, it does not contain recommendations for Scrum meetings, advocate for specific ceremonies, indicate the need for demos, or suggest a demo schedule. All of these are important and should already be in place.

Likewise, Catalyst does not dictate an architectural preference or approach. You will find example patterns, solution architecture templates, and design consideration documents, many of which other architectural frameworks point to. However, Catalyst does not dictate the diagrams required nor does it prescribe what assets should be completed to pass through a stage gate.

Now that we know a little bit more about what Catalyst is, let's look at the foundation and how it is organized.

Catalyst's foundation

Catalyst is organized around three core pillars and each pillar is supported by one or more playbooks:

- Business Outcomes pillar:
  - Business Outcomes playbook
- Technology Delivery pillar:
  - Platform playbook (and delivery approach)
  - Project playbook (and delivery approach)

- Organizational Enablement pillar:
  - C4E (and delivery approach)
  - Internal Support
  - Training

Catalyst augments three of these playbooks with more prescriptive delivery approaches. There is a delivery approach for Anypoint Platform, Anypoint Projects, and C4E. These explicitly define work products to deliver across individual steps. For example, The project delivery approach includes a step for designing a solution that describes using Phillippe Kruchten's 4+1 view model of software architecture. This view is common to many architecture methodologies and is often incorporated into TOGAF deliverables.

The delivery approach also outlines the flow of activities to perform and a **Responsible/Accountable/Consult/Inform** (**RACI**) matrix for each activity. However, even when adopting a specific delivery approach, each organization should understand what is included in these delivery approaches and then take steps to customize the prescription to fit their institutional methodologies.

According to MuleSoft's Catalyst certification course, the Catalyst playbooks differ from the Catalyst delivery approaches not just by structure but also by audience. Both are available to all Anypoint Platform subscribers; however, the playbooks are written from a view specifically intended to be adopted by customers, whereas the audience for the delivery approaches is tailored for **systems integrators** (**SIs**) and delivery organizations.

The playbooks and their associated artifacts are developed and maintained in the Knowledge Hub and are intended to be adopted by MuleSoft customers. But keep in mind that they are not specific to individual products or product offerings. They cover the Catalyst phases of Plan for Success, Establish the Foundation, Build to Scale, and Measure Impact. The individual playbooks provide high-level activities along with individual steps.

Let's briefly take a look at each of these core pillars before digging into their associated playbooks and delivery approaches.

Business Outcomes

Business Outcomes is the guiding light here and the principal pillar that informs and shapes the work to come. Organizations have goals and often a corporate vision statement. When a company undertakes any new venture, it is with an outcome in mind – some future state that helps to achieve this vision or goal. Many, if not all, organizations require a value proposition before undertaking a large program of work to support the goals or vision. The value proposition may include qualitative as well as quantitative values. The business outcomes pillar and the supporting playbook activities document how to align with these business goals, how to recognize success with **key performance indicators** (**KPIs**), what reporting on these will look like, and how to build on the success. Later in this book, we will take a closer look at business outcomes and their relationship with functional requirements.

Technology Delivery

Technology Delivery is also very important. The platform and applications you build today will become the legacy platforms and applications of tomorrow. This pillar is broken into two paths or playbooks:

- Platform
- Project

Platform playbook begins with developing a vision for what the target MuleSoft platform should look like. Here, the platform architect should understand not only the MuleSoft products and how they work together, but they must also understand the following aspects:

- The business outcomes we described earlier
- The business strategy driving the program
- Corporate standards
- Enterprise architecture principals and governance

By understanding the business outcome proposition, we can describe the platform vision by showing how it supports the business outcomes.

Once the platform's future state has been laid out, we can begin to install the platform and the supporting services, such as common logging, alerting, and error handling. We can also establish build and release pipelines to support CI/CD DevOps requirements. And perhaps most importantly, we can begin to measure the impact of the KPIs that are developed as part of the business outcome work, allowing us to refine the platform and identify areas of growth and improvement.

The project playbook describes the activities and steps needed to identify and create a backlog of work based on quick wins based on high business value and/or reusable APIs. This work is usually the responsibility of the project or program manager but should be done with input from the platform and solution architects. The project playbook also defines activities and steps for designing, developing, testing, deploying, and publishing the project or solutions. Many times, this marks the conclusion of a project for the organization. However, Catalyst includes activities to scale as well as monitor and measure the impact of the projects that have been completed. Often, the platform architect may find they have a service that is only called once or twice a quarter or less. If so, it is important to understand why and determine if a different service would be appropriate there.

Much of this book is about understanding these platform capabilities and how they can support different architectural visions. But if done in a vacuum without a complete understanding of the business vision, goals, and outcomes, the platform and applications you build today will not only be the legacy applications of tomorrow, but they may also be a new, expensive, technical debt.

Organizational Enablement

Organizational Enablement is about getting the people and processes set up to create success. This activity can be uncomfortable because it may involve change. To support this change, this pillar is divided into three playbooks:

- C4E
- Internal Support
- Training

One of the reasons organizational work is so difficult and also so necessary is the effects of Conway's law on systems integration. Conway's law is the hypothesis that the communication structure in an organization will be reflected in the system designs. If a company is organized as one large team located in a central space, then the software will most likely be designed as a large monolithic architecture. Likewise, if a company is organized into small teams in different locations, the software is likely to be modular and distributed.

One of the biggest changes recommended within the Catalyst best practices is the establishment of a C4E. In many cases, if not most, creating a C4E will require some reorganization of roles and personnel and potentially adding new resources. We will take a closer look at C4E later in this chapter.

In addition to C4E, we must determine the framework and processes needed to monitor, support, and troubleshoot the MuleSoft platform and all the APIs and applications the platform supports. One caveat here is that some of the material, activities, and steps for the Internal Support playbook in Catalyst are written from a MuleSoft professional services or SI point of view, with activities such as *"set up introduction session with the client."* As mentioned earlier, Catalyst and these playbooks should be seen as an enrichment to the current people, processes, and technology already in place within the organization. The IT organization may decide to leverage their existing internal support team guidelines and only add the activities in this playbook that support identifying and monitoring KPIs related specifically to the MuleSoft platform support.

The Training playbook is the third within Organizational Enablement and, like Internal Support, it also has a heavy SI viewpoint. However, it is critical to the long-term success of the organization to ensure the IT team has the necessary skills to support and continue building MuleSoft components, especially if a third-party SI has been contracted to deliver the initial platform and quick win APIs supporting specific business outcomes. This playbook also identifies activities to expand on the traditional course work through other MuleSoft initiatives such as the Ambassador program, developer workshops, summits and conferences, and online sources such as blogs, forums, and meetup groups.

Playbook organization

There is a second dimension to these pillars, and it helps to further organize the material within each playbook. Catalyst adopted a design-build-scale-optimize approach to development and uses the following names for each phase:

- Plan for Success
- Establish the Foundation
- Build to Scale
- Measure Impact

Table 3.1 shows the relationship between the pillars and playbooks and these phases:

	Plan for success	Establish foundation	Build to Scale	Measure Impact
Business Outcome	• Agree Outcomes and KPIs • Develop Success Plan	• Monitor and manage	• Refresh success plan	• Measure value
Platform	• Define platform vision • Design platform architecture and implementation plan	• Implement platform	• Scale and refine	• Measure platform impact
Project	• Prioritize IT projects • Staff and onboard delivery team	• Define Solution architecture • Execute projects	• Onboard additional delivery teams • Launch additional projects	• Measure impact of projects
C4E	• Assess integration capability • Establish C4E	• Build and Publish core assets • Evangelize	• Drive consumption	• Measure impact of C4E
Internal Support	• Determine support model	• Staff, train, launch team • Publish support guidance	• Support the platform	• Measure impact of support
Training	• Train initial team	• Develop broader training plan • Launch experiential learning	• Train additional teams	• Conduct assessments

Table 3.1 – Catalyst foundation activities by development phase

Within this matrix, the activities needed for the phase are listed below each phase. Each playbook within each pillar contains the activities and steps needed to successfully deliver that phase of a project. For example, within the Platform playbook in the Technology Delivery pillar, the activities associated with the **Plan for Success** phase can be found: defining the platform vision and roadmap and designing the architecture and implementation plan.

Each activity is broken down into specific steps, which are described in detail, along with any artifacts and deliverables this step will produce, including what steps are prerequisites to initiating the step and what roles from the delivery team and account team should work on the step in some form. Finally, many of the steps identify and provide links to physical assets that can be downloaded and used by the project team.

MuleSoft also provides guidance for successful projects through something called Catalyst engagements.

Catalyst engagements

One final note about the foundation of Catalyst: MuleSoft service offerings include working with MuleSoft or partners to execute predefined activities that are organized around the Catalyst phases.

A Catalyst Launch engagement can be very useful for organizations who are just beginning to onboard the MuleSoft platform and develop API applications. Launch combines the activities under **Plan for Success** and **Establish Foundation** across all six playbooks. This engagement is about helping get to the business outcomes. This engagement can also be useful in the initial configuration and setup of the Anypoint Platform and in putting together the first use cases to deliver. Moreover, it establishes a training program to enable the staff identified by the organization through classes specific to their jobs and their day-to-day activities.

Catalyst Scale delivers a program using the activities of **Build to Scale**. So, this engagement focuses on the activities that will allow businesses and organizations to begin driving reuse. This engagement helps identify potential candidates for new use cases, especially those that can benefit from the reusable components initially developed. In this engagement, the teams involved in organizational enablement begin to add to their skill sets through additional training and learn to operate and support the APIs and MuleSoft platform.

Catalyst Optimize uses the **Measure Impact** activities. As the name of the engagement implies, it can be seen as helping move the organization higher along a capability maturity model scale. Activities such as KPI monitoring via newly created dashboards, reporting, and reuse acceleration become embedded into the culture of the organization.

These engagements specifically leverage the different Catalyst product delivery life cycle phases with a prescriptive approach and a long-running effort to achieve business outcomes across the three Catalyst pillars: Business Initiatives, Technology Delivery, and Organizational Enablement. Multiple projects may be initiated and completed within the context of a single Catalyst engagement.

Now, let's consider how we can leverage the Catalyst Knowledge Hub to accelerate and/or enhance an organization's existing methodology.

Leveraging the Catalyst Knowledge Hub

The Catalyst Knowledge Hub is a searchable document store that contains MuleSoft curated assets and content for use on Catalyst engagements. Earlier in this chapter, we described Catalyst as an accelerator and an approach to delivering successful enterprise integration projects; it is not a project or architecture methodology.

> **Note**
>
> In addition to the playbooks and delivery approaches found in Catalyst, MuleSoft has a GitHub account with, at the time of this writing, 158 repos. These repos contain implementation examples of patterns, ranging from a functional monitoring demo to a metrics toolkit to a circuit breaker policy. The account and repo do not require a MuleSoft license to browse and use. The GitHub account is open to anyone looking for examples, demos, and starting frameworks to start their project development with. It can be found here: `https://github.com/orgs/mulesoft-catalyst/repositories`.

One way to leverage the Catalyst Knowledge Hub is to search for examples when you need them. Within the Platform Playbook alone, there are up to 250 asset pages across the phases and activities and many of these have multiple attached files. These files are templates, examples, matrices, videos, PDFs, slides, and more.

As an architect, for example, perhaps you have been asked to develop the Anypoint Platform reference architecture. You search Catalyst for Anypoint Platform and find 347 results. You add in architecture and narrow it down to 117. Checking specifically for **Design Architecture & Implementation**, as shown in *Figure 3.1*, we find a playbook step that may be helpful:

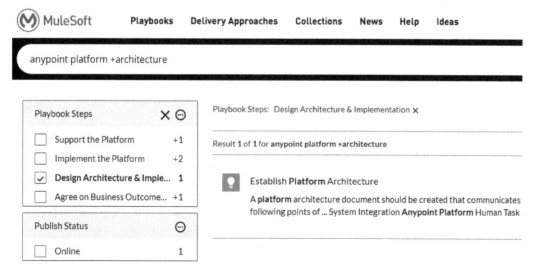

Figure 3.1 – Example of searching the Catalyst Knowledge Hub

We find that there are 25 assets available on the playbook page, one of which is a reference architecture document that has an architecture template. The top four assets on the page are shown in *Figure 3.2*:

Link to Asset Page ↑	⌄	Rating	⌄	Last Modified Date	⌄	Deployment Type
An Approach to Application Load Balanc...		★ ★ ★ ☆ ☆		Jan 19, 2023		PCE
Anypoint Platform APIs		★ ★ ★ ☆ ☆		Jan 19, 2023		Cloudhub;Hybrid;PCE
Anypoint Platform Architecture Template		★ ★ ★ ☆ ☆		Jan 19, 2023		Cloudhub;Hybrid;PCE
Anypoint Platform Reference Architectu...		★ ★ ★ ☆ ☆		Jan 19, 2023		Cloudhub;Hybrid;PCE

Figure 3.2 – Results from the search

> **Note**
>
> The playbook entry itself is more than just a list of reusable assets at the bottom of the page. In the example document in *Figure 3.1*, a review of the 4+1 architecture views can be found.

While searching for specific assets periodically is certainly one way to use the Catalyst Knowledge Hub, a higher leverage option is to fold the approach itself into the project and architecture methodology that's already adopted by the organization by using activities and steps to populate the project Kanban board, Scrum board, or project plan, and using the assets to accelerate and enrich your architecture approach.

The Catalyst approach aligns well with common architectures. Since TOGAF is used by about 80% of organizations, it can provide a good example of combining the principles and concepts of Catalyst with TOGAF.

The TOGAF **Architectural Development Method** (**ADM**) shown in *Figure 3.3* has been augmented with playbooks from the Catalyst approach:

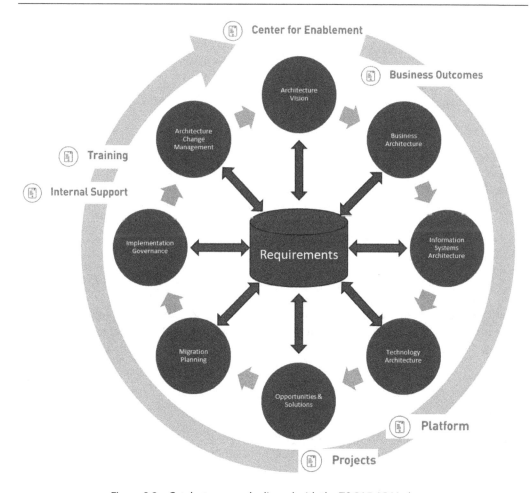

Figure 3.3 – Catalyst approach aligned with the TOGAF ADM phases

In the example shown in *Figure 3.3*, Catalyst Business Outcomes has been aligned with TOGAF Architecture Vision and Business Architecture. Among the TOGAF steps for Architecture Vision and Business Architecture, we have the following:

- Identify stakeholders, concerns, and business requirements
- Confirm and elaborate business goals, business drivers, and constraints
- Select reference models, viewpoints, and tools
- Develop current and target business architecture descriptions

Augmenting these steps or artifacts with Business Outcomes allows the MuleSoft project to align with the Enterprise Architecture along the Catalyst-defined activities:

- Agree on business outcomes
- Identify and align key stakeholders
- Identify dependencies and risks to success

Likewise, as we define Technology Architecture and Opportunities & Solutions, TOGAF looks to deliver an architecture vision, a statement of architecture work, and baseline and target business, data, application, and technology architectures, along with capability assessments that can inform the Catalyst Platform and Project playbooks with steps such as the following:

- Establish the Platform architecture
- Define common services
- Validate the compliance of the architecture

Catalyst Training and Support playbooks have been aligned with implementation governance and change management. These could have a home across all phases of the ADM, similar to how the C4E is positioned as encircling and drawing from the full ADM lifecycle.

Figure 3.3 is just one example of aligning with a pre-existing architecture methodology. The important thing is to understand what is in place, and what building blocks can be extended to support the product life cycle of an API-led integration program.

Integration in general works much better when there is coordination between the business and IT. Integrating the Catalyst process with TOGAF (or any other enterprise architecture method) is no different; sharing over silos between departments is the key. One of the best ways to help drive integration capabilities, encourage reuse, and measure the effectiveness of your APIs across the organization is through the establishment of a C4E. In the next section, we will look at what makes up the C4E and what value establishing a C4E brings to the organization.

Finding value in a C4E

Often, MuleSoft practitioners, architects, and delivery organizations will either dismiss the C4E or – best case – consider it a secondary or even tertiary concern. It is easy to understand why in the following cases:

- Higher priorities have been identified in the statement of work
- Budgets have been set and fixed during annual financial meetings
- The accounting department isn't asking for much; they just want good data they can include on the salary reports

These short-term projects, the tactical fire drills, the siren call of the shiny object, and the drudgery of **yet another governance project** (**YAGP**) are more than enough to distract an organization from putting any effort into something that starts with "Center."

Ironically, when companies disregard not just C4E but the activities and actions it recommends, an organization may exacerbate the problems they sought to fix through the adoption of an API approach and a shiny new MuleSoft platform. Instead of reducing the demand on IT, they've just added to it; instead of leveraging a platform architected for reuse, they find themselves maintaining and operating another platform without training or support, and instead of innovating and accelerating the recently initiated digital transformation program, the business reverts to shadow IT and putting critical business functions in spreadsheets.

The C4E, as defined in Catalyst, is not primarily a governance program. It is not intended to add additional process gates preventing projects from proceeding. It also doesn't have to look the same for every organization. Rather, the C4E is a plan and approach to enable teams to effectively manage the Anypoint Platform, promote the reuse of applications to accelerate innovation, communicate the overall capabilities, and reduce risks through compliance.

Without a vision for long-term platform growth, good organization of resources, and evangelism, a company can quickly begin to produce assets that aren't good building blocks and don't get the reuse that they should have to achieve the value proposition. Let's look at a few of the key elements that go into establishing the C4E, including team enablement, measurement, and staffing.

Team enablement

One of the capabilities and primary activities of the C4E is enabling teams. One of the most effective ways to do this is to provide foundational components, templates, examples, and APIs. Templates and examples can be published to Exchange so that they can be discovered by teams who are looking to start developing a new API.

Templates can also support the codification of best practices in a way that helps ensure the users of the asset will be following the identified best practices. The integration architect for the C4E program, in coordination with the enterprise architect, identifies the best practices, particularly for the common, foundational components of a system. This can include the following:

- Logging
- Error handling
- Security
- Queue management
- Alerts, monitoring, and health checks

Often, an organization may already have a best practice identified for some of the foundation components. For example, an organization may have described a standard for logging that requires all application logs and audit logs to be sent to a standard logging service such as ELK or Splunk. This is great except it generally means every developer will end up figuring out the process for shipping the logs to the aggregator.

However, another best practice is "build once and reuse." These best practices can feed the development of common frameworks that by themselves can be used by other projects. For example, a logging framework can be designed and built to handle any common logging requirements. These common frameworks can then be incorporated into templates for specific integration design patterns such as API, Publish/Subscribe event handler, batch processing, and SOAP service/consumer. And, as stated earlier, each of these can be published and fully documented in Exchange.

Many of the MuleSoft developers and architects can recount having built a logging service, a security component, or a global exception handler multiple times. This is not surprising for consulting companies, SIs, or other partners responsible for delivering the MuleSoft platform for multiple clients, but it should not be the norm within an organization.

Metrics and KPIs

Gathering the metrics for the C4E KPIs is something that can add value to your organization, regardless of whether you have initiated a C4E program or not. They tell you how the organization is performing against the business goals. This information can help the team determine if changes are needed either to the platform or to an API based on its usage.

Catalyst recommends tracking the following KPIs to gain insight into the success of the platform:

- Number of assets in Exchange

- Number of assets in Design Center

- Number of APIs in production

- Developer engagement

- Average rating

- API reuse percentage

- Core usage

One of the more popular repositories in the GitHub account mentioned earlier in this chapter contains a tool that can be helpful here: `https://github.com/mulesoft-catalyst/metrics-toolkit`

This toolkit helps collect and aggregate performance metrics, providing dashboards and charts showing many of the KPIs described here.

> **Note**
>
> In our experience, rating assets in Exchange is rare and even when ratings exist, the volume of ratings for a specific asset does not provide meaningful statistical feedback.

The dashboard shown in *Figure 3.4* shows an example of reporting on the number of assets in Exchange and Design Center:

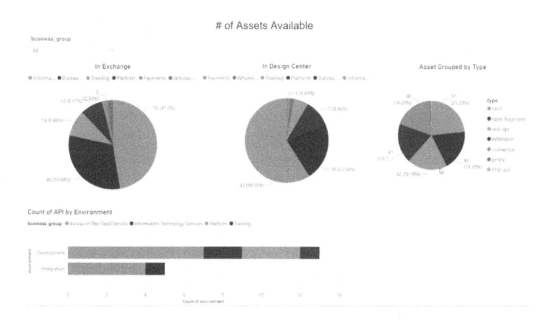

Figure 3.4 – KPI dashboard showing # of Assets Available in Anypoint Platform

The dashboard in *Figure 3.4* can begin to tell a story, albeit incomplete on its own, about which business group is leveraging the platform the most. However, it may also indicate stalled efforts or groups developing APIs but not publishing them to Exchange.

These metrics are by no means a comprehensive list. Capturing KPIs and measuring them can help architects understand the stability and adoption of the platform, how efficiently projects are being delivered, and whether best practices and governance are being followed.

Staffing

First and foremost, there should always be a champion for the program, someone who can sponsor the work and promote (evangelize) the capabilities across the organization. The C4E is designed to operate across functional areas. This means that staffing should be organized to work with the different teams and groups within an organization. Since each organization is different and many are at different levels of maturing for different capabilities, the C4E will not have to look the same for every organization; this extends to how the C4E is staffed. Depending on the size of the organization, some of the defined roles may be part-time. The following list of functional areas is common in most medium to large companies:

- **Project teams**: Often aligned with a product or solution in the business or department. They are responsible for new features, applications, or initiatives.

- **Architecture**: A cross-functional group that may include enterprise, application, data, and infrastructure architects. They are responsible for the organization's architecture roadmap, governance, and compliance.

- **Change control/QA**: They are responsible for ensuring changes to the operating environment are understood, documented, and tested. This is the last line of defense for changes to production.

- **Operations**: The team keeping things running across the infrastructure. It may be subdivided into on-premises and cloud compute support.

- **Security**: Threat protection for possibly the most important and valuable asset the company owns: its data and systems. This may be included in the architecture team or operations and matrixed to project teams.

- **CI/CD**: A comparatively new function that's responsible for the software development life cycle across the organization. It's sometimes included in a change control/QA team.

Ideally, the C4E staffing will include personnel from across any central IT organization and the different business departments. Not only will this provide better visibility into the capabilities being included in the platform, but it should also create better buy-in as each of these teams will have some skin in the game.

Aside from where the staffing will come from, Catalyst identifies three primary roles that will be key to any C4E program:

- **Sponsor**: The champion for the program. They understand and track the business value and are the primary evangelist.

- **C4E lead**: They are accountable for the success of C4E and integration, provide stewardship of the platform assets, and handle all the communication with the stakeholders.

- **Integration architect**: They are responsible for the overall integration architecture vision and roadmap, set the standards and best practices, and liaise with the architecture team as well as project teams. If an API development team is needed, they are responsible for the architecture decisions and direction.

In addition to these roles, consider including roles that line up with the different functional areas identified previously. Here are some examples:

- **Platform liaison**: They will connect with the operations team, specifically infrastructure, and will be responsible for the stable operation of the control plane and the runtime plane.

- **DevOps liaison**: They will connect with the project management teams and CI/CD team. Additionally, they will be responsible for the software life cycle and project approach and will own the API life cycle.

The roles shown here may not fit every organization and every situation. Many organizations depend on individuals wearing multiple hats to get things done while others are very specific about the activities that are expected from a person or a group.

Summary

Among practitioners, I have found there to be many differing opinions about MuleSoft Catalyst. What we have done in this chapter is provide you with a foundation to help you determine how and where the Catalyst approach can help you. This chapter outlined the foundation of Catalyst, what it is, and, importantly, what it is not. You learned how Catalyst is structured, what its principles are, and how its foundation supports the three pillars: Business Outcomes, Technical Delivery, and Organizational Enablement.

We discovered that there are many assets in Catalyst ranging from templates to patterns to examples all wrapped inside best practices for creating the organizational changes to support the work. For organizations just beginning to adopt an API approach to integration, the actions from the playbooks can help inform the organization's project management methodology, and the reference architecture assets and Catalyst principles can shape and address the architecture concerns of business, data, application, and technology.

The chapter also briefly explored the C4E, a key part of the Organizational Enablement pillar. We specifically examined how a C4E helps enable other teams by providing more than just governance. This support also takes the form of best practices, foundation frameworks, and codified best practices in the form of templates and examples We also looked at how the program's success can be measured so that changes can be made where things aren't working while evangelism can communicate these KPIs and measures to stakeholders across the organization. These stakeholders and the key roles needed in a C4E team were described. Staffing for the C4E is usually one of the more challenging aspects and will require support and funding from senior champions of the program within the organization.

Within the establishment of the architecture material of Catalyst, the outgrowth of an application network can be observed and discussed. The next chapter will take a closer look at what the application network is, what the benefits are, and how such a thing can be encouraged to come into existence.

Questions

Answer the following questions to test your knowledge of this chapter:

1. What are the three pillars that form the foundation of MuleSoft Catalyst?
2. Why is it important to identify the business outcome as part of an API delivery project?
3. What is available in the Catalyst Knowledge Hub and is it available to everyone?
4. How does the C4E support successful API project deliveries?

Further reading

To learn more about the topics that were covered in this chapter, take a look at the following resources:

- Alan Dalley, *Another Integration Blog* on Medium posts
- MuleSoft training course and certification: *Delivering Successful Business Outcomes with Catalyst*
- Catalyst secure website for partners and customers: Knowledge Hub,MuleSoft.com
- The C4E Webinar series on Catalyst Foundations
- The MuleSoft blog on COE versus C4E: `https://blogs.mulesoft.com/digital-transformation/coe-c4e-away-teams/`

Answers

Here are the answers to this chapter's questions:

1. MuleSoft Catalyst is built around three pillars: Business Outcomes, Technology Delivery, and Organizational Delivery.
2. The business outcome helps us to identify the priorities for the business. It provides us with an objective or goal the business has identified. It can help shape and promote business initiatives to either modernize or digitally transform the organization. It highlights the value associated with delivering the business outcome. It also allows us to form technical use cases that would support the delivery of the business outcome.

3. The Catalyst Knowledge Hub is available to customers and partners of MuleSoft. It does require a subscription to Anypoint Platform. However, the content within can be used at any time for any project or engagement. The Catalyst Knowledge Hub is organized by pillar, and each pillar contains one or more playbooks. Each playbook defines the activities and each activity's steps across four product development-based categories: Plan for Success, Establish the Foundation, Build to Scale, and Measure Impact. Each step is documented and described, and most steps include assets to support the activity. These assets can be PowerPoint decks to support communication, documents to serve as templates for designs, Visio diagrams with API-led architecture examples, and many others describing best practices, patterns, or network architectures. In addition to the playbooks, there are delivery approaches, which can serve as a prescriptive approach to three of the playbooks: Platform, Project, and C4E.

4. The C4E provides an approach to enabling teams within an organization. The C4E establishes not only governance but also best practices, common services, and other accelerators. The team publishes foundational components and services. The team works with operations, CI/CD, and architecture groups to provide a consistent approach to the SDLC. The C4E monitors KPIs and metrics to determine how well the platform, team, and projects are working and how well APIs are being adopted.

4

An Introduction
to Application Networks

In this chapter, we will consider a different approach to integrating applications and data across an enterprise. We have already taken a high-level look at the different integration patterns that develop over time – point-to-point, publish-subscribe, and **Service-oriented architecture (SOA)**. We also considered some middleware tooling such as the enterprise service bus, hub-and-spoke, message queues, event-driven, and **Extract, transform, and load (ETL)**.

Here, we will take a closer look at the concept of the application network, what differentiates it from these other approaches to integration, and why MuleSoft considers it to be the *next generation of integration middleware*. We will also see how to apply the tools, security, and Mule runtimes to achieve an application network architecture.

In this chapter, we will examine the following topics:

- An introduction to MuleSoft application networks
- Building and implementing an application network
- Benefits and best practices of an application network

In 2019, Andrew Dent, Field CTO, DTO at MuleSoft in Australia, wrote, "*An application network is the way to connect applications, data, and devices through APIs which expose their assets and data on the network.*" In this chapter, we will take a closer look at the concepts and the role of the platform architect in helping define and structure this network.

An introduction to MuleSoft application networks

Understanding the concept of an application network is important. In fact, one of the primary roles of the MuleSoft platform architect is to not only understand it but also act as the composer of this network. Indeed, "Application Network" is the subtitle to the MuleSoft course that prepares students for the Platform Architect exam (*Anypoint Platform Architecture: Application Networks*)! The following URL is a link to this course: `https://trailheadacademy.salesforce.com/classes/ARC720-mulesoft-architecture-application-networks`.

What is an application network?

First, let's understand what an application network is and what it is not. An application network is not an integration architecture. Rather, in the context of API integration at least, it is the landscape that emerges when applications are made available via APIs as a "network node," with connectivity to other application nodes across an organization. It is a collection of connected applications, data, and business process building blocks, with APIs serving as the connective tissue for the network.

In some sense, the origins of a conceptual application network can be partially traced back to Sir Tim Berners-Lee's vision of the **World Wide Web** (**WWW**). Writ large, this network of information and data, spanning every continent, connecting almost every business, enabling devices not yet even imagined at the time, and ushering in the information age, shows how valuable things become when they are connected in a way that makes these connections reusable. The connective tissue of this network is more often than not the verbs of **Representational State Transfer** (**REST**) interacting with the resources, as described in *Dr. Roy Thomas Fielding's seminal doctoral dissertation*.

One of the main issues that emerged from this network is where to find trustworthy information. Any business, entity, and, indeed, bad actor can easily join this network of "applications," sharing false or misleading information and data. In the end, the quality of the data found on this network lowers its overall value. This does not prevent many a high school and college essay or LinkedIn blog from being created with this information, further proliferating the muddy data of this application network. Addressing the quality and trustworthiness of information across the WWW "application network" is now Berners-Lee's latest focus. This also should be the focus of organizations that want to leverage one of their greatest assets, data, to drive innovation.

Trustworthy data across an application network allows us to manage business change, enable agility, innovate new products and solutions, and leverage the best ideas in an organization through reusable components. Almost every application in an organization has some business value associated with it. When these applications are API-enabled and join the application network, the application's intrinsic value increases, as does the value of the network. However, something we can call the *potential value* of the network also increases. This potential value is realized as additional applications enter a network and tap into the data and processes already made available to the new consuming application.

So, let's look closer at what makes up an application network and some of the reasons it's important.

Components and the importance of an application network

The first and most obvious component of an application network is an application or system. However, there are two different kinds of applications:

- **A system of record**: The system of record is the recognized authority for a piece of information or data. For example, there may be many different applications within an organization, all of which use customer data. However, when one specific application is identified as the source of truth for customer data, the other systems must defer to this primary system for validated data.

- **An external, or consumer application**: Many systems within and external to an organization will consume data from multiple sources. In this context, the application is an external consumer application.

The system of record for different data domains can be difficult to identify. Because most organizations have an application landscape that is quite large (some reports place the number of systems at over 900), different business units may utilize similar data but use it in unique ways.

Organizations already have a rudimentary application network without realizing it. When we consider all the applications being utilized in a company and put aside for a moment the connective tissue, such as manual dual-data entry, file downloads, and file uploads, the "network" aspect is invisible. *Figure 4.1* shows a small footprint of various applications that may be used by a company to do their day-to-day business. These applications, of course, will vary from company to company. These could be **Line of Business (LOB)** applications, enterprise-wide applications, or even external applications.

Figure 4.1 - An unintentional application network

We can think of this as an unintentional application network. The ability to leverage the data and process in these applications is unknown. The intrinsic value of an invisible network is not zero; it can end up costing a company significantly financially. For example, consider the cost of manually maintaining data in multiple systems, employing staff to manage and maintain duplicate business functions, not to mention the cost of doing business with unknown data quality. During a strategy and architecture roadmap project for a company, it was discovered that the employee salaries were being downloaded from one application into a CSV file, manually converted to an Excel spreadsheet, manually reviewed and often adjusted by payroll staff in the spreadsheet, and finally, sent off to another third-party company to create the checks. Clearly, several points in this process could result in reputational as well as financial costs.

With a MuleSoft-enabled organization, we can begin to see APIs as the common connective capability across the enterprise, providing accessible data and reusable processes to any of the information systems in this network. *Figure 4.2* is commonly used to represent a MuleSoft platform-enabled application network.

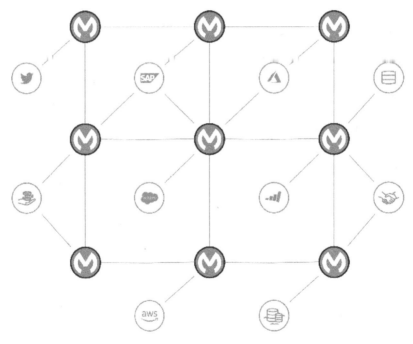

Figure 4.2 - A MuleSoft-enabled application network

This diagram, of course, is very high-level and does not show any specific details of the connections between applications. We can break this down by looking at APIs, the second component of a MuleSoft-enabled application network.

When we talk about the application network in the context of a MuleSoft-enabled organization, the first thing most Mule practitioners will think of is a multi-tiered high-level architecture diagram, typically developed by the API architect to identify what APIs need to be built, where data and processes will come from, and what systems and applications consume particular data and processes.

The API architecture for API-led connectivity is usually drawn as a swim-lane diagram. *Figure 4.3* shows an unpopulated template with each tier, or component layer, identified.

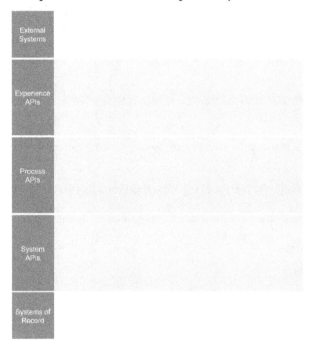

Figure 4.3 - A high-level application network design template

In the template shown in *Figure 4.3*, the first component of an application network, the applications (or systems), are found in the top and bottom swim lanes. The APIs connecting them are found in the middle swim lanes. The components can be identified as follows:

- **External systems**: These are systems that consume the processes and information made available via APIs.

- **Experience APIs**: These APIs are purpose-built to decouple the acquisition of requested data from the formatting and communication required by the external system. For example, the data being acquired may come from various sources, using formats completely foreign to the external system. This experience API takes on the job of presenting it to the external system in a way that makes sense to that specific system.

- **Process APIs**: These APIs can coordinate the acquisition and/or transactions of systems. This coordination can be either orchestration or choreography. Its purpose can also be to aggregate data across different sources or to perform a multi-system business transaction, handling rollbacks and commits manually if needed.

- **System APIs**: These APIs safely and securely expose the data actions to be made available from a system of record. This can include getting, creating, updating, and deleting data in a specific application. Often, the system of record will provide a well-documented and well-designed RESTful API. These APIs can be used directly as a System API, especially if other cost-related factors such as flow count or vCore come up. However, be sure to thoroughly consider any issues of composability, reuse, and coupling that could create technical debt if these systems are swapped out.

- **Systems of record**: This system, as noted earlier, is the agreed-upon source of truth for some piece of information or data.

Next, let's take a look at how we can architect and develop an application network.

Building and implementing an application network

There are three main steps we can consider when thinking about building out the application network.

1. Planning the roadmap
2. Designing and developing
3. Managing and evangelizing reuse

Planning the roadmap

When we begin to think about building an application, especially in an organization that embraces an agile methodology and approach, we usually think about a roadmap with different features emerging, covering different functionality and business use cases. Creating a strategic roadmap should be considered a priority. With no direction or understanding of the desired destination, the future state is left to chance and may or may not support the business outcomes required to support the organization's goals.

As mentioned, this is a regular approach (or should be) when developing the roadmap for an application. This can include an API application as well as a new LOB application. Consider the example project roadmap in *Figure 4.4*. This figure begins with a **Minimum Viable Product (MVP)**, identifying several additional milestones and the functionality included.

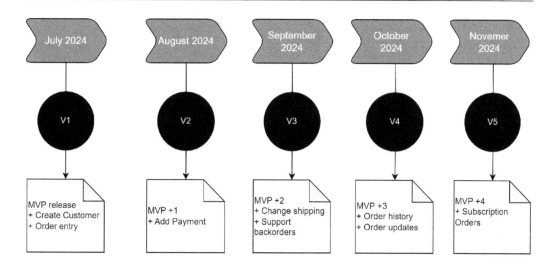

Figure 4.4 - Application roadmap

The roadmap depicted in *Figure 4.4* identifies when we can expect the MVP for an ordering application to be complete, and then it suggests what additional features the users can expect each month following the MVP release.

Likewise, we can begin planning the roadmap of the application network by considering what data and processes should be securely exposed and made available, as well as what applications will begin consuming this data. Consider the high-level architecture designs in *Figure 4.5*. This progression of architecture designs shows how the application network evolves over time.

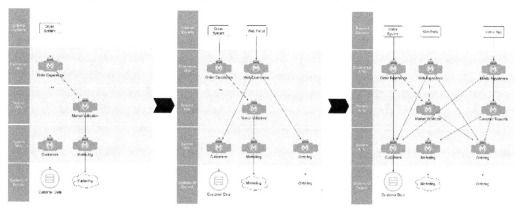

Figure 4.5 - A solution roadmap of an emerging application network

Moreover, the design in these figures also begins to highlight where we will be able to reuse existing APIs, thus extracting part of the value proposition found in MuleSoft Anypoint Platform.

One of the things this solution roadmap should highlight is the importance of an integration architecture driven from the top of the organization. This results in two things:

- An architecture that considers applications from other LOBs, enterprise systems, and organizational goals. Awareness of these cross-functional requirements may not be present within department teams.

- Departmental teams developing integration architectures that begin considering these outside factors and how they can use their systems to provide services in support of organizational goals.

Designing and developing

In this step, we will get a little more granular on what needs to be designed and developed across our now-evolving application network. In the previous section, we began creating a roadmap and provided an approach to seeing how we can reuse different APIs, by observing how future API-led connectivity will introduce new connections and reuse existing connections. Here, we will take those individual connection points and design and develop their details.

Let's consider a quick example using the earlier described use case. We will assume J&J Music has been struggling with poor quality across its customer data, particularly when trying to place orders. The analysis of the music company's operations reveals that customers have had difficulty finding their previous orders because of duplication of their information, or because their information was no longer there. Another issue with this mismanaged data is the inability to gain insights into customers' buying habits so that the company can better meet their needs and deliver a higher level of service, whether shopping in person or online.

The J&J Music CIO decided to address the quality data problem by developing or purchasing a **master data management** (**MDM**) application. This system would govern and promote stewardship of their customer data. We don't have space here to describe the details of the system or its implementation process, but for convenience, let's consider that during the implementation and deployment of the system, data cleanup has occurred and reconciliation with the ordering system was completed. During go-live, the business agreed to declare the MDM application the single source of truth for the customer data.

Ultimately, the desired business outcome is for customers to have a cleaner and less error-prone process when placing orders for their music selections. As the requirements were gathered to define a solution or solutions for this business outcome, the architecture team presented the design you can see in *Figure 4.6*.

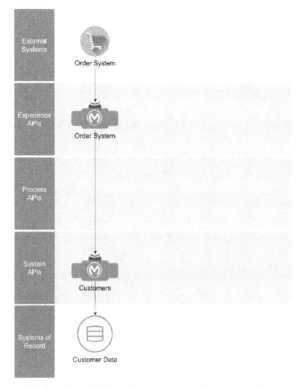

Figure 4.6 - J&J Music's ordering and customer view

Using the swim lane template, the platform architect can identify the ordering system as an external/consuming system. Likewise, the architect has discovered the source of truth for the customer data can be found in the customer MDM system.

The IT team at J&J Music is tasked with developing the APIs to provide controlled access to the data and open the processes through which customer data can be added or edited. Because this data is managed and governed within the MDM solution, we may even need to develop these APIs to integrate with any workflows, policies, notifications, or rules within the MDM solution. This, of course, has immediate present value for the existing Orders application. The Orders application can now take advantage of this curated customer data, ensuring that the source of truth is used when transacting with customers.

However, there is also a "potential value" for any additional application that interfaces with the customer data, and this is what creates the intrinsic value of the application network. This potential value can also be estimated. At a minimum, it is equal to the cost of building the Customer API. By reusing the Customer API instead of rebuilding it, direct cost savings for any other consumer can be achieved. Additionally, although a bit harder to quantify, there is, of course, the value of having good-quality data from a single source of truth.

As we observed in the previous section, as the vision of the roadmap is executed and future functionality is added, the Customer API will be reused. Each time this happens, the organization has cashed in on the value of the application network.

Managing and evangelizing reuse

In the last chapter, we reviewed the concept of a **Center for Enablement** (**C4E**), and we also examined organizational enablement at a high level. The C4E has several roles through which it can provide value to an organization. Monitoring, evangelizing, and promoting reuse are among the most important. Achieving a valuable, reusable application network depends on a company adjusting its IT operating model to begin taking advantage of the connections between applications.

This means that in addition to developing an architecture roadmap strategy and plan, and in addition to designing and developing reusable API services to enable the roadmap strategy, we will need to enable the management of these new assets and find ways to energize the organization to take advantage of the application network as it begins to take shape.

Note that the management activity we describe here is not primarily, or even secondarily, about reviewing code or documentation. This activity is about ensuring the new assets are known more broadly across an organization. Many, if not most, organizations have a difficult time just understanding what systems are in use, especially when we begin counting up the number of shadow-IT systems developed as "skunkworks" applications because IT was having a hard time getting resources allocated for yet another business request. So, in one sense, adding API assets can increase this gap in knowledge of what is out there and how it can be used.

MuleSoft Anypoint Platform can be used to keep the connections of the application network visible, making it clear what parts of the application network are strongest and where weaknesses exist. The following list illustrates some of the basic mechanisms included in Anypoint Platform to make managing an organization's APIs much easier. API portals and dashboards provide metrics on the operation of API on Anypoint:

- Management views of message flow performance
- Management views of APIs
- Architecture and troubleshooting views of APIs (via Visualizer), as shown in *Figure 4.7*

Figure 4.7 - Application network visualization in MuleSoft Anypoint Platform

Views such as the Anypoint Visualizer and the monitoring capabilities discussed in another chapter in this book are tools that are available to highlight good performing APIs across an application network, and they also identify APIs that are either no longer relevant or may be unknown to an organization as a whole. It may be time to retire a particular API, or there may be a need to better promote the data and functionality being exposed by an API collection.

Understanding when to take such actions is dependent on an organization, the future architecture gap transitions, and the adopted best practices of the organization to manage an application network.

In the next section, we will summarize the benefits of the application network and consider some of the best practices to create an application network within an organization.

The benefits and best practices of an application network

In this section, we will review the benefits that application networks offer to an organization, and then we will highlight some best practices to follow when architecting your application network.

Benefits

Connecting and communicating in general have many benefits that are readily observable when looking at the flow of data across applications within an organization. Many of these benefits are quantitative as well as qualitative.

Improved efficiency and agility

When we began this chapter, we referred to the value of the WWW. It is an imperfect comparison to an organization's application network and yet it highlights one of the greatest strengths (and, potentially, a serious weakness) of the application network.

So much data is available via the internet. But much of the best research I believe still comes from a good library and a solid collection of books, such as this one in your hands – material that has gone through editing and research time. However, there is no denying the speed with which we can locate answers to questions once a trustworthy data source has been identified. Likewise, business moves fast. This fact gave birth to the commonly used phrase "*The big don't eat the small; it's the fast that eat the slow*".

This isn't just about being able to locate the data and use it when it's needed. It's about building agility within an IT team by developing building blocks that can be used to build new solutions quickly, without rebuilding the same data pathways over and over again.

Application networks enable you to reuse and recompose existing applications and data, rather than building everything from scratch. This allows you to respond quickly to changing market demands and customer needs, as well as experiment with new ideas and features.

Scalability

Application networks allow you to scale your applications up or down according to the load and demand, without compromising performance or reliability. You can also leverage cloud services and platforms to host your applications and data, reducing the cost and complexity of infrastructure management.

Security

Application networks enable you to enforce consistent security policies across your applications and data, regardless of where they are located or accessed. You can also use encryption, authentication, and authorization mechanisms to protect your data and transactions from unauthorized access or tampering.

Visibility

Application networks provide you with real-time insights into the performance, health, and usage of your applications and data. You can also monitor and troubleshoot issues, as well as optimize your resources and processes.

Best practices

Architects and senior developers have long known the benefit of following established best practices. Doing so can help provide code consistency. Best practices can make it easier for new developers who understand the best practices to step in and be effective, with less knowledge transfer required. They can reveal the easy button, keeping the team from reinventing the wheel.

Here, we will consider eight best practices while architecting an application network and designing the APIs that will power it.

Data strategy

The secret sauce of an application network is understanding and identifying where an organization's data sits and then, safely and securely, enabling the data and processes for consumption and usage as required across any of the other applications, both within the organization and, where appropriate, externally (for example, B2B transactions and messaging).

MuleSoft and Anypoint Platform itself are not part of the data strategy. However, they will help you deliver and execute your data strategy. This is done by opening the door to data that is locked away in various systems of truth. It also helps us deliver this data to consumers safely and securely.

Security and compliance

Security and trustworthiness must be addressed early and often when laying out the architecture roadmap for an application network. Architects and practitioners in architecture and design meetings often use the phrase *"We can expose data from this system and this other system will be able to easily consume it."* Often, this evokes a visceral reaction from the owner of the system being exposed. Even when the intention all along is to secure the data and be intentional about who can access the API and who cannot, far too many times companies have been burned in the public square, if not the marketplace, for exposed data.

Why discuss semantics here? Because security is very important, but if the owner of the data only hears the word "expose" and doesn't yet understand how we design the integration security (both authentication and authorization), we may find a much less cooperative stakeholder.

Innovation and collaboration

The most powerful component of an application may end up being improved collaboration across previously siloed departments, teams, or groups within an enterprise. As the application network grows, we begin to securely unlock data across the enterprise. Without a concerted effort to evangelize these new capabilities, we may end up losing some of the primary benefits behind the application network. As a practical approach to this best practice, the platform architect should encourage open communication. While tools can support much of what we do in integration, the best ideas and innovations come from individuals who understand what services are now available. This communication should be done across functions where possible as well.

Design your APIs with the consumer in mind

Your APIs should be easy to understand, use, and integrate with other applications. You should also follow the principles of **REST** (**representational state transfer**), including resources, methods, status codes, and hypermedia links. With this best practice comes the challenge of finding the balance of functionality and features and what granularity the API should be at.

Document your APIs with clear specifications

Your APIs should have clear and comprehensive documentation that describes their functionality, parameters, responses, errors, and examples. You should also use a standard format to document your APIs, such as **OpenAPI Specification** (**OAS**) or **RESTful API Modeling Language** (**RAML**), which is a widely adopted standard for describing RESTful APIs.

Beyond these specifications, it is critical to provide good developer documentation within Exchange. Stripe and Fiserv's API documentation are often considered the gold standard, and each provides clear examples of how to use their services. We should not be surprised when an API in Exchange is left unused and a new API is developed, as the Exchange entry held nothing more than the resources (functionality) and the operations (GET and PUT). (See the earlier *Innovation and collaboration* section.)

Managing your APIs with Anypoint API Management

While Mulies love to imagine all the APIs within an organization as Mule APIs, the reality is that organizations very often have APIs developed using many different tools. Being able to manage these APIs in a single place also gives us the ability to gain visibility of a full application network, and visibility is one of the key benefits of an application network.

Governing your APIs with policies and standards

With Anypoint API Governance, we can create policies and standards defining how APIs on the application network should be designed, developed, tested, deployed, and maintained. The platform allows us to ensure compliance with these policies and standards, as well as with regulatory requirements and best practices.

Evolving your APIs with feedback and iteration

Your APIs should be constantly improved based on the feedback from your consumers, partners, and stakeholders. You should also adopt an iterative approach to developing your APIs, using agile methodologies such as Scrum or Kanban. This will help you deliver value faster and more frequently, as well as adapt to changing needs and expectations.

Summary

In this chapter, we started learning how to view the problem of integration using a different paradigm – a viewpoint that sees applications and systems across an enterprise, both internal and external, as nodes of a network. We learned that this approach to architecting enterprise integration is something MuleSoft calls an application network. While this approach is not exclusively a MuleSoft idea, the platform presents the architect with the tools, governance, security, and execution needed to enable the application network.

In addition to examining the logical concepts of the application network, we also took some time to examine the physical manifestation of this architecture in the *Building and implementing an application network* section of this chapter. We presented the characteristics of an application network and studied some of the benefits and challenges of architecting and designing these networks. We also looked at what is meant by a composable enterprise and the impact this can have on an IT organization.

Finally, we identified best practices that the platform architect should consider when designing, building, and implementing an application network.

Questions

1. In the context of MuleSoft Anypoint Platform, what are two key components that help form an application network?

2. What is the importance of developing an architecture strategy for an application network?

3. How will a company benefit from developing and/or exposing an application network within the enterprise?

Further reading

- *The New IT Operating Model – Application Networks, Component Exchanges, and Federated Enablement*

- *Catalyst: Projects Delivery – Manage the Solution: Build Solution Roadmap*

- *Why Mule is not your data strategy* (`https://blogs.mulesoft.com/learn-apis/application-network/where-mule-fits-in-your-data-strategy/`)

Answers

1. Two key components of an application network are a system of record applications and external, or consuming applications. The application network acts as the internal nervous system, connecting these different applications with system APIs that securely expose just the right amount of data to process and experience APIs that combine, orchestrate, choreograph, and present this data to approved and authorized consumers.

2. Developing a roadmap allows the platform architect to visually identify APIs that can be reused, based on new consuming applications as they show up on the roadmap.

3. The application network can improve the efficiency of the business as well as the efficiency of the IT team. The application network can create better scalability through reuse and improve the security of the data by locking it down to a single exposed interface, controlled through various authentication and authorization capabilities. Finally, the application network improves the visibility of the flow of data and the reuse of the building blocks that form the network.

5
Speeding with Accelerators

In this chapter, we will examine **artifacts**, **pre-built frameworks**, and **APIs** that are directly available to platform architects and developers from MuleSoft and can be found in Anypoint Exchange. Collectively, these components are referred to as **accelerators**. These accelerators can expedite the progress of a project or an organization in terms of architecture and development. They also highlight and exhibit numerous standards and best practices, which can be studied academically for instructional purposes. For organizations that are just beginning to address their API landscape, these standards and best practices may be sufficient to enhance or enrich existing (or missing) company standards and best practices.

We will cover the following main topics:

- Seeing what accelerators MuleSoft has developed and included in Exchange
- Understanding how using an accelerator can get your organization up and running faster than by starting with nothing
- Learning what building blocks make up these accelerators
- Thinking critically about some of the limitations of the accelerators
- Briefly reviewing additional acceleration artifacts found in Catalyst's GitHub repository

An accelerator is a collection of documentation and technical resources, primarily consisting of API specifications, implementation templates, connectors, and industry-specific accelerators. These API policies expedite the implementation of various use cases that address significant business or industry issues. Accelerators are designed to function like modular construction pieces, allowing clients to modify the endpoints, mappings, and patterns to suit their needs. They represent the best practices that MuleSoft recommends clients follow to accomplish specific use cases. Each use of an accelerator asset saves customers countless hours of discovery, design, development, and testing.

Additionally, custom accelerators and reusable frameworks such as error handling, logging, auditing, custom API rules, and connectors can be created. These are the fundamental components that enable any business to enhance efficiency and expedite the construction of APIs. To use any of the accelerators, you need to log into the Anypoint platform. Anypoint Exchange offers a wide range of pre-built accelerators, including those for the financial services, manufacturing, healthcare, retail, and life sciences sectors. Moreover, there are accelerators available for various systems, such as SAP, OMS, and Data Cloud. To find some of the accelerators offered by MuleSoft, click the following link: `https://www.mulesoft.com/exchange/org.mule.examples/mulesoft-accelerators-introduction/`.

The goal of this chapter is to provide architects with an understanding of how these accelerators can save time across various stages of the API life cycle. You will gain a perspective on how the building blocks in each accelerator can be used and customized, and what different assets, patterns, mappings, and endpoints have been included. Following the previously described use case of our J&J Music Store, you will walk through setting up and customizing parts of the Accelerator for Retail.

In this chapter, we will reference the accelerators found in Anypoint Exchange. The list of these accelerators is described and linked from the following Anypoint Exchange custom asset: `https://anypoint.mulesoft.com/exchange/org.mule.examples/mulesoft-accelerators-introduction/minor/1.0/`.

The specific Accelerator for Retail and Consumer Goods can be found here: `https://anypoint.mulesoft.com/exchange/org.mule.examples/mulesoft-accelerator-for-retail/`.

In addition to these sources in Exchange, we will briefly examine some of the assets under MuleSoft Catalyst in GitHub. Currently, this organization's GitHub account houses 157 repositories, which can be found here: `https://github.com/mulesoft-catalyst`.

To use and review the examples shown in this chapter, you will need to install either Anypoint Studio or Visual Studio Code with the Anypoint Code Builder Extension Pack.

Unpacking the accelerator building blocks

The accelerators of MuleSoft serve as foundational elements designed to expedite and simplify the various stages of the API life cycle. These accelerators, available through Anypoint Exchange, are curated sets of pre-built APIs, connectors, templates, and best practices. Each accelerator is crafted to address specific industry needs, enabling rapid development, integration, and deployment of API solutions.

In this section, we will examine the core components, or *building blocks*, of these accelerators, explaining how they contribute to efficiency and customization. The primary assets include the following:

- Pre-built APIs
- Connectors

- Templates
- Best practices
- Data mapping
- Endpoints

Let's examine each of these assets in more detail, focusing on their descriptions, benefits, and usage examples.

Pre-built APIs

Pre-built APIs are fully functional APIs designed to perform specific tasks relevant to the accelerator's focus area. These APIs can manage data retrieval, processing, transformation, and integration with various systems.

Benefits

The benefits of pre-built APIs are as follows:

- **Time-saving**: This eliminates the need to build APIs from scratch
- **Standardization**: This ensures consistent and best-practice implementations
- **Scalability**: They are designed to handle enterprise-level data volumes and transactions

Usage example: In the Accelerator for Retail, a pre-built API may manage product inventory by interfacing with the store's inventory management system.

Connectors

Connectors facilitate seamless communication between MuleSoft applications and external systems such as databases, SaaS applications, and third-party services.

Benefits

The benefits of connectors are as follows:

- **Ease of integration**: This simplifies the process of connecting disparate systems
- **Flexibility**: It supports a wide range of protocols and data formats
- **Reusability**: Connectors can be used across different projects and applications

Usage example: A connector within the Accelerator for Retail could link the e-commerce platform of the retail music store to its CRM system, enabling synchronized customer data.

Templates

Templates provide pre-configured, reusable integration patterns. They act as blueprints for common integration scenarios, reducing the complexity and time required for setting up integrations.

Benefits

The benefits of templates are as follows:

- **Speed**: It accelerates the initial setup of integrations
- **Consistency** ensures the uniform implementation of integration patterns
- **Customization**: This can be tailored to meet specific business needs

Usage example: The Accelerator for Retail includes a template for synchronizing customer orders between the online store and the fulfillment system.

Best practices

Best practices are guidelines and recommendations embedded within accelerators. They guide users toward optimal API design, security, and governance.

Benefits

The benefits are as follows:

- **Quality assurance**: It promotes high standards in API development and management
- **Security**: It ensures that APIs are designed with robust security measures
- **Efficiency**: This encourages efficient and maintainable code practices

Usage example: The Accelerator for Retail may include best practices for handling sensitive customer data, ensuring compliance with data protection regulations.

Data mappings

Data mappings define how data should be transformed and transferred between different systems and formats. They ensure that data flows smoothly and correctly between integrated systems.

Benefits

The benefits of data mappings are as follows:

- **Accuracy**: This minimizes errors in data translation and transformation.
- **Interoperability**: This ensures that different systems can communicate effectively
- **Customization:** It can be adjusted to accommodate specific data structures

Usage example: The Accelerator for Retail's data mappings can transform sales data from the e-commerce platform into a format suitable for the accounting system.

Endpoints

Endpoints are specific URLs or addresses where APIs are accessible. They define the entry points for API interactions, specifying how and where APIs can be invoked.

Benefits

The benefits of endpoints are as follows:

- **Accessibility**: This provides clear and structured access points for API consumers
- **Control**: This allows for fine-grained management of API access and security
- **Scalability**: This supports the ability to scale API access as needed

Usage example: In the Accelerator for Retail, an endpoint might be established for the API that handles customer feedback. This would enable easy submission and retrieval of reviews.

Customizing MuleSoft accelerators

The customization of MuleSoft accelerators involves modifying the accelerator's pre-built APIs, integration templates, and data mappings to better meet your unique business needs. MuleSoft accelerators can be customized in the following ways:

- **API customization**: MuleSoft creates its APIs with best practices and industry standards in mind. However, every company may have different needs. By modifying the API specifications in the API designer, you can tailor these APIs to meet your specific requirements.
- **Data mapping customization**: MuleSoft accelerators offer pre-made data mappings to transform and map data between various systems. However, as each company has a unique data structure, you may need to modify these mappings to meet your specific requirements.

- **Customization of integration assets**: The accelerators provide integration templates that can be further customized to meet your unique use case requirements. These templates can be modified to add new steps, remove unnecessary ones, or change the way data is transferred between systems.

- **Process flow customization**: Process flows specify the interactions between various systems and processes. You may need to modify these flows to suit your needs.

Keep in mind that, even though customization is effective, it should be done carefully. Ensure that changes are safe, compatible with the rest of the system, and do not inadvertently interfere with other features. If you are unsure, speak with a MuleSoft specialist.

Customizing the Accelerator for Retail – J&J Music Store speeds up

To illustrate how these building blocks come together, consider the use case of a retail music store implementing the Accelerator for Retail. The store aims to streamline its operations by integrating its e-commerce platform, inventory system, and CRM. J&J is looking to implement a few use cases such as real-time inventory sync, customer profile sync, product sync, and sales order sync. J&J is using Salesforce as a CRM system, SAP as an ERP system, and another e-commerce platform for B2C and B2B. The Retail Accelerator provided by MuleSoft covers most of the things that J&J Music is looking to implement.

The following are the steps for using and customizing the Retail Accelerator provided by MuleSoft:

1. **Setting up**: The store utilizes pre-built APIs to manage product inventory, customer data, and sales transactions.

2. **Connecting systems**: Using connectors, the store links its e-commerce platform to the inventory and CRM systems, ensuring data flows seamlessly between them.

3. **Applying templates**: The store utilizes templates to set up data synchronization between its online store and its backend systems.

4. **Following best practices**: The implementation adheres to the best practices for security and data management, ensuring robust and compliant operations.

5. **Mapping data**: Data mappings are configured to translate and transfer data accurately between different systems.

6. **Defining endpoints**: Endpoints are established for APIs, enabling clear and secure access to API functionality.

By leveraging these building blocks, J&J Music Store will not only accelerate its integration process but also ensure a robust, scalable, and efficient system that meets its business needs.

J&J Music decided to build custom frameworks, templates, and connectors to boost overall efficiency and productivity. Why should one build custom frameworks and accelerators? There may be instances where an organization is unable to find the necessary accelerators, connectors, or frameworks in Anypoint Exchange. At the same time, they know that these components will be needed for multiple APIs in the future. This will improve overall reusability across the organization and reduce development efforts.

J&J Music has built the following components and published them to Anypoint Exchange, so they can be leveraged by anyone in the organization. The following components have been built by J&J Music:

- **Error handling framework**: An error handling framework has been built and published to Anypoint Exchange as a Mule plugin. Developers can easily use this framework in their applications by simply adding the Maven dependency in POM.xml. This is a common error handling framework specifically for J&J Music and it ensures consistent error handling across the organization.

- **Logging framework**: J&J Music decided to use the open-source JSON Logger and published it to Anypoint Exchange. They customized the JSON Logger according to their requirements and added additional functionality. The JSON Logger will ensure that logging across the organization is consistent and in the JSON format.

- J&J Music decided to store the application properties in the Azure vault and built an Azure vault properties loader. This loader functions like an out-of-the-box configuration property reader, extracting properties directly from the Azure vault.

- J&J Music has also decided to construct templates for APIs and batch applications. These templates will serve as a starting point for developers when they are building the APIs.

- API fragments are pieces of API specifications that offer a way to reuse parts or fragments of APIs in specs, thus enabling the creation of APIs more quickly. API fragments and reusable APIs are essential for bridging the IT delivery gap.

With the help of common frameworks and assets, the overall productivity and efficiency of J&J Music is improved.

As we saw in the last section, J&J is using the Accelerator for Retail to expedite development and boost output in general. Let's now discuss some of the structural elements and benefits that the MuleSoft accelerators offer.

Essential building blocks for MuleSoft accelerators

MuleSoft accelerators provide several building blocks that help to accelerate the process of constructing application networks. Here are a few of the essential building blocks that make up these accelerators:

- **Pre-built APIs**: These are pre-developed and pre-designed APIs that cover a range of standard business objects and capabilities, including order, provider, patient, and product. These APIs can be quickly and easily imported into any MuleSoft application for immediate use. They also comply with the **RESTful API Modeling Language (RAML)**.

- **Integration assets**: Integration assets comprise pre-built connectors, templates, and examples that facilitate the quick and easy integration of different systems. They also help in reducing development time.

- **API-led connectivity**: This component allows assets to be easily discovered and reused, which can improve the speed of development and reduce the potential for errors.

- **Data mappings**: Predefined data mappings facilitate the conversion of data structures from one format to another, making the exchange of information between systems easier and more seamless.

- **Process flows**: These are premade designs that illustrate how various systems and APIs are typically connected to automate business processes.

- **Best practices**: To guide users effectively, the accelerators integrate MuleSoft and industry best practices into their components.

- **Secure properties**: These properties encrypt and securely store credentials along with other sensitive data. This enables you to secure APIs and integrations.

When combined, these elements provide a solid foundation for using MuleSoft to initiate integration projects efficiently and quickly. Additionally, these components can be modified to meet the unique needs of the company, enhancing the flexibility and utility of MuleSoft accelerators.

The following are the benefits provided by the MuleSoft accelerators:

- **Reducing development time**: Organizations can reduce the time it takes to create integrations from scratch by using pre-built APIs and integration templates. As a result, project timelines are accelerated, enabling quicker implementation and faster time to market.

- **Reducing complexity**: MuleSoft accelerators include predefined data mappings that transform and map data between various systems. This simplifies the process of data transformation and contributes to a reduction in errors and inconsistencies.

- **Enhanced efficiency**: Companies can use integrations more effectively by saving time on developing new integrations and troubleshooting. This can be achieved by making use of pre-existing templates and data mappings.

- **Cost savings**: MuleSoft accelerators can result in medium to long-term cost savings by reducing development time and effort.

- **Compliance and best practices**: MuleSoft accelerators have been designed with compliance and best practices in mind, which means they adhere to industry standards.

- **Speed up digital transformation**: Accelerators enable businesses to swiftly integrate disparate systems and streamline manual procedures, thereby expediting the digital transformation process.

- **Scalability**: MuleSoft accelerators provide enterprises with a scalable integration solution that adapts to their needs. They allow for easy expansion or modification as required.

While MuleSoft accelerators offer many benefits, it's crucial for businesses to also consider any potential drawbacks. These may include the need for customization or the resources required to manage and maintain the MuleSoft platform.

The following are limitations that one may experience while using MuleSoft accelerators, and these entirely depend on the organization's requirements:

- **Technical expertise**: Technical expertise is needed to use MuleSoft accelerators. The MuleSoft Anypoint platform may present a steep learning curve for new users. Due to the platform's extensive integration concept requirements, there could be a barrier to entry and a slower pace of integration.

- **Customization**: MuleSoft offers many accelerators and pre-built APIs. However, these may not always cover one's unique business requirements, leading to the need for customization. This process requires specialized skills and may increase both the project time and cost.

- **Learning curve**: Due to the steep learning curve of MuleSoft's Anypoint platform, fully utilizing a MuleSoft accelerator often requires a solid understanding of it.

- **Maintenance**: Accelerators and pre-built templates expedite initial development and deployment, potentially increasing dependence on MuleSoft for future maintenance and updates. This could lead to higher costs over time.

- **Scalability issues**: With a MuleSoft accelerator, scaling operations quickly might not be possible. This is dependent on the MuleSoft package to which your company is subscribed, as well as whether your package allows a high volume of API calls. Consequently, it may not be able to accommodate requirements for sudden, rapid growth.

- **Cost**: Extra costs may arise from educating employees on how to use the platform, modifying the pre-built integrations, and keeping the integrations up to date.

- **Compatibility issues**: The accelerator is designed to function with a broad spectrum of systems. However, there might be cases where it fails to integrate with newer, sophisticated systems or older, legacy systems.

- The **one-size-fits-all method** of a MuleSoft accelerator offers pre-built data connectors, integration templates, and APIs. However, these may be too general to effectively address specific, specialized, or complicated business needs. Customizing these features to meet requirements can take a considerable amount of time and work.

When determining whether the MuleSoft accelerator is the best investment for their integration needs, organizations must be aware of its limitations.

The MuleSoft Catalyst GitHub repository

MuleSoft Catalyst combines resources, services, and an outcome-driven methodology to optimize return on investment and drive your company's transformation. It is a collection of resources, best practices, and advice that businesses can utilize to expedite digital transformation. Conversely, GitHub is a popular web-based hosting service for version control, where most open-source projects post their publicly available code.

MuleSoft Catalyst GitHub is MuleSoft's official GitHub account where the company shares connectors, pre-built APIs, integration templates, and other components that organizations can leverage to expedite development. MuleSoft simplifies the process for developers to find, use, and contribute to their tools by making these resources publicly available on a platform such as GitHub. This results in quicker and more efficient development cycles. It offers a wealth of resources that can be used to rapidly develop applications. The following components are available in the MuleSoft GitHub repository, which organizations can leverage to increase productivity and accelerate development:

- Pre-built API templates and APIs

- Connectors and properties loader

- Sample applications

- Dataweave examples

- Architectural guides and best practices

- Implementation guides

- Common frameworks such as error plugin

- API policies

- RAML fragments

It is important to understand that access to these resources still necessitates an expert understanding of MuleSoft and its Anypoint platform.

Let's discuss the useful components found in the MuleSoft Catalyst's GitHub repository.

Component Name	Component Type	Description	Link
Metrics Toolkit	MuleSoft Application	The metrics toolkit, formerly known as the metrics accelerator/framework, is a Mule application designed to gather, compile, and load platform metrics into various visual aids. It offers pre-configured visualization options and integrations, such as helpful dashboards and charts.	`https://github.com/mulesoft-catalyst/metrics-toolkit`
Circuit Breaker Policy – Mule 4	API Policy	It is a lightweight API policy to implement the Circuit Breaker pattern in a simpler way.	`https://github.com/mulesoft-catalyst/circuit-breaker-policy-mule-4`
Error Handler Plugin	MuleSoft Plugin	It is an error handling plugin for implementing the error handling in the MuleSoft applications.	`https://github.com/mulesoft-catalyst/error-handler-plugin`
Canary Policy – Mule 4	API Policy	It is an API policy to implement the canary deployment pattern in a simpler way.	`https://github.com/mulesoft-catalyst/canary-policy-mule-4`

Component Name	Component Type	Description	Link
Vault Properties Loader	Mule Connector	It is this connector that is used to load the properties from the vault. This can be customized to connect any vault such as HashiCorp, the Azure vault, and the AWS vault.	`https:// github.com/ mulesoft- catalyst/ properties- loader-vault- mule4`
Mule Sonarqube Plugin	MuleSoft Plugin	With the help of the Mule SonarQube plugin, code inspection, and project metrics collection from Mule projects using SonarQube are made possible.	`https:// github.com/ mulesoft- catalyst/ mule- sonarqube- plugin`
RTF CloudHub Cores Calculator API	MuleSoft Application	Using this API, you can determine how many Runtime Fabric cores your organization and business groups are using. This will help you monitor core usage and ensure that you are not exceeding license limits.	`https:// github.com/ mulesoft- catalyst/ rtf-cloudhub- cores- calculator- api/`
JSON Logger	MuleSoft Connector	The MuleSoft extension JSON Logger is available in this GitHub repository. With the help of the extension's numerous capabilities, you can maximize the value of every log and improve your logging experience.	`https:// github.com/ mulesoft- consulting/ json-logger`

Table 5.1- MuleSoft Catalyst GitHub accelerators

More components are available in the MuleSoft Catalyst's GitHub repository than those listed in the preceding table. They can be found here: `https://github.com/mulesoft-catalyst`.

Summary

This chapter covered the methods by which organizations can utilize MuleSoft accelerators to enhance productivity and expedite development. It also discussed potential drawbacks associated with the use of these accelerators. Furthermore, we examined the components offered by MuleSoft Catalyst GitHub and the necessary building blocks for creating the accelerators.

In the upcoming chapter, we will discuss aligning functional requirements with desired business outcomes.

Further reading

- *MuleSoft Accelerators*: `https://www.mulesoft.com/exchange/org.mule.examples/mulesoft-accelerators-introduction`
- **MuleSoft Catalyst GitHub repository**: `https://github.com/mulesoft-catalyst`

Aligning Desired Business Outcomes to Functional Requirements

A critical step in getting the most out of the MuleSoft platform is to understand the desired business outcomes and turn those outcomes into functional requirements. This chapter looks at how functional requirements line up with the platform's capabilities. You will look at how these functional requirements can influence architecture decisions and design patterns such as data models, granularity, concurrency, and HTTP methods. The chapter will include examples of using bounded context data models versus **Enterprise Data Models (EDMs)**.

In this chapter, we will cover the following topics:

- Developing business outcomes and functional requirements
- Designing for communication
- EDMs versus bounded context data models
- Coarse-grained versus fine-grained APIs
- API concurrency and HTTP verbs
- API callback

Developing business outcomes and functional requirements

Functional requirements in software engineering specify the precise actions or features of a software system. Along with providing requirements for inputs, processes, outputs, and data, they also outline what the system should be able to achieve.

The following are sub-categories of functional requirements:

- **Data input and output**: This describes the kind and format of data that the system should accept as input, as well as the format that the system's output should be in.

- **External interfaces**: This describes how to interact or communicate with external systems.

- **Security**: This describes any security requirements for the application, such as data encryption and user access controls.

- **Error handling**: This describes how the system should handle errors and which error messages should be displayed.

- **Data storage and retrieval**: Since they serve as the foundation for the system's design, testing, and validation, functional requirements are essential for the development of systems. They are frequently headed by business users and are normally described in business terms.

The first step in coordinating functional requirements and desired business outcomes is determining the organization's goals and the technical skills required to reach them.

The following are the steps for determining the functional requirements:

1. **Establish business objectives**: Whether your focus is on boosting sales, increasing customer engagement, or optimizing operational efficiency, first determine your business goals and objectives.

2. **Determine functional requirements**: After the business goals have been established, the next stage is to determine the functional requirements, or the features and functions of a system, that are necessary to achieve the desired results. Software systems, labor skills, and operational procedures may be examples of this.

3. **Consult stakeholders**: When determining functional requirements, it's critical to include important stakeholders. To understand the needs of the company and its clients, this may entail speaking with managers, end users, clients, and tech teams.

4. **Set priorities**: Not every need is the same. Sort the functional requirements into priority lists based on how important they are to the overall strategy.

5. **Map and align**: Align the business outcomes with the functional requirements that have been identified. A business analyst can assist in creating a connection and mapping requirements to outcomes.

6. **Develop and implement**: Create and implement the systems or functions in accordance with the specifications. Make sure that every development project complies with accepted industry norms.

7. **Test and assess**: Make sure that all new features or systems are tested. The better the result, the more mistakes you can correct. Deliver the project in phases, ensuring that each is evaluated considering your business outcomes to guarantee alignment.

8. **Periodic review**: To make sure that the functional requirements and business outcomes remain aligned, ensure that you periodically review both. Your functional requirements and business outcomes will change as your business grows.

Recall that strategic alignment guarantees that an organization's resources contribute to effectively and efficiently accomplishing its goals and objectives. This alignment occurs between desired business outcomes and functional requirements.

Since **Application Programming Interfaces (APIs)** enable communication between various platforms, systems, and technologies, they are frequently a vital part of digital businesses. With the help of APIs, disparate software applications can be universally connected so that they can exchange data, initiate actions, and integrate.

The creation of functional requirements and business outcomes depends heavily on APIs. This is how to do it:

- **Enabling automation**: By enabling direct system-to-system communication, APIs enable automation capabilities. They can create more effective processes and take the place of manual labor, which can increase output and cut expenses.

- **Enabling integration**: APIs enable you to integrate two or more systems for exchanging or unlocking data and establishing secure communications.

- **Improving customer experience**: By enabling the provision of customized services, APIs can improve user experiences. They make it possible to integrate with outside apps to provide customers with distinctive and customized experiences, which raises customer satisfaction and retention.

- **Increasing reach**: Businesses can increase their capabilities and reach by utilizing APIs. They can make company data and services available to outside developers, who can use it to create new applications and open new channels that will allow the company to reach new markets or customers.

The behavior features, capabilities, or functions that an API (Application Programming Interface) must have or offer are referred to as API functional requirements. They serve as representations of the functions or services that an API is meant to offer. These specifications outline the precise functions that the API is allowed to carry out, including data retrieval, record updating, and data deletion. They also describe the sequence of events, the interactions between the API and other software components, and the specifications pertaining to data inputs, outputs, security, error handling, and other topics.

Therefore, the term "API functional requirements" refers to the comprehensive specification of the behavior of the API, including the expected input and responses, the way it responds to different types of requests, and any potential interactions with other systems.

When creating APIs, it's crucial to consider a few non-functional requirements in order to accomplish these business outcomes:

- **Security**: To prevent unwanted access, alterations, or loss of sensitive data, APIs must be secure.

- **Performance**: To guarantee a dependable and effective system, APIs must offer great speed and performance.

- **Scalability**: As a business expands, APIs should be flexible enough to accommodate growing loads

- **Reliability**: To prevent downtime and guarantee uninterrupted operation, APIs must be dependable and accessible.

- **Flexibility**: Changes should be handled by APIs in a way that doesn't interfere with the system.

- **Usability**: Developers should be able to easily utilize APIs with clear documentation and instructions.

- **Interoperability**: To promote integration, APIs should be able to communicate with one another and with software systems.

Businesses can effectively leverage APIs as a strategic tool to propel digital transformation, boost efficiency, broaden customer bases, and improve customer experiences by considering these functional requirements and the business outcomes that APIs can enable.

In the preceding section, we talked about the functional requirements that must match business outcomes. In this section, we'll talk about designing the API for communication.

Designing for communication

The design of APIs, or application programming interfaces, is essential to enabling smooth communication between various software services and components. The following tips detail how an API should be created to promote efficient communication:

- **Clarify goals**: Make sure that you know and understand the API's goals. What kind of information will it process or what kind of service will it offer?

- **Choose the right protocol**: The two primary protocols used for communication in APIs are **Simple Object Access Protocol** (**SOAP**) and **Representational State Transfer** (**REST**). Because of its ease of use, REST is the most popular protocol.

- **URIs**: URIs for your resources should be precisely defined in design endpoints. Always use nouns for defining the API resource path.

- **Use status codes**: In order to inform clients of the outcome of an API request, APIs should return standard HTTP status codes.

- **Provide data in a standard format**: The most widely used format is JSON. The majority of contemporary programming languages support it, and it's lightweight and simple to read and write.

- **Error handling**: Give consistent error handling and informative error messages. It makes for a better user experience to receive explicit instructions on what went wrong and how to fix a bad request sent by a client.

- **Define endpoints clearly**: They are essential for a well-designed API. These endpoints should accurately represent resources and be easy to understand. Your application should have distinct URLs for each resource that can be accessed using HTTP methods.

- **Employ standard HTTP methods**: To manipulate resources in a predictable and understandable way, standard HTTP methods (GET, POST, PUT, DELETE, and so on) should be used.

- **Provide enough documentation**: An API cannot be used unless it has adequate documentation. Every endpoint should be explained, along with its functions, inputs, parameters, potential outcomes, and any exceptions or error messages.

- **Versioning**: In order to prevent applications that use older versions from malfunctioning, APIs should be versioned from the beginning as they are likely to change over time.

- **Pagination and filtering**: These features give clients control over how much data they receive from APIs that return large amounts of data.

- **Security**: Use safe practices when designing your API. Encrypting sensitive data is a must, and proper implementation of authentication is also necessary.

- **Use RESTful principles**: RESTful principles are generally a good choice for web-based APIs, though they are not always appropriate.

- **Authentication and authorization**: An authentication and authorization process, utilizing the OAuth protocol or API keys, should be part of API communication.

- **Rate limiting**: To stop abuse and strengthen and secure your API, think about implementing rate-limiting procedures.

- **Testing**: To make sure the API can handle both intended uses and edge cases, thorough testing is required.

It takes careful planning to ensure that an API for communication is scalable, effective, and well-integrated. By following these guidelines, you can design an API that is user-friendly, adaptable, and helpful in facilitating seamless communication between various software components.

We've talked about the best ways to design in order to facilitate communication between two or more systems. EDMs will be the subject of our next topic.

EDM

An EDM is a kind of integration model that includes all of an enterprise's data—well, most of it. Enterprise-wide conceptual, logical, or physical data models may be included in your enterprise architecture. An EDM is a representation of every data entity and relationship found in an organization's whole data structure. It connects an organization's technical and business understanding of its data and is used as a global view of all data. An organization's strategic data requirements are outlined and standardized by an EDM. It provides a comprehensive and unified perspective of the data within the company to facilitate data governance, reporting, and strategic planning.

Consider a retail establishment as an illustration.

For this retail business, the EDM would comprise data on orders (order ID, order date, product ID, customer ID, quantity, and so on), customers (customer ID, customer name, contact information, and so on), and products (product ID, product name, product description, price, and so on). It would also provide the connections between these entities, such as which product was ordered by which consumer and in what quantity.

Advantages of an EDM

The following are the advantages of EDMs:

- **Standardization**: By providing a unified view of data definitions, relationships, and structures, an EDM improves consistency and standardization throughout an organization

- **Enhanced efficiency**: It makes efficient data sharing between various departments, systems, or applications easier and simplifies data integration

- **Improved decision-making**: It facilitates improved strategic planning and decision-making by offering a lucid and unified view of enterprise data

- **Improved data quality**: By making it possible to identify errors and inconsistencies, an EDM helps improve the quality of data

- **Supported data governance**: It forms an integral part of data governance by assisting in data ownership clarification and providing a roadmap for data management roles and responsibilities

- **Reusability**: It makes reusable data practices between different systems possible

Disadvantages of EDMs

The following are the disadvantages of EDMs:

- **Implementation complexity**: Creating an EDM can be complex, time-consuming, and expensive because it requires a deep understanding of business objectives, processes, and systems

- **Opposition to change**: Organizations may be reluctant to embrace a single data model because they fear losing authority or control over their own data

- **Maintenance**: The model's complexity and cost may increase because of the need to update it frequently as the business changes

- **Limited agility**: Since an EDM necessitates consensus and may impede decision-making processes, it occasionally limits flexibility

- **Skill requirement**: Specialized knowledge and skill sets are needed to implement and maintain an EDM, which may entail further training or resources

Even though an EDM has many advantages, its successful implementation depends on an organization's ability to carefully assess these possible obstacles and take the necessary steps to address them.

The EDM was covered in the preceding section. In the following section, we will discuss the Bounded Context data model and how it differs from the EDM.

Bounded context data model

Domain-driven design coined the term *bounded context*, which describes the process of establishing the limits and responsibilities surrounding a particular model. It concentrates on more manageable micro-models, each of which symbolizes a distinct aspect of the company and thus captures and delineates ownership and boundaries. Each model, or Bounded Context, is used to define the boundaries and provide a context for specific models within the larger system.

Take J&J Inc.'s e-commerce platform, for instance. J&J can be divided into multiple bounded contexts due to its large size and variety of features:

- **User management context**: This context will include user-related data models, such as login credentials, activity logs, and private data. Naturally, the team in charge of this context works on features related to users.

- **Product catalog context**: Data models pertaining to product attributes, such as name, description, price, and category, will be present in this context. Updates, data inputs, and other product-related changes are also covered in this context.

- **Inventory context**: This context keeps track of each product's inventory levels and the quantity that is presently available. Data about incoming and outgoing stock is included.

- **Order management context**: Order processing, order status tracking, and other related tasks are all managed by this context. There will be data models with an emphasis on orders, payment information, order status, and other topics.

- **Shipping context:** This context will oversee the handling of shipping information, including tracking shipments and detailing how orders are delivered to customers.

Each of these scenarios will have its own models and specific characteristics relevant only to that context and be overseen by distinct teams. While similar data may be shared by all contexts, the way in which this data is represented may vary depending on the context. To put it briefly, every bounded context is a highly independent and decoupled component of the system that offers flexibility and ease of use.

A bounded context model for a J&J music store could be broken down into several subcontexts, based on different business functionalities.

- Inventory management: It pertains to the management of all the music products, whether they are digital or physical, that the store sells. It entails tracking sales, maintaining inventory, updating product details, and placing new orders for products as needed.

- Sales and Marketing: In this context, the music store's marketing and sales initiatives are the main focus. It entails tracking sales data and trends, generating marketing campaigns, managing customer relationships, and developing sales strategies.

- Relationship management with customers is the main focus of this context. Customer profiling, order processing, feedback management, exchanges, returns, and complaints are all included.

- Payment Processing: All of the store's transactions are managed by this context. Invoicing, processing refunds, maintaining safe payment gateways, and monthly sales reporting are all part of it.

- Delivery and Shipping: In the event that the music store is physically present, this section handles the customer's product delivery logistics. It includes order tracking, shipping management, and return pickups.

- Website and App Management: In this context, the store's online presence, primarily its website or app, is managed. It entails updating content, monitoring user interaction, administering app/website analytics, and resolving technical problems.

- User Accounts: Managing user authentication, granting access to various users, managing profiles, and enforcing security protocols are all part of this context.

- Music consulting: This refers to services that offer suggestions for songs based on listeners' tastes, new releases, best-sellers, and reviews.

The division of a J&J music store's functions into these bounded contexts allows each team to concentrate on their respective responsibilities, which reduces complexity and facilitates more transparent communication.

Advantages of the bounded context data model

The following are the advantages of the bounded context data model:

- **Independent development**: Teams can work on different system components independently and concurrently in bounded contexts, which speeds up development.

- **Reduced complexity**: By dividing a larger model into smaller, more manageable parts, the complexity of each part is greatly reduced.

- **Enhanced flexibility**: Using various languages, libraries, or databases that are most appropriate for meeting the unique requirements of each context is made possible by bounded contexts.

- **Improved scalability**: Bounded contexts enable more scalability because each context can be scaled independently according to its own requirements. This is especially true when they are integrated with microservices.

- **Better maintenance**: The maintenance process is made simpler by the fact that updates or changes made in one bounded context do not immediately affect others.

Disadvantages of the bounded context data model

The following are the disadvantages of the bounded context data model:

- **Increased complexity**: While bounded context makes each context less complex, it makes communication between contexts more complex.

- **Data inconsistency**: Data inconsistencies between various bounded contexts may arise if improper management is practiced.

- **High initial investment**: Setting up the contexts, creating effective communication channels, and so on can take a substantial amount of initial time, as well as financial and labor commitment, when implementing a bounded context architecture.

- **Difficult refactoring**: It takes more effort and time to refactor across bounded contexts.

- **Dependency on good design**: The degree to which the business domain is comprehended and the boundaries are effectively defined determines how effective a bounded context data model is.

- **Complex communication**: Bounded contexts must communicate with one another through precisely defined interfaces (APIs), which can add to the system's complexity and take some time to define.

Recall that bounded contexts are a relatively sophisticated technique that necessitates careful design and implementation, even though they can offer substantial benefits.

The following table sums up the differences between bounded contexts and EDMs:

Features	Bounded Context data model	EDM
Definition	Aim to delineate specific areas within a larger system, often corresponding to particular business capabilities or services	Focuses on defining and standardizing the data across an entire organization
Ideal Architecture	Ideal for microservices architecture, which allows for the independent evolution of each service	Ideal for large-scale or monolithic systems where consistency is crucial
Complexity	Lessens complexity inside each context but may make communication between contexts more complex	Can make data integration between departments less complicated, but can also be difficult to implement and maintain

Features	Bounded Context data model	EDM
Development	Faster development is possible, as multiple teams can work in parallel	The organization-wide scope necessitates careful planning and comprehension
Adaptability and Agility	Adaptable and agile because modifications made in one context might not have an impact on others	Since they can affect the entire organization, changes can be gradual and need to be carefully considered
Data definition and context	Depending on what is needed, each context may use a different language and database	Regardless of needs, data definitions are standardized throughout the organization
Data management and communication	Demands unambiguous interfaces (APIs) for context-to-context communication	Demands effective Database Management Systems (DBMSs) to manage large amounts of varied data
Uniformity and consistency	Possibility of inconsistent behavior in various situations	Data definitions are uniform throughout the company

Table 6.1 - Bounded context data model versus EDM

The bounded context data model was covered in the preceding part. Coarse- and fine-grained APIs will be covered in the next section.

Coarse-grained APIs

A coarse-grained API is a kind of API design that combines multiple granular-level operations into a single function to provide highly encapsulated services. With fewer, more significant calls, it effectively represents a high-level action or series of actions. A coarse-grained API can complete an equivalent task with fewer requests than a fine-grained API, which needs multiple requests to complete a single task. For instance, a fine-grained API would normally offer distinct endpoints for the creation of new users, the addition of roles to existing users, and the assignment of permissions to existing users within the framework of user management systems. A coarse-grained API, on the other hand, might provide a single endpoint to carry out each of these tasks in a single request.

The following are the key features of coarse-grained APIs:

- **Composite operations**: A single API call can perform several operations using coarse-grained APIs. This "one-stop service" frequently mimics an actual business process, such as setting up an account or submitting an order.

- **Decreased round-trip calls**: It typically requires fewer round-trip calls between the client and server, saving network bandwidth, because it combines multiple operations into a single API call.

- **Higher-level abstraction**: By encapsulating an intricate internal workflow, coarse-grained APIs offer a higher level of abstraction and facilitate easier call and use by client applications.

- **Enhanced security**: A coarse-grained design can help reduce security risks by limiting the number of endpoints that are exposed to the client.

- **Simplicity**: They make interactions with client applications easier by encapsulating complexities and offering a straightforward interface for intricate operations.

Advantages of coarse-grained APIs

The following are the advantages of coarse-grained APIs:

- **Reduced network overhead**: Since coarse-grained APIs have lower latency and require fewer calls, they are better for slow networks

- **Simplified client-side logic**: Client-side logic is frequently easier to understand since there are fewer calls to handle

Disadvantages of coarse-grained APIs

The following are the disadvantages of coarse-grained APIs:

- **Less flexibility**: Coarse-grained APIs might not be as adaptable to varying requirements as they perform broad functions

- **Bloated data**: They might return more information than is required, which would increase memory use and network traffic

The benefits and drawbacks of coarse-grained APIs were discussed in the preceding section. We will discuss fine-grained APIs and how they vary from coarse-grained APIs in the next section.

Fine-grained APIs

A fine-grained API design method involves creating services that are designed to carry out precise, tiny tasks. These APIs are distinguished by their extremely detailed methods, which give clients a great deal of control but necessitate more API calls to carry out intricate tasks.

The following are the key features of fine-grained APIs:

- **Particular operations**: Fine-grained APIs provide endpoints for executing tiny, highly specific tasks. To create a user, assign a role to the user, and set permissions, for instance, separate API calls would be required in a user management system.

- **More API calls**: Since each operation is so detailed and granular, completing a complex task frequently necessitates making more round-trip calls between the client and server, which increases network traffic.

- **Flexibility and control**: Since fine-grained APIs can be used in a variety of ways to carry out complex tasks, they offer a client a high degree of flexibility and control.

- **Complexity**: Managing fine-grained APIs is more difficult. This is because there are more API endpoints to maintain and the need to call multiple APIs to complete a task may result in a more complex client-side application.

- **Enhanced security**: Since you can give each function a specific set of permissions, having more granular control over functions can result in more exact security measures.

Nevertheless, network efficiency and API granularity are trade-offs. Fine-grained APIs have more control and flexibility, but because they make more API calls, they also use more network bandwidth. Therefore, the needs of your application will determine whether to use a coarse-grained (composite) or fine-grained (atomic) API.

Advantages of fine-grained APIs

The following are the advantages of fine-grained APIs:

- **Increased flexibility**: Since developers can precisely select the API calls that they require, these APIs offer a great deal of flexibility

- **Effective data usage**: Since they only provide the information that is needed, they are effective in exchanging data

Disadvantages of fine-grained APIs

The following are the disadvantages of fine-grained APIs:

- **Increased network overhead**: Since fine-grained APIs necessitate more calls, their very nature increases network overhead

- **Complex client-side logic**: Managing fine-grained APIs can result in a higher call count, which in turn can cause more complex client-side logic

It's crucial to remember, however, that a coarse-grained strategy might not always be the best one. If the client only needs to carry out a straightforward operation and the API only offers high-level actions that can accomplish numerous tasks, it could cause needless complexity. Therefore, creating an effective and efficient API requires finding the ideal balance between fine-grained and coarse-grained API design. In conclusion, the use case scenario and project requirements determine which coarse-grained or fine-grained API to use. Fine-grained APIs are better if exact control over the returned data is required. Nevertheless, coarse-grained APIs might be a better choice if network latency is an issue.

The following are the differences between coarse-grained and fine-grained APIs:

	Coarse-Grained APIs	Fine-Grained APIs
Definition	Offer extensive features while utilizing fewer method calls.	Give thorough functionality with more targeted method calls.
Level of detail	High-level, more generalized	Low-level, highly specific
Data transfer	Large amounts of data in a single call	Small amounts of data per call
Server calls	Fewer calls, reduced server overhead	More in number, increased overhead
Network latency	Lower latency due to fewer server calls	Higher latency due to more server calls
Efficiency	Potentially inefficient (extra data may be transferred)	More efficient (only necessary data is transferred)
Suitability	Over the internet where network latency can be an issue	In a high-bandwidth low-latency environment
Control	Less control for the developers as methods are generalized	More control for the developers

Table 6.2 - Coarse-grained APIs versus fine-grained APIs

The following figure shows an illustration of coarse-grained APIs and fine-grained APIs.

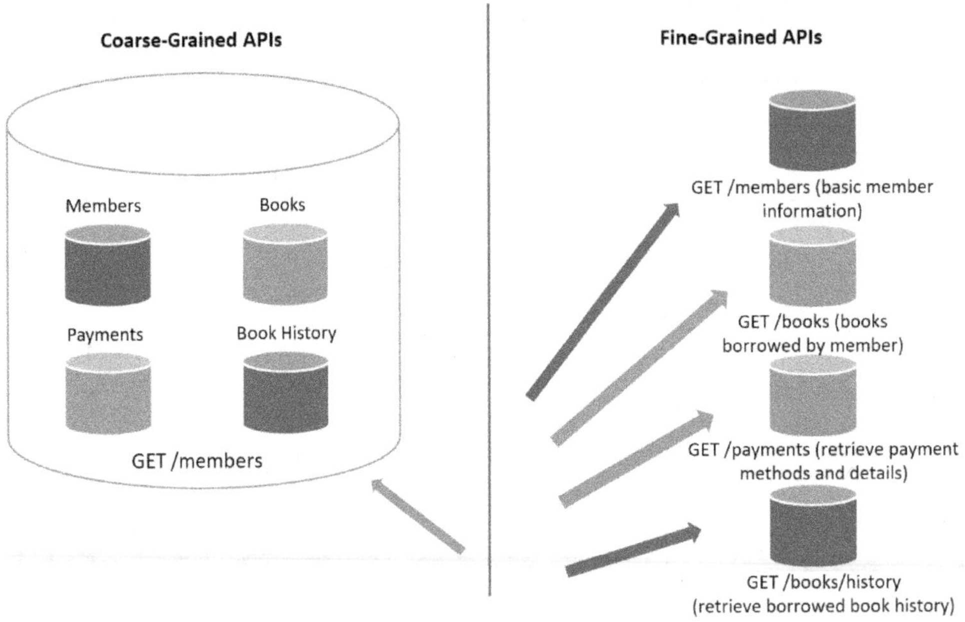

Figure 6.1 - Coarse-grained APIs versus fine-grained APIs

As an example of how coarse-grained and fine-grained APIs differ, let's look at the library management system API shown in *Figure 6.1* in more detail.

Example of a coarse-grained API

An exhaustive amount of data, including the user's contact details, address, list of books they are currently borrowing, borrowing history, any outstanding fines, and registered payment methods, may be returned by a single API call, such as GET /members.

Since it just requires one request and delivers a substantial quantity of data, some of which may not always be needed or utilized, this is a coarse-grained API.

Example of a fine-grained API

A fine-grained method would involve making many API queries to get the same data. API calls such as GET /members (members' basic information), GET /books (books borrowed by a given member), GET /payments (payment methods and details), and GET /books/history (history of books borrowed) would be distinct from one another.

Every API call is unique and yields a targeted collection of information. You can only submit the specified `GetBorrowedBooks` request if all you need to know is which books are borrowed.

> **Note:**
>
> Fine-grained APIs will result in a greater quantity of assets. If you are managing the assets for your APIs using Anypoint Exchange, you will see that there are more assets for fine-grained APIs than for coarse-grained APIs.
>
> In the preceding section, we covered the distinctions between fine-grained and coarse-grained APIs. In the following section, we will delve into API Concurrency and HTTP verbs.

API concurrency

The ability of an API to handle multiple requests at the same time is referred to as API concurrency. It is particularly important in a decentralized system, where lots of independent services communicate with one another through APIs. If the system is overloaded without proper concurrent control, it can lead to race conditions where several processes access and manipulate the same data, leading to inconsistent results.

The following are the ways supported to handle concurrency:

- **Multi-threading**: This is perhaps the most common way to handle concurrency. Each request is handled by a specific thread so that multiple requests can be processed in parallel. The downside is that it may be resource-intensive to manage many threads.

- **Rate limiting**: This is used to control the number of API requests that a client may make during a specified time. This ensures that your API is not overwhelmed with too many requests at once.

- **Queuing**: If the number of concurrent requests exceeds a certain threshold, an application system may create a queue. This ensures that each request is eventually processed, but it may lead to delays if the queue is too long.

- **Caching**: The result of a request can be stored and reused for identical future requests, thus reducing the need for concurrency. It can drastically reduce the load on your API, but it's only applicable to idempotent (read) requests or when you have data that doesn't change frequently.

- **Load balancing**: A load balancer can help the API deal with a lot of requests at once if they are distributed over multiple servers.

It's important to design your APIs with concurrency in mind, as it can significantly impact performance and usability.

HTTP verbs

HTTP verbs, also known as HTTP methods, are commands that specify the desired action to be carried out on a specific resource. While every method implements a different semantic, all the methods share some common features. The most popular HTTP methods are listed here:

- **GET**: Using a given URI, this method retrieves data from the specified server. It is the most widely used technique for sending unencrypted data.

- **POST**: Data from forms is sent to the server using this method. The data sent via POST is not cached by the server.

- **PUT**: This technique uploads the content to replace the existing resource.

- **DELETE**: This command expunges the designated resource.

- **HEAD**: This method is comparable to GET, but it only returns the response's header rather than its body.

- **OPTIONS**: The target resource's communication options are returned by this method.

- **PATCH**: This function partially modifies a resource.

- **CONNECT**: The client uses this method to connect over the network to an HTTP web resource.

- **TRACE**: A message loop-back test is carried out along the route leading to the target resource using this method.

Using HTTP methods, clients can communicate with server resources by submitting, retrieving, and altering data. It is important to remember that the data in these transactions can be encoded in XML, JSON, or even HTML format. The requirements of the client and server often determine the method that is selected.

The following tables lists the HTTPS methods and whether they are safe, idempotent, or both:

HTTP method	Description	Idempotent	Safe
GET	Requests data from specified resources	Yes	Yes
POST	Creates a new resource	No	No
PUT	Updates the existing resource	Yes	No
DELETE	Deletes the specified resource	Yes	No
HEAD	Like GET, but only returns the header section and status line; the resource itself is not returned	Yes	Yes

HTTP method	Description	Idempotent	Safe
OPTIONS	Outlines the target resource's communication options	Yes	Yes
PATCH	Applies a resource's partial modifications	No	No
CONNECT	Used to connect to a resource over a network (typically for SSL tunneling)	No	No
TRACE	Useful for testing and debugging; loops backward along the path to the target resource	Yes	Yes

Table 6.3 - HTTP verbs

The idempotent and safe methods are defined as follows:

- **Idempotent methods**: These methods have the same side effects when called repeatedly as when called only once.

- **Safe methods**: These methods don't change resources when they're called. They shouldn't have any other effects; their sole purpose is to retrieve data.

API callback

An asynchronous API request known as a callback comes from the API server and is delivered to the client in response to one that the client has already made. Callbacks are a useful tool for APIs to provide information about interesting events and to identify them.

The following figure shows an illustration of the API callback.

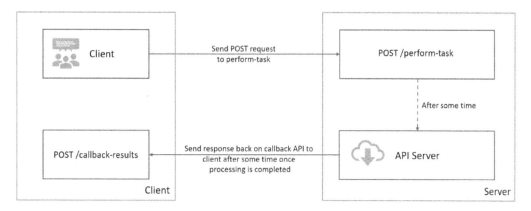

Figure 6.2 - API callback

As shown in *Figure 6.2*, let's imagine that we are developing an API or application that requires a third-party service to perform some heavy processing, and that it is a time-consuming process. In such a case, we would submit the request to the server and not wait for the server to respond immediately. Once the server completes the processing, it will send back the results to the client over the callback URL provided by the client.

The API callback URL can be secured by using a JWT token or by implementing any authentication mechanism on the API callback URL.

There are the mechanisms that can be used to secure an API callback endpoint:

- Implementing the basic authentication on the API callback endpoint
- A HMAC signature can be added to the HTTP header during the callback
- Implementing mutual authentication (mTLS) on the API callback endpoint; the endpoint can verify the client certificate

Although we have discussed a few security measures that can be implemented, the API callback endpoint is subject to additional security measures.

The API callback is beneficial when you anticipate that a request sent to the server may take a while and the client cannot wait for a response. In this situation, the server will acknowledge the client's request and send a technical response indicating that the request has been accepted. After the server finishes processing the client's request, it will send a functional response back to the client using the API callback URL provided by the client.

Summary

In this chapter, we saw how crucial it is to match functional requirements with desired organizational goals and business outcomes. We also discussed the differences between the bounded context data model and the EDM. The differences between coarse-grained and fine-grained APIs were also discussed.

We will discuss microservices, API-led connectivity, and event-driven architecture in the next chapter.

7

Microservices, Application Networks, EDA, and API-led Design

In *Chapter 6*, we learned how to align business outcomes to functional requirements. In this chapter, we will be discussing a few architectural styles, including **microservices**, **event-driven architecture**, and **API-led connectivity architecture** to build a composable application network.

In this chapter, we will cover the following topics:

- Monolithic architecture and its advantages and disadvantages
- Microservices and their advantages and disadvantages
- Microservices design patterns such as Saga and Circuit Breaker, among others
- Event-driven architecture and its advantages and disadvantages
- API-led connectivity
- Application networks and composable enterprises
- Anypoint MQ

Developing an effective integration solution requires the use of architectural design principles. Architects consider factors ranging from business requirements to system constraints to create end-to-end integration solutions. Here are some architectural approaches for integration solutions:

- **Point-to-point integration**: One of the oldest, but least recommended methods due to its simplicity, this approach allows two systems to communicate with each other without intermediaries. However, as systems are added, complexity increases, leading to maintenance problems.
- **Hub and spoke architecture**: This approach connects all systems to a centralized integration hub, enabling efficient communication. Although this simplifies control, single points of failure are possible.

- **Enterprise service bus (ESB) architecture**: This method uses standard interfaces and protocols to translate application functionality into reusable services. This simplifies integration and system management, but the initial installation of an ESB can be complex and expensive.

- **Microservices architecture**: This breaks down large complex systems into small, loosely coupled services. While this allows for flexibility and scalability, it can also introduce data consistency and management issues.

- **Serverless architecture**: This approach focuses on writing individual stateless actions that are triggered by events. It scales automatically and you only pay for what you consume, but it is not recommended for long processes.

- **API-based connectivity**: This architectural approach focuses on developing production APIs that can be reused across the enterprise with security controls in place. This speeds up project delivery and encourages reuse, although it adds complexity.

- **Integrated platform as a service (iPaaS)**: In this architecture, users can develop, operate, and manage integrated workflows in the cloud. Although it offers speed, cost effectiveness, and ease of use, it can have limitations when it comes to handling complex integrations.

- **Hybrid integration**: A combination of on-premises and cloud-based integration models enables flexibility and scalability. However, it can be difficult to manage due to its complex nature.

Each of these architectural approaches has its strengths and weaknesses, and the choice often depends on the organization's specific requirements, constraints, and preferences. Therefore, it is important to understand the nuances of each to make the right choice. In the next section, we will discuss some integration architectures in detail along with their advantages and disadvantages.

Monolithic architecture

Before we move into the microservices architecture, let's make sure we understand the concept of **monolithic architecture**. Breaking down the term "monolithic," *mono* means single, and *lithic* means stone (thus, single stone). So, the monolithic software architectural style is where we encompass all the functionality into one single application, as shown in *Figure 7.1*.

Monolithic architecture unites all business concerns into a single, vast computer network with a single code base. This kind of application involves upgrading the complete stack to make changes, which includes generating and deploying an updated service-side interface and gaining access to the code base.

Figure 7.1 shows that we have a single application containing all the functionality, including the authentication service, order service, payment service, and shipping service, all of which are connected to a database. A typical web application developed with this kind of monolithic architecture will have the user interface, data access layer, and business logic in the same application.

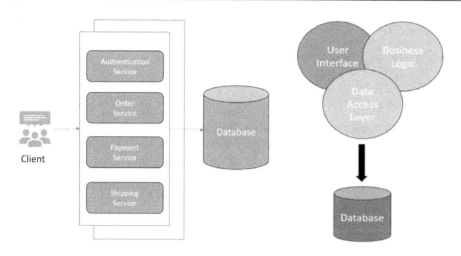

Figure 7.1- Monolithic architecture

Figure 7.2 shows a typical monolithic architecture where the authentication, order, payment, and shipping services are encompassed into a single executable JAR file. These services are tightly coupled and connected to the same database even though they have separate functionality.

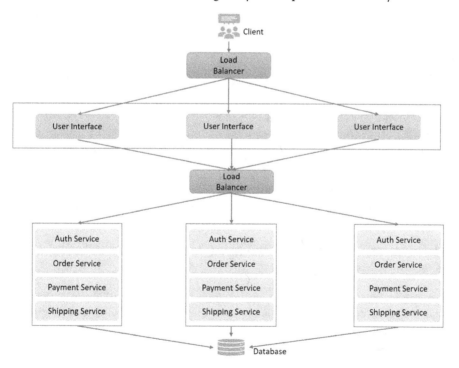

Figure 7.2 - Typical web application architecture

Advantages of a monolithic architecture

The following are the advantages of the monolithic architecture:

- **Easy deployment**: The application can be deployed easily as there is just one single executable file for all the services and user interface

- **Easy application management**: Because a unified application is consolidated, it typically requires less administration, coordination, and orchestration than alternative techniques, making monoliths frequently easier to manage than other solutions

- **Faster end-to-end testing**: The monolithic application is a single, centralized unit, so end-to-end testing can be performed much faster than with distributed applications

Disadvantages of a monolithic architecture

The following are the disadvantages of the monolithic architecture:

- **Single point of failure**: A monolithic architecture encompasses all the required functionality in one single application. This leads to the possibility that the entire application fails in the event of one or more components failing. This can lead to extended downtime for the whole application.

- **Scalability complexity**: Because not every component of a monolithic application can scale independently (since each component has different resource requirements), scaling becomes more difficult as the size of the application increases.

- **Infrastructure cost**: In the event of application performance issues, you need to scale the whole monolithic architecture. This may lead to additional infrastructure costs.

- **Time to market**: Adding and releasing new functionality with monolithic architecture is time consuming. It may take more time to release even simple functionality. This is because the many components in the same application need to be tested to ensure that new changes don't impact the functionality of other components.

- **Complexity in upgrading the application**: Upgrading the application to new versions can be a tedious task. All the components need to be upgraded together and this can be a time-consuming process. In some cases, organizations end up not upgrading the application to avoid this.

- **Deployment complexity**: Even small changes in the application result in the whole application needing to be redeployed.

A monolithic architecture can be suitable for smaller applications because of the faster development, testing, and deployment, and lower infrastructure costs. However, when your system is growing and the functionality required of the application increases, it can result in bottlenecks for the business and lead to the various aforementioned issues.

The monolithic architecture and its advantages and disadvantages are now clear to us. We're going to go over the microservices architecture to see how we can circumvent these limitations of monolithic architecture now.

Microservices architecture

In the case of software composed of small independent services communicating over well-defined APIs, microservices are an architectural and organizational approach to software development. Small, self-contained teams own those services.

A microservices architecture allows teams to create independent, autonomous, loosely coupled, and independently deployable units.

Characteristics of microservices

The following are the characteristics of the microservices:

- Services are independently deployable and loosely coupled units

- Each service has its own code base

- Autonomous services

- Microservices are small and independent

- Each service can scale independently

- Technology agnostic

Microservices are loosely coupled and highly cohesive. A highly cohesive microservice wraps its dependencies, logic, and data, and has a single responsibility inside a well-defined domain. When two systems are constructed so that modifications to one service's implementation, design, or behavior won't affect the other, they are said to be loosely coupled microservices.

A microservices architecture aims to build large software using many small, independently deployable services. In this architecture, service cohesion and loose coupling are the two main functions:

- **Cohesion:** In the context of microservices, cohesion refers to the extent to which the responsibilities of a single service relate to each other. High cohesion within a service is desirable because it increases system maintainability and reduces the complexity of communication between services. A highly unified service performs only one logical function. For example, if you are developing an e-commerce platform, you may have separate services for user authentication, inventory management, order processing, and so on. Each service is unified because it focuses on one area of the system.

- **Coupling**: Coupling refers to the extent to which one service depends on other services to perform its responsibilities. In a microservices architecture, the goal is to create "loosely coupled" services. Loosely coupled services can operate independently of each other, which increases system flexibility and enables easier change management. For example, your order processing service should not fail if your warehouse service goes down. It should still work, although it may not be able to provide real-time inventory data.

By focusing on high cohesion and loose coupling, developers can create microservices systems that are easier to maintain, more resilient, and more scalable than traditional monolithic architectures.

Domain-driven design (**DDD**) and the **single-responsibility principle** (**SRP**) are two important concepts in microservices development:

- **DDD**: This is an approach to software design that focuses on core business logic (the "domain"). In the context of microservices, DDD helps ensure that each service spans a bounded and unified business context. DDD helps to define clear and bounded contexts for each service, ensuring that they are directly related to business characteristics. For example, in an e-commerce application, you can use DDD principles to separate services such as user management, product catalog, ordering, and payment processing. All these services correspond to a specific business area in an e-commerce application.

- **SRP**: This principle states that a class, module, or, in this context, microservice can have only one reason to change. This means that each microservice must handle a single function or process. In the e-commerce example, the user management service should only be responsible for processing users. This should not include activities related to the product catalog, order processing, or payment, as these are different responsibilities. This principle helps maintain high cohesion and low bond strength, resulting in more durable and maintainable systems.

By using DDD and SRP in microservices, you can create a system that effectively separates business logic into individual services, each responsible for one aspect of the entire business domain. This results in a system that is easier to understand, maintain, and extend over time.

The following figure illustrates a microservices architecture where each service runs independently and in separate containers or machines.

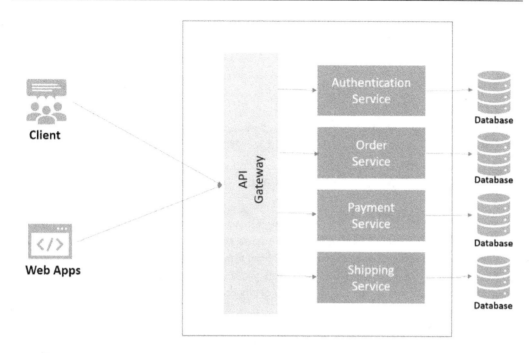

Figure 7.3 - Microservices architecture

Advantages of a microservices architecture

The following are the advantages of a microservices architecture:

- **Agility and faster time to market**: The microservices architecture allows for a rapid time to market because it simplifies the development, testing, maintenance, and evolution of big applications by splitting them into small pieces so they are easier to develop, test, maintain, and expand over time. Thus, teams can speed up their code delivery.

- **Scalability**: Microservices allow you to scale one or more services independently without affecting other services. There's a possibility we might have to scale up the services that don't work very well and microservices allow us to do this on an independent basis.

- **Flexibility and agility**: Each microservice can be developed and deployed independently, so implementing microservices allows nearshore development teams to quickly adjust to changing business needs. This is a more efficient method of getting results in more responsiveness and quicker release cycles.

- **Rapid development**: Microservices make it easier for teams to work on small, focused components, leading to faster development cycles and faster time to market for new features and updates.

- **Continuous deployment**: A microservices architecture allows you to perform continuous deployment and continuous integration effectively and allows for the continuous delivery of software applications.

- **Resource optimization and utilization**: To optimize resource utilization and reduce infrastructure costs, microservices can be run in containerized environments or serverless architectures.

- **Business agility**: The microservices are well aligned with agile methodologies, enabling organizations to react quickly to changing business requirements.

Disadvantages of a microservices architecture

The following are the disadvantages of a microservices architecture:

- **Deployment and scalability complexity**: A microservices architecture allows you to scale and deploy the application independently, but at the same time, scaling and deploying multiple microservices can be challenging to manage and adds complexity. There are tools such as Kubernetes and Docker that help to reduce deployment and scalability complexity, but they come with their own added complexity.

- **Complex and distributed application network**: Managing multiple microservices can be complex. With a greater number of services, it becomes harder to manage and monitor those services. Microservices are inherently distributed, which may result in additional network latency that is difficult to solve, as multiple services may need to be called to serve a single client request.

- **Increased costs**: Microservices can add additional costs because the additional tools used to manage and control microservices, such as Kubernetes, Docker, and API gateways, are often required and come with additional costs.

We have now reviewed the monolithic and microservices architectures and discussed the advantages and disadvantages of both. Next, we will examine a couple of other architectural styles, namely, event-driven architecture and API-led connectivity.

Saga pattern

The **Saga pattern** is a failure management technique that assists in coordinating transactions across several microservices to preserve data consistency and aids in establishing consistency in distributed applications. Data consistency is managed and upheld across numerous microservices using this pattern. A single service completes each transaction, and it broadcasts changes in state to the other services participating in the Saga. Through a series of local transactions, the Saga architectural pattern offers transaction management. A Saga participant's work is represented by a local transaction. A compensatory transaction can roll back every Saga activity. Furthermore, the Saga pattern ensures that the relevant compensation transactions are executed to roll back the previously finished work in case of any failure in between to ensure data consistency or that all activities are completed.

> **Note**
>
> In software, Saga is a design pattern used to manage distributed transactions. It is a series of local transactions where each event updates data in a single service. The term comes from the paper called *SAGAS* written by Hector Garcia-Molina and Kenneth Salem in 1987. The Saga pattern is mainly used in microservices architecture to ensure data consistency across multiple services. Each Saga transaction has a defined recovery process in case of failure. If one transaction fails, rollback processes are performed to maintain data consistency. Saga events are coordinated by an orchestra, which can be either centralized or decentralized.

A local transaction within the Saga pattern refers to a transaction that occurs within a single microservice or database. Each of these local transactions can be executed independently and, if successful, should transition the system from one consistent state to another. The key distinction between local transactions in Saga and traditional distributed transactions is that partial success is acceptable in local transactions. This contrasts with traditional transactions where every part of the transaction must succeed for it to be considered successful.

In the event of a failure in a local transaction, instead of rolling back like in a traditional transaction, the Saga pattern executes a series of compensating transactions. These compensating transactions are designed to undo the changes made by the preceding local transactions in the Saga, thereby maintaining overall system consistency. It is important to note that these compensating transactions themselves are also local transactions.

The following diagram illustrates the Saga design pattern architecture.

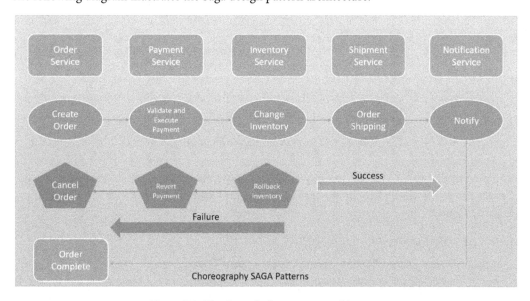

Figure 7.4 - The Saga design pattern architecture

The Saga pattern can be implemented in two ways:

- Saga choreography pattern
- Saga orchestration pattern

Saga choreography pattern

The choreography approach involves a single microservice consuming an event, carrying out the necessary action, and then passing the event on to the subsequent service to consume.

The Saga choreography pattern is used to implement the transaction span across multiple services in a decentralized fashion.

The following figure depicts the Saga choreography pattern.

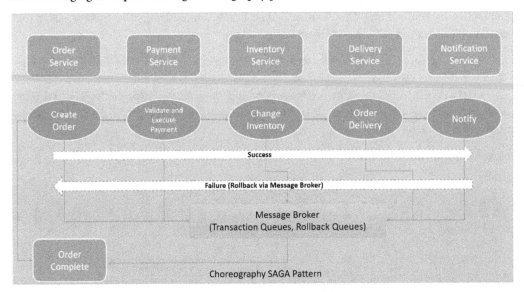

Figure 7.5 - Saga choreography pattern

In the preceding diagram, all the services in the Saga communicate via a message broker for executing the transactions as well as rolling them back. This communication happens asynchronously in a sequenced manner.

Advantages of the Saga choreography pattern

The following are the advantages of the Saga choreography pattern:

- Easily extensible to add new services into the mix, as it works in a decentralized fashion
- Brings with it the advantages of messaging and event-driven architecture, such as loose coupling, asynchronous communication, and reliability

- Enables greater flexibility and evolution, improving scalability and availability, and decreasing coupling between microservices

Disadvantages of the Saga choreography pattern

The following are the disadvantages of the Saga choreography pattern:

- There is no centralized control over the transaction processing, so it becomes complex to manage and understand the process if it spans multiple services

- Transaction rollback is complex as each service in a Saga must have transaction rollback capabilities

- Monitoring and controlling the interactions between the microservices in a choreographed system can be more challenging in the absence of a central coordinator

Saga orchestration pattern

In the orchestration pattern, the application is completed by connecting each service to the centralized coordinator, which arranges the services in a predetermined sequence. A centralized Saga orchestrator instructs Saga players to carry out local transactions using command messages in an orchestration-based Saga.

The following diagram illustrates the Saga orchestration pattern:

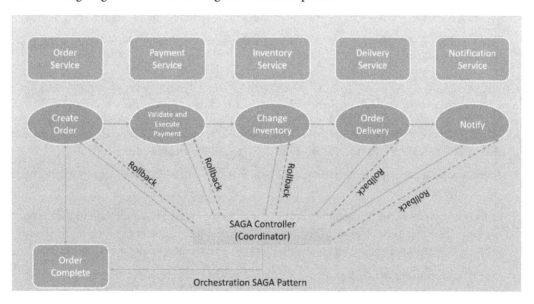

Figure 7.6 - Saga orchestration pattern

Using a centralized controller, a distributed transaction may be implemented using the Saga orchestration microservice design. The calls between the Saga participants are coordinated using this centralized controller to carry out a transaction.

Saga controllers manage communication with the service, perform transactions, and are responsible for notifying services in Saga to perform a rollback in case of any failures.

Advantages of the Saga orchestration pattern

The following are the advantages of the Saga orchestration pattern:

- More control of the processing of transactions when they are explicitly executed through the orchestration pattern
- Monitoring and controlling the interactions between the microservices in an orchestrated system is made simpler with a central coordinator

Disadvantages of the Saga orchestration pattern

The following are the disadvantages of the Saga orchestration pattern:

- Adding new services or processes to the Saga is much more complicated as changes are required in the Saga controller
- Because orchestration is often more tightly coupled, the system may be less resilient and scalable
- In an orchestrated system, the central coordinator may serve as a single point of failure, reducing the system's resilience.

Using the fictitious use case of an e-commerce application, let us demonstrate a simplified example of how MuleSoft can be utilized to implement Saga choreography:

1. **Microservices creation**: Assume that a MuleSoft application has three separate microservices built into it: the Order service, the Payment service, and the Delivery service.

2. **Event creation**: The Order service initiates a new Saga and publishes `OrderCreatedEvent` upon receiving an order.

   This can be done in the MuleSoft application by adding a `POST HTTP` method to the Order service, which will cause an event to be triggered following the creation of an order. An Anypoint MQ service or a message broker such as RabbitMQ or ActiveMQ could receive this event.

3. **Event subscription**: `OrderCreatedEvent` has a subscription from the Payment service. It attempts to process the payment after receiving this event, and if it is successful, it publishes a `PaymentProcessedEvent`. This could be done in MuleSoft by configuring an Anypoint MQ subscriber in the Payment service to listen for `OrderCreatedEvent` and initiate the appropriate payment processing flow when it is detected. It adds a new event to its queue after processing is complete.

4. **Orchestration**: `PaymentProcessedEvent` is a subscribed service for the Delivery service. It begins the delivery procedure as soon as it receives this event. The Delivery service can have an MQ subscriber that listens for `PaymentProcessedEvent` and initiates delivery, just like the Payment service.

5. **Compensating transactions**: The Payment service issues `PaymentFailedEvent` if the payment procedure is unsuccessful. The order would then be canceled through a compensating transaction initiated by the Order service that has subscribed to this event. An order cancellation flow can be initiated by setting up an additional MQ subscriber in the Order service, which will listen for `PaymentFailedEvent`.

This is merely a simplified example; the actual implementation will be far more complicated, considering a few additional factors such as managing transactional consistency between service calls and handling communication failures between services.

Implementing Saga choreography would require MuleSoft's ability to manage APIs and seamlessly integrate various systems.

The Saga pattern for creating microservices has been demonstrated in the previous section. Next, we shall discuss the Competing Consumers pattern in this part.

The Competing Consumers pattern

Multiple consumers from the same channel can process messages in parallel thanks to the Competing Consumers pattern. When multiple consumers of the same pool instance need to process several small tasks in parallel and asynchronously, this pattern comes in handy.

In a normal scenario, the traffic coming to the message broker from the publisher is low, and the consumer can process messages at the rate at which they come from the publisher, as shown in *Figure 7.7*.

Figure 7.7 - Competing Consumers pattern for low traffic

There might be a scenario where the ingress traffic increases, such as when publishers start sending more messages to the queue or the number of publishers increases. In this case, the rate at which messages are published to the queue is faster than that at which they are consumed.

If this happens, we can increase the number of consumers listening to a message stream and allow more than one consumer per queue to process messages simultaneously. This way, the traffic is distributed amongst several consumers to enable the simultaneous processing of messages, with one message being transmitted to a single consumer regardless of how many consumers are listening to the same queue.

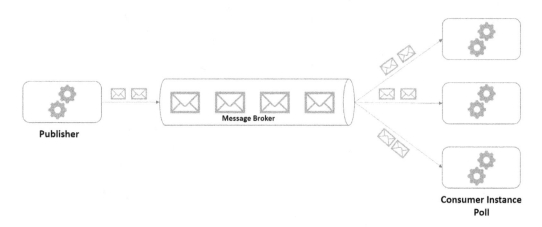

Figure 7.8 - Competing Consumers pattern for high traffic

In *Figure 7.8*, we have added more consumers to the pool to process traffic coming at the same rate at which it comes from the publisher.

Benefits of implementing the Competing Consumers pattern

The following are the benefits of implementing the Competing Consumers pattern:

- **Scalability**: Depending on the traffic from publishers in message channels, consumers may be added or deleted. Increasing the number of consumers will allow the distribution of traffic between multiple consumers and each message can be processed asynchronously and independently.

- **High availability**: The same message channel is being listened to by several consumers. Other consumers can process messages if one of the consumers fails or stops.

- **Reliability and resilience**: If the message processing fails for one of the messages, the message will be returned to the queue and will be available for reprocessing again by other consumers.

We can use the Competing Consumers pattern in a variety of applications:

- When distribution of traffic is necessary, as it cannot be handled by a single consumer, such as when there are very high and variable transport volumes. We may be able to have several consumers processing messages at the same time under these circumstances.

- Where reliability of the message, fault tolerance, and availability are necessary.

- If the process is split into a small set of tasks and each task can be executed asynchronously or independently in concurrent execution mode.

Circuit Breaker pattern

Another design pattern used in software development is the Circuit Breaker pattern. In microservices, the **Circuit Breaker design pattern** prevents service failures by keeping an eye on interactions, establishing thresholds, and momentarily stopping or suspending traffic to malfunctioning services. It guarantees dependable performance in distributed architectures by assisting in the prevention of cascade failures and preserving system stability.

It is named after the electrical circuit breaker that stops the flow of electricity when there is a fault detected. In software, the circuit breaker pattern is used to detect failures and to define the logic of preventing the failure from reoccurring, during maintenance, temporary external system failure, or unexpected system problems.

That's how it works, you know. When a system encounters a certain number of failures (e.g., it fails to call a microservice), the Circuit Breaker trips. The Circuit Breaker pattern will prevent any interaction with the service during a specified period and return an error without delay. The Circuit Breaker will allow a limited number of test requests to be passed once the timeout has expired. If they are successful, the Circuit Breaker will restart its usual operation; if it is unsuccessful, a timeout period shall be resumed.

The Circuit Breaker pattern protects the system against allocating resources to operations that may fail, prevents overloading, and gives it a chance to recover.

Circuit Breaker states

The following are the various Circuit Breaker states:

- **Open**: When the configured trip timeout has been reached, the Subscriber source does not attempt to retrieve messages and does not skip messages silently.

- **Closed**: The starting state in which messages are normally obtained from MQ based on the configuration of the Subscriber source.

- **Half-open**: After trip timeout elapses, the Subscriber source goes to a Half-Open state. In the next poll for messages, the Subscriber source retrieves a single message from the service and uses that message to check whether the system has recovered before going back to the normal Closed state.

The following diagram illustrates the architecture of the Circuit Breaker pattern.

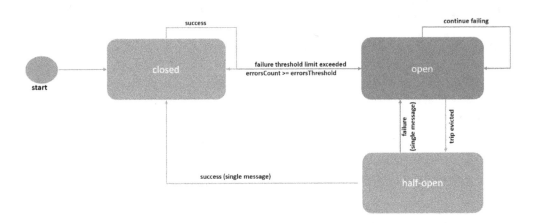

Figure 7.9 - The Circuit Breaker pattern

MuleSoft allows us to implement the Circuit Breaker pattern using Anypoint MQ or by applying the Circuit Breaker policy to the API. This policy can be downloaded from MuleSoft Catalyst and published to your organization's Anypoint exchange.

Anypoint MQ

Anypoint MQ is a multitenant, cloud-based managed queuing service provided by MuleSoft for exchanging data between your applications asynchronously. The Anypoint MQ broker allows an application to publish the message to the queue so that another application can consume the message from the queue. Anypoint MQ is fully integrated with the Anypoint platform, offering access control, client management, and connectors.

Mule applications can use Anypoint MQ Connector to publish and consume messages from the queue, whereas non-Mule applications can use Anypoint MQ REST APIs for publishing and consuming messages from the queues.

Message exchanges and queues

Message queues are temporary storage where publishers can publish messages and consumers can consume messages. Message queues enable reliable and scalable communication between multiple applications.

Figure 7.10 - Anypoint MQ (queue)

Message exchanges allow you to bind multiple queues to send the same copy of messages to all the queues bound to the exchange. The following figure illustrates how messages flow from the exchange to all associated queues.

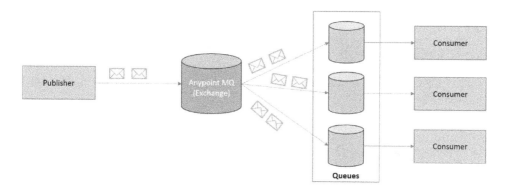

Figure 7.11 - Anypoint MQ (exchange)

With an exchange, messages are routed intelligently to certain queues using message routing rules. The following figure illustrates how messages flow to specific queues depending on the routing rules.

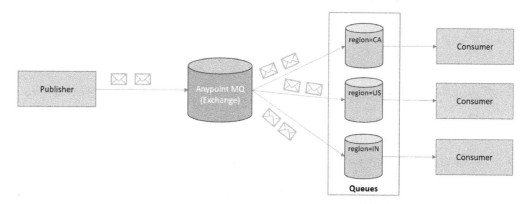

Figure 7.12 - Anypoint MQ (exchange intelligent routing)

The following are a few considerations to keep in mind while using message exchanges:

- 450 queues can be bound to the message exchange
- Only 10 queues can be bound to a message exchange that has intelligent routing enabled
- One queue can be bound to multiple queues

Anypoint MQ supports **first in first out (FIFO)** queues. Ordered delivery of your messages is guaranteed by these queues. Applications that demand exactly one delivery and precise message ordering but not fast delivery speed are best suited for FIFO queues.

10 in-flight messages per message group in a FIFO queue are supported by Anypoint MQ. There is no maximum number of message groups in a FIFO queue in Anypoint MQ.

The following are the features supported by Anypoint MQ:

- Up to 120,000 in-flight messages supported by standard queues and 10 in-flight messages supported by FIFO queues

- Anypoint MQ can be configured in multiple regions in the US, Europe, and APAC

- Encryption is supported for storing messages in the queues

Cross-region failover for Anypoint MQ standard queues

Anypoint MQ automatically creates a fallback queue in a fallback region when you enable failover for a queue. A Mule application will publish and consume messages from the fallback queue if it is unable to connect to an Anypoint MQ server in that area.

As soon as the connector determines that the main region is unavailable, it changes to publish and consume new messages from the fallback queue and periodically verifies that the main region is operational again.

The following are the considerations for cross-region failover:

- Failover is supported for standard queues but not for FIFO queues and message exchanges.

- Failover is not supported in the Anypoint government cloud as it supports only one region. The Anypoint government cloud is discussed in *Chapter 13*.

- Either Anypoint MQ Connector 4.0.5 or later is required for failover support.

- In some countries, Anypoint MQ is available in just one area. The data is stored in a region outside the country until the primary region is available if failover is enabled for the queues in these regions and the primary region is down.

- Failover is not enabled by default. Once failover is enabled, it will create the queue with the `_fb` suffix in the failover region. For example, if you have a queue called `myOrderQueue` in the primary region, it will create `myOrderQueue_fb` in the failover region.

Dead-letter queues

You can make sure that undeliverable messages are routed to a **dead-letter queue** (**DLQ**) using Anypoint MQ. After that, you can examine the messages that were sent to the DLQ to ascertain why they were not delivered. A DLQ only receives undelivered messages; otherwise, it functions similarly to any other queue. When creating the queue, you can set the delivery delay, encryption, and **time-to-live** (**TTL**) value.

The following are other capabilities provided by Anypoint MQ:

- It provides out-of-the-box Anypoint MQ Connector for publishing and consuming messages with the message exchange and queues.

- Non-MuleSoft applications or third-party applications can use Anypoint MQ REST APIs to publish and consume messages from the Anypoint MQ.

- It can transfer substantial payloads, up to 10 MB. Anypoint MQ converts the payload to a string before sending if it contains any format other than text (such as CSV, HTML, JSON, and XML), which increases the size of the payload. A payload too large error may occur if the payload is larger than the 10 MB maximum payload size because of this conversion.

The Circuit Breaker pattern with Anypoint MQ

A Circuit Breaker capability is provided by the Subscriber source, allowing you to regulate how the connector responds to errors that arise during the processing of a consumed message. You can use the Circuit Breaker to handle any outage of an external service that you connect to. The Circuit Breaker enables the external service to recover under a lower load and permits the system to cease making requests. The following figure shows the configuration of the Circuit Breaker pattern on Anypoint MQ.

Figure 7.13 - The Circuit Breaker pattern with Anypoint MQ

The following are the parameters that need to be configured on Anypoint MQ to enable the Circuit Breaker pattern:

- `onErrorType`: This determines the kinds of errors that are considered failures when the flow is being executed. Only when the flow concludes with an error propagation does an error occurrence count. Every error is automatically interpreted as a circuit failure.

- `errorsThreshold`: This determines the number of `onErrorType` errors that must be encountered by the Circuit Breaker to open.

- `tripTimeout`: If `errorsThreshold` is reached, the circuit shall remain open for a time that can be specified with this value.

- `circuitName`: The name of the Circuit Breaker that will be bound to this specification. Each queue has its own Circuit Breakers by default.

Event-driven architecture (EDA)

Modern applications constructed with microservices frequently employ EDA, which makes use of events to trigger and communicate between decoupled services. An event is an update or change in status, such as when a product is added to a shopping cart in an online store.

Let's now discuss decoupling and loose coupling within EDA.

Decoupling and loose coupling are related but distinct concepts within EDA. **Decoupling** is a way to eliminate the dependencies between the different components of the system. In the context of the EDA, publishers generate event data without knowing the consumer of the messages. This allows the publisher and consumer to communicate independently without knowing each other.

Loose coupling attempts to lessen the coupling between components (rather than totally separate them) by reducing their level of interdependence. While components in a loosely coupled system may communicate with one another, they do so without developing any kind of dependency.

Benefits of EDA

The following are the benefits of EDA:

- **Parallel processing**: Multiple processes can be triggered by a single event to be executed independently of each other. The key feature of EDA is its ability to handle messages asynchronously. This means that it can distribute workloads and support parallel processing. A broker can receive any number of events from various event producers and deliver them to various components for processing.

- **Improved responsiveness**: Services can communicate asynchronously without waiting for instant answers by exchanging events. This method improves responsiveness, permits more parallelism, and lowers system latency.

- **Scalability**: A single incident prompts several responses from various customers, enhancing performance. Decoupling makes it easier to add, update, or remove event producers and consumers, enabling rapid modifications in response to changing needs.

- **Fault tolerance and resilience**: EDA can be resilient and fault tolerant by design. Other components can keep working on their own even if one breaks down or stops responding. This increases the application's overall availability and dependability by guaranteeing that the system continues to function even in the event of a breakdown.

Limitations of EDA

The following are the limitations of the EDA:

- **Message ordering**: The key principle of EDA is to process messages asynchronously and independently, and it becomes challenging to maintain the order and consistency of the events, especially when events are processed in a distributed environment

- **Error handling**: In EDA, errors and exceptions may be handled differently, as events may be handled at different times and in different locations

- **Complexity**: In terms of understanding the flow of events, relationships between events, and problems with troubleshooting, EDA can create complexity

- **Debugging challenges**: In EDA, especially when events lead to a chain of interactions between components, it can be hard to identify the source of problems

We have discussed Anypoint MQ in this chapter, and it can be used to implement EDA. Another messaging system, such as JMS, AMQP, or Kafka, can be used to implement EDA.

API-led connectivity and EDA together

EDA and API-led connectivity are two potent software architecture techniques that work well together. With API-led connectivity, the software's essential building blocks are the APIs. Because all the devices, systems, and applications are linked and communicate with one another via APIs, the systems are manageable, reusable, and modular. In contrast, the design paradigm known as EDA involves software components that respond to and create events. These occurrences indicate a modification in an application's state, which sets off events in other system components.

When combined, these two strategies can greatly improve the way an application is designed and runs.

- **Enhanced scalability**: API-led connectivity can facilitate the addition of new system components, while EDA can assist in managing the real-time flow of information.

- **Enhanced efficiency**: The effective reuse of software components can be made possible by the combination of EDA and API-led connectivity, which can expedite and lower the cost of development.

- **Flexibility**: While EDA enables real-time responsiveness to changes, enabling a flexible and dynamic system, API-led connectivity offers the flexibility to connect different applications, systems, and devices.

- **Real-time processing**: While APIs can offer real-time access to the services and resources required for event processing, EDA makes it easier to process events in real time.

- **Simple maintainability**: Updating and maintaining systems is made easier by the modular design of API-led connectivity. This is enhanced by EDA, which connects loosely coupled services and facilitates easy system modification.

In conclusion, EDA combined with API-led connectivity can yield a stable, scalable, and adaptable software architecture that effectively manages real-time data flow and dynamic task processing.

Experience API

As the name implies, an Experience API in API-led connectivity describes the experience of a particular user or system. An Experience API's primary goal is to deliver data in the format needed by a specific device, web application, or channel. For its end user, system, or channel—be it a mobile app, a desktop website, or even another application—each Experience API offers a particular view that is appropriate. Because of this, developers can alter the user interface or the device's data source without changing the underlying systems and procedures. We must modify experience APIs to meet the unique needs of each customer as they are optional and should only be utilized if they are unable to use our APIs.

For instance, the information shown on a web-based application will not be the same as the information displayed on a mobile application. Experience APIs can help in this situation. They retrieve identical information from System or Process APIs, but their presentation varies according to the intended device or channel. Experience APIs provide great flexibility in terms of changing user interfaces and experiences without interfering with the business processes of the backend systems. This enables companies to promptly adjust to evolving consumer demands, market trends, and preferences.

Process API

In API-led connectivity, a **Process API** is used to coordinate data from System APIs and carry out a particular business function. These APIs can be reused across various channels and applications because they are made to handle business use cases and processes. An order process for a customer, for instance, could be managed by a Process API. It could use System APIs to calculate pricing, verify inventory, get product details, and oversee the life cycle of an order. Different Experience APIs (the third layer in API-led connectivity) can then use this Process API to obtain the data in the format needed by each channel or platform (such as a mobile app, web portal, or other customer touchpoints). Process APIs are optional and should only be used when gathering information from multiple System APIs for a particular entity.

With the help of these Process APIs, the customer-facing application (Experience API) can abstract away the process of retrieving data from multiple systems, increasing process reusability and streamlining. In this manner, modifications to the underlying systems have no direct impact on how well customer-facing apps operate. Process agility, service reusability, and optimized data processes are all provided by using Process APIs in API-led connectivity, which facilitates and expedites application development.

System API

A **System API** is the kind of API that facilitates communication with databases, underlying systems, and other services in API-led connectivity. This kind of API doesn't have any business logic or procedures; instead, it just serves as a mechanism for data retrieval and storage. With the help of system APIs, it is possible to efficiently encapsulate the technical details of the systems and only expose the necessary information. An instance of a System API could be the ability to retrieve customer information from a database or the features of a particular software program. System APIs are optional and should be used only in case the backends we are using do not already expose good RESTful APIs.

To access a database, ERP, or email system, for instance, a system API might be developed. Higher-level process APIs or Experience APIs would then use this API to supply functionality for various user interfaces or processes.

The following is the architecture of API-led connectivity:

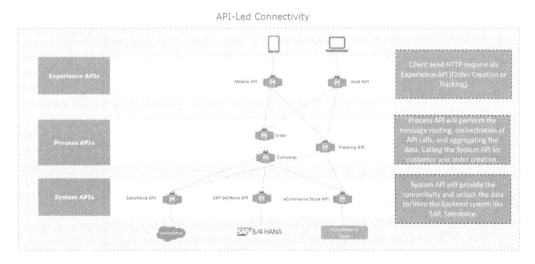

Figure 7.14 - API-led connectivity architecture

In *Figure 7.14*, the communication between the Experience, Process, and System APIs happens via HTTP. Benefits such as better productivity, efficiency, agility, and flexibility are afforded by API-led connectivity. It allows organizations to create configurable and reused APIs, use new technologies, and streamline processes that allow them to maintain links with legacy IT systems.

Let's talk about API-led connectivity and EDA together. API-led connectivity and EDA complement each other, but they are two distinct styles of architecture.

The following are some differences between EDA and the REST API:

- EDA is asynchronous, whereas the REST API is synchronous

- EDA is loosely coupled, whereas the REST API is tightly coupled

- EDA communicates via a message broker, whereas the REST API communicates over HTTP

The following diagram shows EDA and API-led connectivity architecture together.

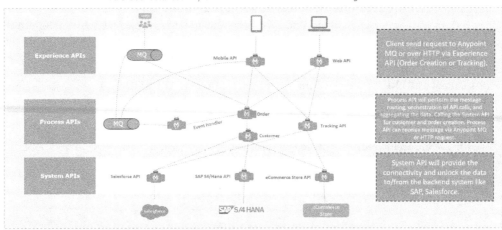

Figure 7.15 - API-led connectivity architecture and EDA together

In *Figure 7.15*, we have combined EDA and API-led connectivity architecture to receive messages via Anypoint MQ or HTTP. We can ensure zero message loss, reliability, and guaranteed delivery with EDA, and we can make use benefits of both architectures when they are implemented together.

Application networks and composability

A set of capabilities in an approach called the **MuleSoft composable enterprise** is offered by the company that focuses on integration and API management solutions. The core of the composable enterprise concept is to create a flexible and configurable architecture that allows enterprises to rapidly adjust and evolve their systems.

Application networks and APIs, which make an organization more flexible and enable quick responses to changing market dynamics, technological disruption, or business needs, are key elements of composable enterprises. An application network can assist a company in becoming more flexible, adjusting its pace of business, and adapting to shifts in its industry, market, and customer base without compromising its core values.

Every newly built API can contribute additional value to your whole application network and marketplace when your composable organization adopts an API-led approach.

The following are the key enablers of the composable enterprise concept:

- **API-led connectivity**: MuleSoft advocates the API-led connectivity architecture that allows you to manage, design, and implement reusable APIs to connect data, applications, and systems. APIs are building blocks for integrations that allow the composition of various services and components.

- **Reusable assets**: The composable enterprise concept emphasizes building reusable components, assets, and building blocks such as APIs, templates, connectors, and frameworks. This allows us to create new APIs rapidly, reducing the length of the development cycle and minimizing overall development efforts. This means new features can be released much faster. These reusable assets can be stored in Anypoint Exchange, which allows the discovery of assets by other developers.

- **Hybrid integration**: The composable enterprise supports hybrid implementations that allow organizations to connect on-premises and cloud-based systems. MuleSoft provides the connectors, platform components, and other services that enable connectivity with databases, services, and devices running on the cloud and on-premises.

- **Application networks**: Building application networks—where APIs are arranged and shared in a regulated way—is a concept that MuleSoft advocates. This enables businesses to increase their connectivity capabilities by utilizing already-existing APIs and developing new ones.

- **Universal API management**: Universal API management allows the creation, management, securing, and governing of APIs located anywhere or following any architecture or written in any technology. Most organizations have APIs running on multi-cloud and on-premises and probably have APIs based on different technologies. These businesses are unable to manage and coordinate these dissimilar APIs, and they lack visibility as information moves between these platforms. This is one of the issues that MuleSoft aims to resolve in universal API management, which, according to MuleSoft, is the capacity to extend full life cycle management capabilities to APIs that are developed and implemented anywhere.

- **Automation**: Automation is one of the critical key enablers of the composable enterprise, which allows organizations to automate manual business processes and improve overall productivity by reducing manual tasks. LOB teams and non-technical users can independently create integration applications from central IT-created components with MuleSoft Composer. The creation of more feature-rich components is made simpler for builders via MuleSoft Robotic Process.

Summary

This chapter has covered a variety of architectural styles that are crucial to understanding when creating a network using modular architecture. Along with other contemporary architectural styles such as EDA and API-led connectivity, we also reviewed the monolithic and microservices architectures.

Several microservices design patterns, such as the Saga, Circuit Breaker, and Competing Consumers patterns, were also examined. Additionally, we now know how to use MuleSoft's Anypoint MQ component to implement a messaging architecture or EDA.

In the next chapter, we will be talking about the influence of non-functional requirements in shaping architecture.

8

Non-Functional Requirements Influence in Shaping the API Architecture

This chapter will discuss the influence of non-functional requirements in shaping the architecture. Non-functional requirements are crucial for implementing an API solution that will ensure data security at rest and in transit, enabling a less risky or safer deployment model, API performance, and security.

In this chapter, we will cover the following topics:

- Common non-functional requirements
- Meeting performance requirements in the platform
- Applying security to the API design
- Data encryption in transit and at rest
- Deployment strategies such as blue-green deployment and canary deployment

Common non-functional requirements

Non-functional requirements aid in balancing the trade-offs between various features, guiding the design and methodology according to what's essential for the target audience and the intended use of the API. It establishes a norm for the behavior of the API.

Often referred to as *quality attributes*, **non-functional requirements (NFRs)** are the standards that evaluate a system's functionality rather than its particular behaviors or functions.

Each architect has a set of NFRs that they need to manage. These NFRs outline a solution's technical limitations and specify how it should operate. The most common NFRs are availability, scalability, performance, security, observability, maintainability, resiliency, reliability, consistency, and quality.

Some NFRs, such as scalability, high availability, fault tolerance, and disaster recovery, will be discussed in *Chapter 16*. In this chapter, we will be discussing some of the NFRs related to API performance, security, and so on.

Meeting performance requirements in the platform

The speed at which an API can receive, handle, and process requests to communicate with or supply data to other applications or services is referred to as API performance.

The API performance can be measured by the following factors.

Response time

This is the duration it takes for an API to respond to a request. Payload size, server processing, and network latency are some of the variables that affect it. It is a crucial indicator of user effectiveness and satisfaction.

Throughput

This is the number of requests an API can handle in a given amount of time. The throughput is affected by concurrency, load balancing, and server resource allocation. It is an essential indicator of dependability and scalability.

Error rates

This is the percentage of errors returned by your API in a given amount of time. The error rates are affected by factors such as the quality of code, exception handling, quality checks, and validation.

Availability

This is the amount of time your API is up and running., measured as a percentage. The availability is affected by factors such as downtime, uptime, and maintenance. Availability of the API is crucial for the enterprise to ensure business continuity.

Latency

This gauges how long it takes to get a response from the API once a request has been performed. Higher performance is usually a consequence of lower latency.

Scalability

This is the ability of the API to process more requests and transactions without seeing a decrease in performance. The API must be flexible enough that it can be scaled independently during the traffic load.

We have just seen the different factors that can be used to measure the performance of the APIs. The following are the factors that enable you to improve the overall performance of the MuleSoft APIs.

Resource allocation

There is a need to allocate the right resources to your application when deploying to any MuleSoft environment. The resource allocation may vary from environment to environment for the same application. For example, an application deployed to CloudHub, compared to one deployed on-premises, may require more or fewer computing resources. MuleSoft provides a runtime plane that allows you to increase or decrease computing resources by just increasing or decreasing the number of workers (replicas in the case of CloudHub 2.0) and worker size (the replica size in the case of CloudHub 2.0). This can be achieved with zero downtime. Increasing the computing resources means you will be able to accept more API requests to be processed and can improve overall performance during peak hours. APIs deployed on Runtime Fabric can be allocated with more computing resources by adding more replicas or increasing the replica size.

In contrast to CloudHub and Runtime Fabric, scaling the Mule APIs installed in an on-premises Mule environment is more difficult. Individual applications cannot be scaled in an on-premises Mule environment; instead, the entire server must be scaled by adding more instances or resources. Scaling the Mule environment on-premises might necessitate downtime.

Performance testing

You need to assess both the Mule applications and their running environment to get the best possible performance out of them. Performance testing is a type of non-functional software testing that assesses an application's responsiveness, speed, scalability, and stability under a specific workload. This crucial step guarantees the quality of the software. Performance testing is also known as stress testing. Apache JMeter is an Apache project that allows you to execute performance testing on the APIs to measure and analyze their API responsiveness and throughput.

Performance testing will also help you to identify the right computing resources required to run your APIs.

Performance monitoring

APIs must be monitored continuously to validate the resources consumed by them during testing. This will allow you to understand the CPU or memory consumed by each API during performance testing or standard testing. MuleSoft provides out-of-the-box components such as Anypoint Monitoring or Runtime Manager metrics to validate CPU or memory usage and network usage by APIs.

Alerts can be configured for CPU or memory usage that exceeds the threshold limit, or if an API is not responsive. This will ensure the application's maintainability and availability.

Load balancing

The process of dividing up network traffic evenly among a pool of resources to support an application is known as load balancing. By increasing response times and reducing network latency, load balancing improves application performance. An intelligent component called a load balancer distributes client requests or network load efficiently across multiple servers.

The load balancer will make sure that traffic is only routed to servers that are online, healthy, and less crowded. This will guarantee the APIs' dependability and accessibility.

The following are the algorithms for the load balancers to distribute network traffic:

- **Round-robin load balancing**: Cycles of client requests are sent to available servers. The optimal conditions for round-robin server load balancing are roughly equal processing and storage capacities across servers.

- **Least connection load balancing**: Here, a client request is sent to the servers that have the least active connections or aren't as busy. This will ensure that busy servers are not overloaded with more client requests.

- **Weighted round-robin load balancing**: A numerical value is assigned to each server. When assigning sessions to servers, the load balancer makes use of this. The server with the higher weighting receives the new request if two servers have the same number of active connections. The weighting value is disregarded if the servers with the fewest connections all have the same weight.

> **Note**
> In most cases, the algorithm uses a round-robin mechanism to distribute requests to a dedicated load balancer, but it's not always correct. The algorithm is trying to split traffic evenly, but based on the performance of the **dedicated load balancers (DLB)** and applications it's adjusting.

Application caching

The cache is a sort of temporary data storage that automatically stores information to expedite data retrieval the next time an application is accessed. To save a round trip to the database or another system call for the subsequent API request, we typically cache data in APIs that is static or doesn't change frequently. This will improve the API's overall performance and response time.

Caching in MuleSoft can be achieved in the following ways:

- By applying the caching policy to APIs on Anypoint API Manager, server-side implementation in MuleSoft can be achieved.

- A component called cache scope lets you store the outcome of a transformation or operation in memory for a predetermined period. This can decrease the number of times the operation needs to be performed, which can enhance the performance of your application.

Many other factors can improve the overall performance of APIs:

- **Configuration and tuning**: To prevent performance degradation, it is important to properly configure essentials such as thread pools, timeouts, memory and CPU utilization, and **garbage collection (GC)** tuning.

- **Using batch processing**: To increase the overall effectiveness and performance of the API for heavy-load processing, think about utilizing batch processing techniques as an alternative to real-time processing.

- **Effective exception handling**: Include effective error-handling procedures in the design of your Mule application. Performance can be severely impacted by error propagations that are not managed or controlled.

- **Optimizing DataWeave transformations**: To maximize the efficiency of DataWeave transformations, only transform the necessary data, and make use of pagination and streaming when working with larger datasets.

- **Asynchronous processing**: By enabling parallel process execution, asynchronous processing can greatly enhance MuleSoft API performance.

- **Monitoring and logging**: Accurate monitoring and timely logging will assist in identifying and resolving any performance problems.

We will discuss more about NFRs in upcoming chapters. Scalability, high availability, disaster recovery, fault tolerance, and so on will be discussed in *Chapter 16*.

We've seen how to enhance API performance generally and the variables that may contribute to API performance problems. Now, we will explore a number of several deployment techniques that can be used to guarantee trouble-free API deployment and simple API rollback procedures.

API security

Preventing malicious attacks and the misuse of APIs is a practice known as API security. Due to their inherent vulnerability to application logic and sensitive data, including **personally identifiable information (PII)**, APIs can be the target of cyberattacks.

The following are ways to apply security to API design:

- **Authentication and authorization**: To manage who may use your APIs, put in place robust authentication and authorization procedures. Standard protocols such as OAuth 2.0, OpenID Connect, or JWT-based authentication can be used to do this.

- **Encryption**: Use SSL/TLS encryption to protect all data while it is in transit. APIs should decline to exchange data via unencrypted routes.

- **Throttling and quotas**: Reduce the possibility of a **distributed denial-of-service (DdoS)** attack by setting quotas or rate limiting (throttling) on your API. This limits the number of requests a customer may submit in a certain period of time.

- **Access control**: To guarantee that only authorized users have access to certain resources, APIs should include robust, detailed access control mechanisms. One popular method is **role-based access control (RBAC)**.

- **Validating and filtering the data**: Input data should be validated and output data filtered to prevent common web threats such as injection attacks and **cross-site scripting (XSS)**.

- **Error handling**: Sensitive information should not be exposed in API error messages, as this could provide attackers with the means to exploit the system.

- **Logging and monitoring**: Extensive logging should be implemented to monitor API activity, aiding in issue detection, diagnosis, and identification of suspicious activity.

- **API versioning**: Proper versioning should be used when updating or making changes to the API to avoid breaking applications relying on older versions.

- **Securing the API endpoints**: API endpoints should be secured by implementing the principle of least privilege to limit access. It is advisable to use (Universal Unique Identifier) UUIDs instead of auto-incrementing IDs to mitigate unauthorized access.

- **Penetration testing and regular audits**: Conduct regular audits and penetration testing on your APIs to proactively identify and address security vulnerabilities and weaknesses. You can utilize tools such as OWASP ZAP and Postman to perform routine API testing.

It is important to note that creating a secure API requires more than just implementing authentication and authorization. Every aspect, including the data structure and the use of HTTP status codes, contributes to the security of the entire system. It is crucial to take into account every security concern and potential weakness in the APIs when designing them. MuleSoft offers tools for securing APIs that can be used from the design stage through the deployment stage. For instance, to guarantee API consistency and quality and enforce API governance throughout the company, we can apply an API governance ruleset to **Rest API Modeling Language (RAML)** or **Open API Specification (OAS)** during the design phase. This will also guarantee that the OWASP Top 10 has been addressed. Security API policies can be applied to the deployed API during the deployment phase.

Let's now discuss how to secure the rest of the API while it is in transit.

Data security in motion or in transit

Data in transit or motion means transferring data from one location to another location over a network. This includes transferring information over HTTP, via emails, or collaboration platforms. Given that it is exposed while traveling across the internet or a private corporate network, this data is typically less secure than inactive data. Data in transit is, therefore, a highly vulnerable point of attack.

The following approaches can be used to protect data in transit or motion:

- **Data encryption**: The most popular technique to safeguard data while it is in transit is data encryption. In addition to shielding your data from hackers, end-to-end encryption makes sure that even if it is intercepted, the recipient would be unable to decrypt it without the encryption key.

- **Virtual private network (VPN)**: A VPN is another popular technique to secure data as it's sent. By using a VPN, you can establish a secure tunnel between the servers you interact with and your internet connection. This obscures your IP address and shields your data from prying eyes, making it more difficult for hackers to follow your online activity.

- **SSL and TLS**: Cryptographic technologies called **Secure Socket Layer** (**SSL**) and **Transport Layer Security** (**TLS**) are designed to offer network security. They function by establishing an encrypted connection between a client and a server to thwart tampering and unwanted access.

- **Using a private network**: When sending sensitive data, try to stay away from public or unprotected networks. Data interception is less likely when private or protected wireless networks are used.

- **Employ secure file transfer options**: Always choose services that provide secure file transfers while transferring files. For instance, the **Safe File Transfer Protocol** (**SFTP**) supports safe authentication in addition to encryption.

- **Frequent system/software updates**: Software developers increase security and address security gaps with each release. Your system may become open to intrusions if you fail to upgrade.

- **Multi-factor authentication (MFA)**: By demanding many kinds of verification to authenticate a user, MFA adds an extra layer of protection.

- **Put in place a policy for data loss prevention (DLP)**: A DLP policy minimizes the chance of data leaks by monitoring, detecting, and blocking data in use, in motion, and at rest.

TLS establishes an encrypted connection between a web server and a browser. This guarantees the privacy and security of all data transferred between the web server and the browser. "One-way TLS" describes a process in which the client authenticates just the server, ensuring that the client is certain that the server is what it says it is.

To accomplish this, the client verifies the trustworthiness of the server's TLS certificate as well as the chain of certificates that lead to it. In this instance, the encryption is one-way (from client to server), rather than two-way, and the server does not know the client's identity (although it will know that the data the client sends will be safely encrypted). When the client is open to the public (such as a web browser) and does not require a unique identity, this kind of configuration is usually employed.

The following figure illustrates one-way TLS:

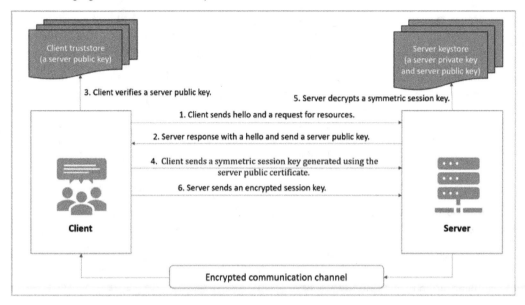

Figure 8.1 - One-way TLS

In contrast, two-way TLS, also referred to as mutual or client authentication SSL, ensures a higher level of security by having the client and server authenticate and validate each other's identities.

Two-way TLS is a mode of communication that requires both the client and the server to authenticate themselves to each other before any data exchange takes place. Because two-way TLS verifies the reliability of both parties involved in the data transmission, it can provide a higher level of security. In situations where private or sensitive data is transferred or stored, this is crucial. Two-way TLS is frequently used by businesses that deal with sensitive personal data, financial transactions, or private company information to reduce the risk of a data breach.

The following figure illustrates two-way TLS:

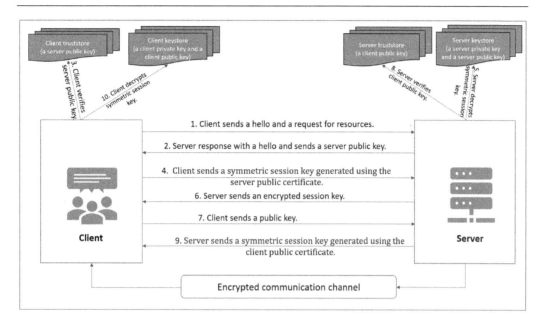

Figure 8.2 - Two-way TLS (mutual authentication)

In this section, we saw how to use methods such as one-way and two-way TLS to secure data while it is in transit. The secure connection between the client and server is established using this method. We will talk about securing the data at rest in the next section.

Data security at rest

Securing data that is physically stored in any digital format, such as spreadsheets, databases, data warehouses, archives, tapes, off-site backups, and mobile devices, is referred to as "protecting data at rest."

The following actions can be taken to guarantee the security of this data:

- **Strong access controls**: Make sure that data is only accessible to those who have a specific need. RBAC, biometric verification, and complicated passwords can all help achieve this.

- **Data masking**: To prevent sensitive information from being seen by unauthorized parties, employ data masking, which involves de-identifying or scrubbing it up.

- **Updates and security patches**: Consistently apply the most recent security patches to your systems and software.

- **Utilize DLP tools**: These tools can identify critical data, keep track of where it moves to, prevent unauthorized access, and stop it from leaving your organization.

- **Frequent audits**: Keep track of who has access to data on a regular basis, audit it, and change permissions as necessary. This can also assist you in spotting any oddities or patterns that might point to a security breach.

- **Data encryption**: Data encryption is the process of transforming data into a different format, or code, that is only readable by those who possess a secret key or password. It's among the best methods for protecting data while it's not in use.

- **Use of strong authentication techniques**: Preventing unwanted access to data can be achieved by putting MFA and other techniques into place.

To completely secure their sensitive and vital data, organizations must protect their data both in transit and at rest. In this section, we saw how to use data encryption, data masking, and other techniques to secure data while it is at rest, and there will be more discussion on API security in upcoming chapters. The topic of deployment strategies will be covered in the upcoming section. It is important to choose the appropriate deployment strategies when deploying an application.

Deployment strategies

Deploying APIs can be challenging and complex, as there are numerous deployment strategies available. Selecting the right deployment strategy is crucial, depending on an organization's requirements and the nature of the APIs that you are deploying. It is also important to consider how to minimize the risk of deployment failure or quickly switch back to a previous version of APIs without causing any downtime.

To ensure that software applications are deployed reliably and efficiently, with minimal user disruption, deployment strategies are needed. These strategies help to reduce the risks of disruption, data loss, and security breaches, as well as improve the quality and performance of software applications for organizations.

There are three important deployment strategies used by organizations to minimize the risk of deployment failures:

- Rolling update deployment

- Blue-green deployment

- Canary deployment

We will discuss all three deployment strategies in detail.

Rolling update deployment

A rolling update ensures that application deployment can be achieved with zero downtime. In rolling update deployment, a new version of an application is slowly released in all previous instances. In brief, this approach replaces the existing instances of the application instances with new ones, one by one. Using this approach, we can gradually update various system components over time. We introduce the updated version of the application to the production environment gradually through a staged rollout.

The following figure shows how rolling update deployment works.

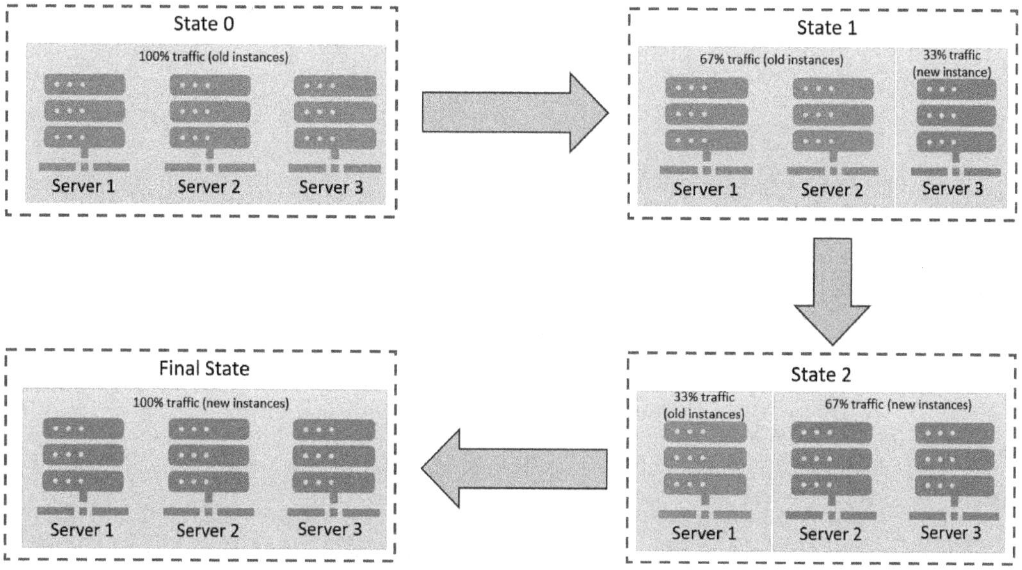

Figure 8.3 - Rolling update deployment

Figure 8.3 shows how each server is deployed with an application, one at a time, with traffic to each new instance of the application growing over time.

Blue-green deployment

Blue-green deployment is the deployment strategy where two identical production environments run in parallel, with one environment named the blue environment and the other environment named the green environment. Blue is the current production environment, whereas green is the new production environment.

The following is the process for blue-green deployment:

1. Deploy the latest changes or enhancements to the green environment.

2. Execute the regression test, manual test, or automated test to ensure that the green environment works as expected and functions correctly.

3. Once the green environment is tested and ready, switch traffic from blue to green.

4. Keep an eye on the green environment's performance to find any problems or defects in the green environment, and roll back traffic to the blue environment.

Blue-green deployment runs two identical production environments concurrently, reducing the chance of downtime and service interruptions. It is possible to swiftly revert to the blue environment if problems with the green environment are found, protecting end users in the process.

The following figure shows how blue-green deployment works.

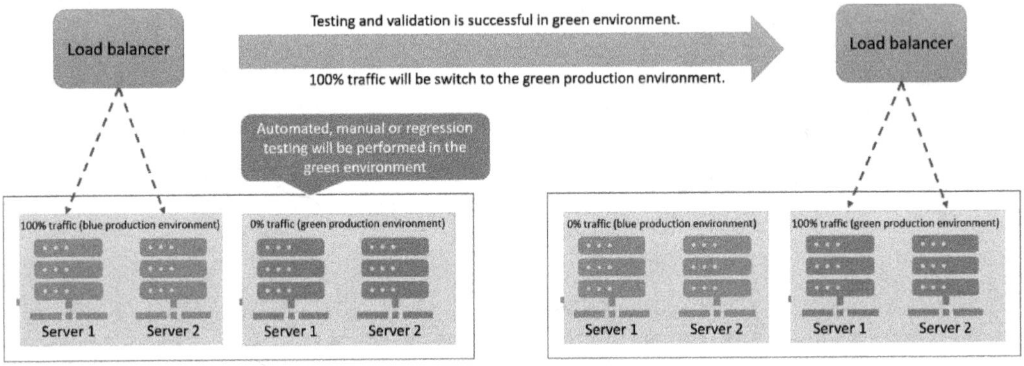

Figure 8.4 - Blue-green deployment

Canary deployment

A canary release enhances observability, limits the impact of new components on the current service, and gradually rolls out traffic to a new version of the software, all of which help organizations lower the risks associated with software introduction.

One method for lowering the risk involved in the release of new software versions is canary deployment. Before making the new software version available to all users, it is first shown to a limited, select group of users in a live setting. Teams may test how a new version will function in a real-world setting, reduce risk, and enhance software quality through canary deployments, all of which work toward improving user experience. The following is the process for canary deployment:

1. Decide which users or systems will get the update or feature first and by a small percentage.

2. Give the canary group access to the update or feature.

3. Keep an eye on the canary group's performance to spot any problems or bugs.

4. Increase the percentage of users or systems that receive the update or feature progressively if the canary group performs well.

5. Before deploying to more users or systems, address any issues found and roll back the deployment.

The following figure shows how canary deployment works.

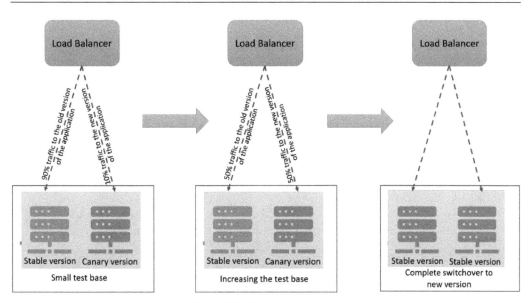

Figure 8.5 - Canary deployment

A crucial component of continuous delivery strategies, canary deployments come in handy when introducing updates and new functionalities for cloud-based apps. Canary deployments, so named for the historical method of using canaries in coal mines to identify harmful gases before they affect people, assist in identifying software flaws before they affect every user.

MuleSoft Catalyst provides an API policy that allows you to implement a canary deployment. A Mule canary deployment API policy that switches the API implementation host dynamically enables a gateway proxy to support a canary release strategy.

Summary

This chapter discussed the necessary NFRs for implementing a strong architecture. We examined the factors that impact API performance and proposed solutions to enhance it. Additionally, we delved into API security and deployment strategies, including the use of one-way and two-way SSL for secure communication between client and server. It is crucial to prioritize API security and performance when designing APIs.

In the next chapter, we will discuss how to leverage CloudHub 1.0 to host MuleSoft APIs.

Further reading

- One-way and two-way SSL – `https://dzone.com/articles/implementing-one-way-and-two-way-ssl-mutual-authen`

- API security – `https://www.mulesoft.com/resources/api/api-security`

- API performance – `https://blogs.mulesoft.com/tag/api-performance/`

9

Hassle-free Deployment with Anypoint iPaaS (CloudHub 1.0)

In this chapter, we'll learn how to run, manage, and deploy MuleSoft applications in the CloudHub 1.0 environment. We will also look at the different features and capabilities provided by CloudHub 1.0 and the different platform architecture approaches for running and deploying the application within CloudHub 1.0 in the Anypoint Platform.

In this chapter, we will cover the following topics:

- What is CloudHub 1.0?
- What capabilities are provided by CloudHub 1.0?
- Architecture capabilities of CloudHub 1.0
- Networking and hosting options
- High availability, scalability, fault tolerance, and disaster recovery with CloudHub 1.0

Technical requirements

For this chapter, you'll require access to the Anypoint Platform. You can sign up for a 30-day free trial account at `https://anypoint.mulesoft.com/login/signup`.

You'll also need to download MuleSoft Anypoint Studio (visit `https://www.mulesoft.com/lp/dl/anypoint-mule-studio`).

What is CloudHub 1.0?

CloudHub 1.0 is a modern multitenant cloud-based integration **Platform-as-a-Service (PaaS)** that's globally located in 12 regions to run the MuleSoft application. It allows businesses to create APIs using existing data sources, integrate on-premises services into the cloud, and deploy applications in the cloud. Applications deployed to CloudHub 1.0 can be managed by the Runtime Manager in the Anypoint Platform. Applications in CloudHub 1.0 can be deployed using Anypoint Studio, Anypoint CLI, CloudHub 1.0 APIs, or the Mule Maven plugin. CloudHub 1.0 uses the AWS cloud as the underlying infrastructure, and the availability of CloudHub 1.0 depends on the availability of the AWS cloud. CloudHub 1.0 provides a managed runtime plane for deploying and running APIs in the cloud.

CloudHub 1.0 is elastic; it can be scaled on demand. You can start with small workloads that can be scaled up as and when required. This can be achieved without experiencing any downtime of the applications or APIs.

We discussed the control plane and the runtime plane in the previous chapters. When you are deploying an application to CloudHub 1.0, it means you are using the MuleSoft-managed control and runtime plane. CloudHub 1.0 provides Runtime Manager for managing, monitoring, and deploying MuleSoft applications. Before we dive into some of the use cases, let's talk about various features supported by CloudHub 1.0.

Workers and worker size

A worker is a dedicated instance where you can run the MuleSoft application. The worker size is the amount of memory and storage that is configured on the application during deployment. It is available in various sizes, as shown in *Table 9.1*:

Worker Size (vCores)	Worker Memory (GB)	Heap Memory (GB)	Disk Storage Size (GB)
0.1	1	0.5	8
0.2	2	1	8
1	4	2	12
2	8	4	40
4	16	8	88
8	32	16	168
16	64	32	328

Table 9.1 - Worker size available with CloudHub 1.0

The minimum storage allocated to the worker is **8 GB** for applications and systems, out of which **3 GB** is used by the operating system and the Mule runtime. The initial metaspace allocated to the application deployed to CloudHub 1.0 is **128 GB** and the metaspace limit for the application deployed to the CloudHub 1.0 is unlimited, regardless of the worker size. Allocating **0.1** vCores and **0.2** vCores to the application means it will handle a small workload for the application. If you want better performance and to handle large workloads, then more vCores can be allocated to the applications, depending on various factors, such as the number of requests per second and the size of the payload. Worker size can be scaled at any time without any downtime for the applications. To enable horizontal scaling, increase the number of workers for the application. To enable vertical scaling, increase the worker size of the applications:

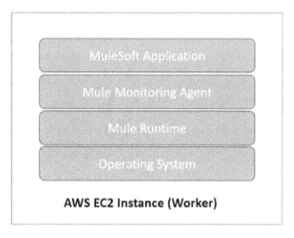

Figure 9.1 - CloudHub 1.0 worker

Figure 9.1 shows a MuleSoft Worker as a dedicated EC2 instance created on AWS by installing Linux, the Mule runtime, the Monitoring agent, and the MuleSoft application.

Shared load balancer

CloudHub 1.0 provides a default load balancer for any application deployed to Runtime Manager. It provides basic functionality, such as TCP load balancing, and it is also equipped with rate limiting to ensure platform stability. MuleSoft continuously monitors the load balancer and scales these limits whenever necessary. Rate limits can differ from region to region. If the rate limit is exceeded on the shared load balancer, you may receive a 429 error code from the shared load balancer for a certain time.

The shared load balancer has no support for configuring custom domains or certificates. It supports TLS 1.1 and TLS 1.2 in transit.

Region

At the time of writing, CloudHub 1.0 allows you to deploy applications across 12 regions globally. Organizations can deploy their applications in the CloudHub 1.0 region that is nearest to their corporate data center or system. *Table 9.2* provides a list of regions that are available in CloudHub 1.0:

Regions	Region Alias	URL
US East (N. Virginia)	us-e1	<app_name>.us-e1.cloudhub.io
US East (Ohio)	us-e2	<app_name>.us-e2.cloudhub.io
US West (N. California)	us-w1	<app_name>.us-w1.cloudhub.io
US West (Oregon)	us-w2	<app_name>.us-w2.cloudhub.io
Canada (Central)	ca-c1	<app_name>.ca-c1.cloudhub.io
South America (Sao Paulo)	br-s1	<app_name>.br-s1.cloudhub.io
Asia Pacific (Singapore)	sg-s1	<app_name>.sg-s1.cloudhub.io
Asia Pacific (Sydney)	au-s1	<app_name>.au-s1.cloudhub.io
Asia Pacific (Tokyo)	jp-e1	<app_name>.jp-e1.cloudhub.io
EU (Ireland)	ir-e1	<app_name>.ir-e1.cloudhub.io
EU (Frankfurt)	de-c1	<app_name>.de-c1.cloudhub.io
EU (London)	uk-e1	<app_name>.uk-e1.cloudhub.io

Table 9.2 - CloudHub 1.0 regions

DNS records

CloudHub 1.0 supports multiple DNS records for enabling internal and external communication:

DNS Record	Description

<myapp>.<region_alias>.cloudhub.io	The publicly accessible URL of the shared load balancer, configured to accept both HTTP traffic on port 80 and HTTPS traffic on port 443, will redirect to the designated ports of ${http.port} and ${https.port}.
	
	`http.port=8081`
	
	`https.port=8082`

DNS Record	Description
mule-worker-<myapp>.<region_alias>.cloudhub.io	This DNS can be accessed publicly, providing the external IP addresses for workers and exposing the HTTP application on port ${http.port} and the HTTPS application on port ${https.port}.
mule-worker-internal-<myapp>.<region_alias>.cloudhub.io	This DNS is accessible within the Anypoint Virtual Private Cloud (VPC), and it offers internal IP addresses for workers. The HTTP application is accessible through port ${http.private.port} and the HTTPS application can be accessed through port ${https.private.port}.

Table 9.3 - DNS records

Table 9.3 shows a list of default DNS records that have been created for the application and deployed to the CloudHub 1.0 worker. They can be used to access the APIs over public or private networks.

Intelligent healing (single-region disaster recovery)

Applications deployed to CloudHub 1.0 can recover automatically from any failures or crashes. MuleSoft provides a mechanism known as self-healing, where applications recover if an availability zone goes down or the underlying infrastructure fails. In such cases, the application will restart in another availability zone or try to recover automatically.

Let's see what happens with an application that's deployed to one worker:

- The application will be deployed automatically to one availability zone in the selected region.

- If the availability zone fails, the application will restart in another availability zone. There may be minor downtime until the application restarts in another availability zone:

If the Availability Zone fails, the application will be switched to another
Availability Zone in the same region.

Figure 9.2 - Intelligent healing (single instance of an application)

Now, let's see what happens with an application deployed to multiple workers:

- An application deployed on multiple workers means that the application will be deployed to multiple availability zones in the selected region.

- If the availability zone fails, the application will restart in another availability zone and another instance of the application in another availability zone will continue to serve requests. The failed instance will try to restart in another availability zone:

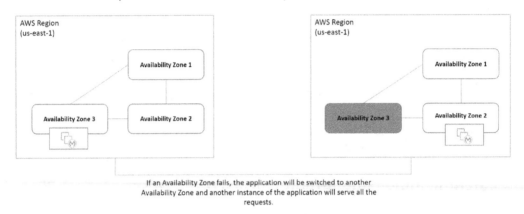

If an Availability Zone fails, the application will be switched to another
Availability Zone and another instance of the application will serve all the
requests.

Figure 9.3 - Intelligent healing (multiple instances of an application)

Zero downtime updates

An application can be redeployed, or application configurations such as worker size, workers, or any other settings can be modified without any downtime. In the case of application redeployment, the user will never experience any downtime. When we redeploy the application to CloudHub 1.0, the old instance of the application keeps running and the domain is pointed to the old instance of the application until the new application is successfully deployed to CloudHub 1.0.

High availability

Applications deployed on CloudHub 1.0 are highly available. To ensure the high availability of the application, it must be deployed on more than one worker. When you deploy an application on one worker, the application will be deployed to one availability zone in AWS. Minor downtime can be expected if the availability zone goes down or if the application is trying to recover from any failures.

When you deploy an application on more than one worker, the application will be available in multiple availability zones in AWS. There will be zero downtime when one of the availability zones goes down because the application is available in another availability zone. If the region goes down, you will experience downtime until one of the availability zones in the region comes up again.

Scalability

Scalability is crucial for any application to achieve high performance. Applications deployed to CloudHub 1.0 can be scaled easily by increasing the number of workers (horizontal scaling) or the size of the workers (vertical scaling). This can be achieved using zero downtime.

CloudHub 1.0 provides features such as autoscaling. To enable autoscaling in CloudHub 1.0, you must have an Enterprise License Agreement. In the Runtime Manager console of Anypoint Platform, you can define policies for the application to auto-scale depending on memory and CPU usage.

Persistent Queues

Persistent Queues is a cloud-based service that allows messages published to VM queues to be stored externally in the application. This feature is directly tied to the CloudHub 1.0 application and can be enabled at the application level. It allows developers to design VM queues to distribute loads among the workers by enabling the persistent queue; it will ensure that if the worker goes down, the message will persist. In multiple-worker deployment environments, if one of the workers fails, then the message will be read by another worker to ensure service continuity.

Persistent Queues can be enabled if your application deployed to CloudHub 1.0 is using VM queues. Messages can be stored in persistent queues as encrypted messages by enabling **Encrypt persistent queues**:

☑ Automatically restart application when not responding

☑ Persistent queues | ☑ Encrypt persistent queues

☑ Use Object Store v2

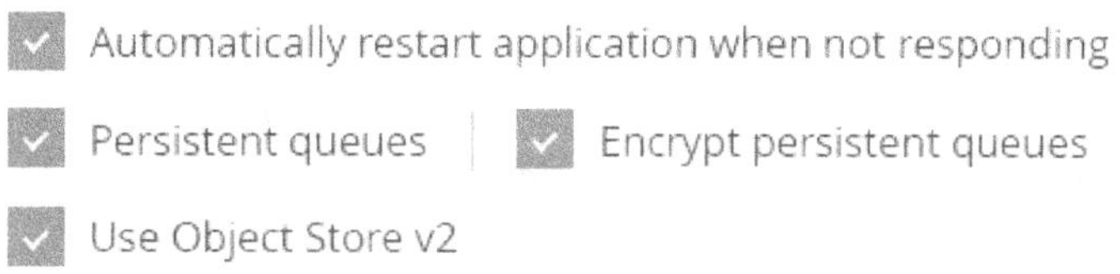

Figure 9.4 - Enabling Encrypt persistent queues

Figure 9.4 shows how to enable Persistent Queues for applications deployed to CloudHub 1.0.

Persistent Queues has the limitation that it can degrade the performance of the application by up to 10x compared to not using Persistent Queues. Performance can further degrade if you choose the **Encrypt persistent queues** option. If you are not using Persistent Queues, messages will be stored in memory or the local file of the worker. In such cases, messages will be lost when the application restarts or is redeployed.

Managing schedules

CloudHub 1.0 allows you to manage and view the scheduler components that are configured within the Mule flow of the deployed application. In Runtime Manager, you can use the **Schedules** tab in the application to view the frequency of the scheduler, change the frequency of the scheduler, or enable/disable the scheduler without changing or redeploying the running application.

The following tasks can be performed on the **Schedules** tab:

- Trigger the job at any time, irrespective of what schedule has been set up on the application or without modifying the scheduler

- Disable the scheduler in case of any maintenance in the underlying system that the scheduler application is connected to

- Schedulers can be updated at any time without modifying or redeploying the application

Object Store V2

Object Store V2 allows applications deployed to CloudHub 1.0 to store data and share the state of batch processes, Mule applications, and components within the application or by using the Object Store REST API. Here is a list of features of Object Store V2:

- Object Store V2 will be in the same region as your worker.

- It allows an unlimited number of entries. There is no restriction on the total size of the object store.

- It can store values up to 10 MB (Base64 encoded) in size.

- It is available in all the regions and all the availability zones in the region.

- It provides a MuleSoft Object Store connector for retrieving and storing data.

- The Object Store REST API v2 can be used by external applications to access object stores in other MuleSoft applications.

- The Object Store REST API supports Connected Apps to authenticate with Anypoint Platform using APIs:

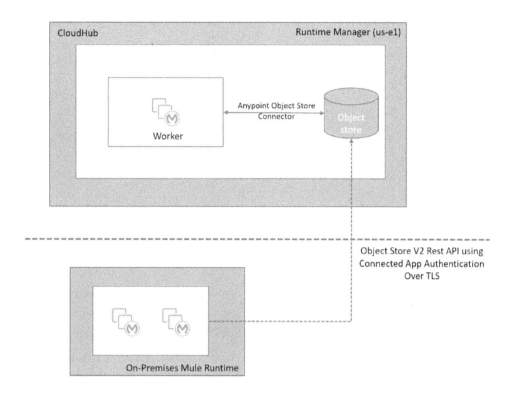

Figure 9.5 - Accessing Object Store between CloudHub 1.0 and an on-premises Mule runtime

Figure 9.5 shows a MuleSoft application that's been deployed to CloudHub 1.0 and is accessing the Object Store. To access the Object Store within the application, an Object Store connector can be used. To access Object Store from another application deployed in CloudHub 1.0 or on-premises, you can use Object Store REST APIs.

Static IP address

By default, an IP address is allocated to any application deployed to CloudHub 1.0 from the AWS EC2 IP pool. Every time we restart or redeploy the application, the IP address will be dynamically changed. You can find a list of available AWS EC2 IP pool IP addresses at `https://docs.aws.amazon.com/vpc/latest/userguide/aws-ip-ranges.html`. CloudHub 1.0 allows us to configure static IP addresses for applications on the **Settings** page of the Runtime Manager UI.

The main reason for having a static IP address for an application is so that it can be whitelisted for other services. For example, MuleSoft wants to connect to an SFTP location where the source needs its IP to be whitelisted to connect to SFTP securely.

The static IP address that's allocated to any organization = 2 * the number of production vCores:

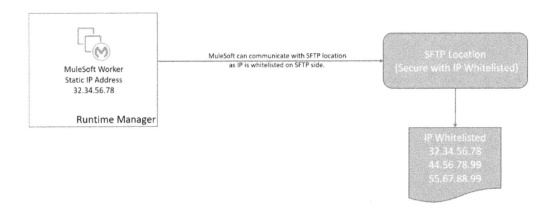

Figure 9.6 - An application communicating with an external service using a static IP address

Static IP addresses can only be changed in the following scenarios:

- If the application has been deleted and deployed again. Deleting the application will delete the static IP address assigned to the application. Whenever you deploy an application with the same name, it will be assigned a new static IP address dynamically.

- If the application is redeployed to a different region.

- If the application is moved from one environment to another.

- Releasing the unused IP addresses and then enabling **Use static IP** later:

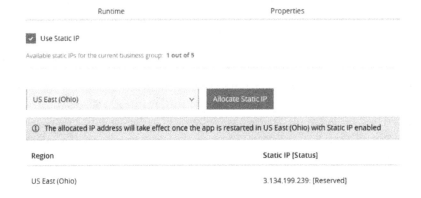

Figure 9.7 - Enabling a static IP address for an application that's been deployed to CloudHub 1.0

Figure 9.7 shows how to enable a static IP address for an application that's been deployed to CloudHub 1.0.

In this section, we've gone through the features and capabilities provided by CloudHub 1.0, including scalability, high availability, regions, DNS records, static IP addresses, workers, worker size, and more.

By default, CloudHub 1.0 doesn't support custom domains and certificates or mutual authentication, and it can't connect the resources behind the firewall. However, CloudHub 1.0 does allow you to create Anypoint VPC, which supports features such as mutual authentication, custom domains, and certificates. It can connect the resources behind the firewall and allows you to create your own isolated and separate network segment in CloudHub 1.0. Let's discuss Anypoint VPC and its components in detail.

Anypoint VPC

Anypoint VPC allows you to set up a secure, isolated, separate, and private network in CloudHub 1.0 where you can host your MuleSoft applications in a dedicated space for your organization. Anypoint VPC can be created in the 12 different AWS regions mentioned previously. A region can be chosen while creating Anypoint VPC. Let's take a look at some key points regarding this service:

- Anypoint VPC can connect securely with your own data centers or public cloud

- It connects CloudHub 1.0 to the resources behind firewalls

- Supports vanity domains and custom certificates

- Supports the dedicated load balancer to route the traffic to the application deployed within Anypoint VPC

- Supports mutual authentication

With Anypoint VPC, you can configure specific inbound firewall rules to control inbound traffic. The default firewall rules that can be configured on Anypoint VPC are listed here:

${http.port}	8081	This will accept public traffic from the shared load balancer over HTTP
${https.port}	8082	This will accept public traffic from the shared load balancer over HTTPS
${http.private.port}	8091	This will accept local network traffic from the internal VPC over HTTP
${https.private.port}	8092	This will accept local network traffic from the internal VPC over HTTPS

Table 9.4 - Anypoint VPC default inbound firewall rules

Anypoint VPC architecture

The following diagram shows the default Anypoint VPC architecture. In this architecture, port 8081 (`http.port`) is allowed to accept HTTP traffic, and 8082 (`https.port`) is allowed to accept HTTPS traffic from the shared load balancer. Port 8091 is allowed to accept HTTP traffic and 8092 is allowed to accept HTTPS traffic from internal applications or internal users:

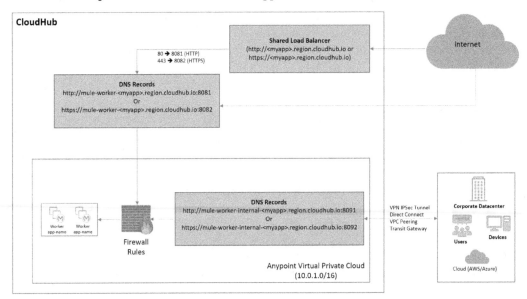

Figure 9.8 - Anypoint VPC architecture with a shared load balancer

The application in the local private network cloud can access the MuleSoft application running within Anypoint VPC using internal DNS (`mule-worker-internal-<myapp>.<region_alias>. cloudhub.io:port`). Those internal applications or users must establish the connection with Anypoint VPC using VPC peering, VPN IPsec tunneling, Direct Connect, or Transit Gateway. MuleSoft applications deployed within Anypoint VPC on CloudHub 1.0 can access services, applications, and databases located in the corporate data center, the private cloud, or on-premises:

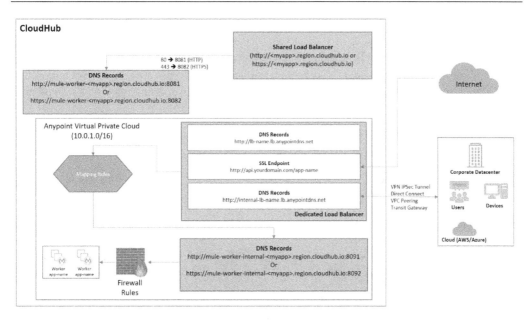

Figure 9.9 - Anypoint VPC architecture with a dedicated load balancer

In the architecture shown in *Figure 9.9*, we are blocking traffic from the shared load balancer, which means we will be not allowing any traffic on ports 8081 and 8082, and those rules will be removed from Anypoint VPC. This means applications deployed on CloudHub 1.0 are on private port 8091 or 8092. To route traffic to applications deployed on these private ports, you need a dedicated load balancer within Anypoint VPC.

Now, let's talk about VPC connectivity methods. Anypoint VPC can connect to private networks using one of the following approaches, depending on where your system is located and running:

- VPN IPsec tunnels
- VPC peering
- Transit Gateway
- Direct Connect

VPN IPsec tunnels

Virtual Private Network (VPN) IPsec tunnels allow Anypoint VPCs to connect to on-premises data centers. It is one of the recommended solutions for connecting Anypoint VPC to on-premises data centers. It ensures there's an encrypted and secure connection between an Anypoint VPC and an on-premises data center:

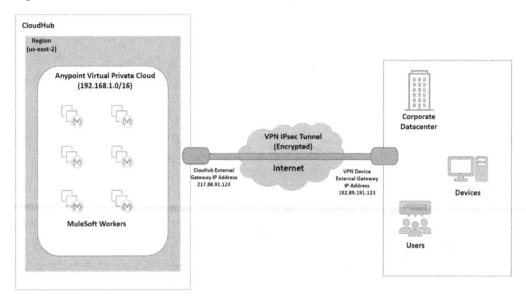

Figure 9.10 - Anypoint VPN

VPN IPsec tunneling enables the connection between Anypoint VPC and an on-premises data center or private network over the internet via an encrypted tunnel. Anypoint Platform VPN IPsec tunneling supports two types of routing: static and dynamic.

Static routing is non-adaptive as it doesn't update or modify the route table automatically; it needs to be updated. Static routing doesn't use any complex algorithms and is more secure than dynamic routing.

Dynamic routing uses a complex algorithm to choose the best path in the network topology. Dynamic routing uses **Border Gateway Protocol (BGP)**.

Anypoint VPN high availability

Anypoint VPN creates two tunnels that terminate in the two different availability zones in the AWS region. This ensures that if one of the tunnels is down due to the availability zone being maintained or upgraded, AWS will route the traffic to the tunnel in the other availability zone. It is recommended to configure both tunnels in the customer gateway for redundancy. If one of the tunnels goes down, AWS will route the traffic to another tunnel for that VPN connection:

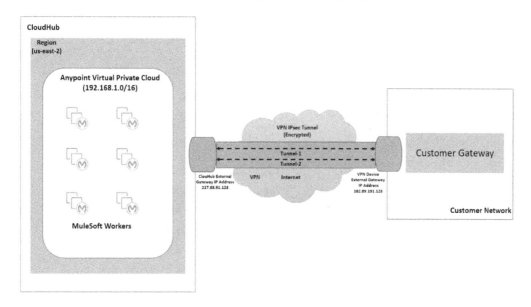

Figure 9.11 - Anypoint Virtual Private Network High Availability

Figure 9.11 illustrates the VPN with two tunnels to ensure high availability.

Anypoint VPN disaster recovery

Anypoint allows us to associate up to 10 VPNs with Anypoint VPC. Anypoint VPN gateways can be configured in the same or different physical location to the customers. To avoid a single point of failure, customer gateways must be in different locations or cities. It is recommended to use the second location as the disaster recovery location:

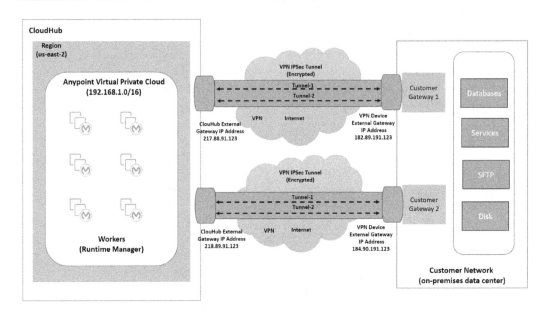

Figure 9.12 - Anypoint VPN disaster recovery

In the architecture shown in *Figure 9.12*, the VPN is configured in such a way that it will be used in the following order if there is a failure:

- VPN-1 Tunnel-1

- VPN-1 Tunnel-2

- VPN-2 Tunnel-1

- VPN-2 Tunnel-2

This is configured as an automatic failover to another VPN tunnel or another VPN connection in the event of any failures. This VPN solution will be resilient and robust. Dynamic routing can promote the route from VPN-1 to VPN-2 automatically, and it also supports static routing, where VPN-2 will be on standby mode in case VPN-1 fails.

Here are some example use cases for VPN IPsec tunneling:

- Connecting Anypoint VPC with a customer's private data center or private network

- Connecting Anypoint VPC with a non-AWS cloud, such as Azure, GCP, or Oracle Cloud

Here are some recommendations for configuring the VPN connection:

- Always implement highly available VPN solutions to prevent any kind of downtime during AWS security updates to the VPN

- It is best practice to have separate VPN tunnels for production and non-production environments

VPC peering

VPC peering is the connectivity option provided by CloudHub 1.0 to peer two or more VPCs in the same AWS region. VPC peering is the quickest way to enable communication between Anypoint VPC and an AWS VPC in the same region as it can be easily created by submitting a support ticket and providing the network details in the template provided by MuleSoft. Here is the official MuleSoft documentation describing how to submit a support request: `https://docs.mulesoft.com/cloudhub-1/to-request-vpc-connectivity`.

The template can be found in the official MuleSoft documentation: `https://docs.mulesoft.com/runtime-manager/_attachments/VPC-form-v9.3-template.xlsx`.

VPC peering can be configured using IPv4 or IPv6 IP addresses:

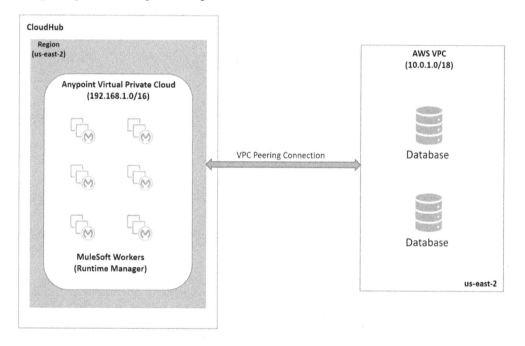

Figure 9.13 - Anypoint VPC peering

Transit Gateway Attachments

Transit Gateway Attachments is another option provided by MuleSoft to connect AWS Transit Gateway. Transit Gateway in AWS can connect to the AWS VPC or any public/private cloud or on-premises data centers. CloudHub 1.0 can attach the Transit Gateway available in AWS to enable a connection with on-premises data centers, the public/private cloud, and so on.

Transit Gateway is the router in the AWS cloud that simplifies the network configuration and allows you to connect VPCs or Private Space in AWS or Anypoint Platform, as well as establish a VPN connection with on-premises, Azure Cloud, or any third-party private network in a secure manner.

CloudHub 1.0 allows you to attach multiple Transit Gateways in your organization, but this depends on the number of Transit Gateway licenses your organization is entitled to:

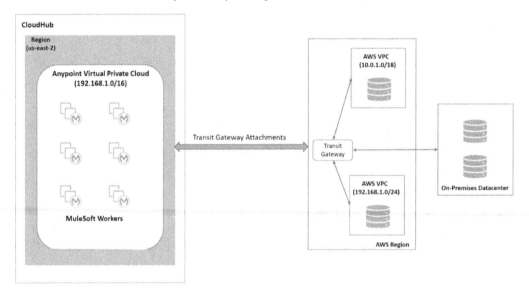

Figure 9.14: Transit Gateway Attachment

In *Figure 9.14*, we are connecting AWS VPCs to the on-premises data center via Transit Gateway in AWS and creating a Transit Gateway Attachment in Anypoint Platform. In this way, we can connect AWS VPCs and on-premises data centers via AWS Transit Gateway.

Note that Transit Gateway can only be created in the AWS instance that will be connecting to on-premises data centers, the public/private cloud, and so on. CloudHub 1.0 can take advantage of connecting the Transit Gateway by attaching with Anypoint VPC.

AWS Direct Connect

AWS Direct Connect allows you to create a dedicated network line between your private network and one Direct Connect location. Once you have enabled Direct Connect connectivity in your AWS account, you can establish connectivity with your AWS VPC or an on-premises data center. This connectivity can be set up with the help of MuleSoft's support team. Direct Connect uses BGP for dynamic routing:

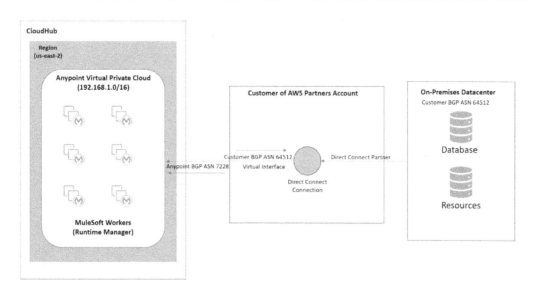

Figure 9.15: AWS Direct Connect

Calculating a CIDR mask for Anypoint VPC

Classless Inter Dynamic Routing (CIDR) is a method of allocating IP addresses that improves data routing efficiency and replaces the old method of allocating IP addresses based on Class A, Class B, and Class C networks. The minimum block size supported is /24 and the maximum block size is /16:

CIDR Block Size	Number of IP Addresses
/24	256
/23	512
/22	1024
/21	2048
/20	4096
/19	8192
/18	16384
/17	32768
/16	65536

Table 9.5 - CIDR block size

Let's learn how to calculate the CIDR block for Anypoint VPC. Consider the following requirements and calculate the CIDR block size:

- Two non-production environments: Development and UAT
- One production environment
- Applications in the development environment will be deployed on one worker
- Applications in the UAT environment will be deployed on two workers
- Applications in the production environment will be deployed on two workers
- Around 10 applications will be deployed to each environment
- A separate Anypoint VPC is required for the production and non-production environments

Always multiply the number of applications by 10 to ensure we select the maximum CIDR block size – once the VPC has been created, it cannot be updated. The only way to increase the CIDR mask of Anypoint VPC is to delete it and start again:

Environment	Production	Non-Production
Development		10 (Applications) * 10 * 1 (Worker) = 100
UAT		10 (Applications) * 10 * 2 (Worker) = 200
Production	10 (Applications) * 10 * 2 (Worker) = 200	
Total	200	300
Additional IP Addresses (50% of total) for Zero Downtime	100	150
IP Addresses Reserved for Infrastructure	2	2
Total IPs	302	452

Table 9.6 - Anypoint VPC sizing

From *Table 9.6*, we have concluded that the total number of IP addresses required for production is 302, which can be provided with a CIDR block size of /23. The total number of IP addresses required for non-production is 452, which can be provided with a CIDR block size of /22.

The following are the recommendations and best practices for creating Anypoint VPC:

- Always choose a high CIDR range – Anypoint VPC doesn't allow you to update the CIDR mask later. To modify the CIDR mask, the VPC must be deleted and created again with a new CIDR mask.

- It is recommended to have separate Anypoint VPCs for production and non-production environments.

- The CIDR mask chosen for your Anypoint VPC must not overlap within your IP ranges in your network or data centers.

- Multiple environments can be mapped with a single Anypoint VPC.

- One environment cannot be associated with multiple Anypoint VPCs.

- Multiple business groups can be mapped with Anypoint VPC. It is recommended to create Anypoint VPC in a parent business group and share it with sub or child business groups.

Anypoint dedicated load balancer

Once Anypoint VPC has been created and the application has been deployed to Anypoint VPC on the private ports, we need to access it. To access the application that's been deployed on the private ports within Anypoint VPC, we need to configure a dedicated load balancer.

Dedicated load balancers are components that allow you to route traffic to MuleSoft applications running in CloudHub 1.0 on an Anypoint VPC on the private port. It is an optional component that may not always be required.

A dedicated load balancer will expose two A records for accepting traffic from local private networks and public networks. One of these records is internal (`internal-<lb-name>.lb.anypointdns.net`), while the other is external (`<lb-name>.lb.anypointdns.net`).

A dedicated load balancer allows you to select several workers. For a higher number of requests that are coming via a dedicated load balancer, you can select more workers while configuring the dedicated load balancer. You can also increase the number of workers.

CNAME records can be created in the corporate DNS nameserver with a user-friendly domain such as `api.domainname.com` to mask A records, which are exposed during the creation of the dedicated load balancer:

A Record	CNAME
<lb-name>.lb.anypointdns.net	api.domainname.com
internal-<lb-name>.lb.anypointdns.net	api-internal.domainname.com

Table 9.7 - Dedicated load balancer CNAME and A record mapping

An application deployed on the private ports (8091 and 8092) within Anypoint VPC can receive traffic from the dedicated load balancer. This means that the dedicated load balancer can only route traffic to the application running on the private port within Anypoint VPC:

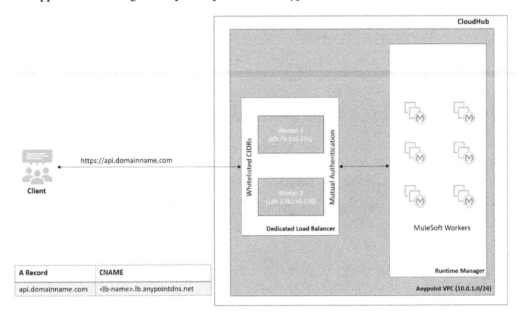

Figure 9.16 - Dedicated load balancer architecture

Allowlist CIDRs

Dedicated load balancers can accept traffic from external or third-party applications over the internet. We may need to allow traffic from some of the IP ranges on the dedicated load balancer and drop traffic from those IP addresses that are not permitted.

We have the CIDR allowlist option, where you can add IP addresses that are allowed to send traffic on the dedicated load balancer. By default, all external traffic is allowed because the CIDR allowlist is 0.0.0.0/0. You need to ensure that the default CIDR block 0.0.0.0/0 is removed and add the allowed IP range to allow external traffic from certain ranges of IP addresses:

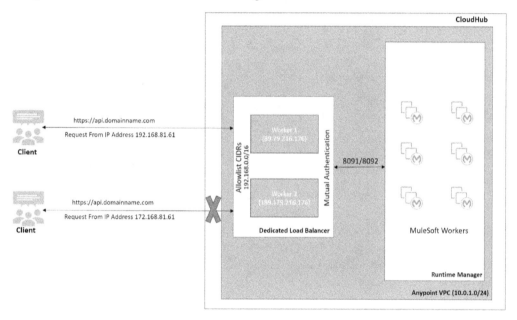

Figure 9.17 - Dedicated load balancer Allowlists

In *Figure 9.17*, the allowed IP range on the dedicated load balancer is 192.168.0.0/16. Client requests coming from IP address 192.168.81.61 are accepted and client requests coming from 172.168.81.61 are blocked by the dedicated load balancer because it is not on the allowlist.

SSL certificates

Dedicated load balancers allow you to add multiple domain certificates. It's mandatory to have at least one domain certificate associated with the dedicated load balancer.

Figure 9.18 shows that there can be multiple domain SSL certificates associated with a single dedicated load balancer and that each SSL certificate configured on the dedicated load balancer is associated with one or more mapping rules:

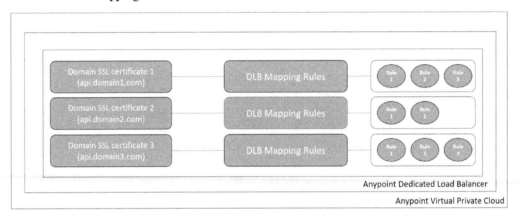

Figure 9.18 - Dedicated load balancer SSL certificate and mapping rules

A dedicated load balancer allows you to configure the wildcard certificates so that they support subdomain requests. For example, `*.domain.com` is the domain that's allowed on the dedicated load balancer, which means it will allow any subdomains, such as app1.domain.com, app2.domain.com, and so on.

More details on SSL certificate configuration on a dedicated load balancer can be found in the MuleSoft documentation.

Mutual authentication

Dedicated load balancers provide additional security in that you can upload client certificates to enable two-way authentication:

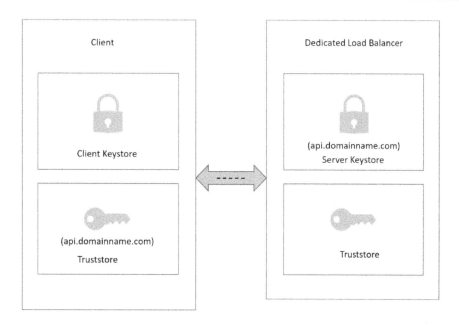

Figure 9.19 - Dedicated load balancer – mutual authentication

To allow more clients to send requests via a dedicated load balancer with two-way authentication, add a client certificate to the existing truststore of the dedicated load balancer, as shown in *Figure 9.20*:

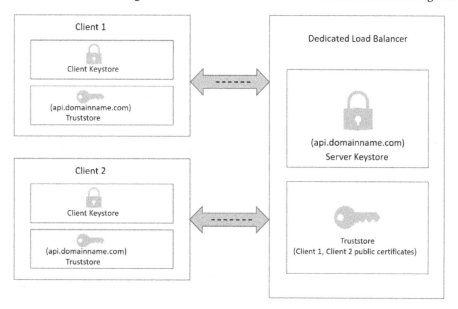

Figure 9.20: Dedicated load balancer – mutual authentication

The private key is configured on the server side (server keystore). It is never shared with anyone, and it is used to decrypt the data. The server keystore will have server private and server public keys. The public key is configured on the client side (client truststore) and generally client store server public certificate. It is used to encrypt the data.

In the same way, Keystore and Truststore are configured on the client side. Keystore will be on the client side and will contain client private and public keys, whereas Truststore will only contain a server public key.

Dedicated load balancer sizing

By default, dedicated load balancers run in a high availability configuration of two workers. Each worker has a size of 2 vCores + 3.5 GB memory. The other sizes for dedicated load balancers are 4, 6, and 8 workers. The round-robin algorithm is used to distribute requests to workers of the dedicated load balancer. Sometimes, it may use another algorithm where requests can be distributed to the dedicated load balancer workers depending on the traffic load.

A dedicated load balancer is allocated with two workers by default. There are a few points that need to be considered while sizing a dedicated load balancer:

- The number of requests coming to the dedicated load balancer.

- The number of downstream APIs behind the dedicated load balancer.

- The response time from downstream APIs. A longer response time means it will be holding the resources of the dedicated load balancer.

- The size of the payloads in incoming requests that are passing through the dedicated load balancer.

In most cases, two workers will fulfill the requirements of performance. However, in some cases, you may have to configure more workers for the dedicated load balancer for higher traffic.

Dedicated load balancer timeout

By default, the dedicated load balancer response timeout is 300 seconds (5 minutes). This can be increased or decreased in the dedicated load balancer configuration in Runtime Manager.

Dedicated load balancer mapping rules

Mapping rules are associated with the domain certificate that has been configured on the dedicated load balancer, and there can be multiple mapping rules associated with each domain certificate. If there are multiple rule matches, it will always execute the first matching rule for incoming requests to the dedicated load balancer.

Mapping rules will translate the URI of incoming requests to route requests to the target application deployed to CloudHub 1.0 within Anypoint VPC. There are a few parameters that need to be understood before configuring the mapping rules:

- **Input Path (inputUri):** This is the URI that the client requests – for example, /{app}/.

- **Target App (appName):** This is the MuleSoft application running in CloudHub 1.0 within Anypoint VPC. This is where the dedicated load balancer will route the request, depending on the incoming request URI.

- **Output Path (appUri):** This is the URI string that passes to the target application deployed within Anypoint VPC.

- **Protocol** – This is the protocol with which the target (downstream) application is listening. It can be HTTP, HTTPS, WS, and so on.

The values defined in the curly brackets ({ }) in the input path of the mapping rules are the variables. These variables cannot be used in the output path but can be used in the target app parameter for the application's name.

In the case of multiple mapping rules defined on the dedicated load balancer, it will always apply first matching rules to incoming requests regardless of the multiple matching rules available.

Let's understand how to define the mapping rules on the dedicated load balancer.

Example 1

The application's name can be passed in the URL of incoming requests, and it can be used to route requests to the application deployed in CloudHub 1.0. Input requests are sent via `https://api-dev.domainname.com/invoice-app-dev/v1.0/invoices` to fetch invoices. Here is the configured mapping rule:

Input Path	Target App	Output Path	Protocol
/{app}/	{app}	/	https

Table 9.8 - Dedicated load balancer mapping rules

`{app}` is the variable, and the value will be `invoice-app-dev`. HTTPS is the protocol for the downstream API. So, the dedicated load balancer's mapping rules will translate the URL to `https://mule-worker-internal-invoice-app-dev.us-e1.cloudhub.io:8092/v1.0/invoices`:

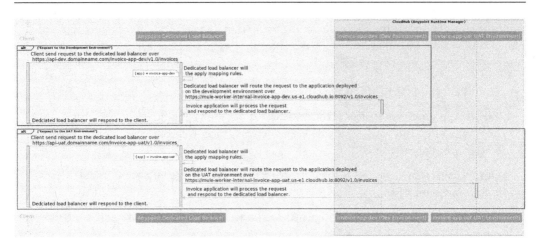

Figure 9.21: Dedicated load balancer URL translation with mapping rules

Example 2

In *Example 1*, we saw how to route requests using the application name via the dedicated load balancer.

In this example, we will learn how to route requests using the subdomain. Generally, there is a different subdomain name for each environment. All non-production environments will be mapped to non-production Anypoint VPCs, and production environments will be mapped to production Anypoint VPCs:

Domain	Subdomain	Anypoint VPC	Environment
api-dev.subdomain.com	api-dev	VPC-1	Development
api-uat.subdomain.com	api-uat	VPC-1	UAT
api.subdomain.com	api	VPC-2	Production

Table 9.9 - API domains

Let's consider the following mapping rules, which have been configured to route requests to the application deployed in CloudHub 1.0. Input requests come via `https://api-dev.domainname.com/invoice/v1.0/invoices` to fetch invoices. Here's the configured mapping rule:

Input Path	Target App	Output Path	Protocol
/{app}/	{app}-{subdomain}	/	https

Table 9.10 - Dedicated load balancer mapping rules

{app} is the variable, the value will be `invoice`, and {subdomain} will be `api-dev`. HTTPS is the protocol for the downstream API. So, the dedicated load balancer mapping rules will translate the URL to `https://mule-worker-internal-invoice-api-dev.us-e1.cloudhub.io:8092/v1.0/invoices`:

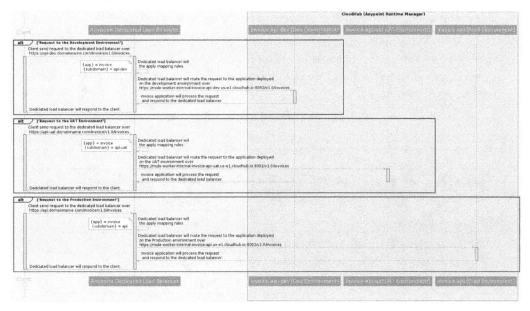

Figure 9.22 - Dedicated load balancer URL translation with mapping rules

HTTP inbound mode

One of the critical configurations on the dedicated load balancer determines how to route incoming HTTP requests. It can either accept the HTTP or HTTPS request, silently drop the HTTP request, or redirect the request to the downstream API on HTTPS.

The following options can be configured on a dedicated load balancer to ensure that incoming traffic will be accepted and sent to the downstream APIs:

- **Off**: The dedicated load balancer will silently drop all the incoming HTTP traffic and only accept requests on HTTPS

- **On**: The dedicated load balancer will accept incoming requests on HTTP on default SSL endpoints

- **Redirect**: The dedicated load balancer will always route traffic to the downstream API via HTTPS

Recommendations

Here are some recommendations that you can follow while configuring a dedicated load balancer:

- All environments associated with Anypoint VPC will be mapped to the dedicated load balancer. This means a single dedicated load balancer can route requests to multiple environments.

- Multiple CNAMEs can be mapped to the single dedicated load balancer or single A records, such as `api-dev.domainname.com` for the development environment, `api-uat.domainname.com` for the QA environment, and `api.domainname.com` for the production environment.

- Always create separate load balancers for production and sandbox environments.

Let's look at the differences between dedicated load balancers and shared load balancers:

Features	Shared Load Balancer	Dedicated Load Balancer
Custom Domain	Not Supported	Supported
Custom Certificates	Not Supported	Supported
Mutual Authentication	Not Supported	Supported
Whitelisted CIDRs	Not Supported	Supported
Rate Limiting	Applicable	Not Applicable

Table 9.11 - Shared load balancer versus dedicated load balancer

Dedicated load balancers for public and private traffic

APIs deployed to Runtime Manager may receive traffic from external and internal consumers. It may be necessary to protect some of the APIs from external consumers or not provide external access to those APIs. It is recommended to have a separate dedicated load balancer for private and public traffic for security reasons. We may need some APIs to be accessible internally, or some APIs may be public-facing. Here, we will see an example of API-led connectivity where Experience APIs must be publicly facing APIs and Process and System APIs must be private.

There are multiple solutions to achieve this:

- A single dedicated load balancer for public and private APIs
- Separate dedicated load balancers for public and private APIs

Approach 1 – single dedicated load balancer for public and private APIs

In this approach, we will be setting up a single dedicated load balancer that will give two A records: `<lb-name>.lb.anypointdns.net`, which accepts external traffic, and `internal-<lb-name>.lb.anypointdns.net`, which accepts private local network traffic. You can upload multiple certificates on the dedicated load balancer and create CNAME records that point to these A records.

Here's an example of CNAME and A record mapping in the DNS registry:

- `api.domainname.com` => `<lb-name>.lb.anypointdns.net` (A record)
- `api-internal.domainname.com` => `internal-<lb-name>.lb.anypointdns.net` (A record)

Each certificate will have its own mapping rules. You can create mapping rules that direct traffic to the public application when the request comes via `api.domainname.com`, and another set of mapping rules that direct traffic to the private application when the request comes via `api-internal.domainname.com`. When the dedicated load balancer receives a request, it looks for the host header in the request to match the request against the certificate endpoint and subsequent mapping rules. For example, suppose the public request comes from the client on the dedicated load balancer via `http://api.domainname.com`. In this case, the host value in the header will be api.domainname.com, and the dedicated load balancer will match the certificates with the host and apply subsequent mapping rules. Traffic will be forwarded to the APIs.

The issue with using a single dedicated load balancer for both public and private traffic arises when a bad actor targets access to the private application via the public domain of the dedicated load balancer using a modified host header.

For example, a bad actor can send a request to `api-internal.domainname.com` with the host header set to `api-internal.domainname.com`. This request will match the private certificates and execute subsequent mapping rules, allowing access to the private application via the public domain of the dedicated load balancer:

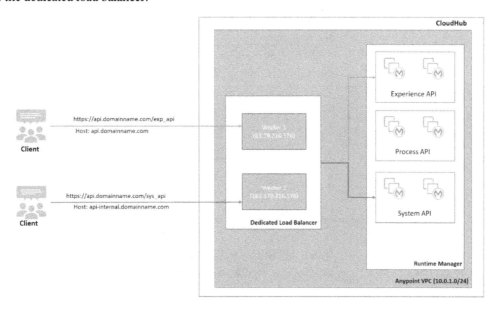

Figure 9.23 - Single dedicated load balancer for public and private APIs

In *Figure 9.23*, you can see how a bad actor can access a private application via the public domain of a dedicated load balancer sending the host value of `api.domainname.com`. Another issue is that allowlist CIDRs are global to the dedicated load balancer. If the same allowlist CIDRs are applied to both the public and private domains of the dedicated load balancer, then you cannot add specific private IP ranges. To do so, you would need to remove `0.0.0.0/0`, which means public traffic will not be allowed.

Approach 2 – separate dedicated load balancers for public and private APIs

To overcome the issues of using a single dedicated load balancer, you should use separate dedicated load balancers for public and private APIs. With this approach, you must configure separate certificates for private and public domains in separate dedicated load balancers with unique mapping rules. Apart from this, you can configure separate whitelisted CIDRs for both dedicated load balancers:

- **Dedicated load balancer (public) and whitelisted CIDRs (0.0.0.0/0)**: Allow access to everyone.

- **Dedicated load balancer (private) and whitelisted CIDRs (192.168.1.0/24, 10.0.1.0/22)**: Allow access to private ranges of IP addresses:

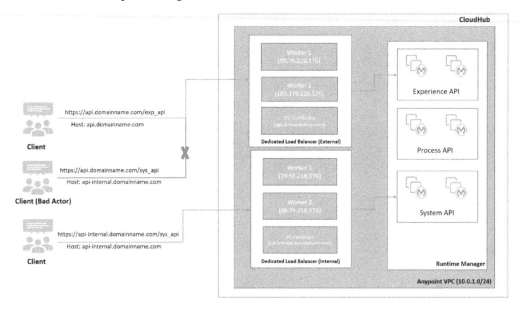

Figure 9.24 - Separate dedicated load balancers for public and private APIs

Requests by a bad actor to access a private API using a public dedicated load balancer will be blocked because no certificates match the public dedicated load balancer with the host header. Allowlist CIDRs are separate for public and private dedicated load balancers. This means you can completely stop public traffic and allow traffic only from a specific range of private IP addresses for a private dedicated load balancer.

Different options for deploying a MuleSoft application to CloudHub 1.0 Runtime Manager

MuleSoft provides multiple ways to deploy an application to CloudHub 1.0, and all these ways can be integrated with a CI/CD pipeline for automatic deployment of the MuleSoft application to CloudHub 1.0. Let's explore all the ways we can deploy an application to CloudHub 1.0.

The Mule Maven plugin

The Mule Maven plugin is one of the most important Maven plugins for deploying, undeploying, and packaging MuleSoft applications into CloudHub 1.0. Let's discuss the Mule Maven plugin in more detail. The following plugin can be configured in the POM.xml file of your application with all the attributes that are needed to deploy and run the application in CloudHub 1.0:

```
<plugin>
  <groupId>org.mule.tools.maven</groupId>
  <artifactId>mule-maven-plugin</artifactId>
  <version>3.8.6</version>
  <extensions>true</extensions>
  <configuration>
    <cloudHubDeployment>
      <uri>https://anypoint.mulesoft.com</uri>
      <muleVersion>${app.runtime}</muleVersion>
      <username>${anypoint.username}</username>
      <password>${anypoint.password}</password>
      <applicationName>${application.name}</applicationName>
      <environment>${mule.environment}</environment>
      <region>${mule.region}</region>
      <workers>${mule.workers}</workers>
      <workerType>${mule.workerType}</workerType>
      <properties>
        <key>value</key>
      </properties>
    </cloudHubDeployment>
  </configuration>
</plugin>
```

In the preceding Mule Maven plugin, values defined with $ { } are parameters that you can pass in the mule deploy command, as shown here:

```
mule deploy -DmuleDeploy -Dapp.runtime=4.3.0 -Danypoint.
username=anypointusername -Danypoint.password=password -Dapplication.
name=music-api-dev -Dmule.environment=Sandbox -Dmule.workers=1 -Dmule.
workerType=MICRO
```

Here are the attributes that can be configured in the Mule Maven plugin while you're deploying your application to CloudHub 1.0:

Attributes	Description	Required	Default Value/ Example
cloudHub Deployment	Root element.	Yes	
uri	Your Anypoint Platform URI.	No	
muleVersion	The Mule runtime engine version to run in your CloudHub 2.0 instance.	Yes	For example, 4.3.0
username	CloudHub username.	Only when using Anypoint Platform credentials to log in	
password	CloudHub password.	Only when using Anypoint Platform credentials to log in	
applicationName	The title of the application to be implemented in Runtime Manager.	Yes	
artifact	The absolute path of the JAR file to be deployed.	No	
environment	The CloudHub environment where the application will be deployed.	Yes	
properties	Properties can be passed that need to be set during application deployment.	No	
workers	The number of workers.	No	1
workerType	The size of each worker.	No	MICRO
region	Region of worker clouds.	No	us-e1
objectStoreV2	Enables Object Store V2.	No	true
persistentQueues	Enables persistent queues.	No	false
businessGroup	Business group path of the deployment.	No	
businessGroupId	Business group ID or organization.	No	

Attributes	Description	Required	Default Value/ Example
deployment Timeout	The permitted duration, measured in milliseconds, for the deployment process. This refers to the time between the commencement of deployment and the confirmation of successful artifact deployment.	No	1000000
server	The Maven server is integrated with the Anypoint Platform credentials. The server's ID can be found in the `settings.xml` file, which is linked to a user's Anypoint username and password.	No	
skip	When enabled, it bypasses the deployment goal of the plugin.	No	false
skipDeployment Verification	When enabled, it bypasses the confirmation of the status of your deployed application.	No	false
authToken	Specifies the authorization token to access the platform.	Only when using an authorization token to log in	
connected AppClientId	Specifies the Connected App ClientID value.	Only when using Connected Apps credentials to log in	
connectedApp ClientSecret	Specifies the Connected App client secret key.	Only when using Connected Apps credentials to log in	
connected AppGrantType	Specifies the only supported connection type: client credentials.	Only when using Connected Apps credentials to log in	
applyLatest RuntimePatch	When enabled, the application will be first updated with the latest version of Mule Runtime, before being deployed to CloudHub.	No	false
disableCloud HubLogs	When set to `true`, this feature will disable the CloudHub logs.	No	false

Table 9.12 - Mule Maven plugin attributes

More details on the Mule Maven plugin can be found in the MuleSoft documentation: `https://docs.mulesoft.com/mule-runtime/4.5/mmp-concept`.

You can use the following commands to deploy and undeploy the application:

```
mvn clean deploy -DmuleDeploy (Deploy Application to CloudHub 1.0)
mvn mule:undeploy (Undeploy Application from CloudHub 1.0)
```

The Mule Maven plugin can use one of the following authentication mechanisms to deploy applications to CloudHub 1.0:

- Anypoint Platform username and password
- Server
- Anypoint Connected App
- Auth token

Anypoint CLI

The Anypoint CLI can be used to deploy, undeploy, or redeploy a MuleSoft application to CloudHub 1.0. The Anypoint CLI is a scripting and command-line tool for Anypoint Platform. The Anypoint CLI can manage various features of Anypoint Platform, such as CloudHub 1.0, API Governance, Anypoint dedicated load balancers, Anypoint VPC, Exchange, Design Center, and API Manager. To use the Anypoint CLI, you need to set up the npm package for the Anypoint CLI.

Here is the documentation from MuleSoft to set up the Anypoint CLI: `https://docs.mulesoft.com/anypoint-cli/4.x/install`.

The Anypoint CLI can use one of the following authentication mechanisms to manage Anypoint Platform:

- Anypoint Platform username and password
- Client ID and client secret
- Bearer token – command line only

A list of commands for managing CloudHub 1.0 can be found in the MuleSoft documentation: `https://docs.mulesoft.com/anypoint-cli/4.x/cloudhub-apps`.

You can use the following command to deploy an application to CloudHub 1.0:

```
runtime-mgr:cloudhub-application:deploy  <name> <zipfile> [flags]
```

The following flags can be passed with this command:

Flag	Description	Default Value
`--runtime`	Provide the name and version of the runtime environment.	
`--workers`	Number of workers.	`1`
`--workerSize`	Size of the workers in vCores.	`0.1`
`--region`	Name of the region.	`us-east-1`
`--property`	Set a property (`name:value`) – for example, `--property "https.port:8082"`.	
`--propertiesFile`	All properties in this file should be overwritten with their corresponding values. Ensure that the absolute path of the properties file is specified on your local hard drive.	
`--[no-]persistentQueues`	Enable or disable persistent queues.	`disabled`
`--[no-]persistentQueuesEncrypted`	Enable or disable persistent queue encryption.	
`--[no-]staticIPsEnabled`	Enable or disable static IPs.	`disabled`
`--[no-]objectStoreV1`	Enable or disable Object Store V1.	
`--[no-]objectStoreV2`	Enable or disable Object Store V2.	
`--[no-]autoRestart`	The application will be automatically restarted in the event of unresponsiveness.	`enabled`
`--output`	Specify the desired format for the response. The available options are `table` and `json`.	`table`
`--help`	Output usage information.	
`--timeout`	Set the timeout value in milliseconds. This should be within the range of `60000` to `300000`.	

Table 9.13 - Anypoint CLI attributes for deploying applications to CloudHub 1.0

More details on Anypoint CLI for deploying applications to CloudHub 1.0 can be found in the MuleSoft documentation: `https://docs.mulesoft.com/anypoint-cli/4.x/cloudhub-apps`.

CloudHub 1.0 API

The CloudHub 1.0 API allows you to deploy and manage your MuleSoft application. You can deploy your MuleSoft application, manage schedules and queues, and view logs about the application. Here is the REST API provided by MuleSoft for deploying applications to CloudHub 1.0:

Method	POST
API Endpoint	`https://anypoint.mulesoft.com/cloudhub/api/v2/applications`
Request Body	```json\n{\n "domain": "api-dev",\n "muleVersion": {\n "version": "4.4.0"\n },\n "region": "us-east-1",\n "monitoringEnabled": true,\n "monitoringAutoRestart": true,\n "workers": {\n "amount": 2,\n "type": {\n "name": "Medium",\n "weight": 1,\n "cpu": "1 vCore",\n "memory": "1.5 GB memory"\n }\n },\n "loggingNgEnabled": true,\n "persistentQueues": true,\n "objectStoreV1": true\n}\n```
Authentication	Basic or OAuth 2.0 (Connected App or Anypoint username and password)
Header	X-ANYPNT-ENV-ID (environment ID of Anypoint Platform), Content-Type (application/json)

Table 9.14: Platform API attributes for deploying applications to CloudHub 1.0

More details on API requests for deploying applications to CloudHub 1.0 can be found on the Anypoint Platform Developer portal: `https://anypoint.mulesoft.com/exchange/portals/anypoint-platform/f1e97bc6-315a-4490-82a7-23abe036327a.anypoint-platform/cloudhub-api/`.

Summary

In this chapter, we explored the capabilities and features offered by CloudHub 1.0 and how they can be utilized to run and manage MuleSoft applications. We examined various features, such as high availability, fault tolerance, scalability, and disaster recovery. Furthermore, we gained knowledge about Anypoint VPC, which allows us to create isolated and separate network segments within CloudHub 1.0. We also understood the significance of Anypoint VPC. Additionally, we explored different network connectivity options, including VPC peering, VPN IPsec tunneling, AWS Direct Connect, and Transit Gateway Attachments, which enable us to connect resources behind firewalls or on public/private clouds. Moreover, we learned how to leverage the Mule Maven plugin, Anypoint CLI, and Platform APIs to deploy MuleSoft applications in the CloudHub 1.0 environment.

In the upcoming chapter, we will discuss CloudHub 2.0, which allows us to run MuleSoft applications in a containerized environment based on Kubernetes.

Further reading

The CloudHub 1.0 reference list includes the following sources:

- MuleSoft documentation: CloudHub Architecture | MuleSoft Documentation

- YouTube series: `https://youtube.com/playlist?list=PL5GwZHHgKcuDQ 6vWarTLgVbrPEQipzbOM&si=xKjv6f7f10VRkyjg`

- Medium article: Anypoint Virtual Private Cloud, Virtual Private Network and Dedicated Load Balancer Libraries and Resources | by Jitendra Bafna | Medium

- A few tables in this chapter were referenced from MuleSoft's official documentation: `https:// docs.mulesoft.com/`

10

Hassle-Free Deployment with Anypoint iPaaS (CloudHub 2.0)

In *Chapter 9*, we learned about the capabilities and features of CloudHub 1.0. In this chapter, we will learn about the architectural capabilities provided by CloudHub 2.0 for managing MuleSoft applications. It will also cover how CloudHub 2.0 differs from CloudHub 1.0.

In this chapter, we will cover the following topics:

- What is CloudHub 2.0?

- What are the different capabilities provided by CloudHub 2.0?

- Architectural capabilities of CloudHub 2.0

- Networking and hosting options such as private space and shared space

- High availability, scalability, fault tolerance, and disaster recovery with CloudHub 2.0

What is CloudHub 2.0?

We learned about CloudHub 1.0 in *Chapter 9*. In this chapter, we will be learning about another hosting option (i.e., CloudHub 2.0) provided by MuleSoft for running the application independently and securely.

CloudHub 2.0 is a cloud-based **integration platform as a service** (**iPaaS**) similar to CloudHub 1.0. It is a managed, multi-tenant service and is located globally over 12 regions for running the MuleSoft application in a containerized environment based on Kubernetes.

CloudHub 2.0 is elastic in nature; it can be scaled on demand. You can start with smaller workloads that can be scaled up as and when required. This can be achieved without experiencing any downtime in the applications or APIs.

Why CloudHub 2.0?

There are various reasons for choosing CloudHub 2.0, and those reasons are listed as follows:

- CloudHub 2.0 uses a Kubernetes-based architecture that allows you to achieve container-based application isolation. Each application deployed to CloudHub 2.0 runs in a separate container and is independent of others.

- It simplifies the network to enable connectivity with on-premises data centers, **Amazon Virtual Private Cloud** (**VPC**), and other clouds such as **Azure** or **Google Cloud Platform** (**GCP**).

- It supports inbound firewall rules as well as outbound firewall rules and you can set up a maximum of 80 inbound and 80 outbound firewall rules per private space. It provides better firewall controls.

- It provides out-of-the-box security that allows all internal services to communicate with each other securely and secures sensitive data with encrypted secrets.

- It supports multiple public endpoints for a single application deployed to CloudHub 2.0.

- It supports an out-of-the-box ingress load balancer that routes the traffic to the application deployed to CloudHub 2.0. The ingress load balancer auto scales depending on the workload.

- It has a dynamically scalable infrastructure with built-in services to support high volumes.

The following is a list of capabilities provided by CloudHub 2.0:

- It can be deployed in a private or shared space.

- It provides container-based application isolation.

- It is available in 12 regions, globally.

- It can be deployed on multiple replicas to enable high availability and fault tolerance.

- It has more granular virtual core (vCore) options; four vCores per replica is the maximum that can be allocated.

- It can be deployed in clustered mode; a minimum of two replicas are required for clustering.

- It has support for both the rolling update and recreate deployment model.

- Horizontal scaling is achieved by increasing the number of replicas, and vertical scaling is achieved by increasing the number of vCores. The ingress load balancer scales automatically depending on the workload.

- It supports features such as intelligent healing and zero-downtime updates.

- It stores up to 200 MB of log data per configuration or stores it for up to 30 days, whichever limit is reached first.

Let's discuss a few of the features provided by CloudHub 2.0 in more detail.

Replicas and replica size

A replica is a dedicated instance in which you can run the MuleSoft application in the containerized environment. Replica size is the amount of memory and storage configured on the application during deployment. It is available in various sizes, as listed here:

vCore size	Total memory (GB)	Heap memory (GB)	Storage (GB)
0.1	1.2	0.6	8
0.2	2	1	8
0.5	2.6	1.3	10
1	4	2	12
1.5	6	3	20
2	8	4	20
2.5	9.5	4.75	20
3	11	5.5	20
3.5	13	6.5	20
4	15	7.5	20

Table 10.1 - Replica sizes

Replicas with fewer than one vCore provide limited CPU and I/O for small workloads. To handle larger workloads with consistent performance, use a higher number of vCores in the application.

Region

CloudHub 2.0 currently allows you to deploy the application across 12 regions globally. Organizations can deploy the application in the CloudHub 2.0 region that is near their corporate data center or systems.

These are the DNS records for the US region control plane:

Region	DNS record
US East (N. Virginia)	`<appName>-<uniqId>.<shard>.usa-e1.cloudhub.io`
US East (Ohio)	`<appName>-<uniqId>.<shard>.usa-e2.cloudhub.io`
US West (N. California)	`<appName>-<uniqId>.<shard>.usa-w1.cloudhub.io`
US West (Oregon)	`<appName>-<uniqId>.<shard>.usa-w2.cloudhub.io`

Region	DNS record
Canada (Central)	`<appName>-<uniqId>.<shard>..can-c1.cloudhub.io`
South America (Sao Paulo)	`<appName>-<uniqId>.<shard>.bra-s1.cloudhub.io`
Asia Pacific (Singapore)	`<appName>-<uniqId>.<shard>.sgp-s1.cloudhub.io`
Asia Pacific (Sydney)	`<appName>-<uniqId>.<shard>.aus-s1.cloudhub.io`
Asia Pacific (Tokyo)	`<appName>-<uniqId>.<shard>.jpn-e1.cloudhub.io`
EU (Ireland)	`<appName>-<uniqId>.<shard>.irl-e1.cloudhub.io`
EU (Frankfurt)	`<appName>-<uniqId>.<shard>.deu-c1.cloudhub.io`
EU (London)	`<appName>-<uniqId>.<shard>.gbr-e1.cloudhub.io`

Table 10.2 - CloudHub 2.0 regions

This is the DNS record for the US government region control plane:

Region	DNS record
US Gov West	`<appName>-<uniqId>.<shard>.usg-w1.gov.cloudhub.io`

Table 10.3 - CloudHub 2.0 US government region

These are the DNS records for the EU region control plane:

Region	DNS record
EU (Ireland)	`<appName>-<uniqId>.<shard>.irl-e1.eu1.cloudhub.io`
EU (Frankfurt)	`<appName>-<uniqId>.<shard>.deu-c1.eu1.cloudhub.io`

Table 10.4 - CloudHub 2.0 EU control plane regions

In these records, `uniq-id` is a 6-digit value appended to the app name to ensure uniqueness, such as `b9cdfr`, and `shard` is a 6-digit value associated with the private space that the app is deployed to, such as `p7oprc`. However, for a shared space, `shard` will be a six-digit value followed by a hyphen (`-`) and number, e.g., `r7oprb-2`.

Clustering

CloudHub 2.0 supports clustering and provides scalability, workload distribution, and reliability. An application deployed on more than one replica allows us to enable clustering while deploying the application to CloudHub 2.0. With clustering enabled, replicas for the same application can share the Object Store and VM queues, and replicas can share the data within the same application. A minimum of two replicas are required to enable clustering between replicas:

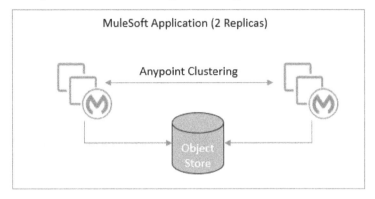

Figure 10.1 - Anypoint clustering in CloudHub 2.0

High availability

CloudHub 2.0 allows you to deploy the highly available application and ensure business continuity. Deploying an application on more than one replica will create multiple instances of the application, and that will ensure the high availability of the application in the event of one or more replicas crashing or failing.

Application isolation

CloudHub 2.0 provides application isolation by deploying the application into separate containers. Each replica of the application will be run in a separate container. This will ensure an issue in one replica will not impact other replicas and that all replicas are independent of each other.

Intelligent healing

An application deployed to CloudHub 2.0 may fail due to an underlying hardware failure; in such a case, the replica automatically recovers as it supports self-healing mechanisms. If a replica crashes due to code issues or memory issues, the platform will automatically identify the issue and redeploy the replica automatically.

Zero-downtime updates

CloudHub 2.0 supports two types of deployment models—rolling update and recreate:

- The rolling update model allows you to deploy the application with zero downtime by updating replicas incrementally

- The recreate deployment model terminates the old replica first and then deploys a new replica

- The rolling update model ensures that the old application replica is available until a new application is redeployed

- The recreate model is faster than the rolling update one and it can be used when you can deploy an application with downtime or deploy a new application

Scalability

The ingress load balancer at the front of the application auto-scales depending on the application workloads and it is a completely managed service. An application running in CloudHub 2.0 can be scaled horizontally and vertically by increasing the number of workers and worker size, respectively.

Supported Mule runtime

The Mule runtime engine allows you to run MuleSoft applications and supports domains and policies. CloudHub 2.0 supports Mule runtime engine versions 4.3x through 4.4x. Mule 3.x is not supported. During application deployment on CloudHub 2.0, it automatically pulls the selected version of the Docker image from the repository.

Granular vCore options

CloudHub 2.0 supports configuring granular vCores while deploying applications. The minimum number of vCores that can be allocated to a replica is 0.1 and the maximum number is 4. Other vCore sizes that can be allocated to the replicas are 0.2, 0.5, 1, 1.5, 2, 2.5, 3, and 3.5.

Object Store v2

Object Store v2 allows the application deployed to CloudHub 2.0 to store data and share the state of batch processes, Mule applications, and components within the application or by using the Object Store REST API. The following is a list of features provided by Object Store v2:

- It will be in the same region as your worker.

- It allows an unlimited number of entries. There are no restrictions on the total size of the Object Store.

- Each entry stores a single value in a key-value pair up to 10 MB (Base64 encoded) in size.

- It is available in all regions and availability zones.

- It provides a MuleSoft Object Store Connector for retrieving and storing data.

- The Object Store REST API v2 can be used by external applications to access object stores available in other MuleSoft applications.

- The Object Store REST API v2 supports connected apps to authenticate with Anypoint Platform using APIs.

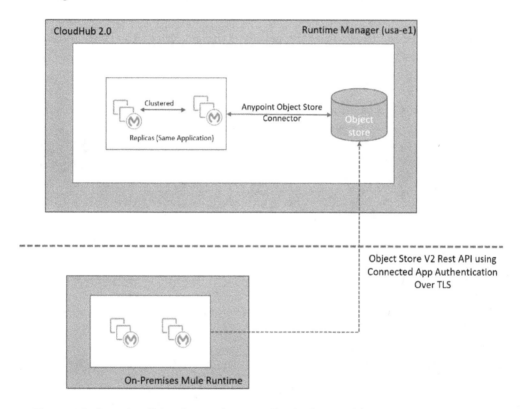

Figure 10.2 - Accessing Object Store v2 between CloudHub 2.0 and on-premises Mule Runtime

In *Figure 10.2*, a MuleSoft application with an Object Store v2 deployed to CloudHub 2.0 can use the Object Store Connector component to store and retrieve the data.

Applications deployed to the on-premises Mule runtime, or any external application, can access the Object Store using REST APIs v2.

Managing schedules

CloudHub 2.0 allows you to manage and view the scheduler components that are configured within the Mule flow of the deployed application. From Runtime Manager, use the **Schedule** tab in the application to view the frequency of the scheduler, change the frequency of the scheduler, or enable/disable the scheduler without changing or redeploying the running application.

Various other tasks can be performed from the **Schedule** tab, as follows:

- You can trigger the job at any time irrespective of what schedule has been set up on the application or without modifying the scheduler

- Disable the scheduler in case of any maintenance in the underlying system that the scheduler application is connecting

- Schedulers can be updated at any time without modifying or redeploying the application

Figure 10.3 shows how to update the scheduler in the CloudHub 2.0 application settings:

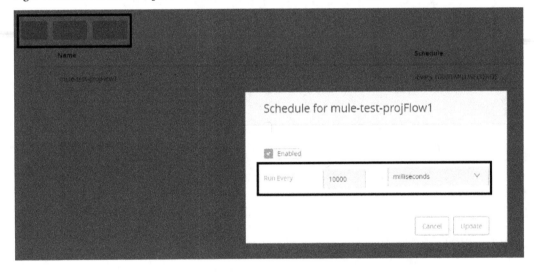

Figure 10.3 - Managing the scheduler for CloudHub 2.0 application

Last-mile security

An application deployed within a shared space supports last-mile security. Last-mile security enables traffic between ingress and the application deployed on worker nodes over HTTPS. An application deployed to CloudHub 2.0 supports a single listener port for HTTP traffic, that is, 8081 for both an HTTP and HTTPS workload. That option can be enabled on the Runtime Manager console under the Ingress tab:

CloudHub 2.0
Private Space
(192.168.0.0/24)
INGRESS
https (443)
https (8081)
Client
MuleSoft Application

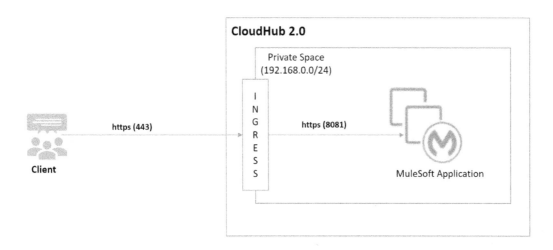

Figure 10.4 - Last-mile security in CloudHub 2.0

Figure 10.5 shows how to enable last-mile security in the Runtime Manager for the application deployed to CloudHub 2.0:

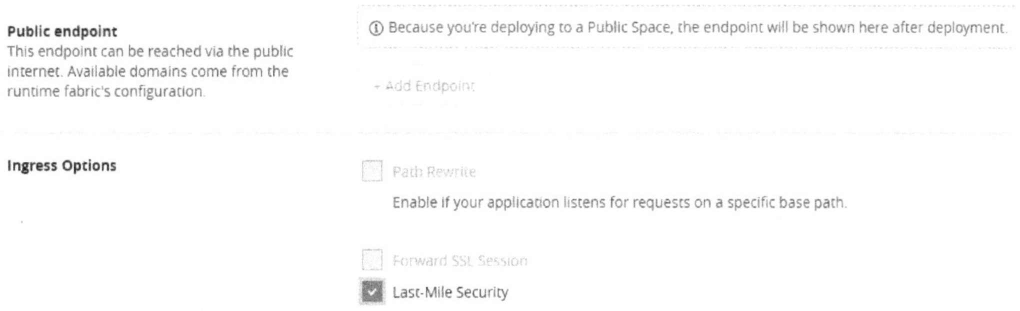

Public endpoint
This endpoint can be reached via the public internet. Available domains come from the runtime fabric's configuration.
Because you're deploying to a Public Space, the endpoint will be shown here after deployment.
+ Add Endpoint
Ingress Options
Path Rewrite
Enable if your application listens for requests on a specific base path.
Forward SSL Session
Last-Mile Security

Figure 10.5 - Enabling last-mile security for applications in CloudHub 2.0

CloudHub 2.0 supports shared spaces and private spaces for deploying and running MuleSoft applications in a containerized environment. Let's explore the shared and private spaces.

Shared space

A shared space enables you to run the Mule instance in a multitenant environment. CloudHub 2.0 provides one shared space in each region to deploy your MuleSoft application.

This is when to use a shared space:

- You don't have a requirement to use a vanity domain and can continue to use cloudhub.io
- You are not required to use custom certificates and custom domains

- You don't want to access resources, services, or databases located in the on-premises data center or the private/public cloud

- You don't have the requirement of running the application in isolation from the public cloud

You should not use a shared space if any of the following applies to you:

- You want to run your application in a single-tenant environment or isolated mode

- You are required to use a vanity domain

- You need custom certificates

- You need private endpoints

- You need to connect to the resources, services, or databases located in the on-premises data center or the private/public cloud

Figure 10.6 shows the high-level architecture of the shared space:

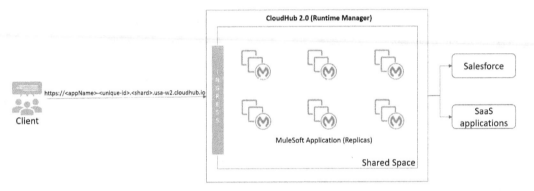

Figure 10.6 - High-level shared space architecture

Private space

Private space is a virtual, private, and isolated space in CloudHub 2.0 to run your MuleSoft application. You can create multiple private spaces in single or multiple regions in CloudHub 2.0 for single or multiple business groups. A range of allowable IP addresses for the apps in your private space is required.

This is when to use a private space:

- You want to connect one or more resources, services, or databases located in the on-premises data center or the private/public cloud. You can use the Anypoint VPN or transit gateway; however, there is no support for AWS Direct Connect and VPC peering in CloudHub 2.0.

- You want to enable private endpoints to accept traffic from private locations.

- You want to configure custom certificates and your own vanity domains.
- You want to configure inbound as well as outbound firewall rules.

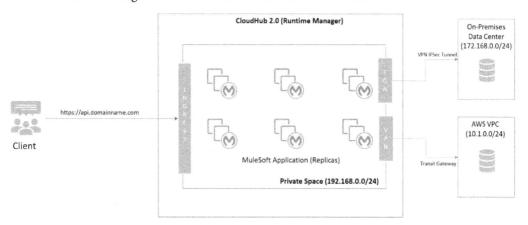

Figure 10.7 - High-level private space architecture

You need a CIDR mask to create a private space, and we can use the same logic from *Chapter 9* for calculating the CIDR block. Once the private space is created, it will provide the following information shown in *Figure 10.8*:

Figure 10.8 - Private space details

Let's look at attributes in more detail shown in *Figure 10.8*:

- **Region**: This is the region in which the private space is created.
- **CIDR block**: This is the IP range that was provided while creating the private space.
- **Internal DNS servers**: Internal DNS servers allow you to do host and IP address mapping.
- **Public DNS target and Private DNS target**: It will provide two domains by default; one is for public traffic and the other for internal traffic. The public domain can be used by applications to accept traffic from external clients, whereas the private domain can be used to accept traffic within the private network, VPN, or transit gateway.

- **Inbound Static IPs and Outbound Static IPs**: In CloudHub 2.0, inbound as well as outbound static IPs will be allocated at the private space level, not the application level. Inbound static IPs are allocated to your public domain, and you can use them to map more public domains. Outbound static IPs allocated to the private space can be useful when an application deployed to the private space wants to communicate with any external systems, such as SFTP, where IP whitelisting is needed to enable the communication. In such cases, all outbound static IPs can be whitelisted on external systems. The number of inbound IP addresses assigned depends on the number of availability zones in the region. For example, if the `usa-east-1 region` has three availability zones, then three inbound and three outbound static IP addresses will be allocated.

- **Route Table**: **Route Table** allows you to configure routes to determine where traffic will be directed from private space. *Figure 10.9* shows the default route that will be added while creating a private space:

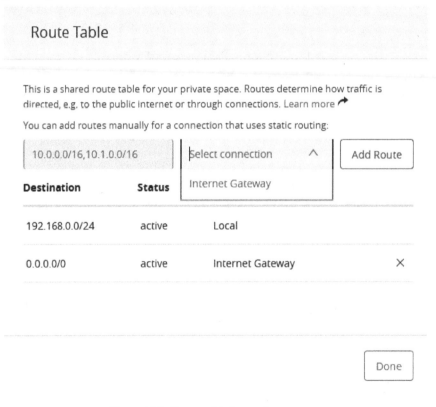

Figure 10.9 - Route table for a private space

The preceding figure shows that traffic within the local network is allowed, as well as traffic to the internet. If you want to disable traffic over the internet, just remove the 0.0.0.0/0 route that is accessible via Internet Gateway, but note that API Manager, Anypoint MQ, and Object Store require internet access from the private space. You can add more accessible subnet routes to the Route Table or remove the routes from the Route Table if you no longer want the subnet to be accessible through transit gateway or VPN connections.

AWS service role

A service role is a position that an AWS service takes on to carry out tasks for you.

You can link **identity and access management (IAM)** roles to your private space if you have them set up in AWS. The IAM position in AWS grants the private space access to resources and permissions. To set up this function on AWS, do the following:

- Make use of the distinct AWS IAM role name that Anypoint Platform generated.
- Utilise the organization ID of the company that set up the private area.
- This feature requires outgoing traffic on port 443 to be enabled.

Inbound and outbound traffic rules

CloudHub 2.0 allows you to configure inbound and outbound traffic rules in the private space. The following figure shows the default inbound and outbound rules available in the private space:

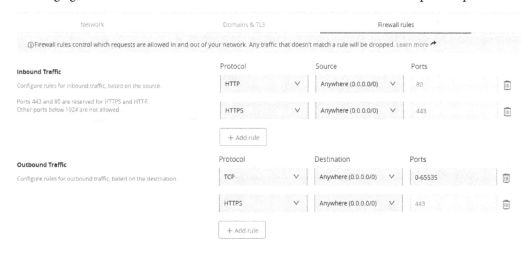

Figure 10.10 - Inbound and outbound firewall rules for a private space

In *Figure 10.10*, we can see that inbound traffic is allowed on HTTP and HTTPS from anywhere. If you want the private space to only accept traffic on HTTPS, remove the rule that accepts HTTP traffic.

If you want to accept HTTPS traffic from the internal network, change **Source** to **Local private network**, as shown in the following figure:

Figure 10.11 - Configuring the inbound firewall rule for a private space

A private space allows you to add new inbound firewall rules or modify existing inbound firewall rules, depending on your requirements. You can add up to 80 inbound firewall rules.

Outbound traffic decides how an application deployed to the private space will communicate with the external services. By default, it allows TCP connection over port 0 to 65535 and HTTPS connection over port 443.

A private space allows you to add new outbound firewall rules or modify the existing outbound firewall rules depending on the requirements. You can add up to 80 outbound firewall rules.

If you want TCP and HTTPS to only communicate with local services within your network, change **Source** from **Anywhere** to **Local private network**, as shown in the following figure:

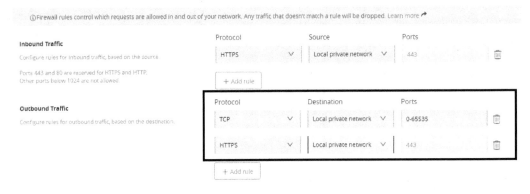

Figure 10.12 - Configuring the outbound firewall rule for a private space

TLS context and domains

Private spaces, by default, provide TLS contexts with one public and one private domain. If you are looking to configure additional TLS contexts to support a custom domain, it is possible to create additional TLS contexts by uploading a domain certificate in PEM or JKS format:

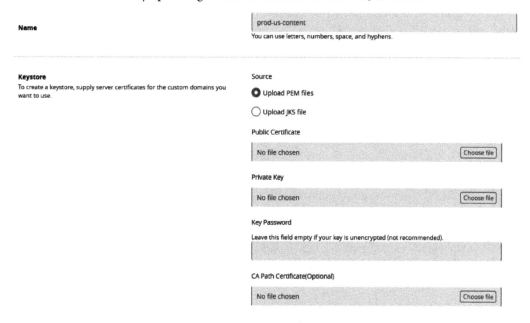

Figure 10.13 - Configuring TLS context for a private space

Public and private endpoints

CloudHub 2.0 creates two endpoints by default when an application is deployed. One is a public endpoint and the other is a private endpoint. Public endpoints can accept traffic from external clients, whereas private endpoints accept traffic from private networks, VPNs, or transit gateways. Multiple public endpoints are supported, and you need to configure the TLS context in the private space settings to enable multiple public endpoints on applications. To disable traffic from external clients, you need to delete the public endpoints from the application deployed to CloudHub 2.0

Ingress load balancer

CloudHub 2.0 supports an ingress load balancer to route traffic to applications deployed in private spaces and shared spaces. The ingress load balancer automatically scales depending on the number of inbound requests coming to it or the traffic load. Private spaces allow you to download logs to the ingress load balancer whenever required for troubleshooting. The default read/response timeout for the ingress load balancer is 300 seconds and it can be increased or decreased depending on the requirements.

The default log level is **Error**, but it supports other log levels such as **Debug**, **Trace**, and **Info**.

HTTP requests

HTTP requests CloudHub 2.0:HTTP requests" define how requests are handled by the ingress load balancer. There are three ways in which traffic will be handled. They are as follows:

- **Redirect to HTTPS**: Redirect incoming HTTP requests to the same URL using the HTTPS protocol
- **Accept HTTP**: Allow incoming requests on the default SSL endpoint using the HTTP protocol
- **Drop HTTP**: Drop the HTTP request silently and accept only traffic on HTTPS

Figure 10.14 shows how to configure the HTTP requests, response timeout, and log downloads for the ingress load balancer in the private space:

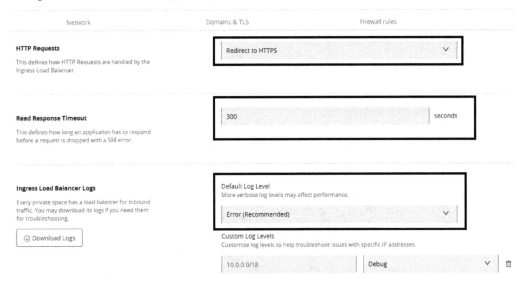

Figure 10.14 - Configuring HTTP requests for a private space

VPN connection

To connect a private space to the external network, a VPN connection can be established between them that includes an on-premises data center. It will create a secure and highly available connection between the private space and on-premises data center:

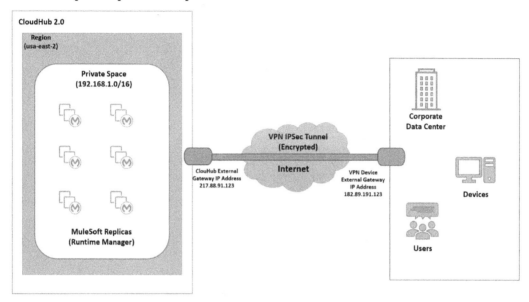

Figure 10.15 - VPN IPSec tunnel for a private space

VPN high availability

A private space allows you to create a second VPN connection if you have created only one VPN connection, and this is known as a redundant VPN. It is strongly recommended to create a redundant VPN as it will ensure high availability and will inherit some of the settings from the initial VPN, such as the routing type, ASN, and so on.

It is recommended to have two VPN connections to the customer gateway in case of any updates on one VPN connection or any failures. In such cases, the other VPN connection will ensure connectivity between the Anypoint Platform and the on-premises data center:

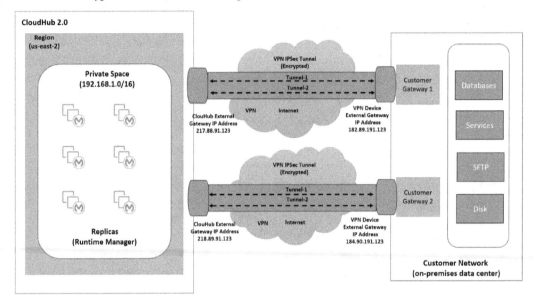

Figure 10.16 - VPN high availability

In the preceding architecture, the VPN is configured in such a way that it will be used in the following order in the event of any failures:

1. VPN-1 Tunnel-1
2. VPN-1 Tunnel-2
3. VPN-2 Tunnel-1
4. VPN-2 Tunnel-2

This is configured as an automatic failover to the other VPN tunnel or connection in the event of any failures. This VPN solution will be resilient and robust. Dynamic routing can help in advertising the route from VPN-1 to VPN-2 automatically, and it also supports static routing where VPN-2 will be on standby mode in the event that VPN-1 fails.

Transit gateways

AWS Transit Gateway is like a router that helps you to simplify the network configuration and allows you to connect private spaces in AWS or Anypoint Platform, establishing the VPN connection toward on-premises or the Azure cloud or any third-party private network in a secure manner.

CloudHub 2.0 allows you to attach multiple transit gateways in your organization, depending on the number of transit gateway license entitlements for your organization:

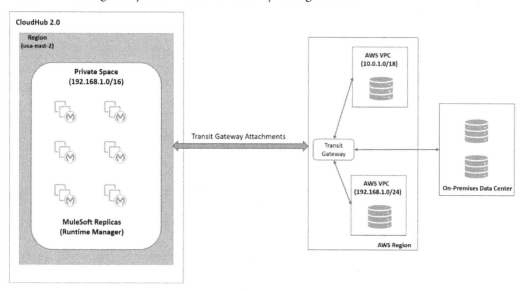

Figure 10.17 - Transit Gateway attachments

In *Figure 10.17*, we are connecting the private space to the on-premises data center via AWS Transit Gateway by creating a transit gateway attachment in Anypoint Platform.

Private space network architecture

The following figure shows how applications deployed in the private space can communicate with the services or applications in the external or local network or over the internet. As we have discussed, local services can communicate with applications deployed in the private space via private endpoints, and external clients can communicate using public endpoints. You can configure public and private endpoints while deploying the application to the private space:

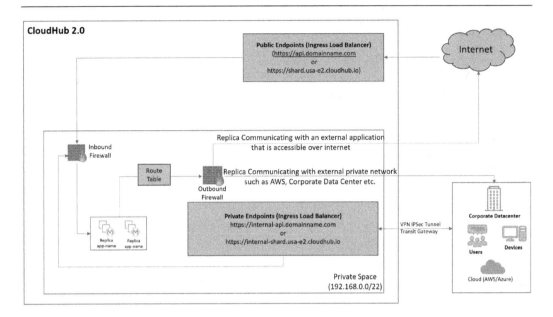

Figure 10.18 - Private space network architecture

If you need to have a custom domain, you need to create a TLS context in the private space and add a domain certificate in JKS or PEM format. In the following figure, we have custom private (`internal-api.domainname.com`) and public (`api.domainname.com`) domains. To enable traffic to reach the application deployed in the private space over the custom domains, create a CNAME record in the vanity domain pointing to your private space **fully qualified domain name (FQDN)**:

Custom domain (CNAME)	FQDN (A record)	Domain type
`internal-api.domainname.com`	`internal-<shard>.usa-e2.cloudhub.io`	Private
`api.domainname.com`	`<shard>.usa-e2.cloudhub.io`	Public

Table 10.5 - CNAME ⇔ A record mapping

The private space will validate incoming requests against the inbound firewall rules, and all outgoing requests going from the private space will be validated by outbound firewall rules.

Multiple environments in private spaces

Private space allows you to map a sandbox or production environment in the business group and its child group:

Figure 10.19 - Mapping multiple environments for a private space

If you want to map the production and sandbox environments with the same private space, you can choose **Any environment**. However, it is recommended to have a separate private space for the sandbox and production environment.

Multiple domains in private spaces

Private space allows you to create multiple TLS contexts to support multiple domains. For example, the sandbox is mapped to one private space having two environments: development and QA.

In such cases, we can configure two TLS contexts with the domain `api-dev.domainname.com` for the development environment and `api-uat.domainname.com` for the uat environment, as shown in *Table 10.6*.

CNAME	Private space – public domain target (A record)	Environment	Domain type
`api-dev.domainname.com`	`<shard>.usa-e2.cloudhub.io`	Development	Public
`api-qa.domainname.com`	`<shard>.usa-e2.cloudhub.io`	QA	Public

Table 10.6 - CNAME ⇔ A record mapping for multiple environments

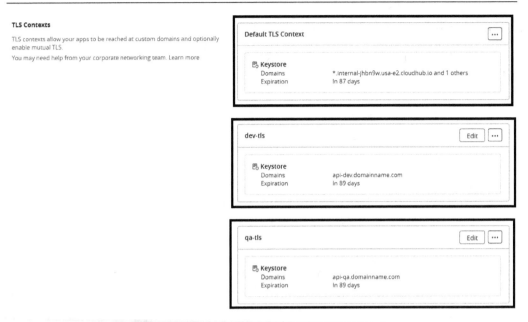

Figure 10.20 - TLS context for a private space

We have three TLS contexts. One is the default TLS context that was created automatically while creating the private space. Then, we have two more TLS contexts for the development and QA environments.

Now, whenever we deploy an application to the development environment, we can select the host (`https://api-dev.domainname.com`) under the **Ingress** tab that is related to development, and whenever we deploy an application to the QA environment, we can select the host (`https://api-qa.domainname.com`) under the **Ingress** tab that is related to QA:

Figure 10.21 - Application endpoints for a private space

Different options for deploying MuleSoft applications to CloudHub Runtime Manager

MuleSoft provides multiple ways of deploying applications to CloudHub, and all options can be used to integrate with the CI/CD pipeline for the automatic deployment of MuleSoft applications to CloudHub. Let's explore all the options that can be used to deploy applications to CloudHub.

Mule Maven plugin

The Mule Maven plugin is one of the important Maven plugins for deploying, un-deploying, and packaging MuleSoft applications into CloudHub 2.0. Let's discuss the Mule Maven plugin in more detail. The following plugin can be configured in the POM.xml file of your application with all the required attributes that are needed for deploying and running the application in CloudHub:

```
<plugin>
  <groupId>org.mule.tools.maven</groupId>
  <artifactId>mule-maven-plugin</artifactId>
  <version>3.8.6</version>
  <extensions>true</extensions>
  <configuration>
    <cloudhub2Deployment>
      <uri>https://anypoint.mulesoft.com</uri>
      <provider>MC</provider>
      <environment>${environment}</environment>
      <target>${target}</target>
      <muleVersion>${app.runtime}</muleVersion>
      <username>${anypoint.username}</username>
      <password>${anypoint.password}</password>
      <applicationName>${application.name}</applicationName>
      <replicas>${replicas}</replicas>
      <vCores>${replicaSize}</vCores>
      <deploymentSettings>
        <http>
          <inbound>
            <publicUrl>${publicURL}</publicUrl>
            <forwardSslSession>true</forwardSslSession>
            <lastMileSecurity>true</lastMileSecurity>
          </inbound>
        </http>
      </deploymentSettings>
    </cloudhub2Deployment>
  </configuration>
</plugin>
```

In the preceding Mule Maven plugin, the values defined with ${} are the parameters that you can pass from the `mule deploy` command, as shown here:

```
mule deploy -DmuleDeploy -Dapp.runtime=4.4.0 -Danypoint.
username=anypointusername -Danypoint.password=password -Dapplication.
name=music-api-dev -Denvironment=Sandbox -Dworkers=1 -
DworkerType=MICRO -Dreplica=1 -DreplicaSize=0.1 -DpublicUrl=https://
api-dev.domainname.com -Dtarget=jj-dev-ps
```

The following table shows the attributes that can be configured on the Mule Maven Plugin while deploying the application to CloudHub:

Parameter	Description	Required	Default value/ example
`cloudhub2 Deployment`	This is the top-level element.	Yes	
`uri`	This is your Anypoint Platform URI.	No	`https:// anypoint. mulesoft. com`
`muleVersion`	This is the Mule runtime engine version to run in your CloudHub 2.0 instance	Yes	e.g., 4.3.0
`username`	This is your Anypoint Platform username.	Yes (only when using Anypoint Platform credentials)	
`password`	This is your Anypoint Platform password.	Yes (only when using Anypoint Platform credentials)	
`application Name`	This is the title of the application to be implemented in the Runtime Manager.	Yes	e.g., `invoice-api-dev`
`scopeLogging Configurations`	This is the package of the logging library to use. `logLevel:` is the log level. Allowed values are NONE, ERROR, WARN, INFO, DEBUG, and TRACE.	No	
`target`	This is the target where the application is to be deployed. It can be a shared or a private space.	Yes	

Parameter	Description	Required	Default value/example
provider	Set to MC for CloudHub 2.0.	Yes	MC
environment	This is the CloudHub 2.0 environment where applications are to be deployed.	Yes	
replicas	This is the number of replicas to be created for applications.	Yes	
vCores	This is the size of the replica, and the allowed values are 0.1, 0.2, 0.5, 1, 1.5, 2, 2.5, 3, 3.5, and 4.	No	0.1
businessGroup	This is the business group path of the deployment.	No	
businessGroupId	This is the business group ID of the deployment.	No	
deployment Timeout	This is the permitted duration, measured in milliseconds, for the deployment process. This refers to the time between the commencement of deployment and the confirmation of successful artifact deployment.	No	10,00,000.00
server	The Maven server is integrated with the Anypoint Platform credentials. The server's ID can be found in the settings.xml file, which is linked to a user's Anypoint username and password.	No	
properties	Properties can be passed to set during application deployment.	No	
secure Properties	Secure properties can be passed to set during application deployment.		
skip	When set to true, it skips the plugin deployment goal.	No	false
skipDeployment Verification	When set to true, it skips the status verification of your deployed app.	No	false
authToken	Specifies the authorization token to access the platform.	Only when using an authorization token to log in	

Parameter	Description	Required	Default value/ example
`connectedApp ClientId`	Specifies the Connected App clientID value.	Only when using onnected App redentials to log in	
`connectedApp ClientSecret`	Specifies the Connected App secret key.	Only when using onnected App redentials to log in	
`connectedApp GrantType`	Specifies the only supported connection type: `client_ credentials`.	Only when using Connected App redentials to log in	

Table 10.7 - Mule Maven plugin attributes

A few other parameters that can be passed under **deploymentSettings** are listed next:

Paramter	Description

`enforce Deploying Replicas AcrossNodes`	This setting ensures that replicas are deployed across distinct nodes with the default value being set to false.
	
	`<deploymentSettings>`
	`  <enforceDeployingReplicasAcrossNodes>false`
	`  </enforceDeployingReplicasAcrossNodes>`
	`</deploymentSettings>`

`updateStrategy`	The value of `updateStrategy` can either be `recreate` or `rolling`.
	
	`<deploymentSettings>`
	`  <updateStrategy>recreate</updateStrategy>`
	`</deploymentSettings>`

Paramter	Description
clustered	This setting allows for clustering to be enabled across multiple replicas of the application. By default, it is set to `false`. ``` <deploymentSettings> <clustered>true</clustered> </deploymentSettings> ```
http	**Public URL**: This refers to the web address of the deployed application. **Last-mile security**: By enabling this feature, HTTPS connections will be forwarded and decrypted by the application. **Forward SSL Session**: When set to true, this option enables SSL forwarding during a session. The default value is `false`. ``` <deploymentSettings> <http> <inbound> <publicUrl>https://myapp.anypoint.com </publicUrl> <lastMileSecurity>true</lastMileSecurity> <forwardSslSession>true</forwardSslSession> </inbound> </http> </deploymentSettings> ```
generateDefault PublicUrl	CloudHub 2.0 will generate a public URL for the deployed application when the `set to true` option is selected.

Table 10.8 - Mule Maven Plugin deployment settings parameter

The following commands are used to deploy and undeploy the application:

```
mvn clean deploy -DmuleDeploy (deploy the application to CloudHub 2.0)
mvn mule:undeploy (undeploy the application from CloudHub 2.0)
```

The Mule Maven plugin can use one of the following authentication mechanisms to deploy applications to CloudHub:

- Anypoint Platform username and password
- Server
- Anypoint connected app
- Authorization token

Anypoint CLI

The Anypoint CLI can also be used to deploy, undeploy, or redeploy MuleSoft applications to CloudHub 2.0. The Anypoint CLI is a scripting and command-line tool for Anypoint Platform. The Anypoint CLI is capable of managing various features of Anypoint Platform, such as CloudHub 1.0, CloudHub 2.0, API governance, Anypoint dedicated load balancers, Anypoint VPC, Exchange, Design Center, API Manager, and so on. To use the Anypoint CLI, you need to set up an npm package for it. Here is the documentation from MuleSoft to set up the Anypoint CLI:

```
https://docs.mulesoft.com/anypoint-cli/4.x/install
```

The Anypoint CLI can use one of the following authentication mechanisms to manage Anypoint Platform:

- Anypoint Platform username and password
- Client ID and client secret
- Bearer token (command line only)

A list of commands for managing CloudHub can be found in the MuleSoft documentation here:

```
https://docs.mulesoft.com/anypoint-cli/4.x/cloudhub2-apps
```

The following command can be used to deploy applications to CloudHub 2.0:

```
runtime-mgr:application:deploy <appID> <deploymentTargetID>
<runtimeVersion> <artifactID> [flags]
```

You can deploy the application mentioned in the app ID to the deployment target using the following values:

Value	Description	Example
`--artifactId`	The application's Artifact ID was sourced from the exchange.	`--artifactId mule-error-plugin`
`--deployment TargetId`	Identify the deployment target.	`--deploymentTargetId cloudhub-us-east-2`
`--name`	Specify the name of the application that needs to be deployed on CloudHub 2.0.	`--name testcloudhubapp`
`--runtimeVersion`	This is the required runtime version for the deployment of the application.	`--runtimeVersion 4.3.0`
`--secureProperty`	This sets an encrypted property	`--secureProperty secureTestProperty:true`

Table 10.9 - Anypoint CLI application deployment values

Flags that can be passed with the `runtime-mgr` deployment command are listed as follows:

Flag	Description	Example
`--assetVersion`	This is the asset version in the exchange.	`--assetVersion 3.0.5`
`--[no-]clustered`	This enables the utilization of clustered nodes, necessitating a minimum of two replicas	`--no-clustered`
`--[no-]disableAmLogForwarding`	This disables application logs forwarding to Anypoint Monitoring.	`--disableAmLogForwarding`
`--[no-]forwardSslSession`	This enables SSL session forwarding.	`--no-forwardSslSession`
`--groupId`	This is the group ID of the asset to deploy.	`--groupId org.mule.test`
`--[no-]lastMileSecurity`	This enables last-mile security.	`--no-lastMileSecurity`
`--[no-]objectStoreV2`	This enables Object Store v2.	`--no-objectStoreV2`
`--pathRewrite`	This provides the anticipated base path for the HTTP listener within your application.	`--pathRewrite /http://localhost:8000`
`--property`	This sets a property.	`--property testproperty:true`
`--propertiesFile`	All properties are substituted with values from a designated file.	`--propertiesFile /Users/mule/Documents/dev-properties.txt`
`--publicEndpoints`	This provides access points accessible through the worldwide web.	`--publicEndpoints my-superapp-example:/status?limit=50`
`--replicas`	This is the quantity of replicas to be deployed.	`--replicas 3`
`--replicaSize`	This is the size of replicas in vCores.	`--replicaSize 0.1`
`--scopeLoggingConfig`	This defines scope logging.	`--scopeLoggingConfig testscope1:WARN, testscope2:DEBUG`

Flag	Description	Example
`--scopeLoggingConfig File`	This uploads a file to define scope logging.	`--scopeLoggingConfigFile /Users/mule/Documents/ cert.txt`
`--updateStrategy`	This updates the strategy used.	`--updateStrategy recreate`

Table 10.10 - Anypoint CLI application deployment flags

Technical enhancements from CloudHub 1.0 to CloudHub 2.0

- Allows you to configure the clustering for deployments with more than one replica.
- Allows for application deployment using containers to control resource usage, guarantee application availability, and facilitate scalability.
- Allows AWS service role for resources access control.
- Granular vCore allocation options—CloudHub 2.0 supports deploying applications on granular vCores.
- Allows you to configure more than one private or public endpoint.
- Allows you to download ingress self-service logs. This can be accessed via private space. Titanium users can access logs via Anypoint Monitoring also.
- Support for inbound and outbound firewall rules.
- In CloudHub 1.0 applications, names must be unique for each control plane, whereas in CloudHub 2.0, application names must be unique per private space.
- VPC peering and AWS Direct Connect are deprecated in CloudHub 2.0. Transit Gateway can be leveraged instead of VPC peering and AWS Direct Connect.
- HTTP and HTTPS traffic uses port 8081.
- You can associate a private space with multiple environments based on the type of the environment, such as a sandbox and production. This is not possible in the Anypoint Virtual Private cloud where you have to associate each individual environment to the Anypoint Virtual Private cloud.
- By default, VPN is enabled with high availability in CloudHub 2.0.
- CloudHub 1.0 application workers and CloudHub 2.0 application replicas with the same vCore sizes may show a difference in performance metrics and they cannot be compared.

The following are functions or features not supported by the CloudHub 2.0:

- Mule versions prior to 4.3.0

- CloudHub Connector

- TLS 1.0 is not supported. Use TLS 1.2 or TLS 1.3

- Creating custom notifications

- Anypoint Functional Monitoring

- Persistent queues; use Anypoint MQ for persistent queues and other queue management

Summary

In this chapter, the provided capabilities and features of CloudHub 2.0 have been explored, highlighting its differences from CloudHub 1.0. The discussion has encompassed various features such as high availability, fault-tolerance, and a scalable architecture, all supported by CloudHub 2.0.

Furthermore, the utilization of both Shared and Private spaces in CloudHub 2.0 for running MuleSoft applications has been demonstrated. Additionally, the deployment of MuleSoft applications in the CloudHub 2.0 environment has been explained, utilizing tools such as the Mule Maven Plugin and Anypoint CLI.

The upcoming chapter will delve into the Runtime fabric manager, which operates on self-managed Kubernetes and baremetal servers. This manager can be leveraged to run MuleSoft applications in a containerized environment based on Kubernetes.

Further reading

The CloudHub 2.0 reference list includes the following sources:

- MuleSoft documentation: `https://docs.mulesoft.com/cloudhub-2/ch2-architecture`

- YouTube series: `https://youtube.com/playlist?list=PL5GwZHHgKcuDaUn FQymi85AbUVbvJBtsA&si=GvCy64jOsw3PoYT4`

- A few tables in this chapter referenced from MuleSoft official documentation: `https://docs.mulesoft.com/`

11

Containerizing the Runtime Plane with Runtime Fabric

In this chapter, we will discuss how to run and manage the MuleSoft application in a Kubernetes-based containerized environment. MuleSoft provides Runtime Fabric on bare-metal servers/**virtual machines** (**VMs**) and Runtime Fabric on self-managed Kubernetes so that you can manage and run a MuleSoft application in containerized environments.

In this chapter, we will be covering the following topics:

- Kubernetes architecture and its components
- Runtime Fabric on bare-metal servers/VMs
- Runtime Fabric on self-managed Kubernetes
- Runtime Fabric on Red Hat OpenShift
- Anypoint Security

Technical requirements

For this chapter, you'll require the following:

- Enterprise Anypoint Platform access with Runtime Fabric enabled for your organization.

- A Runtime Fabric setup license key.

- EKS/GKE/AKS in case you're planning to set up Runtime Fabric on self-managed Kubernetes.

- VMs/bare-metal server to fulfill all the prerequisites. A link for this can be found in the *Further reading* section at the end of this chapter.

- Red Hat OpenShift in case you're planning to set up Runtime Fabric on OpenShift.

Kubernetes architecture

First, we'll discuss the high-level architecture of a Kubernetes cluster before looking at Runtime Fabric, which is provided by MuleSoft. Kubernetes clusters follow the master-slave architecture for running a containerized application and are faster and more lightweight compared to applications deployed on VMs. They are also easily manageable and scalable.

Kubernetes comprises master nodes and worker nodes to run application workloads and manage container orchestration. The master node is generally the decision-maker and manages the Kubernetes cluster. It is the entry point for any administrative tasks, and you can easily communicate with the master node via APIs, the CLI, or the Kubernetes GUI. To ensure the high availability and fault tolerance of the architecture, there must be more than one master node in the cluster.

Master node components

Master nodes comprise the following components:

- **kube-apiserver**: The API server performs all the administrative tasks on the master node. The user can interact with the API server via an HTTP REST call, at which point the API server validates and executes the request. The client can interact with the API server to leverage the Kubernetes functionality.

- **Etcd**: etcd is a highly available and distributed key-value store that's used for storing all cluster data, such as the current state, desired state, resource configurations, and runtime data. etcd is used by the Kubernetes cluster to store all the configuration data, its state (current and desired state of the cluster), and metadata. etcd is written in Golang.

- **kube-scheduler**: The scheduler watches for newly created Pods with no assigned worker node and selects the node for the Pod. Simply put, the scheduler decides which node container will be deployed, depending on the available resources.

- **Controller manager**: The controller manager is responsible for managing various controllers that continuously watch the state of clusters and ensure the current state of the cluster is close to the desired state. Various controllers are available:

  - **Node controller**: The node controller is responsible for onboarding new nodes to the cluster and managing the desired state of the nodes. It handles situations where the node becomes unavailable to keep the application running.

  - **Replica controller**: The replica controller monitors the replica sets and ensures the desired number of Pods is available in the replica set. If a Pod crashes or dies, it will create a new Pod automatically. It will always ensure that the desired number of Pods, or at least one Pod, is up and running.

  - **Deployment controller**: The deployment controller manages the deployment of the application. It ensures that the pod runs at a desired number of replicas and also ensures that unhealthy replicas get replaced with new, healthy replicas. This will guarantee that at least one instance of your application is maintained to serve requests.

  - **Job controller**: The job controller communicates with the API server to remove or add new Pods and doesn't run a job itself. A job is a Kubernetes task that runs on one or more Pods to carry out a task and then terminates:

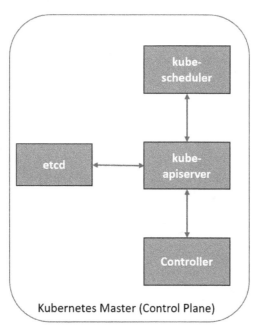

Figure 11.1 - Kubernetes master node

Figure 11.1 depicts the components of the master node in the Kubernetes control plane.

Worker node components

There will always be more than one worker node in the cluster to ensure its high availability and fault tolerance. Worker nodes are responsible for running the containerized application. They comprise the following components:

- **kube-proxy**: This is a network proxy that runs on each worker node of the cluster. kube-proxy manages network rules on the nodes, and these network rules allow your Pods to communicate with a network session inside or outside of your cluster.

- **kubelet**: kubelet runs on each worker node to communicate with master nodes in the cluster. It is responsible for managing how Pods are deployed to the Kubernetes cluster. It receives commands from the API server and instructs the container to start or stop.

- **Container runtime**: The container runtime is responsible for running and managing your application in the Pod.

Figure 11.2 depicts the components in the worker node:

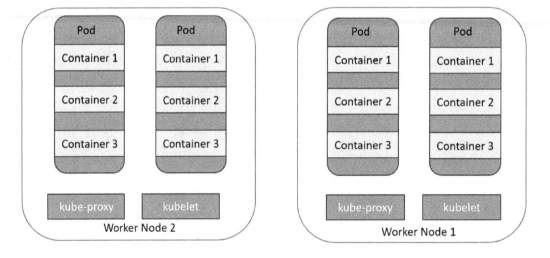

Figure 11.2 - Kubernetes worker nodes

Figure 11.3 depicts the complete Kubernetes architecture:

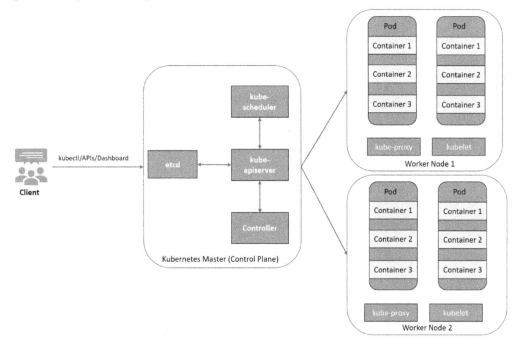

Figure 11.3 - Kubernetes architecture

In this section, we looked at Kubernetes architecture. The next section describes Runtime Fabric. Runtime Fabric runs on top of Kubernetes and is a service that's provided by MuleSoft for running Mule applications and proxies.

What is Runtime Fabric?

Runtime Fabric is a container service that's built on top of Kubernetes by MuleSoft to run and manage MuleSoft applications on the cloud (Azure/AWS/Google) and in on-premises data centers. Runtime Fabric can be set up on bare-metal servers/VMs, self-managed Kubernetes (such as **Azure Kubernetes Service (AKS)**, **Elastic Kubernetes Service (EKS)**, or **Google Kubernetes Engine (GKE)**), and Red Hat OpenShift.

When we set up Runtime Fabric on self-managed Kubernetes, bare-metal servers/VMs, or Red Hat OpenShift, there is a difference in the customer's and MuleSoft's responsibilities for managing Runtime Fabric. In the following sections, we will understand which responsibilities belong to MuleSoft and which belong to the customer when Runtime Fabric is set up in any of the instances mentioned previously.

Runtime Fabric on bare-metal servers/VMs

Runtime Fabric on bare-metal servers/VMs comprises a set of VMs for the cluster. Each VM can be served as a controller node or worker node.

A controller node is a dedicated VM for operating Runtime Fabric and includes an orchestration service, an internal load balancer, and services that allow you to monitor the cluster from Anypoint Platform (the control plane). A worker node is a dedicated VM for running the Mule application and API gateway.

The following is the typical architecture of Runtime Fabric in a development environment with one controller node and two worker nodes:

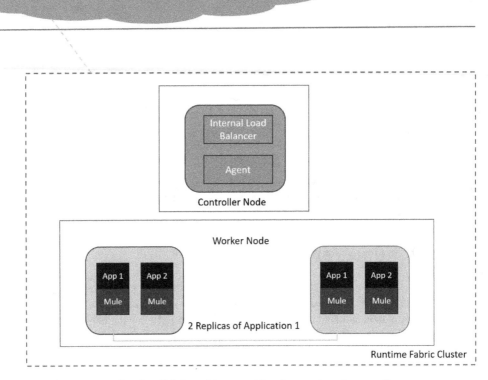

Figure 11.4 - Runtime Fabric architecture (development environment)

The following is the typical architecture of Runtime Fabric in a production environment, which provides high availability and fault tolerance. The Runtime Fabric architecture has three controllers and three workers. The three controller nodes enable fault tolerance if one controller is lost:

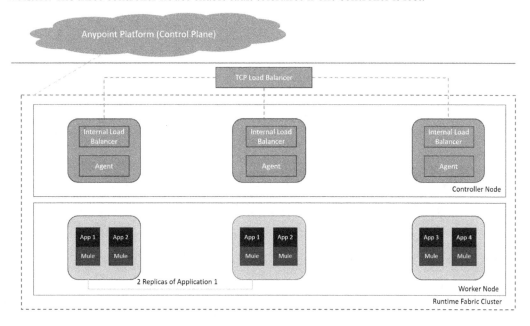

Figure 11.5 - Runtime Fabric architecture (production environment)

To provide further fault tolerance if two controller nodes are lost, a total of five controllers should be set up. This configuration can be set up for a production environment. For a development environment, you can set up one controller node and two worker nodes. Communication between Anypoint Platform and an agent on the controller node is always outbound. The agent is always available on the controller and the controller only runs an internal load balancer. The Mule application is deployed on the worker. Multiple replicas of the application can be run across the worker nodes. The maximum number of control nodes in a cluster is 5 and the maximum number of worker nodes in a cluster is 16. For a development environment, we can use one, three, or five control nodes. For a production environment, we can use three or five control nodes.

Network architecture

A TCP load balancer is used to load balance requests within an internal load balancer on each controller node. The internal load balancer distributes traffic among the replicas of the application running on the worker nodes. An external client can send requests to the TCP load balancer via a public domain:

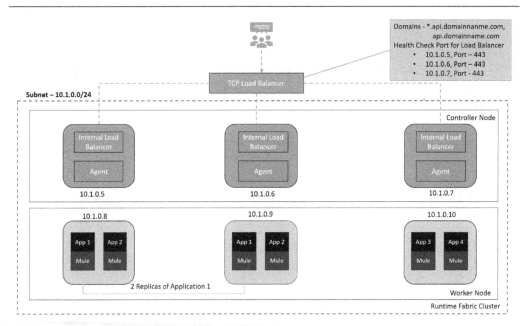

Figure 11.6 - Runtime Fabric network architecture

Figure 11.6 depicts the network architecture of Runtime Fabric.

Shared responsibility between the customer and MuleSoft

It is critical to understand what the customer's and MuleSoft's responsibilities will be in terms of managing Runtime Fabric. The following diagram depicts the customer's and MuleSoft's responsibilities:

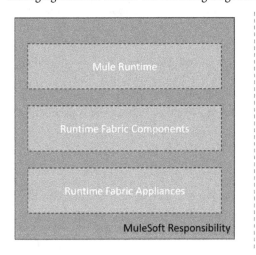
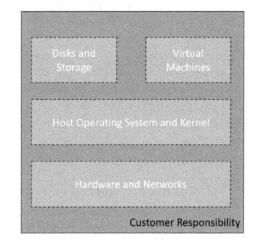

Figure 11.7 - Shared responsibility model

Figure 11.7 depicts Runtime Fabric's shared responsibility model between MuleSoft and Customer.

It is the customer's responsibility to manage infrastructure components such as the disk, storage, VMs, network ports, synchronization of system times across all the VMs, and server patching. It is MuleSoft's responsibility to manage the Mule runtime, Runtime Fabric-related components, and Runtime Fabric appliances.

The concept of etcd in Runtime Fabric

etcd is a reliable and distributed key-value pair data store. It maintains the cluster configuration data, the current state, and the metadata associated with it. etcd is available on all the controller nodes of Runtime Fabric and copies the same data across all the controller nodes:

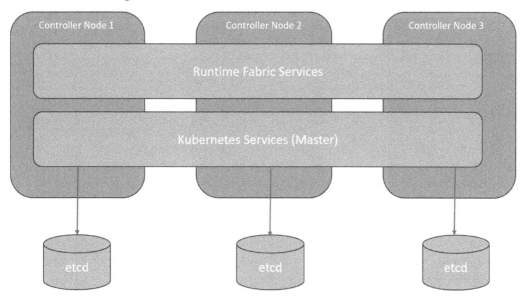

Figure 11.8 - etcd configuration

Runtime Fabric information is stored in JSON or YAML format. etcd will ensure that there is consistent information across all the nodes and that the same information will be available, no matter from which node you are accessing the information. The controller generally writes or reads into etcd files. Reading is an easy operation as the same copy of etcd is available on all the controller nodes.

Writing is a complex operation. For example, if you get multiple requests to write to etcd at the same time, which request will go through? Not all controllers perform the write operation in the etcd cluster; only one controller node will perform the write operation, and that is known as a leader node. Other nodes in the cluster are known as follower nodes. In the etcd cluster, one of the nodes will be elected as a leader among them and the rest will be followers.

If any controller node receives a write request, it will be forwarded to the leader node, and the leader node will perform a write operation to `etcd`. After that, it will ensure that followers receive the same copy of the data. This process will be marked as complete by the leader when it receives confirmation from all the followers.

Quorum management

One of the key ideas in figuring out how many controller nodes the Runtime Fabric cluster needs to operate correctly and successfully write to the `etcd` file is quorum management.

Quorum management is the minimum number of nodes required in the cluster to perform the write operation in `etcd` and function properly. The formula for calculating the quorum is `floor (n/2) + 1`, where `n` is the number of controller nodes in the cluster. Let's calculate the quorum and understand how it fits into the Runtime Fabric architecture:

- When we have one controller node, the quorum will be `floor (1/2) + 1 = 1`. This means that when the control node goes down, the whole system will be down. This configuration is only okay for a development environment.

- When we have two controller nodes, the quorum will be `floor (2/2) + 1 = 2`. This means that when one controller goes down, there is still one controller node available and the quorum is 2. In this case, there will be no fault tolerance and the write operation will not be performed. This means a controller with one node and a controller with two nodes provide similar availability of the cluster. So, there is no point in having a cluster with two nodes.

- When we have three controller nodes, the quorum will be `floor (3/2) + 1 = 2`. This means that when one controller goes down, there are still two controller nodes available and the quorum is 2. In this case, there will be two controller nodes available, as well as the quorum. In this case, we can afford to have one controller node unavailable, and we'll still have two controller nodes to keep doing the work.

- When we have four controller nodes, the quorum will be `floor (4/2) + 1 = 3`. This means that when one controller goes down, there are three controller nodes available and the quorum is 3. This means the cluster will keep working. However, if we lose one more controller, there will be two controller nodes available, and the quorum will be 3. This means that a controller with three nodes and a controller with four nodes provide similar availability of the cluster. There is no point in having a cluster with four nodes.

- When we have five controller nodes, the quorum will be `floor (5/2) + 1 = 3`. This means that when one controller goes down, there are controller nodes available and the quorum is 3. This means that the cluster will keep working. However, if we lose one more controller, there will be three controller nodes available, and the quorum will be 3. In this case, there will be three controller nodes available, as well as the quorum. In this case, we can afford for two controller nodes to be unavailable as we'll still have three controller nodes to keep doing the work.

Generally, it is recommended to set up an odd number of controller nodes (that is, one, three, or five) in the cluster. The following table illustrates the fault tolerance that's provided by a specific number of controller nodes:

Number of Controller Nodes	Quorum	Fault Tolerance
1	1	0
2	2	0
3	2	1
4	3	1
5	3	2

Table 11.1 - Quorum and fault tolerance association

Scalability

Scaling can be achieved at the infrastructure level and the application level.

Horizontal scaling can be done in two ways:

- Add or remove a controller or worker node in the Runtime Fabric cluster
- Add or remove replicas of the application

Vertical scaling can be done in two ways:

- Increase or decrease the computing resources, such as memory or CPU, on the nodes (controller and worker) in the cluster
- Increase or decrease the CPU resources (reserved CPU or CPU limit) on the replicas of the application

High availability

High availability in Runtime Fabric can be achieved by running multiple controller and worker nodes, as we discussed previously, in the Runtime Fabric architecture.

To run the application in high-availability mode, deploy more than one replica of the application. This will ensure the high availability of the application.

Fault tolerance

An application that's deployed to Runtime Fabric is fault tolerant by default. Consider a case where you have deployed one or more replicas of the application. If one of the replicas crashes due to JVM failures or is unavailable due to a node going down, this unhealthy replica will be replaced with a new replica on another node or the same node if it is available. We previously covered the Kubernetes architecture, where there is a controller that ensures the desired state of the cluster.

Inbound load balancer (ingress load balancer)

An inbound load balancer is available on all the controller nodes that distribute traffic to replicas of the application in the worker node. By default, inbound traffic is disabled to avoid unnecessary consumption of resources. It can be enabled from Anypoint Runtime Manager. This load balancer is responsible for TLS termination, and the number of resources required to scale the load balancer is dependent on the number of incoming requests and the size of the payload for each request.

The internal load balancer can be configured in shared mode or dedicated mode:

- **Shared mode** allows you to specify the CPU cores and amount of memory for the internal load balancer. Shared mode is the default setting and it is distributed among all the control nodes.

- **Dedicated mode** doesn't allow you to specify CPU cores and the amount of memory for the internal load balancer, but it uses all the resources dedicated to the internal load balancer. In this mode, the internal load balancer is deployed to the dedicated internal load balancer nodes.

The internal load balancer's sizing depends on the response time latency, number of requests, and payload size:

- 0.5 GB is the default internal load balancer size, which can handle up to 500 active connections

- 1.5 GB can handle more than 500 active connections and is needed when security policies are enabled

The inbound load balancer can define how traffic will be accepted from the client and forwarded to the application running in Runtime Fabric:

- **Accept HTTPS requests**: Accept only traffic on the HTTPS protocol and drop all inbound HTTP traffic:

  - **Redirect HTTP to HTTPS**: Accept traffic on HTTPS and send traffic to Runtime Fabric on HTTP. Respond with 302 to redirect traffic on HTTPS on port 443 in case traffic is coming on HTTP.

- **Accept HTTP request**: Accept traffic on HTTPS and send the request to Runtime Fabric on HTTP port 80.

    - **Drop HTTP request**: Accept traffic on HTTPS. Traffic sent to Runtime Fabric on HTTP will be ignored or dropped.

- **Accept HTTP requests only**: Accept traffic on HTTP. This is not a secure way to allow traffic on HTTP.

Anypoint Security

Anypoint Security enables you to apply security at the edge to secure application networks by enforcing policies and proxying all the inbound and outbound connections to mitigate any risks or threats. Various edge policies can be applied in front of Runtime Fabric to protect the application network from external threats:

- **Denial of Service (DoS) policy**: This policy ensures that traffic will only be accepted from legitimate sources and prevents attackers from flooding your application network with requests. DoS means sending the request continuously with a large payload to your application network to consume the server resources and bandwidth of the network.

- **IP Allowlist policy**: As its name suggests, the IP Allowlist policy will allow traffic to an application network from the IP addresses that have been allowed in the policy, and traffic coming from the IP addresses that are not in the allowlist will be dropped.

- **HTTP limit policy**: This policy allows you to configure the size of the payload and the number of headers that are allowed on the application network. Attackers will try to send a large payload to consume server resources, causing DoS, and consume the network bandwidth, which leads to the degradation of the server's performance. With an HTTP policy, you can control the size of incoming messages.

- **Web Application Firewall (WAF) policy**: A WAF policy will protect request and response traffic to provide security at the web application level.

Application performance metrics

The following figure represents the application performance of a Mule application for different vCPU cores on a simple 10 KB payload:

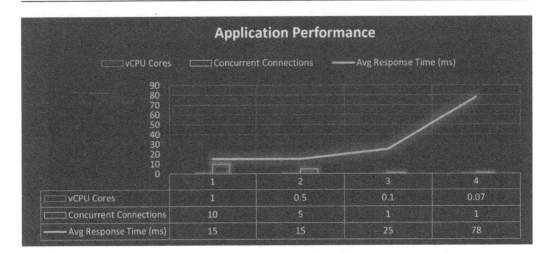

Figure 11.9 - Runtime Fabric application performance metrics

Internal load balancer performance metrics

The following figure represents the performance of the internal load balancer on the controller node on AWS EC2 M4 instances:

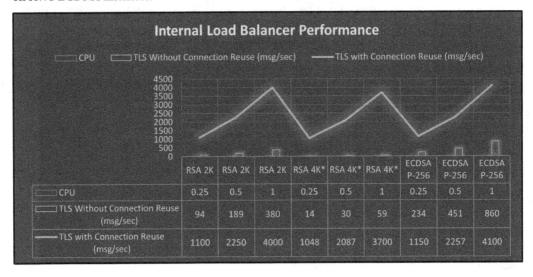

Figure 11.10 - Internal load balancer performance metrics

The preceding application and load balancer performance metrics were taken from the official MuleSoft documentation (`https://docs.mulesoft.com/runtime-fabric/1.13/deploy-resource-allocation`).

With that, we've covered the architecture of Runtime Fabric on bare-metal servers and VMs. Next, we'll look at the architecture of Runtime Fabric on self-managed Kubernetes.

Runtime Fabric on self-managed Kubernetes

MuleSoft provides the option to set up Runtime Fabric on self-managed Kubernetes (EKS/AKS/GKE). Runtime Fabric on self-managed Kubernetes allows you to deploy and manage Mule applications and API proxies to a Kubernetes cluster that has been created, configured, and managed by you. This option allows you to **Bring Your Own Kubernetes** (**BYOK**); MuleSoft will provide Runtime Fabric services, the Mule runtime, and other components required to run the applications. In this section, we are going to discuss how EKS on AWS can be leveraged to run Runtime Fabric. However, before we do that, we need to understand the EKS architecture and its capabilities.

EKS architecture

EKS is a fully managed service from AWS that provides Kubernetes to run workloads and manage the Kubernetes control plane.

Control of EKS is fully managed by AWS, and AWS is responsible for the availability, scalability, fault tolerance, and durability of the Kubernetes control plane. The control plane generally hosts the controller nodes in the AWS-managed **Virtual Private Cloud** (**VPC**). The Kubernetes control plane communicates with the worker nodes in the cluster via the EKS-managed **Elastic Network Interface** (**ENI**). ENI is in multiple Availability Zones to provide fault-tolerant and high-availability architecture.

ENI is the virtual bridge that connects instances within an AWS virtual private cloud to the networks to allow secure inbound and outbound traffic.

The following is the typical EKS architecture you can set up. However, it is not necessary to use a similar architecture; it will vary depending on your organization's requirements:

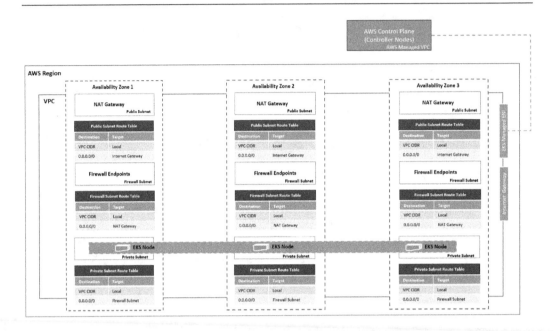

Figure 11.11 - Elastic Kubernetes architecture for Runtime Fabric

In *Figure 11.11*, we have chosen the region where we need to set up the Kubernetes cluster. We have set up VPC in that region, which has three subnets, as follows:

- **Private subnet**: This is the subnet where the worker node (AWS EC2 instances) will be hosted, and the worker node will be spun up across all the Availability Zones to provide high availability and fault tolerance. The worker node's size is decided depending on your application workload.

- **Firewall subnet**: This subnet will restrict the egress (outbound) traffic from the private subnet. By default, all outbound traffic will be allowed from the private subnet if you have associated the NAT gateway with the private subnet. If you have requirements specifying that you can connect to a few applications available on the internet, in such cases, you can allow those application domains or IP addresses in the firewall policies of the firewall subnet. This means you are not allowing all traffic from the private subnet toward the internet. The firewall subnet is optional and it mostly allows you to define stateful and stateless rules.

- **Public subnet**: This subnet is associated with the internet gateway and allows ingress (inbound) and egress (outbound) traffic to and from the internet. The NAT gateway will be set up in the public subnet to allow only egress (outbound) traffic from the private subnet toward the internet.

Each subnet is spun up across all the Availability Zones to ensure scalable, highly available, and fault-tolerant architecture. The route table associated with each subnet is used to define the rules where the traffic will be directed from the subnet.

With EKS set up, the Kubernetes control plane (controller nodes) is automatically set up in the AWS-managed VPC. It is managed by AWS and takes care of scaling, high availability, fault tolerance, and more. It also enables EKS-managed ENI across the Availability Zones to establish communication between the control plane and worker nodes in the Kubernetes cluster.

A bastion host can be set up in the public subnet to connect the worker nodes in the private subnet.

Data stored on `etcd` is encrypted using Amazon's **Key Management Service** (**KMS**). Controller nodes are distributed among the various Availability Zones and traffic is distributed by **Elastic Load Balancer** (**ELB**).

Runtime Fabric architecture on EKS

Let's take a look at the Runtime Fabric on self-managed Kubernetes architecture. This architecture and how its many components interact and coordinate are shown in the following figure:

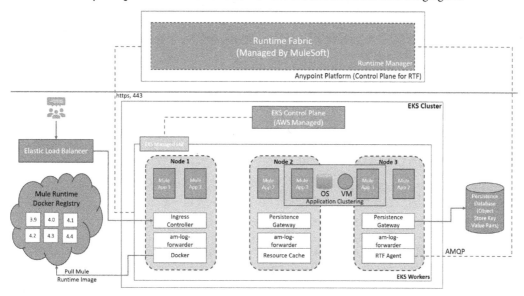

Figure 11.12 - Runtime Fabric architecture on EKS (self-managed Kubernetes)

Figure 11.12 shows various components and how they interact with each other:

- The Persistence Gateway is responsible for storing object store data in a persistent data store. The application must be clustered to share the data, such as in an object store or VM queues across the replicas. The Persistence Gateway will ensure that this data doesn't vanish if the application restarts or is deployed and recovers from any crashes.

- The Docker Pod is the worker node that's responsible for pulling the specific version of the Mule runtime from the Mule Docker registry.

- The log forwarder agent will forward logs to external systems, such as Splunk, CloudWatch, ELK, or Anypoint Monitoring.

- Two kinds of clustering can be achieved: at the infrastructure level and application level. Infrastructure clustering involves groups of nodes that work together in the cluster to run the MuleSoft applications and ensure the high availability, scalability, and fault tolerance of the architecture.

- Application clustering can be enabled when we are deploying more than one replica of the application, and this can be enabled during application deployment. This will improve application performance and allow data to be shared across the replicas of the application.

- Replicas of applications deployed on Runtime Fabric are fault tolerant. They are recovered automatically after the JVM crashes or a worker node is down.

- Auto-scaling is supported by adding a worker node to the auto-scaling group. It can scale depending on whether the memory and CPU usage exceeds the configured value.

Installing Runtime Fabric on self-managed Kubernetes

Runtime Fabric can be set up on self-managed Kubernetes using the `rtfctl` or `helm` utility.

Here is the official MuleSoft documentation for installing Runtime Fabric on self-managed Kubernetes using `rtfctl` or `helm`:

- `rtfctl`: `https://docs.mulesoft.com/runtime-fabric/1.13/install-self-managed`

- `helm`: `https://docs.mulesoft.com/runtime-fabric/1.13/install-helm`

Shared responsibilities between the customer and MuleSoft

It is critical to understand what the customer's and MuleSoft's responsibilities will be in terms of managing Runtime Fabric on self-managed Kubernetes. The following diagram depicts the customer's and MuleSoft's responsibilities:

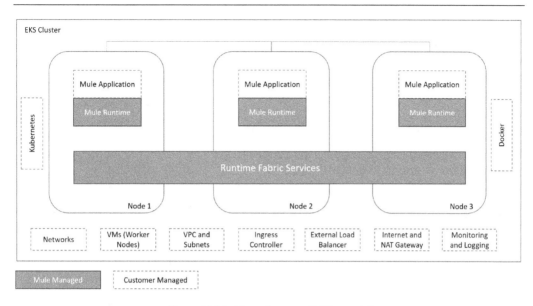

Figure 11.13 - Shared responsibility model

MuleSoft provides Runtime Fabric services, the Mule runtime, and other components for deploying and running Mule applications on self-managed Kubernetes.

The customer will be responsible for managing the Mule application, infrastructure, Kubernetes, networks, load balancers, monitoring and logging to external platforms, and so on.

Ingress

Runtime Fabric allows you to specify a custom ingress configuration for ingress using a resource template. In a resource template, you can define the annotation, class name, and HTTP and HTTPS routing rules. Ingress is responsible for TLS termination and tunneling, load balancing, and routing. The ingress controller can be an NGINX ingress controller, AWS load balancer controller, and so on:

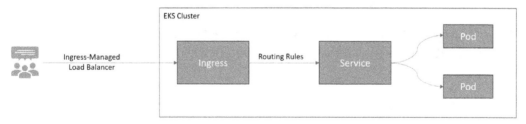

Figure 11.14 - Ingress-managed load balancer

> **Note**
>
> The following documentation explains how you can configure ingress on Runtime Fabric on self-managed Kubernetes: `https://developer.mulesoft.com/tutorials-and-howtos/runtime-fabric/runtime-fabric-aws-elastic-kubernetes-service/`.

High availability and fault tolerance

Whenever you set up Runtime Fabric on self-managed Kubernetes, the control plane is completely managed by the cloud provider, and it is highly available to ensure business continuity and performance. A minimum of three worker nodes should be set up, as per the quorum, to ensure fault-tolerant and highly available architecture. An application can be highly available by deploying multiple replicas and clusters together.

An application that's deployed to Runtime Fabric on self-managed Kubernetes is fault tolerant and will automatically recover from any failures or worker nodes that go down.

Scalability

The control plane scalability of self-managed Kubernetes is managed by the cloud provider. Worker nodes can be scaled horizontally by adding or removing the nodes and can be scaled vertically by adding or removing computing resources such as CPU or memory.

A worker node can be added to an auto-scaling group to auto-scale in case memory or CPU usage increases or decreases.

An application that's been deployed to Runtime Fabric on self-managed Kubernetes can be scaled horizontally by adding or removing the replicas and scaled vertically by increasing or decreasing the replica size. Auto-scaling is not supported for the application, but it can be scaled from the Runtime Manager UI, the Mule Maven plugin, or the Platform API with zero downtime.

How will an application deployed to self-managed Kubernetes communicate with an external service for which IP whitelisting is required?

You may come across a situation where your application must communicate with external services. To establish a successful connection with external services, your application's IP address must be whitelisted on the external services.

Here, we will consider applications that have been deployed to AWS EKS to communicate with an external service where IP whitelisting is a must.

Scenario 1 – worker nodes running in the public subnet

In this case, a worker node is running in the public subnet, which means the worker node will get the public IP address and a Pod will be allocated an IP address from the public subnet IP range.

A Pod can communicate with external services using the public IP of the worker node as the Pod's IP address will be SNATed with the worker node IP address. You just need to provide the public IP address of all the worker nodes in the cluster to be whitelisted for successful communication between the Pod running on the worker node and external services. **SNAT** stands for **source network address translation**:

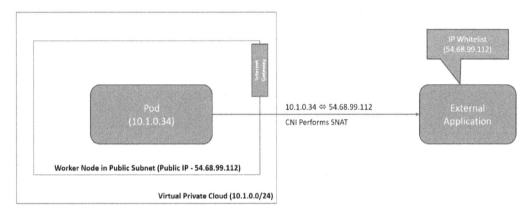

Figure 11.15 - Worker node running in the public subnet

Scenario 2 – worker nodes running in the private subnet

In this case, worker nodes are running in the private subnet, which means the worker will only get a private IP address, and worker nodes can communicate with the outside world using the NAT gateway.

The Pod IP address will be SNATed with the NAT gateway's public IP address to communicate with the external service; only the NAT gateway's IP address needs to be whitelisted in the external system to establish successful communication between the Pod and the external application via the NAT gateway in a public subnet:

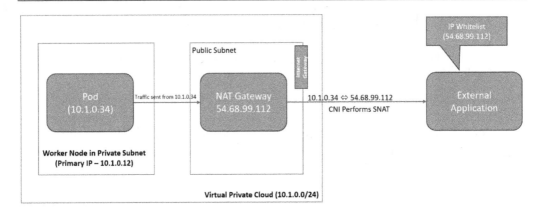

Figure 11.16 - Worker nodes running in the private subnet

Simply put, Pods communicate with the external application through service abstraction.

The difference between Runtime Fabric on self-managed Kubernetes and bare-metal/VMs

The differences between Runtime Fabric on bare-metal/VMs and Runtime Fabric on self-managed Kubernetes are illustrated in the following table:

Attributes	Runtime Fabric (Bare-Metal/VMs)	Runtime Fabric (EKS/AKS/GKE)
Kubernetes	MuleSoft-provided	BYOK.
Ingress	Included	Not included.
OpsCenter UI	Included	Not included.
Node Type	Bare-metal or VMs	VM-based instances are supported. Fargate is not supported.
Last Mile Security	Supported	Supported.
Tokenization Service	Supported	Supported.
Anypoint Clustering	Supported	Supported.
Persistence Gateway	Supported	Supported.
Anypoint Security	Supported	Not supported.
Runtime Fabric Services	Included	Included.
Mule Runtime	Included	Included.
Maximum Number of Business Group	50	50.

Attributes	Runtime Fabric (Bare-Metal/VMs)	Runtime Fabric (EKS/AKS/GKE)
Maximum Number of Worker Nodes	16	30.
Replicas Per Application	8	8.
Replica Per Worker Node	40	40.
Maximum Number of Controller Nodes	5	Self-managed controller nodes.
Kapacitor Alerts	Included	Not included.
Installation Options	VMs or bare-metal server	EKS, GKE, AKS.
Controller Node Accessibility	Can access controller node	Not accessible.
Maximum Number of Environments Associated Per Runtime Fabric Cluster	50	100.
Docker	MuleSoft-provided	**Bring Your Own Docker** (BYOD).
Application Port	8081	8081.

Table 11.2 - The difference between Runtime Fabric on self-managed Kubernetes and bare-metal/VMs

Now that we've covered the architectural differences between Runtime Fabric on self-managed Kubernetes and bare-metal/VMs, let's look at a few helpful services that can be used to manage and execute Runtime Fabric.

rtfctl

`rtfctl` is a utility that's provided by MuleSoft for installing and managing Runtime Fabric from a local machine, bastion host, or any computer. This `rtfctl` utility is available for Runtime Fabric on bare-metal servers/VMs and self-managed Kubernetes.

> **Note**
>
> The following documentation from MuleSoft explains how to install and use `rtfctl`:
>
> `https://docs.mulesoft.com/runtime-fabric/2.3/install-rtfctl`.

Tokenization services

A tokenization service allows you to protect sensitive data. For example, let's say an incoming message contains sensitive data such as credit card numbers or Social Security numbers. This data can be tokenized using a tokenization service. MuleSoft provides a tokenization and detokenization policy that can be configured at the API gateway level.

To enable a tokenization and detokenization policy in API Manager, you should deploy a tokenization service in Runtime Fabric.

The following diagram shows how to tokenize sensitive data such as Social Security numbers:

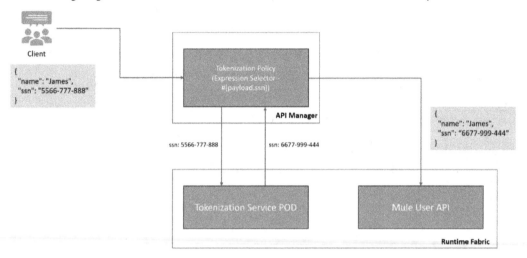

Figure 11.17 - Tokenziation with Runtime Fabric

The following diagram shows how to detokenize the data that was tokenized in the preceding example:

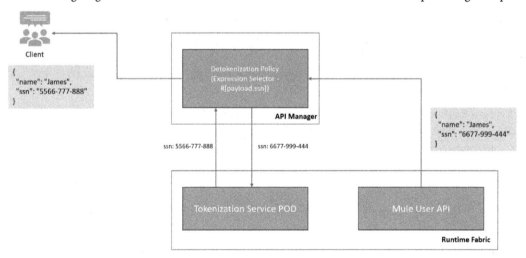

Figure 11.18 - Detokenziation with Runtime Fabric

Secrets Manager

Anypoint Security provides Secrets Manager so that you can store secrets, TLS, key stores, and trust stores that can be used by your deployments. Secrets Manager supports the TLS context for Runtime Fabric ingress.

CPU bursting in Runtime Fabric

Runtime Fabric CPU bursting is a concept based on Kubernetes CPU bursting technology. Whenever we deploy the application to Runtime Fabric, we need to allocate the correct resources, such as vCPU and memory, to the application to ensure that it can handle the required workloads.

When we deployed the application to Runtime Fabric, it deployed in the isolated Pod. Each replica of the application runs in a separate Pod. Each replica has its own Mule runtime, and resources such as vCPU and memory need to be allocated for each replica. We also need to determine the number of replicas that need to be created during deployment.

We need to allocate the following resources for the replica while deploying the application:

- **Reserved CPU**: Guaranteed vCPU that's available for the replica of the application.
- **CPU limit**: The maximum CPU that can be used by the replica of the application (the level to which the CPU can burst).
- **Memory**: The amount of memory that can be used by the replica of the application (in GiB). The minimum memory that can be allocated to the replica of an application is 0.7 GiB on Mule 4 and 0.5 GiB on Mule 3.

Whenever the amount of reserved CPU and CPU limit are equal, it means the CPU is allocated to the replica in the guaranteed model. This will ensure the consistent performance of the application.

If the CPU limit that's allocated to the replica is greater than the reserved CPU, it means CPU bursting has been activated and a replica of the application is ready to consume more CPU if the application is overloaded with requests. This CPU will be taken from spare CPU resources available on the worker nodes.

When you are using CPU bursting, the minimum reserved CPU must be 0.02 vCPUs and the minimum CPU limit must be 0.07 vCPUs. An application with high workloads may require additional CPU capacity to perform better. If the application's deployment fails when using the minimum CPU limit, then increase the CPU limit and redeploy the application.

For applications with critical performance requirements, never utilize vCPU bursts as it doesn't guarantee burst vCPU will be available as and when needed. In such a case, go with the guaranteed CPU model, where you can keep the reserved CPU equal to the CPU limit.

You need to ensure that you don't consume more CPU than what you have paid for, even if you are using CPU bursting. Check out `https://docs.mulesoft.com/runtime-fabric/1.8/deploy-resource-allocation#cpu-and-licensed-cores` for more details.

The CPU limit is bound to the upper limit of the number of CPU cores provided on the worker nodes, which means the CPU limit that's provided to replicas should not exceed the CPU cores of worker nodes.

The following diagram illustrates how CPU bursting works during application overload, as well as the number of requests, and then goes back to normal once the number of requests reduces or goes back to normal:

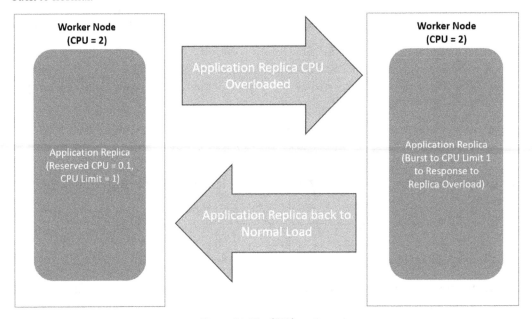

Figure 11.19 - CPU bursting

The CPU limit is not always guaranteed but it can burst to a defined limit if, and only if, a spare CPU is available; other replicas of the application that are deployed might also be competing for the unallocated CPU on the worker node.

Runtime Fabric runs a few services on the worker nodes that consume CPU between 0.3 to 0.5 vCPUs by default.

For example, let's say you have three worker nodes, and each worker node has two vCPUs, which means a total of six vCPUs in the cluster. A minimum of 0.3 vCPUs will be used by worker nodes for other processes, which means a total of 0.9 vCPUs is reserved for worker nodes and the remaining 5.1 vCPUs are available for use.

Pod

A Pod can hold one or more applications in the Kubernetes cluster. A Pod is ephemeral; if Pod execution fails, Kubernetes will automatically create a replica of the Pod to replace unhealthy instances. Runtime Fabric Pods can consist of only one MuleSoft application. Deploying more than one application in a Pod is not allowed. The following diagram shows how a Pod can be set up in Runtime Fabric:

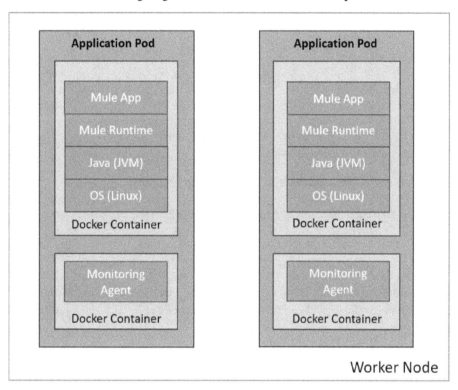

Figure 11.20 - Runtime Fabric Pod

Last-mile security

Last-mile security allows you to enable HTTP traffic between the edge and your application on Runtime Fabric. An application that's been deployed on Runtime Fabric always listens on port 8081; no other ports are supported. To enable last-mile security, you need to configure a TLS context with a server keystore on the HTTPS listener of the application that's been deployed to Runtime Fabric with the HTTPS protocol and enable last-mile security in the **Ingress** tab of the application settings in Runtime Manager:

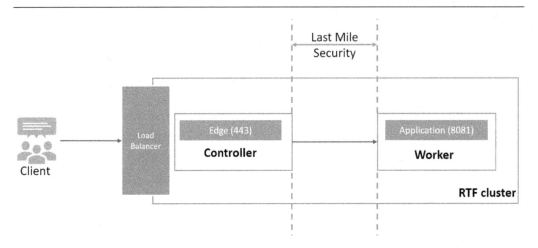

Figure 11.21 - Last-mile security

Internal service-to-service communication

DNS is created for each application that's deployed to the cluster in the `cluster.local` domain. The fully qualified domain name is `<service>.<namespace>.svc.cluster.local`.

For example, the `invoice-sys-api` application is deployed to the Runtime Fabric cluster listening on port 8081 using the HTTPS protocol. The domain will be `invoice-sys-api.e893e8e9-f802-4346-9dd8-ce958efb1979.svc.cluster.local`, where `invoice-sys-api` is the application name and `e893e8e9-f802-4346-9dd8-ce958efb1979` is the namespace of Runtime Fabric:

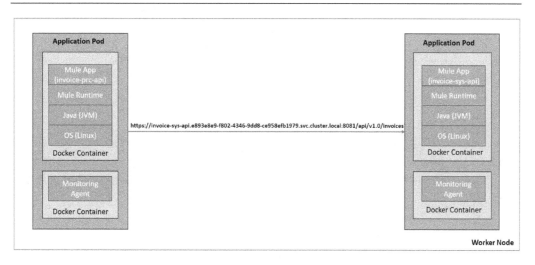

Figure 11.22 - Internal service-to-service communication

Persistence Gateway with Runtime Fabric

The Persistence Gateway allows the MuleSoft application to store and share the data across the multiple replicas deployed to Runtime Fabric. With the Persistence Gateway, data will not be lost in the case of an application restart or redeployment:

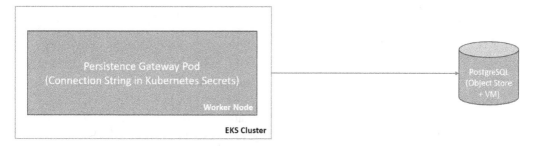

Figure 11.23 - Persistence Gateway with Runtime Fabric

Always deploy multiple replicas of the Persistence Gateway to ensure high availability and scalability. PostgreSQL databases are the only databases that are supported by the Persistence Gateway on Runtime fabric.

Deployment strategy

Two types of deployment strategy are supported on Runtime Fabric:

- Rolling Update
- Recreate

Rolling Update allows you to redeploy the application with zero downtime. An existing replica of the application is available until a new replica of the application is deployed and the client can continue to send the request. Once a new replica has been successfully deployed, the old replica is terminated.

The following diagram depicts how rolling updates work:

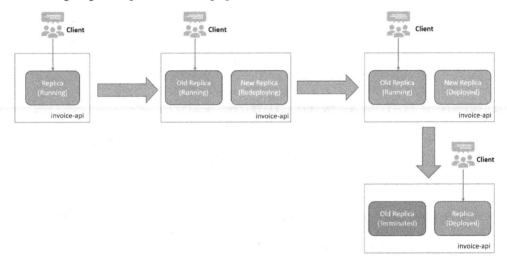

Figure 11.24 - Rolling Update deployment strategy

Recreate will terminate the existing replica of the application and then deploy a new replica of the application. The application will not be available during the deployment.

The following diagram depicts how Recreate works:

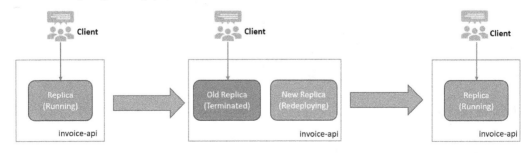

Figure 11.25 - Recreate deployment strategy

Clustering

To enable clustering for an application that's been deployed to Runtime Fabric, there must be a minimum of two replicas. Clustering can be enabled from the Runtime Manager UI or can be specified in the Mule Maven plugin when you're deploying the application.

Deploying replicas across nodes

This option ensures that an application with multiple replicas is deployed across the nodes in the cluster. This option can be enabled from the Runtime Manager UI or can be specified in the Mule Maven plugin when you're deploying the application.

Backing up and restoring Runtime Fabric

It is critical to back up the Runtime Fabric cluster so that it can be restored in the event of any failures. Data in Runtime Fabric is distributed across the Kubernetes cluster.

It is important to preserve the application that's been deployed to Runtime Fabric in the event of any failures so that it can restore all the applications, its configuration, and its state:

- Always store a backup in external storage that is outside Runtime Fabric
- It is a best practice to back up Runtime Fabric every hour

When to use the backup and restore process

There are a few use cases where the backup and restore process can be used:

- During the hardware upgrade of Runtime Fabric, where you can add more computing resources and migrate to the new operating system
- Migrating Runtime Fabric from on-premises to the cloud or one cloud provider to another
- Migrating Runtime Fabric from one data center to another
- Adding more nodes to scale the Runtime Fabric cluster
- When you're failing over the cluster in the event of disaster recovery

What's backed up?

Runtime Fabric backs up services and components related to the Runtime Fabric cluster, but it doesn't back up anything related to the Anypoint Platform cluster. The following is a list of things that are backed up:

- Application details, including replica sets, Pods, application metadata, and properties configured in the Runtime Manager UI
- All data in Runtime Fabric and applications, which includes ingress, secrets, role and cluster bindings, services and service accounts, and deployments
- The current `rtfctl` version running on the Runtime Fabric cluster
- The current agent version on the Runtime Fabric cluster
- Data related to the MuleSoft configurations, such as object store, Anypoint Monitoring, and external load forwarders
- Controller and worker node configuration

Backing up and restoring

The backup and restore process is simple via `rtfctl`. Just by executing a single-line command, you can back up and restore Runtime Fabric.

To back up Runtime Fabric, use the following command:

```
./rtfctl backup <path_to_store_backup>
```

To restore Runtime Fabric, use the following command:

```
./rtfctl restore <path_to_backup_store>
```

Different options for deploying a MuleSoft application to Runtime Fabric

MuleSoft provides multiple ways of deploying an application to Runtime Fabric. Every option can be integrated with a CI/CD pipeline so that a MuleSoft application can be automatically deployed to Runtime Fabric. Let's explore all the options that can be used to deploy applications to CloudHub.

The Mule Maven plugin

The Mule Maven plugin is an important Maven plugin for deploying, undeploying, and packaging MuleSoft applications into Runtime Fabric. Let's discuss it further. The following Mule Maven plugin can be configured in the POM.xml file of your application with all the attributes that are needed to deploy and run the application in Runtime Fabric:

```xml
<plugin>
  <groupId>org.mule.tools.maven</groupId>
  <artifactId>mule-maven-plugin</artifactId>
  <version>3.8.6</version>
  <extensions>true</extensions>
  <configuration>
    <runtimeFabricDeployment>
      <uri>https://anypoint.mulesoft.com</uri>
      <muleVersion>${app.runtime}</muleVersion>
      <username>${username}</username>
      <password>${password}</password>
      <applicationName>${app.name}</applicationName>
      <target>rtf</target>
      <environment>${environment}</environment>
      <provider>MC</provider>
      <replicas>${replicas}</replicas>
      <properties>
        <key>value</key>
      </properties>
      <deploymentSettings>
        <enforceDeployingReplicasAcrossNodes>false
        </enforceDeployingReplicasAcrossNodes>
        <updateStrategy>recreate</updateStrategy>
        <clustered>false</clustered>
        <forwardSslSession>false</forwardSslSession>
        <lastMileSecurity>false</lastMileSecurity>
        <resources>
          <cpu>
            <reserved>${reserved.cpu}</reserved>
            <limit>${cpu.limit}</limit>
          </cpu>
          <memory>
            <reserved>${reserved.memory}</reserved>
          </memory>
        </resources>
        <http>
          <inbound>
```

```
              <publicUrl>${public.url}</publicUrl>
           </inbound>
        </http>
     </deploymentSettings>
  </runtimeFabricDeployment>
 </configuration>
</plugin>
```

In the preceding Mule Maven plugin configuration, values defined under $ { } are the parameters that you can pass with the mule deploy command, as shown here:

```
mule deploy -DmuleDeploy -Dapp.runtime=4.3.0
-Dusername=anypointusername -Dpassword=password -Dapp.name=music-
api-dev -Denvironment=Sandbox -Dreserved.cpu=20M -Dcpu.limit=1500M
-Dreserved.memory=700Mi -Dpublic.url=https://api-dev.domainnanme.com
```

The following attributes can be configured in the Mule Maven plugin while deploying an application to Runtime Fabric:

Parameter	Description	Required	Default Value/ Example
runtimeFabricDeploy-ment	Top-level element.	Yes	
uri	Your Anypoint Platform URI.	No	
muleVersion	The Mule runtime engine version to run in your Runtime Fabric instance.	Yes	
username	Your Anypoint Platform username.	Only when using Anypoint Platform credentials to log in	
password	Your Anypoint Platform password.	Only when using Anypoint Platform credentials to log in	

Parameter	Description	Required	Default Value/ Example
applicationName	The application name that's displayed in Runtime Manager after the app deploys.	Yes	
target	The Runtime Fabric target name to deploy the app.	Yes	
provider	Set to MC, for Runtime Fabric.	Yes	
environment	Target Anypoint Platform environment.	Yes	
replicas	This specifies the number of replicas, or instances, of the Mule application to deploy. The maximum number of replicas per application is 8.	Yes	
businessGroup	The business group path of the deployment.	No	
businessGroupId	The business group ID of the deployment.	No	
deploymentTimeout	The allowed elapsed time, in milliseconds, between the start of the deployment process and the confirmation that the artifact has been deployed.	No	1000000
server	Maven server with Anypoint Platform credentials.	No	
properties	Top-level element.	No	
secureProperties	Top-level element.	No	
skip	When set to true, it skips the plugin deployment goal.	No	
skipDeploymentVeri-fication	When set to true, it skips the status verification of your deployed app.	No	

Parameter	Description	Required	Default Value/ Example
`authToken`	Specifies the authorization token to access the platform. You can use this authentication method instead of setting the username and password.	Only when using an authorization token to log in	
`connectedAppClientId`	Specifies the connected app client ID value.	Only when using Connected Apps credentials to log in	
`connectedAppClient-Secret`	Specifies the connected app secret key.	Only when using Connected Apps credentials to log in	
`connectedAppGrant-Type`	Specifies the only supported connection type: `client_credentials`.	Only when using Connected Apps credentials to log in	
`deploymentSettings`	The deployment setting is defined in the following table.	No	

Table 11.3 - Mule Maven Plugin attributes

There are a few other parameters that can be passed under **deploymentSettings**, as shown here:

Parameter	Description	Example

`enforceDe-ployin-gRepli-casAc-rossNodes`	Enforces the deployment of replicas across different nodes. The default value is `false`.	`<deploymentSettings>`
		   `<enforceDeployingReplicasAcrossNodes>false`
		   `</enforceDeployingReplicasAcrossNodes>`
		`</deploymentSettings>`

`updat-eStrategy`	The updat eStrategy value can be recreate or rolling.	`<deploymentSettings>`
		   `<updateStrategy>recreate</updateStrategy>`
		`</deploymentSettings>`

Parameter	Description	Example
clustered	Enables clustering across two or more replicas of the application. The default value is false.	``` <deploymentSettings> <clustered>true</clustered> </deploymentSettings> ```
http	URL of the deployed application.	``` <deploymentSettings> <http> <inbound> <publicUrl>https://api-dev.domainname. com</publicUrl> </inbound> </http> </deploymentSettings> ```

Table 11.4 - Deployment settings attributes

The following commands can be used to deploy and undeploy an application:

- `mvn clean deploy -DmuleDeploy` (deploys the application to Runtime Fabric)
- `mvn mule:undeploy` (undeploys the application from Runtime Fabric)

The Mule Maven plugin can use one of the following authentication mechanisms to deploy applications to Runtime Fabric:

- Anypoint Platform username and password
- Server
- Anypoint connected app
- Auth token

It is possible to deploy a MuleSoft application from the Runtime Manager UI of Anypoint Platform.

The benefits of Runtime Fabric

The following benefits are provided by Runtime Fabric:

- Runtime Fabric allows you to run a MuleSoft application in lightweight containers.

- Runtime Fabric can be set up on EKS, AKS, GKE, Red Hat OpenShift, and bare-metal servers/VMs on-premises or in any cloud.

- Multiple versions of the Mule runtime are supported in the same Runtime Fabric.

- It supports zero-downtime deployments or updates.

- The minimum replica size supported on Runtime Fabric is 0.02 vCores.

- It provides container-based application isolation. Each container is independent of each other.

- It supports features such as high availability, fault tolerance, scalability, and automatic recovery of replicas.

- Hazelcast-based clustering is supported to store and share data across replicas.

- Each application can be scaled independently of others and each application can be deployed on a different replica size.

Runtime Fabric on Red Hat OpenShift

Previously, we saw that Runtime Fabric can be installed on VMs/bare-metal servers and self-managed Kubernetes (EKS/AKS/GKE). Runtime Fabric can be also set up on Red Hat OpenShift as a Kubernetes (K8s) operator. Runtime Fabric as a Kubernetes operator can be set up on the following platforms:

- Red Hat OpenShift Service on AWS

- Microsoft Azure Red Hat OpenShift

- Red Hat OpenShift Dedicated

- Red Hat OpenShift on IBM Cloud

- Self-managed Red Hat OpenShift editions (Performance Plus, OCP, and Kubernetes Engine)

We won't do a deep dive into the Runtime Fabric architecture as a Kubernetes operator in Red Hat OpenShift, but if you plan to install Red Hat OpenShift Runtime Fabric services, it supports the aforementioned platforms.

The following is a high-level architecture for setting up Runtime Fabric on Red Hat OpenShift:

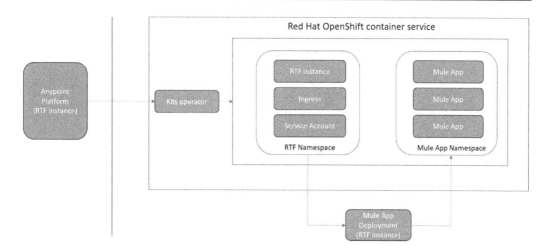

Figure 11.26 - Runtime fabric on Red Hat OpenShift

For more details on Runtime Fabric on Red Hat OpenShift, refer to the link provided in the *Further reading* section.

Summary

This chapter described the functionality provided by Runtime Fabric and how it can be used with VM/bare-metal servers, self-managed Kubernetes, and Red Hat OpenShift. We also covered various components, such as ingress, last-mile security, tokenization services, deployment strategies, zero downtime deployments, and non-functional requirements such as scalability, fault tolerance, and high availability. In the next chapter, we will explain how to set up the Mule runtime in your data center so that you can run Mule applications.

Further reading

To learn more about the topics that were covered in this chapter, take a look at the following resources:

- *Runtime Fabric overview*: https://docs.mulesoft.com/runtime-fabric/latest

- *Runtime Fabric prerequisites (bare-metal/VMs)*: https://docs.mulesoft.com/runtime-fabric/1.13/install-prereqs

- *Runtime Fabric license key installation*: https://docs.mulesoft.com/runtime-fabric/1.13/install-manual

- *Persistence Gateway*: https://docs.mulesoft.com/runtime-fabric/2.3/persistence-gateway

- *Runtime Fabric on Red Hat OpenShift*: https://docs.mulesoft.com/runtime-fabric/latest/install-openshift

12

Deploying to Your Own Data Center

In this chapter, we will discuss how to run, manage, and deploy the MuleSoft application in your own data center. We will also be looking at the different features and capabilities provided by the Mule runtime when running the MuleSoft application in your own data center, as well as different platform architecture approaches for running and deploying the application on an on-premises Mule runtime.

In this chapter, we are going to cover the following list of topics:

- Hardware and software requirements for setting up the Mule runtime on-premises
- Managing the Mule server from the control plane
- Anypoint Private Cloud Edition
- Anypoint clustering and server groups
- High availability and disaster recovery
- What are the different ways a Mule runtime can be set up?

Technical requirements

- Access to Anypoint Platform – a 30-day-free-trial account can be created here: `https://anypoint.mulesoft.com/login/signup`
- Download MuleSoft Anypoint Studio (visit `https://www.mulesoft.com/lp/dl/anypoint-mule-studio`)

Hardware requirements

The following are the minimum requirements for running the MuleSoft application on a Mule runtime, but you can scale depending on the latency and performance requirements:

- 2 GHz CPU or 1 virtual CPU in virtualized environments
- 1 GB of RAM
- 4 GB of storage

MuleSoft supports x64 and x86 architectures but does not yet support ARM.

Software requirements

MuleSoft can run on any operating system that is enabled with the **Java Runtime Engine** (**JRE**) from the supported JDK.

Why an on-premises Mule runtime?

An on-premises Mule runtime is widely used by organizations that have a requirement for a high level of privacy and security where they don't allow the setting up of anything outside their organization's data center. In such cases, you can leverage an on-premises Mule runtime.

With an on-premises Mule runtime, you have complete control over the runtime plane and underlying infrastructure for running the Mule application. You are completely responsible for managing the underlying infrastructure, networks, load balancers, and so on.

Let's understand the responsibilities of both MuleSoft and the customer when you choose an on-premises Mule runtime:

- The customer is responsible for setting up and configuring the Mule runtime as the customer has full control over the on-premises instance.
- The Mule runtime will be provided by MuleSoft.
- The customer is responsible for managing and configuring the underlying infrastructure, load balancers, server security, networks, and so on.
- The runtime plane will be managed by the customer and the control plane will be managed by MuleSoft. Anypoint Platform can be the control plane if you are not going with Anypoint Platform **Private Cloud Edition** (**PCE**). With Anypoint Platform PCE, you can set up the control plane in your own data center.

Running applications in an on-premises Mule runtime

The following are the considerations for running a Mule application in an on-premises Mule runtime:

- An on-premises Mule runtime allows you to run multiple applications within a single Mule runtime.

- You can deploy multiple versions of applications in the same Mule runtime.

- The Mule runtime allows you to share configurations across multiple applications using domains.

- The runtime supports clustering, which allows you to group servers together to form a cluster that can act as a single unit.

- To load balance the HTTP workloads between multiple instances of applications, there is a need for an external load balancer.

- The runtime supports server groups for running applications in distributed mode, but applications are completely isolated from each other. This is useful when you want to deploy applications on all servers.

Let's talk about how to achieve non-functional requirements.

High availability

Clustering the Mule runtime ensures high availability by default. If any servers in the cluster are unavailable due to planned downtime or failure, then other nodes in the cluster will continue processing existing events or messages. We will discuss Anypoint clustering further later in this chapter.

Scalability

An on-premises Mule runtime can be scaled horizontally as well as vertically. To implement horizontal scaling, more servers with a Mule runtime can be added to or removed from the cluster or group. Adding more servers to the existing cluster or group will automatically deploy all the applications that are available on existing servers in the cluster or group to the newly added server.

Vertical scaling can be achieved by adding more computing power to the existing server, such as RAM and storage.

Load balancer

To enable HTTP workloads, an external load balancer needs to be set up in front of a group or cluster of servers. This will ensure that requests are load balanced across all the servers behind the load balancer. It will improve the performance and enable high availability for HTTP workloads.

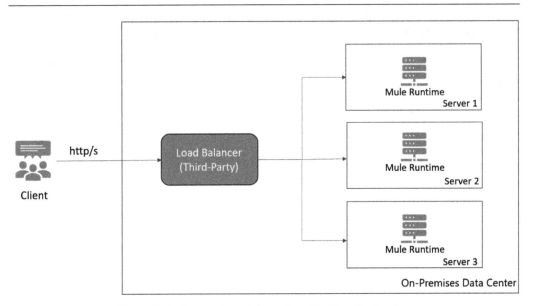

Figure 12.1: On-premises Mule runtime HTTP load balancing

In *Figure 12.1*, we have three servers with a Mule runtime, and they have been load balanced using an external load balancer for HTTP workloads.

In this section, we have gone through the various features of an on-premises Mule runtime, such as high availability, scalability, and load balancing.

In the next sections, we will go through various important concepts of the on-premises Mule runtime, such as Anypoint clustering, server groups, and domain projects.

Anypoint clustering

Anypoint clustering refers to a group of Mule runtimes set up on servers that act as a single unit. In Anypoint clustering, all the Mule runtimes in the cluster communicate with each other and share their status and information via a distributed shared memory grid. Anypoint clustering uses Hazelcast.

There is an open source in-memory data grid called Hazelcast. It offers distributed in-memory computing that is elastically scalable, which is widely acknowledged as the quickest and most scalable method for enhancing application performance.

The Mule Hazelcast server implements a customized version of the Hazelcast distribution that is tailored to the requirements of the Mule runtime. This customized implementation does not modify the Hazelcast behavior in any way. It simply implements the basic configuration that the Mule runtime requires, plus the default logging configuration using Log4j.

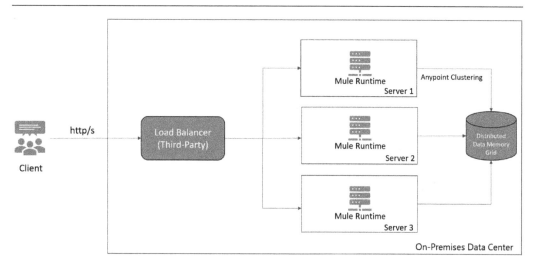

Figure 12.2: On-premises Mule runtime with Anypoint clustering

The following are the benefits of implementing clustering for the on-premises Mule runtime:

- Anypoint clustering distributes traffic among the nodes in the cluster, and this improves the overall performance of the application

- Horizontal scaling can be achieved easily by adding additional nodes to the cluster, and it automatically deploys all the applications that are available on the existing nodes in the cluster on the new node

- Anypoint clustering supports the automatic coordination of access to resources by the Mule runtime, such as files, databases, and FTP

- It improves the overall performance of the application, uses automatic failover, and supports high availability to ensure business continuity

Anypoint clustering supports two different types of clustering that can be leveraged depending on your organization's network settings:

- **Unicast clustering**: In unicast clustering, you need to configure the IP address of the nodes in the cluster to establish communication between nodes. In unicast clustering, ports start from `5701` and it auto-increments from that port in sequence to establish the communication between nodes.

- **Multicast clustering**: In multicast clustering, you don't have to configure the IP address of nodes in the cluster explicitly as it automatically detects other servers in the cluster and enables communication between them. To implement multicast clustering, additional network privileges are needed and you need to contact the network administrator to ensure that multicast clustering is supported in your organization's network. Multicast clustering must be enabled on the IP address `224.2.2.3` and UDP port `54327` to implement it. In multicast clustering, all nodes in one cluster must be in the same network segment. Adding new nodes to the cluster or removing existing nodes from the cluster doesn't require restarting the cluster.

Concurrency issues

Anypoint clustering solves concurrency issues such as the following:

- **File-based connector**: All Mule instances will access the same folders, and this leads to duplicate file processing or may lead to a processing failure if a file is modified or deleted by another Mule application.
- **JMS topics**: All Mule instances listening to the topic will get the same copy of the message, and this leads to the duplication of message processing.
- **JMS request/reply queues**: All the Mule instances might be listening to the same response queue. There might be a chance that the response obtained by a Mule instance is not correlated with the request that it sent and that may lead to an incorrect response or timeout.

There are many other concurrency issues that can be caused by the Salesforce Streaming API, multicast connector, and so on that can be solved by enabling Anypoint clustering.

Setting up Anypoint clustering manually

Anypoint clustering allows you to cluster servers without registering on Anypoint Platform by adding `mule-cluster.properties` to `$MULE_HOME/.mule` on all the servers with the following properties:

```
...
mule.cluster.nodes=192.168.11.22,192.168.11.23,192.168.11.24
mule.cluster.multicastenabled=false
mule.clusterId=<ClusterId>
mule.clusterNodeId=<ClusterNodeID>
...
```

The following are the cluster configuration properties that can be added to `mule-cluster.properties` in `$MULE_HOME/.mule`:

Property Name	Description	Required	Comments
`mule.clusterId`	Unique identifier for the cluster. It can be any alphanumeric string.	Yes	
`mule.cluster-NodeId`	Unique ID of the node within the cluster.	Yes	
`mule.cluster-Size`	The number of nodes that belong to the cluster.	Yes	It can be any integer between 1 and the number of nodes in the cluster.

Property Name	Description	Required	Comments
`mule.cluster.networkinter-faces`	Comma-separated list of interfaces for use by Hazelcast. Wildcards are supported.	No	192.168.2.*,192.168.99.99
`mule.cluster.nodes`	The nodes that belong to the cluster, in the form `<host:port>`.	No	For example, `172.16.9.24:9000`. Specifying just one IP address enables the server to join the cluster.
`mule.cluster.quorumsize`	Enables you to define the minimum number of machines required in a cluster to remain in an operational state.	No	
`mule.cluster.multicastena-bled`	(Boolean) Enable/disable multi-cast. Set to `false` if using fixed IP addresses for cluster node discovery (see the `mule.cluster.nodes` option).	No	If set to `true`, do not set IP addresses in `mule.cluster.nodes`.
`mule.cluster.multicastgroup`	Multicast group IP address to use.	No	
`mule.cluster.multicastport`	Multicast port number to use.	No	
`mule.cluster.jdbcstoreurl`	The JDBC URL for connection to the database.		Required only when storing persistent data.
`mule.cluster.jdbcstoreuser-name`	Database username.		Required only when storing persistent data.
`mule.cluster.jdbcstorepass-word`	Database user password.		Required only when storing persistent data.
`mule.cluster.jdbcstore-driver`	JDBC Driver class name.		Required only when storing persistent data.
`mule.cluster.jdbcstorequer-ystrategy`	SQL dialect for accessing the stored object data.		Required only when storing persistent data. This property can take three different values: `mssql`, `mysql`, and `postgresql`.

Property Name	Description	Required	Comments
`mule.cluster.jmxenabled`	(Boolean) Enable/disable monitoring.	No	
`mule.cluster.listenersenabled`	(Boolean) Enable/disable membership listener.		

Table 12.1: Anypoint cluster configuration properties

Quorum Management in Anypoint clustering

When you set up Anypoint clustering manually, Quorum Management allows you to define the minimum number of nodes in the cluster required for the cluster to be in an operational state. The minimum number of nodes in the cluster for Quorum Management can be defined by adding properties (`mule.cluster.quorumsize`) in `mule-cluster.properties` in `$MULE_HOME/.mule`.

Setting the minimum quorum size allows you to achieve better consistency and protect the cluster in case of the unexpected loss of nodes from the cluster. For example, say you have set up a cluster of seven nodes. You have set a minimum quorum size of five nodes, which means for the cluster to be operational, a minimum of five nodes must be active in the cluster.

A quorum cluster is only applicable to components using Object Store. Whenever `QuorumException` occurs, it is important to catch it and perform appropriate actions, such as retrying the message, stopping the process, sending the email, or logging the error details. If the number of servers in the cluster is less than the quorum size, the operation will be rejected, and it will throw `QuorumException`.

Setting up Anypoint clustering on Anypoint Platform

In this case, Anypoint Platform will act as a control plane and Anypoint clustering can be easily set up from the Runtime Manager console without doing any manual steps. To set up Anypoint clustering, servers must be registered on Anypoint Platform. Now, you can easily create clusters from Anypoint Platform and add all the required servers to be part of the cluster. While creating Anypoint clusters, you can choose the type of clustering you want to set up and it will automatically create `mule-cluster.properties` in `$MULE_HOME/.mule` on all the nodes in the cluster with all the required properties.

Make sure the Mule runtime version is the same across all the nodes in the cluster.

Persistent object store

By default, Anypoint clustering is non-persistent (transient). Data stored in an object store and VM queues will be lost when the application or the Mule runtime is restarted. But MuleSoft provides an option where you can set up persistent Anypoint clustering by using a JDBC database. This JDBC database will be shared across all the nodes in the cluster. This data will persist if the application or Mule runtime is restarted. The following is a list of JDBC databases supported:

- MySQL 5.5+

- PostgreSQL 9

- Microsoft SQL Server 2014

To enable an object store, you need to add the following properties to `mule-cluster.properties` in `$MULE_HOME/.mule` on all the servers in the cluster:

`mule.cluster.jdbcstoreurl`: JDBC URL connection string

`mule.cluster.jdbcstoreusername`: Database username

`mule.cluster.jdbcstorepassword`: Database user password

`mule.cluster.jdbcstoredriver`: JDBC Driver class name

`mule.cluster.jdbcstorequerystrategy`: SQL dialect

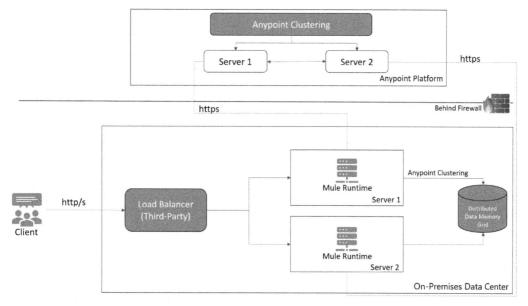

Figure 12.3: Anypoint clustering

Primary node and secondary nodes

Anypoint clustering has the concept of a primary node and secondary nodes, where one of the nodes in the cluster is the primary node and the other nodes in the cluster are secondary nodes. In the event of a primary node failure, one of the secondary nodes will become the primary node.

Whenever an application deployed to the cluster has a scheduler component, scheduler polling only works in the primary node.

For other sources or listeners, if you want the primary node to listen to messages, there is the primaryNodeOnly=true attribute, which can be configured during connector configuration:

```
<flow name="jmsListener_flow">
    <jms:listener config-ref="jmsConfig" destination="listen-queue"
    primaryNodeOnly="true"/>
    <logger message="#[payload]"/>
</flow>
```

In the preceding connector configuration of a JMS listener, the message will only be picked up by the primary node. This configuration can be handy when you are using topics because it has properties to deliver the message to all listeners. With the primaryNodeOnly=true property, it will ensure that the message is delivered to the topic listener on the primary node.

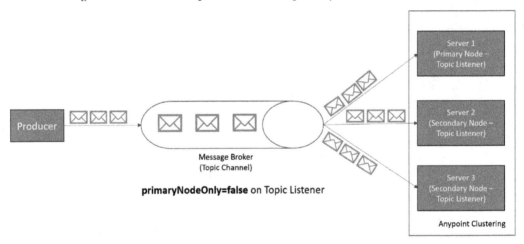

Figure 12.4: JMS topic listener (primaryNodeOnly=false)

In *Figure 12.4*, which depicts the JMS topic listener, primaryNodeOnly=false means the same message in the topic will be delivered to all the active topic listeners in the cluster. So, it will lead to the processing of the same message multiple times. A topic has a property to deliver a message to all the active listeners.

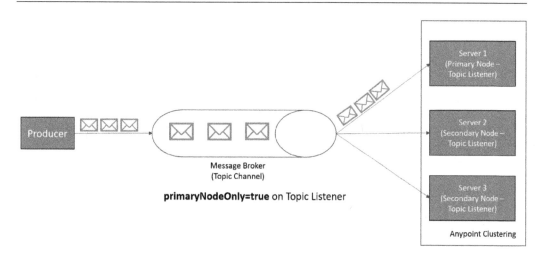

Figure 12.5: JMS topic listener (primaryNodeOnly=true)

In *Figure 12.5*, which depicts the JMS topic listener, `primaryNodeOnly=true` means a message in the topic will be delivered to one topic listener on the primary node in the cluster. In the event of primary node failures, one of the secondary nodes will become the primary and continue to process messages from the topic.

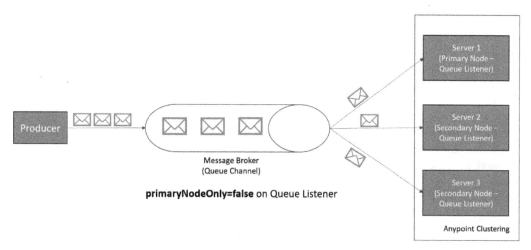

Figure 12.6: JMS queue listener (primaryNodeOnly=false)

In *Figure 12.6*, which depicts the JMS queue listener, `primaryNodeOnly=false` means messages will be load balanced among all the nodes in the cluster, but no messages will be delivered to multiple nodes in the cluster. Queues have a property that means messages will be delivered to one of the active queue listeners in a round-robin fashion, and it provides load balancing of messages among the multiple nodes in the cluster.

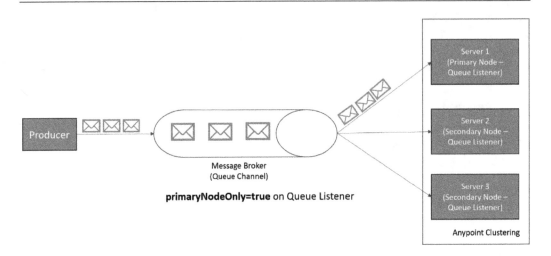

Figure 12.7: JMS queue listener (primaryNodeOnly=true)

In *Figure 12.7*, which depicts the JMS queue listener, `primaryNodeOnly=true` means messages in the queue will be delivered to one queue listener on the primary node in the cluster. In the event of primary node failures, one of the secondary nodes will become the primary and continue to process messages from the queue.

Let's understand how to implement the Competing Queue Consumer pattern with Anypoint clustering. The Competing Queue Consumer pattern enables the parallel processing of messages by multiple consumers from the same channel. Multiple consumers can listen to the same queue to process messages in parallel.

There is a use case where messages are sent to the queue by producers at a very high rate – higher than the rate at which messages are consumed by the consumer. To ensure the messages are processed at a fast rate, we may require more instances of consumers who can consume the messages in parallel from the queue. We can scale up by adding more consumers (queue listeners) to increase the message consumption rate, and this way, traffic is distributed among the multiple queue listeners.

In Anypoint clustering, this pattern can be implemented by having multiple nodes in a cluster with `primaryNodeOnly=false`. This will ensure that all nodes with a queue listener are listening to the queue and messages will be read from the listeners in parallel, and that is how it will improve the overall performance.

The Competing Queue Consumer pattern provides the following list of benefits:

- **Scalability**: Consumers can be added or removed depending on the rate at which messages are published by the publisher. By increasing the number of consumers, messages will be distributed among the consumers to ensure the messages are processed independently and at a faster rate.

- **High availability**: Multiple consumers listen to the same queue. If one of the consumers crashes or shuts down, there are other consumers that will continue to process the messages.

- **Reliability and resilience**: If message processing fails on one of the nodes, the message will be delivered back to the queue, ensuring it can be reprocessed.

VM queues in Anypoint clustering

VM queues can be used to load balance requests between clusters. For example, your application contains a sequence of child flows, and the cluster can assign each successive child flow to the Mule runtime that is free and less busy in the cluster. A message entering the cluster can be processed by multiple nodes as it passes through VM endpoints, as shown in the following figure:

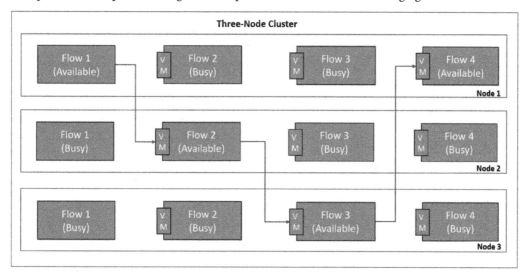

Figure 12.8: Three-node cluster

In *Figure 12.8*, we have deployed an application that has four flows, and each flow communicates via VM queues:

- Flow 1 on node 1 receives and processes the message and sends it to the VM queue

- Flow 2 on node 2 is available and reads the message from the VM queue, completes the processing, and publishes it to the VM queue

- Flow 3 on node 3 is available and reads the message from the VM queue, completes the processing, and publishes it to the VM queue

- Flow 4 on node 1 is available, reads the message from the VM queue, and completes the processing

Anypoint server group

An Anypoint server group is a group of servers that acts as a single deployment target for deploying an application, so you don't have to deploy the application on each server individually. For example, when you want to deploy an application, you just need to select the server group as the target, and it will deploy the application to all the servers in the group.

Servers added to the server group are isolated from each other and they don't share status. To distribute an HTTP workload, you can use a load balancer, which can distribute traffic among the servers in the server group.

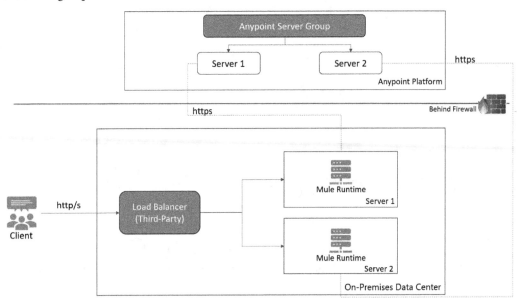

Figure 12.9: Anypoint server group

To enable a server group, make sure all nodes have the same version of the Mule runtime, and nodes must be registered on Anypoint Platform. Server groups are not suitable whenever there are concurrency issues, such as a topic listener on both nodes receiving the same message, ending up duplicating the processing of messages.

We have just learned about Anypoint clustering and server groups, which can be implemented with an on-premises Mule runtime. We have also seen how to register servers in Anypoint Platform, which are managed by MuleSoft, as well as creating server groups or clusters from Anypoint Platform.

The following is a comparison between Anypoint server groups and clustering:

Comparison Factors	Anypoint Server Group	Anypoint Clustering
Required third-party load balancer for HTTP traffic	Yes	Yes
Avoid concurrency issues	No	Yes
Nodes are aware of each other, share common information, and synchronize their statuses	No	Yes
Improves application performance by dividing the workload between nodes in the cluster	No	Yes
Nodes are independent and isolated from each other	Yes	No
All nodes must have the same version of the Mule runtime in the group or cluster	Yes	Yes
Automatic coordination of access to resources, such as files, databases, and FTP sources	No	Yes
Automatic load balancing of processing within a cluster or group	No	Yes

Table 12.2: Anypoint clustering versus server groups

In the next section, we will be talking about Anypoint Platform PCE, which can be set up in an on-premises data center to manage clusters, server groups, and servers.

Anypoint Platform Private Cloud Edition

With Anypoint Platform PCE, you can set up an Anypoint Platform control plane within your own data center, and it allows you to manage, run, or deploy a MuleSoft application on your local servers using your organization's security policies and compliance.

For example, there is a requirement where you want the MuleSoft control plane and data plane within your own data center and don't want to interact with external systems or public internet connectivity. In such cases, you can run the Anypoint Platform software locally within your own data center using Anypoint Platform PCE.

All security and other policies are available locally and can easily be applied to an application from Anypoint Platform PCE located within your own data center.

The following are components included with Anypoint Platform PCE:

Component	Included	Not Included	Description
Anypoint Runtime Manager	X		Enables you to track and manage your deployed Mule applications.
Runtime Fabric management (including Security Edge and tokenization)		X	Automates the deployment and orchestration of customer-hosted Mule applications and API gateways.
Anypoint API Manager	X		Enables you to manage your registered APIs.
Secrets Manager		X	Stores and manages secrets for supported Anypoint Platform services.
Anypoint Exchange	X		Enables your organization to share various assets for reuse across integration projects.
Access Management	X		Enables you to create your Anypoint Platform account or configure an externally federated identity.
Anypoint Design Center, excluding Flow Designer	X		Enables you to create API specifications in several modeling languages and to create RAML API fragments.
Anypoint Analytics – Insights		X	Provides in-depth visibility into business transactions and events on your Mule apps deployed to CloudHub and on-premises servers.
Anypoint Analytics – Anypoint Visualizer	X		Enables you to explore your application network via an application network graph.
Anypoint Analytics – API		X	Provides insight into how your APIs are being used and how they are performing.
Anypoint Monitoring	X		Provides visibility into integrations, Mule flows, and components in your application network.
Object Store		X	Object Store v2 allows CloudHub applications to store data and states across batch processes, Mule components, and applications, either from within an application or by using the Object Store REST API.

Anypoint MQ		X	A multi-tenant cloud messaging service that enables you to perform advanced asynchronous messaging scenarios between tenant applications.
API Testing		X	Provides a testing framework that enables you to easily build automated tests for your integrations and APIs.

Table 12.3: Anypoint Platform PCE components (Source: MuleSoft official documentation: https://docs.mulesoft.com/)

Anypoint Platform PCE supports 4-Node and 7-Node configurations to ensure high availability and stable performance. 4-Node configuration is the smallest configuration supported by Anypoint Platform PCE. This is the minimum number of nodes required to ensure high availability and failover.

Figure 12.10 refers to the control plane and data plane running an on-premises data center with Anypoint clustering enabled between the servers.

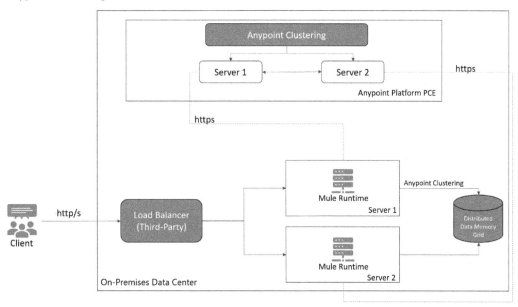

Figure 12.10: Anypoint control plane and runtime plane on-premises data center with Anypoint clustering

Running on-premises Mule runtime use cases

A Mule runtime can be set up on a single node or multiple nodes on-premises. Running a Mule runtime on a single node is not recommended if you are looking for better performance, high availability, and business continuity.

There are multiple ways you can set up the Mule runtime:

- Runtime plane on-premises and no control plane

- Runtime plane on-premises and control plane on Anypoint Platform

- Runtime plane on-premises and control plane on Anypoint Platform PCE (fully on-premises)

Mule runtime plane on-premises and no control plane (standalone)

In this approach, the Mule runtime will be set up on-premises without registering the server to Anypoint Platform. This means we don't have a control plane to manage the Mule runtime. With this approach, we will not be able to apply any API policies and cannot leverage Anypoint Monitoring for the application deployed to the Mule runtime on-premises. It is possible to cluster the servers using a manual approach, as discussed earlier in this chapter.

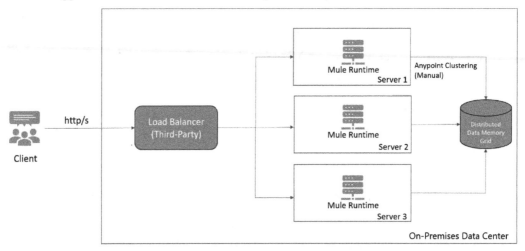

Figure 12.11: Mule runtime plane on-premises and no control plane (standalone)

The preceding architecture shows manual clustering on a runtime plane without registering the server to the control plane on Anypoint Platform.

Mule runtime plane on-premises and control plane on Anypoint Platform (hybrid)

In this approach, the Mule runtime will be set up on-premises and all the servers will be registered on Anypoint Platform. The Anypoint Platform control plane is outside the firewall of the organization, and there is a need to allow communication between the on-premises servers and the control plane on Anypoint Platform. The on-premises servers will send metadata to the control plane, and this will generate metrics on the control plane such as CPU utilization and memory utilization. With the control plane, you can manage the on-premises servers, such as by starting and stopping the Mule runtime and application and viewing the status of the servers.

The following figure shows how a Mule runtime on-premises will communicate with the control plane on Anypoint Platform.

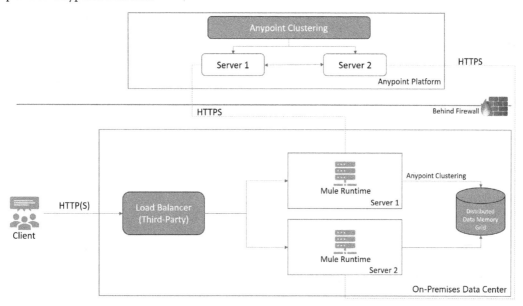

Figure 12.12: Mule runtime plane on-premises and control plane on Anypoint Platform (hybrid)

We have discussed Anypoint clustering, and it is possible to cluster all servers to act as a single unit. It can be easily done from Runtime Manager in Anypoint Platform. *Figure 12.12* shows a Mule Runtime setup with Anypoint clustering with a control plane. With this approach, metadata will leave the organization's data center to generate metrics such as CPU and memory utilization and manage the clusters, servers, and server groups.

Mule runtime plane on-premises and control plane on Anypoint Platform PCE (fully on-premises)

With this approach, you have the runtime plane and control plane both located in your own data center. We discussed Anypoint Platform PCE earlier, which is available locally, and an application deployed to an on-premises Mule runtime can connect to Anypoint Platform PCE without any public internet connectivity. The following are a few capabilities provided by Anypoint Platform PCE:

- Anypoint Platform PCE supports using Runtime Manager to manage applications deployed to an on-premises Mule runtime and set up Anypoint clustering, server groups, and so on

- Anypoint Platform PCE supports using API Manager to manage the life cycle of APIs deployed to an on-premises Mule runtime, such as applying API policies and managing API instances

- Anypoint Platform PCE supports Anypoint Monitoring and Anypoint Visualizer

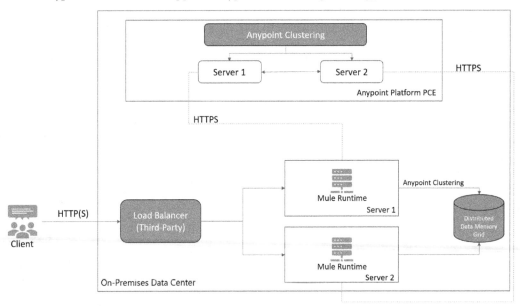

Figure 12.13: Mule runtime plane on-premises and control plane on Anypoint Platform (hybrid)

In *Figure 12.13*, you can see both the control plane and runtime plane located in the same data center and there is no need for public internet connectivity to establish the communication between the control and runtime planes. With this approach, you need to manage the whole infrastructure networks for the control and runtime planes as both are in your own data center. This solution is mostly used when your organization has strict compliance and security requirements that mean they cannot use a cloud-based solution.

This approach can be useful when your organization has a strict compliance policy where your data or metadata must not leave your organization's data center that is hosted on-premises and you have a strong team for managing underlying infrastructure and networks.

Running multiple MuleSoft applications on a single port (Mule domain)

A Mule domain allows you to share resources among applications deployed on an on-premises Mule runtime. You may have to share the connector configuration, shared properties, and error handlers among the multiple applications, and domain projects are the only way to share resources among applications.

When deploying Mule on-premises, you can specify global configurations such as default error handling, shared properties, scheduler pools, and connector configuration to be shared across all applications deployed on the same domains. To use Mule, you need to create a domain and then link to it from every application. This means that each app now assigned to your Mule domain will have access to shared resources in that domain.

Domain usage significantly improves performance when you're deploying multiple services to the same Mule on-premises runtime engine. Since domains provide a central point for all shared resources, they make the class-loading process faster, especially since the domain dependencies defined in POM. xml are also shared within the domain apps.

The following are the shared configuration can be part of the domain project:

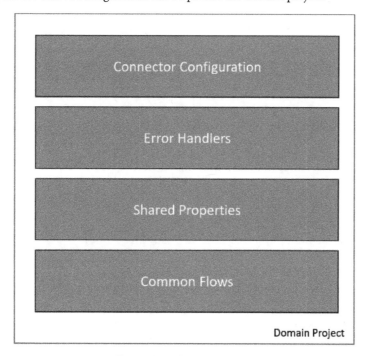

Figure 12.14: Domain project

Let's consider deploying applications on an on-premises Mule runtime that has an HTTP listener. Each application must be deployed on a different port, and they must not overlap with other applications' ports. This adds the complexity of managing multiple ports. To solve this problem, we can use a domain project by adding an HTTP listener connection configuration on any port (for example, 8081). An application can reference the domain project and refer to the HTTP listener configuration from the domain project. This way, all the applications can refer to the domain project and the HTTP listener configuration – you don't have to configure a separate port for each project, and you can easily refer to the connector configuration from the domain project.

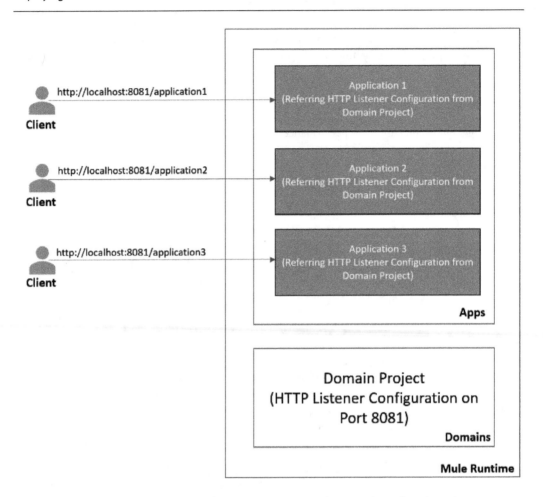

Figure 12.15: Running MuleSoft applications on a single port using a domain project

In the preceding diagram, each application deployed to the Mule runtime refers to the domain project to use the HTTP listener connector configuration, so the applications can run on a single port, 8081.

How to use a domain project in API-led connectivity architecture

As we are aware, there are three layers in API-led connectivity: the experience API, the process API, and the system API. We usually have a requirement not to expose the system and process APIs externally and only the experience API can be called by external consumers.

To achieve this, we will use three domain projects: `exp-domain-project-8081`, `prc-domain-project-8082`, and `sys-domain-project-8083`. Each domain project will have an HTTP listener connector configuration with a different port, as shown in the following table.

Layer	Domain Project	HTTP Listener Configuration – Port	Load Balancer
Experience API	`exp-do-main-pro-ject-8081`	8081	External load balancer
Process API	`prc-do-main-pro-ject-8082`	8082	Internal load balancer (optional)
System API	`sys-do-main-pro-ject-8083`	8083	Internal load balancer (optional)

Table 12.4: Domain project configuration

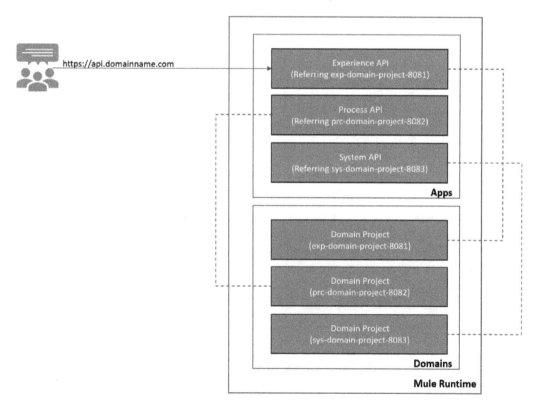

Figure 12.16: Domain project with API-led connectivity

In *Figure 12.16*, the experience API running on port 8081 is exposed to the external load balancer, whereas the system and process APIs can be exposed to the internal load balancer, so the experience API can communicate with the process API using an internal URL and the process API can communicate with the system API using an internal URL. If an internal load balancer has been set up in front of the process API and the system API, then an internal load balancer can be used for internal communication.

Deploying a MuleSoft application on-premises using the Mule Maven plugin

The Mule Maven plugin is an important Maven plugin for deploying, un-deploying, and packaging MuleSoft applications on-premises. Let's discuss the Mule Maven plugin some more. The following plugin can be configured in POM.xml of your application with all the attributes that are required for deploying and running the application on-premises:

```
<plugin>
  <groupId>org.mule.tools.maven</groupId>
  <artifactId>mule-maven-plugin</artifactId>
  <version>3.8.6</version>
  <extensions>true</extensions>
  <configuration>
    <standaloneDeployment>
      <muleHome>${mule.home }</muleHome>
      <muleVersion>${app.runtime}</muleVersion>
    </standaloneDeployment>
  </configuration>
</plugin>
```

In the preceding Mule Maven plugin, values defined under ${ } are the parameters that you can pass with the mule deploy command as follows:

```
mule deploy -DmuleDeploy -Dapp.runtime=4.3.0 -Dmule.home=/opt/mule/bin
```

The following are the attributes that can be configured on the Mule Maven plugin while deploying an application on-premises:

Parameter	Description	Required
standaloneD-eployment	Top-level element.	Yes
application-Name	Specifies the application name to use during deployment.	Yes

muleVersion	The Mule version running in your local machine instance. If this value does not match the Mule version running in your deployment target, the plugin raises an exception. The Mule Maven plugin does not download a Mule runtime engine if these values don't match.	Yes
muleHome	The location of the Mule instance in your local machine.	Yes
deployment-Timeout	The allowed elapsed time, in milliseconds, between the start of the deployment process and the confirmation that the artifact has been deployed. The default value is 1,000,000.	No
skip	When set to true, skips the plugin deployment goal. Its default value is false.	No

Table 12.5: Mule Maven plugin attributes

The Mule Maven plugin supports **Anypoint Runtime Manager** (**ARM**) deployment to deploy applications on the target, such as servers, clusters, or server groups registered on Anypoint Platform. The following plugin can be configured in POM.xml of your application with all the attributes that are required for deploying and running the application using ARM:

```
<plugin>
  <groupId>org.mule.tools.maven</groupId>
  <artifactId>mule-maven-plugin</artifactId>
  <version>3.7.1</version>
  <extensions>true</extensions>
  <configuration>
    <armDeployment>
      <muleVersion>${app.runtime}</muleVersion>
      <uri>https://anypoint.mulesoft.com</uri>
      <target>${target}</target>
      <targetType>${target.type}</targetType>
      <username>${username}</username>
      <password>${password}</password>
      <environment>${environment}</environment>
      <properties>
        <key>value</key>
      </properties>
    </armDeployment>
  </configuration>
</plugin>
```

In the preceding Mule Maven plugin, values defined under $ { } are the parameters that you can pass with the `mule deploy` command as follows:

```
mule deploy -DmuleDeploy -Dapp.runtime=4.3.0 -Dtarget=test-
cluster -Dtarget.type=cluster -Dusername=Anypoint_Username
-Dpassword=Anypoint_Password -Denvironment=Sandbox
```

The following are the attributes that can be configured on the Mule Maven plugin while deploying applications using ARM.

Parameter	Description	Required
armDeployment	Top-level element.	Yes
application-Name	Specifies the application name to use during deployment.	Yes
muleVersion	The Mule version required for your application to run in your deployment target.	Yes
uri	The Anypoint Platform URI.	No
target	The name of the server where your Mule instances are installed.	Yes
targetType	The type of target to which you are deploying. Valid values are cluster, server, and server-Group.	Yes
username	Your username for the server where your Mule instances are installed.	Only when using Anypoint Platform credentials to log in
password	Your password for the server where your Mule instances are installed.	Only when using Anypoint Platform credentials to log in
environment	The environment name for the server where your Mule instances are installed. This value must match any environment configured in your Runtime Manager account.	Yes
businessGroup	The business group path of the deployment.	No
business-GroupId	The business group ID of the deployment.	No
deployment-Timeout	The allowed elapsed time, in milliseconds, between the start of the deployment process and the confirmation that the artifact has been deployed. The default value is 1000000.	No

Parameter	Description	Required
server	The Maven server with Anypoint Platform credentials. This is only needed if you want to use your credentials stored in your Maven settings.xml file. This is not the Mule server name.	No
properties	Top-level element.	No
skip	When set to true, skips the plugin deployment goal. Its default value is false.	No
skipDeploy-mentVerifica-tion	When set to true, skips the status verification of your deployed app. Its default value is false.	No
authToken	Specifies the authorization token to access the platform. You can use this authentication method instead of setting a username and password.	Only when using an Authorization token to log in
connectedAp-pClientId	Specifies the Connected Apps clientID value.	Only when using Connected Apps credentials to log in
connectedAp-pClientSecret	Specifies the Connected Apps secret key.	Only when using Connected Apps credentials to log in
connectedAp-pGrantType	Specifies the only supported connection type: client_credentials.	Only when using Connected Apps credentials to log in

Table 12.6: Mule Maven plugin attributes while deploying with ARM

Here are the commands to deploy and undeploy an application:

```
mvn clean deploy -DmuleDeploy (deploy application on-premises)
mvn mule:undeploy (undeploy application from on-premises)
```

Deploying a MuleSoft application on-premises using the Anypoint Runtime Manager (ARM) REST API

MuleSoft provides the ARM API for deploying applications on cluster or server groups or servers registered on Anypoint Platform. It also provides endpoints for managing servers, clusters, and server groups and supports many other operations via the ARM REST API. Here is the full list of operations: https://anypoint.mulesoft.com/exchange/portals/anypoint-platform/f1e97bc6-315a-4490-82a7-23abe036327a.anypoint-platform/arm-rest-services/.

The following table showcases deploying an application to the target using the ARM API:

Method	POST
API endpoint	`https://anypoint.mulesoft.com/hybrid/api/v1/applications`

Request body	`{`
	`    "applicationSource": {`
	`        "source": "EXCHANGE",`
	`        "groupId": "com.mulesoft.hybrid",`
	`        "artifactId": "platformApp",`
	`        "version": "0.0.1"`
	`    },`
	`    "targetId": 101,`
	`    "artifactName": "test-app"`
	`}`

Authentication	OAuth 2.0 (Connected Apps or Anypoint username and password)
Header	X-ANYPNT-ORG-ID (organization ID of Anypoint Platform), X-ANYPNT-ENV-ID (environment ID of Anypoint Platform), and Content-Type (application/json)

Table 12.7: ARM API

More details on the ARM API can be found on the Anypoint developer portal. Here is the link: `https://anypoint.mulesoft.com/exchange/portals/anypoint-platform/f1e97bc6-315a-4490-82a7-23abe036327a.anypoint-platform/arm-rest-services/minor/1.0/console/method/%231517/`

Deploying Mule for high availability and disaster recovery strategies

The downtime of an application can occur at any time. It could be planned due to the maintenance of the application and infrastructure, or it could be unplanned due to JVM failures or crashes, hardware failures, or network issues. Due to the global shift toward e-commerce, businesses want their applications to run with 100% uptime, be highly available, and be able to recover quickly from any disaster without having an impact on the business.

There are various ways to address high availability and disaster recovery strategies, and one method is Anypoint clustering, providing basic failover, which we already discussed earlier in this chapter. With Anypoint clustering, in the event of the primary node failing, the secondary node becomes the primary node to resume the processing.

MuleSoft provides four options for implementing high availability:

- Cold standby

- Warm standby

- Hot standby – active-passive

- Active-active

Cold standby

In the cold standby approach, one or more operating systems are not running. This is basically a backup of the production environment or virtual machines. In the event of any outages being detected, the backup operating system and Mule runtime are started. Some downtime will occur while starting the backup operating system and Mule runtime and redirecting traffic to the backup.

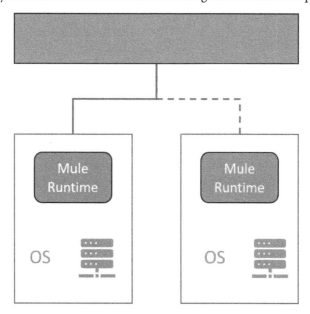

Figure 12.17: Cold standby

Warm standby

In the warm standby approach, the backup operating system is running but the Mule runtime is not running. In the event of any outages being detected, the backup Mule runtime is started. A little downtime can occur while starting the runtime and redirecting traffic to the backup.

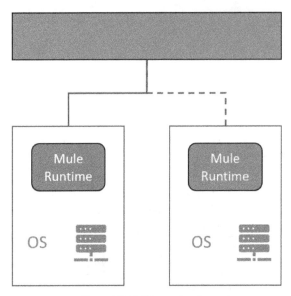

Figure 12.18: Warm standby

Hot standby – active-passive

In this approach, the backup Mule runtime and operating system are operational and running. However, they are not processing any requests. In the event of any outages being detected, the backup will start processing the requests. Minimal downtime can occur when redirecting traffic to the backup.

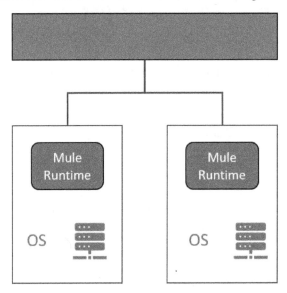

Figure 12.19: Hot standby – active-passive

Active-active

In this approach, the backup Mule runtime and operating system are operational and running. Environments are clustered and a load balancer routes the traffic to all the environments. There is no downtime with this approach.

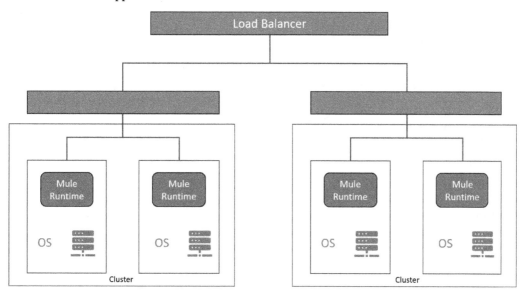

Figure 12.20: Active-active

It is also possible to load balance a single-cluster environment, and it will ensure zero downtime of the service. To implement this approach, the network latency between environments must be less than 10 milliseconds.

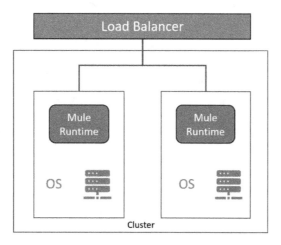

Figure 12.21: Active-active – single-cluster

Upgrading a Mule runtime or scaling the underlying infrastructure without any downtime

We generally have requirements to upgrade a Mule runtime or make hardware changes such as increasing the memory or storage, and these things must be achieved with zero downtime to ensure business continuity. It is also important to ensure the stability of the Mule runtime after an upgrade or making hardware changes. The current Mule runtime can be considered as a baseline production environment, and a new environment is created when the runtime configuration changes and hardware is upgraded.

To gain confidence in the new environment, we will use the canary deployment approach, where we will send a small amount of traffic to the new environment and the rest of the traffic to the baseline environment. Slowly, we will increase the traffic to the new environment as we gain confidence on the newly deployed application.

Once 100% of the traffic is being routed to the new environment, the baseline environment will be terminated, and the new environment will become the baseline production environment. The following is an illustration of how traffic can increase slowly in a new environment, eventually terminating the old environment.

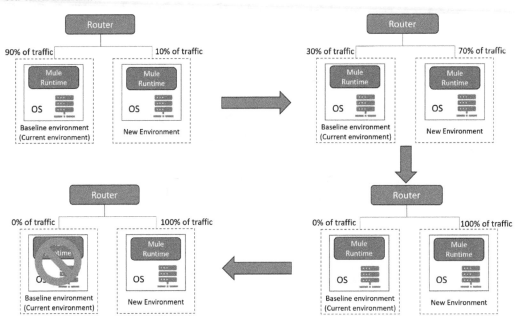

Figure 12.22: Upgrading a Mule runtime or scaling the underlying infrastructure without any downtime

In this approach, temporary costs can be incurred for running the extra instance (this may be for a few minutes, hours, or days).

Mule runtime on-premises security

Security is critical for any business to ensure that information stored and retrieved via software applications is secure and protected, and it must be secured from unauthorized users. Information such as credit card details and Social Security numbers should be accessed in a secure way to perform any transaction, and it must only be accessible to legitimate or authorized users.

The Mule runtime provides various tools for implementing security:

- A cryptography module for encrypting and decrypting data. Supported strategies are JCE, PGP, and XML to encrypt and sign data.

- Secure configuration properties for storing credentials or sensitive data in a properties file in encrypted form.

- Enabling a FIPS 140-2 certified environment

- Out-of-the-box API policies such as JWT validation tokens, client credentials enforcement policy, and other security policies that can be enabled on APIs for authorization and authentication.

- TLS security configuration – a Mule application can be secured in transit by configuring TLS. TLS 1.1 and TLS 1.2 are supported.

- Spring Security for enabling basic authentication or basic authentication with an LDAP provider.

Summary

In this chapter, our understanding has expanded regarding the attributes and functionalities of the on-premises Mule runtime. Moreover, we have explored important topics such as Anypoint clustering, server groups, domain projects, and non-functional prerequisites such as high availability, scalability, and load balancing. Additionally, we have explored subjects such as upgrading the Mule runtime, implementing security measures, and disaster recovery alternatives. Looking ahead, the forthcoming chapter will concentrate on Government Cloud and EU Control Plane, with a specific focus on distinctive factors to be taken into account.

Further reading

- Anypoint Platform PCE supported configurations: `https://docs.mulesoft.com/private-cloud/3.2/supported-cluster-config`

- FIPS 140-2 compliance support: `https://docs.mulesoft.com/mule-runtime/4.5/fips-140-2-compliance-support`

- Security: `https://docs.mulesoft.com/mule-runtime/4.5/securing`

- Clustering: `https://docs.mulesoft.com/runtime-manager/cluster-about`

- A few tables in this chapter have been taken from the MuleSoft official documentation: `https://docs.mulesoft.com/`

Government Cloud and the EU Control Plane – Special Considerations

This chapter will show you some important differences that come into play when working with Government Cloud versus the EU control plane. The chapter will give a brief introduction to FedRAMP compliance. You will also learn about how Government Cloud is deployed in a special AWS Region that is FedRAMP-compliant.

In this chapter, we will cover the following topics:

- FedRAMP requirements and compliance
- Government Cloud considerations
- EU compliance with the EU control plane

FedRAMP compliance

A standardized method for the security assessment, authorization, and ongoing monitoring of cloud products and services is offered by the **Federal Risk and Authorization Management Program (FedRAMP)**, which is a government-wide initiative in the United States. For cloud deployments and service models at the low- and moderate-risk impact levels within federal agencies, it is an obligatory program. MuleSoft Government Cloud is designed to be FedRAMP-compliant. Here's what that means:

- **Security assessment**: To make sure MuleSoft Government Cloud satisfies FedRAMP requirements, it has undergone a thorough security evaluation. Demonstrating efficient defense against data breaches and other security incidents is part of this.

- **Authorization**: MuleSoft Government Cloud has obtained authorization indicating that the platform has satisfied FedRAMP requirements following the successful completion of the security assessment.

- **Continuous monitoring**: MuleSoft keeps an eye on Government Cloud's security to make sure FedRAMP regulations are being followed. Regular reporting and security control updates are part of this.

- **Data protection**: MuleSoft Government Cloud offers strong data protection features, such as secure data transfer, access controls, and data encryption. These steps are intended to satisfy the strict security requirements outlined by FedRAMP.

- **Transparency**: MuleSoft keeps its security procedures open and honest as part of its dedication to maintaining FedRAMP standards. Users can confirm that the appropriate precautions are taken thanks to this.

In effect, FedRAMP compliance means MuleSoft Government Cloud is a trusted cloud service provider that meets stringent security standards, making it suitable for use by US government agencies and their partners.

A **third-party assessment organization** (**3PAO**) carried out the security assessment in compliance with FedRAMP and NIST 800-53A regulations. This assessed the effectiveness of the security controls in place to safeguard the availability, confidentiality, and integrity of MuleSoft's Government Cloud, as well as the data it handles, transfers, and stores.

The Government Cloud environment of MuleSoft is set up in **Amazon Web Services** (**AWS**) on AWS GovCloud. AWS GovCloud is an **International Traffic in Arms Regulations** (**ITAR**) -compliant, FedRAMP high-authorized environment with provisional DOD IL2, IM4, and IA5 authorizations. To protect the confidentiality, integrity, and availability of government data properly, MuleSoft Goverment cloud has reinforced its configuration in AWS by ensuring compliance with FedRAMP special requirements.

What is MuleSoft Government Cloud?

MuleSoft's Government Cloud is a customized version of the Anypoint Platform, created especially for government organizations. It offers a safe, FedRAMP-compliant environment in which to create and implement integrations and APIs. All data and application traffic stays behind a secure network barrier for improved security, guaranteeing adherence to laws requiring limited access and data privacy.

The following are the key features of Government Cloud:

- **FedRAMP-authorized**: MuleSoft's Government Cloud conforms to the regulatory standard imposed by the government, which incorporates sophisticated security safeguards

- **Safe, isolated platform**: To offer the highest level of data protection for sensitive information, Government Cloud runs inside an isolated network

- **Design, build, deploy, and manage APIs**: Government Cloud gives users the same capabilities as the basic Anypoint Platform, enabling them to plan, develop, implement, and oversee APIs and integrations all within one package

- **Connectivity to any system**: Any system, service, or data source can be connected securely thanks to Government Cloud

- **High availability**: It provides a zero-downtime automated capacity scaling and management of cloud data flow

MuleSoft Government Cloud encompasses all the runtime plane capabilities (services and the Mule runtime engine) of Anypoint Platform, together with a portion of the control plane (browser-based administration of APIs and instances of the Mule runtime engine) functionality. End-to-end API life cycle management and the whole API-led connection technique are supported by Government Cloud. Government organizations can use MuleSoft's Government Cloud to build, deploy, and manage integrations and APIs while adhering to stringent security and compliance requirements. MuleSoft's Government Cloud is a powerful API-led connectivity tool.

Government Cloud considerations

When contemplating MuleSoft Government Cloud, it's important to bear in mind the following:

- **Compliance**: All cloud services used by the US government must comply with FedRAMP, which is met by MuleSoft Government Cloud.

- **Enhanced security**: To safeguard sensitive data, MuleSoft Government Cloud provides cutting-edge security features and protocols. They consist of data protection, access controls, and strong network security.

- **Data residency**: All data and metadata are located inside US borders, which is advantageous for government organizations with stringent requirements regarding data residency.

- **Integration capabilities**: MuleSoft offers robust API-led connectivity features, such as safe system, service, and data source connections.

- **Dedicated environment**: To ensure higher dependability and performance, Government Cloud offers a dedicated environment that isolates capacity.

- **High availability**: To ensure uptime, the platform is built with multiple active instances for high availability.

- **Scalability**: The platform provides scalable solutions, including adjustments for variations in data volume and user count, to satisfy agencies' evolving needs and requirements.

- **Frequent updates**: To maintain compliance with changing security and regulatory standards, MuleSoft updates its Government Cloud platform regularly.

- **Non-functional requirements**: Aside from functional requirements, other factors that may affect the user experience are system performance, latency, and uptime.

By keeping in mind these factors, government organizations can make the most of MuleSoft Government Cloud while maintaining legal compliance and providing citizens with better digital services.

Security in MuleSoft Government Cloud

As stated, MuleSoft Government Cloud meets all the FedRAMP security requirements, compliance, and standards. MuleSoft Government Cloud also adheres to the following additional security protocols:

- **Federal Information Processing Standards** (FIPS 140-2)
- **Transport Layer Security** (TLS) 1.2 encryption
- **National Institute of Standards and Technology** (NIST) 800-53
- **Commonwealth of Independent States** (CIS) benchmarks

Anypoint Virtual Private Cloud and Virtual Private Network in MuleSoft Government Cloud

MuleSoft's Government Cloud uses Anypoint **Virtual Private Cloud** (**VPC**) and **Virtual Private Network** (**VPN**) to isolate Mule applications and offer safe, private connections between those apps and on-premises networks:

- **Anypoint VPC**: This lets you create a virtual network that is under your control and is like a private, isolated area inside MuleSoft's Government Cloud. A VPC allows you to create a virtual private network, with resources such as apps and APIs that are completely isolated from all other resources in Government Cloud.

- **Anypoint VPN**: VPNs extend a private network and allow resources to send and receive data as if they were directly connected to the private network. Anypoint VPN guarantees the security and encryption of all data transferred over the public internet between your Anypoint VPC and your on-premises network.

An additional degree of security is added by isolating your application data from public view using Anypoint VPC. Anypoint VPN connects securely your on-premises network to your VPC, allowing you to access your information from your private network without worrying about data getting intercepted during transit. By offering secure, private data ingress and egress points, Anypoint VPC and VPN work together to increase system security and privacy.

They offer advantages, including improved network performance, data security, and more network customization options.

These tools are particularly significant in the context of Government Cloud because they address the higher security and compliance requirements that are inherent to government organizations.

A dedicated load balancer in MuleSoft Government Cloud

A Government Cloud environment includes a dedicated load balancer, which is a cloud-based service that distributes incoming network traffic to multiple MuleSoft application workers in Government Cloud. This ensures that the load is distributed evenly across the environment, thereby promoting effective resource use, optimum performance, and greater availability of applications.

The following are the key benefits of the presence of a dedicated load balancer in MuleSoft Government Cloud:

- **Improved performance**: By evenly distributing network traffic, load balancers help prevent any single application worker from becoming a bottleneck of performance.

- **Increased reliability and availability**: The load balancer reroutes traffic to other operational servers so that your application remains available when there is a problem with an operation worker.

- **Secure Sockets Layer (SSL) termination**: Support for SSL termination is provided by a separate load balancer. This implies that the load balancer handles SSL handshakes with a user session, which frees up resources for backend application workers and improves system performance.

- **Supports scaling**: Dedicated load balancers also work effectively in scalable environments, dynamically distributing network loads across numerous instances as they go in and out of service.

- **Custom domains**: You can also configure routing rules that allow traffic to be directed to specific domains or multiple domains using a dedicated load balancer.

The use of a dedicated load-balancing server is especially important to maintain high availability and performance, where mission-critical applications are frequently housed in Government Cloud.

The dedicated load balancer in Government Cloud exposes two A records to accept traffic from local private networks and public networks. One of these records is internal (`internal-<lb-name>.lb-gprod-rt.anypointdns.net`) and the other is external (`<lb-name>.lb-gprod-rt.anypointdns.net`).

The MuleSoft Government Cloud control plane

MuleSoft Government Cloud supports Anypoint Platform as a control plane that is FedRAMP-compliant. The control plane is where you design, deploy, share, and manage APIs and applications.

The following components are included in the control plane:

- Anypoint Design Center to design API specifications

- Anypoint Management Center to manage users, APIs, and integrations

- Anypoint Exchange is a marketplace to publish and share API specifications, APIs, and integration

- Anypoint Runtime Manager for the deployment of API and integration into the cloud or data centers

The MuleSoft Government Cloud runtime plane

APIs and Mule applications are deployed and made available to users on the runtime plane component of Anypoint Platform. The Mule runtime server, Anypoint connectors, and support services are part of the running plane.

Standalone Mule support in MuleSoft Government Cloud

MuleSoft Government Cloud deployment permits the deployment of Mule runtime engine instances into an on-premises environment (standalone Mule instances). Standalone Mule instances, and MuleSoft support for them, are outside the scope of FedRAMP. This means the customer is responsible for ensuring that all data exchanged with Salesforce complies with any applicable data protection principles, requirements, and standards. Review the MuleSoft System Security Plan for the FedRAMP scope.

Mule runtime version 4.1.x or later and the runtime agent version 2.4.9 or later are required for FIPS compliance. Standalone Mule support enables federal, state, and local government customers to deploy standalone Mule instances inside their private clouds or on-premises environment and manage them, using the MuleSoft Government Cloud control plane.

The following components are not supported by MuleSoft Government Cloud:

- Anypoint Analytics
- Anypoint Code Builder
- API Data Gateway
- API Governance
- Anypoint Flex Gateway
- Anypoint Runtime Fabric
- Anypoint Security
- Anypoint Service Mesh

Deployment models for MuleSoft Government Cloud

There are two options when deploying Government Cloud. The first option is the fully managed model, where the control and runtime planes are in the cloud. The second option is to have the control plane in the cloud and the runtime plane in the customer's data center. If the control plane is in the cloud and the runtime plane is hosted in the MuleSoft cloud or the customer's data center, you can also use a combination of both options.

A fully managed deployment model (the control plane and the runtime plane managed by MuleSoft)

In this deployment model, the control and runtime planes will be managed by MuleSoft. Customers don't have to worry about the underlying infrastructure, and it is completely FedRAMP-compliant.

Figure 13.1 shows the architecture of the fully managed deployment model.

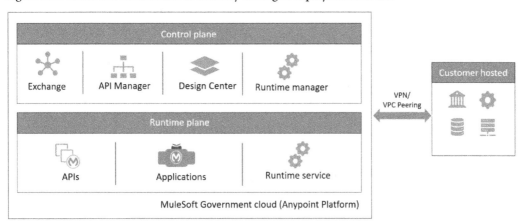

Figure 13.1: The fully managed deployment model

The following are the benefits of the fully managed deployment model:

- It supports high availability, scalability, and an intelligent healing mechanism
- 99.99% uptime
- It's able to manage multiple Mule runtime versions
- FedRAMP-compliant
- Fault-tolerant
- MuleSoft is responsible for managing the underlying infrastructure to run MuleSoft applications
- Application isolation
- Government Cloud can connect to on-premises data centers or private clouds using Anypoint VPN and VPC peering

The following is the primary limitation of the fully managed deployment model:

- Latency can be experienced while connecting to on-premises data sources, services, and resources

The hybrid deployment model (the control plane managed by MuleSoft and the runtime plane managed by customers)

With the hybrid option, users can host the Mule runtime server and associated APIs in a self-managed environment and can use the MuleSoft control plane to manage the APIs. The Mule runtime server can be installed in a third-party cloud such as AWS, Microsoft Azure, GCP, OCI, or another cloud infrastructure provider, or it can run on a physical server or virtual machine.

The customer is also in charge of providing the infrastructure and the framework for high availability, failover, clustering, and load balancing when using customer-hosted runtimes.

Figure 13.2 shows the architecture of the hybrid managed deployment model.

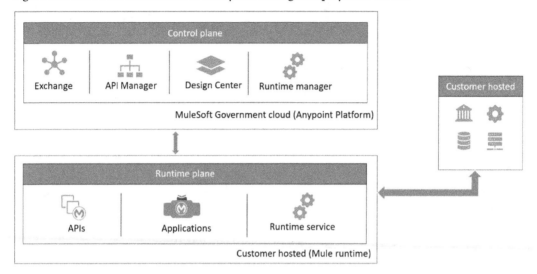

Figure 13.2: The hybrid managed deployment model

The following are the benefits of the hybrid managed deployment model:

- Low latency when connecting on-premises resources, data sources, and services
- Supports a variety of servers and **virtual machines** (**VMs**) for on-premises and cloud data centers' runtimes
- Data will not leave the customer's data center
- One of the most flexible deployment models

The following are the limitations of the hybrid managed deployment model:

- The customer is responsible for managing and provisioning the infrastructure for running Mule applications
- The customer is responsible for managing non-functional requirements such as high availability, scalability, and other network and firewall configurations

We have discussed Government Cloud, a platform provided by MuleSoft for government agencies to manage and run APIs. In the next section, we will examine the EU control plane.

The EU control plane

MuleSoft gives you the alternative of hosting Anypoint Platform completely in the EU region. For the purposes of EU geolocation-based data storage regulations, MuleSoft provides a European Anypoint Platform control plane (an EU control plane). Customers in Europe who are compelled by law to keep all their data processing and storage in physical locations within the EU can use this platform.

All aspects of the runtime plane, including management, integration, and API control, are located within EU borders. The EU retains control over all data, including runtime management, control traffic, and data in transit and at rest. Additionally, it guarantees that users adhere to the strictest security guidelines and the EU's **General Data Protection Regulation (GDPR)**.

MuleSoft hosts Anypoint Platform entirely in the EU region (with data centers based in the cities of Dublin and Frankfurt). This enables you to manage and deploy the MuleSoft APIs and their related data within the EU.

In addition to the EU control plane, MuleSoft allows you to deploy Mule applications in the EU region, which means you can host the runtime plane in the EU region. This ensures that you can meet the EU regulatory requirements and compliance.

> **Note**
>
> The EU control plane can be accessed at `https://eu1.anypoint.mulesoft.com`. EU control plane usage is limited to eligible clients only and requires an application.

EU control plane considerations

There are various things to consider before using MuleSoft's EU control plane, including the following:

- **Compliance**: The EU control plane assists in making sure that your data complies with GDPR and other strict EU data protection regulations.

- **Data residency**: All application data remains within the EU while it is in transit and at rest. For organizations that must adhere to regulations regarding data sovereignty, this is especially crucial.

- **Security standards**: MuleSoft makes sure that your data is well protected by adhering to the strictest security standards.

Nevertheless, there are also disadvantages, such as the following:

- **Restricted geographic coverage**: Currently, MuleSoft's EU control plane is only accessible within the European Union. If your company conducts business outside of the EU, you may need to investigate other regional or global control plane options.

- **Performance**: Selecting the EU control plane may affect latency, depending on where your users or systems are located.

- **Service availability**: MuleSoft's capabilities and service availability may differ from the US control plane, depending on the infrastructure and support provided in the area.

- **Costs**: Using the EU control plane rather than the default US plane may incur additional costs based on your contract and usage.

- **Data transfer**: It may be difficult and time-consuming to move your data from MuleSoft's US control plane to the EU control plane if you currently use the US control plane.

Deploying applications to the EU control plane

Deploying an application to the EU control plane is just like with the US control plane. During deployment, you need to make sure that you select a region that falls inside the EU. There are two regions supported, Dublin and Frankfurt. The topic of deploying applications to CloudHub 1.0 and CloudHub 2.0 was covered in *Chapters 9* and *10*, so refer to those chapters for more information if required.

Object Store in the EU control plane

Object Store V2 is used by default by Mule applications created in the EU control plane. To utilize this version, there are no platform or application configuration changes required. The EU control plane does not support Object Store V1.

Moving from the US control plane to the EU control plane

There is no automated migration process or tool to move an organization from the US control plane to the EU control plane for current customers who already have applications, resources, and assets deployed in the US control plane and wish to move/migrate to the EU version.

These platforms are purposefully kept apart from one another, and so any apps, resources, and other assets must be created from scratch in the EU control plane. As any customer with significant deployments in the US control plane is likely to find this to be a labor-intensive task, check with your account executive about the possible use of MuleSoft services to help with migration planning.

Anypoint VPC and VPN in the EU control plane

The EU control plane enables the use of Anypoint VPC to create virtual, isolated networks to run MuleSoft applications. The EU control plane also supports network connectivity options such as Anypoint VPN to access the resources from on-premises data centers or private networks. Other network connectivity options such as VPC peering and AWS Transit Gateway are also supported in the EU control plane.

Refer to *Chapter 9* for additional details on the Anypoint VPC and network connectivity options, such as Anypoint VPN, VPC peering, and Transit Gateway configurations.

Anypoint Dedicated Load Balancer (DLB) in the EU control plane

Anypoint DLB is an optional component of the EU control plane. It is used to route HTTP/HTTPs traffic to applications deployed within Anypoint VPC.

A dedicated load balancer in the EU control plane exposes two A records to accept traffic from local private networks and public networks. One of these records is internal (`internal-<lb-name>.lb-prod-eu-rt.anypointdns.net`) and the other is external (`<lb-name>.lb-prod-eu-rt.anypointdns.net`).

Refer to *Chapter 9* for additional details on Anypoint DLB configurations if required.

Summary

In this chapter, we walked you through Government Cloud and the EU control plane that MuleSoft provides. We discussed the considerations around Government Cloud and the EU control plane. We also saw how Government Cloud and the EU control plane support several different deployment models.

In the next chapter, we're going to examine Anypoint monitoring and alerts.

Further reading

- MuleSoft Government Cloud: `https://docs.mulesoft.com/gov-cloud/`
- The MuleSoft EU control plane: `https://docs.mulesoft.com/eu-control-plane/`

Functional Monitoring, Alerts, and Operation Monitors

In this chapter, we will discuss how to monitor MuleSoft applications that have been deployed to CloudHub, on-premises, and Runtime Fabric. Application monitoring is critical for gaining visibility into the performance, availability, and correctness of applications. MuleSoft provides Anypoint Monitoring, which monitors MuleSoft applications and provides application performance visibility.

In this chapter, we will cover the following topics:

- What is Anypoint Monitoring?
- Anypoint Monitoring capabilities
- Functional Monitoring
- API alerts and notifications
- API logging and troubleshooting
- API Manager monitoring
- Runtime Manager monitoring

Why is API monitoring required?

API monitoring ensures that APIs are working as expected and are available. In the modern era, most organizations are engaged in digital transformation, and they are relying on APIs to enable this digital transformation. Most organizations depend on APIs for critical business transactions. For organizations, their APIs must always be available to ensure business continuity, and it is vital to implement robust monitoring systems for APIs to ensure their performance and correctness.

Monitoring APIs helps developers discover any issues before they escalate and mitigate any risks that might result in revenue loss.

For example, let's say that an API related to payment is not responding and is impacting the payments that customers are making from your eCommerce application. This may lead to revenue loss for your business. Monitoring can troubleshoot the issue and fix it quickly to prevent any further revenue loss.

Anypoint Monitoring

Anypoint Monitoring is the out-of-the-box feature provided by MuleSoft for monitoring APIs or applications that are deployed to CloudHub, the on-premises Mule runtime, and Runtime Fabric. This tool can identify and troubleshoot issues related to MuleSoft APIs, measure the performance of APIs, and resolve issues quickly.

Any organization's DevOps team can use Anypoint Monitoring to diagnose issues and identify solutions quickly. With this tool, the overall time to identify issues will be reduced. It also helps to resolve issues through alerts, a data visualization tool, aggregated metrics, and more.

The monitoring and analytics capabilities of Anypoint API Manager

Anypoint API Manager provides built-in analytics dashboards that show **Requests by Location**, **Requests by Date**, **Requests by Platform**, and **Requests by Application** for a certain period. They show the performance of the APIs and how they are being used. Policy violations can be also included in API analytics dashboards and API charts. API Manager analytics are retained for 30 days:

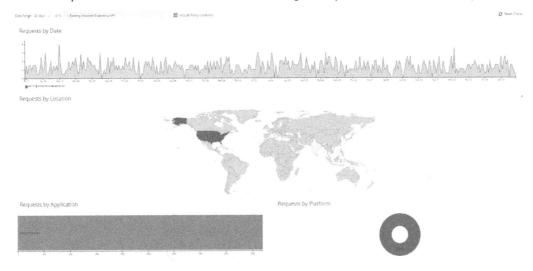

Figure 14.1 - API monitoring and analytics with API Manager

Figure 14.1 shows an out-of-the-box dashboard showing **Requests by Application**, **Requests by Location**, **Requests by Platform**, and **Requests by Date**.

API Manager allows you to create custom dashboards for metrics such as **Request Size**, **Requests**, **Response Size**, and **Response Time**, as shown in *Figure 14.2*:

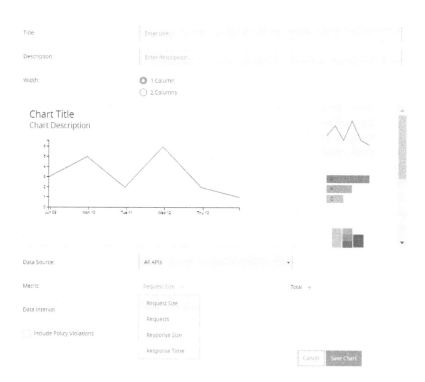

Figure 14.2 - Custom dashboard in API Manager

Figure 14.2 shows how to create a customer dashboard for the various metrics, such as request and response size, response time, and number of requests.

Understanding Mule API analytics charts

API Manager provides three different charts for each API instance: **Requests Summary**, **Top Apps**, and **Latency**.

Understanding the Requests Summary chart

This chart shows the number of requests received for the duration you choose.

The default duration is 1 hour:

Figure 14.3 - Requests Summary chart

Let's take a look at what the different graph lines are for:

- **Green**: Successful request that returned HTTP status code 1xx to 3xx

- **Gray**: Failed request that returned HTTP status code 4xx (client error)

- **Blue**: Failed request that returned HTTP status code 5xx (server error)

Understanding the Top Apps chart

The **Tops Apps** chart shows the total number of requests made to the API instance by each application for the top 5 applications calling that API instance:

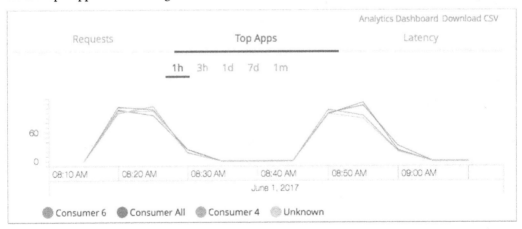

Figure 14.4 - Top Apps chart

Each color in the charts represents one of the top five applications.

Understanding the Latency chart

The **Latency** chart displays the average response time for a selected period. This helps us understand the performance of the API:

Figure 14.5 - Latency chart

The higher the response time (high latency), the worse the performance.

API Manager alerts

API Manager allows you to set up various alerts for the API instance that you have created. Alerts can be set up for **Request Count**, **Response Code**, **Policy Violation**, and **Response Time**. This can be easily set up in API Manager for the API instance:

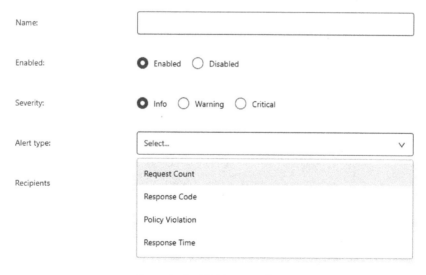

Figure 14.6 - API Manager alerts

To set up alerts, you must configure the required alerts in your API Manager instances and provide target recipients that should receive the alert notifications.

Understanding the Mule Analytics Event API

The Mule Analytics Event API allows you to generate reports or charts. Reports can be generated for a specific environment for multiple APIs, or different reports can be generated for the same APIs. The Analytics Event API has a retention policy of 30 days and a data availability delay of up to 10 minutes. This API enforces a usage limit of 10 requests per minute, with a maximum of 20,000 events per request. Request rates of more than 10 requests per minute will be throttled.

API reports

API Manager allows you to create API reports, which can identify events such as a policy violation due to IP blacklisting or JWT validation failure:

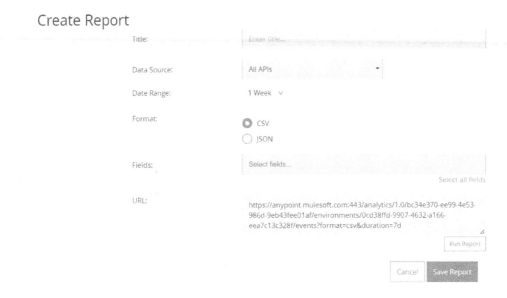

Figure 14.7 - Anypoint Monitoring report

Reports can be generated in CSV or JSON format for all APIs or individual APIs.

Understanding Anypoint Monitoring

Anypoint Monitoring is integrated with Anypoint Platform so that it can monitor applications deployed on-premises, on CloudHub, and Runtime Fabric. Anypoint Monitoring provides built-in dashboards and allows you to create custom dashboards for various metrics.

The following are the benefits of Anypoint Monitoring:

- Monitor all microservices, applications, and APIs from a single pane of glass
- Reduce the **mean time to resolution (MTTR)**
- Understand the application's performance and health instantly
- Set up alerts for things such as **Response Time Exceeded** and **CPU and Memory Utilization Exceeded**
- Proactively identify issues and resolve them quickly without much impact

Dashboards

Anypoint Monitoring provides a built-in dashboard that provides information about application metrics. The dashboard also contains metrics about inbound and outbound requests, application performance, failure metrics, and infrastructure-related metrics for applications deployed to CloudHub. The following figure shows the built-in chart provided by Anypoint Monitoring:

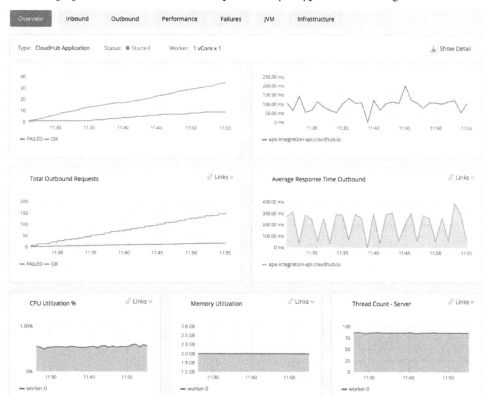

Figure 14.8 - Anypoint Monitoring dashboard

This dashboard helps you identify anomalies, troubleshoot issues in the application, and resolve issues instantly.

Anypoint Monitoring allows you to configure custom dashboards based on various metrics. You can easily configure custom dashboards via the Anypoint Monitoring console:

Figure 14.9 - Anypoint Monitoring custom dashboard

The following custom dashboards can be configured with Anypoint Monitoring:

- **Graph**: A wide variety of metrics can be displayed as time series data. This custom dashboard supports query language.

- **Singlestat**: Displays summary statistics (a single total or number) for a single grouping of time series data.

- **Table**: A wide variety of metrics can be displayed as time series data in tabular format.

- **Text**: Displays textual information in HTML format, such as adding a header to a chart.

Anypoint Monitoring event-driven alerts

Anypoint Monitoring provides out-of-the-box alerts that you can configure to notify others of any abnormalities in your application network. For example, imagine that you want to add an alert when the response time is exceeded; this can easily be configured in the Anypoint Monitoring alert console:

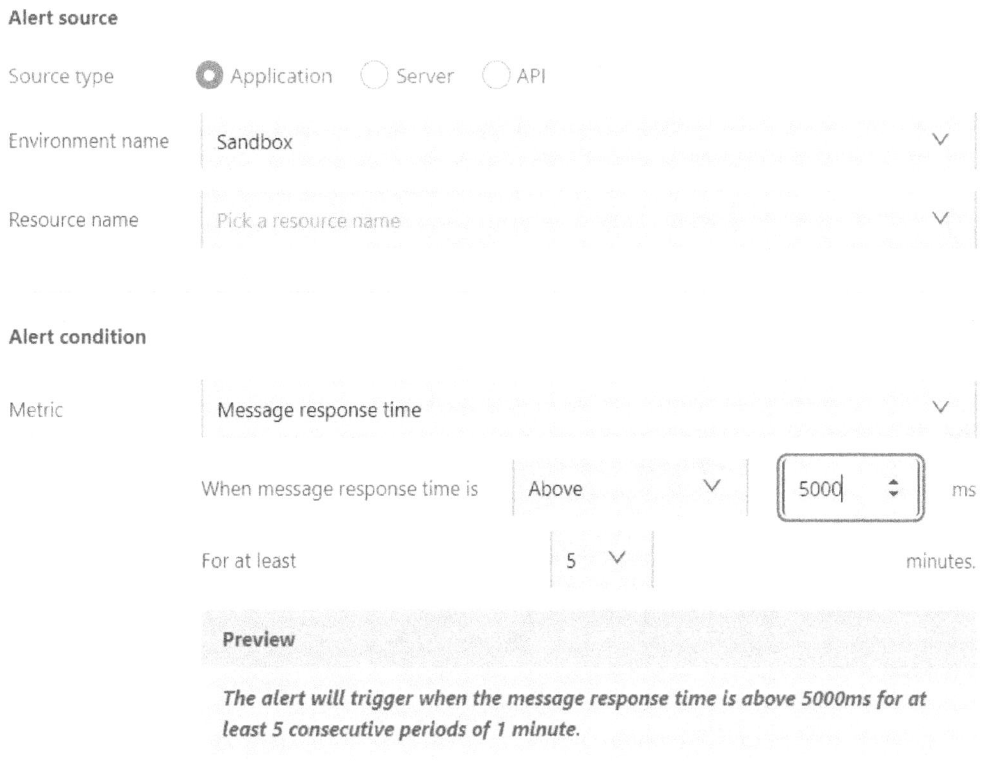

Alert source

Source type   ⦿ Application   ◯ Server   ◯ API

Environment name   Sandbox   ⌄

Resource name   Pick a resource name   ⌄

Alert condition

Metric   Message response time   ⌄

                     When message response time is   Above   ⌄ | 5000 ⬍ | ms

                     For at least   5   ⌄   minutes.

┌───┐
│ Preview   │
└───┘

*The alert will trigger when the message response time is above 5000ms for at
least 5 consecutive periods of 1 minute.*

Figure 14.10 - Anypoint Monitoring event-driven alerts

The alert will be triggered when the message response time is above 5 ms for at least 5 consecutive periods of 1 minute:

Figure 14.11 - Anypoint Monitoring event-driven alerts

In the same way, you can configure other alerts, such as **Message count**, **CPU utilization**, **Memory utilization**, and **Message error count**.

Enabling Anypoint Monitoring for applications deployed to CloudHub

There are two ways to enable Anypoint Monitoring for applications deployed to CloudHub. Let's take a look.

Using the Anypoint Monitoring console

On the **Settings** tab of Anypoint Monitoring, you can select **CloudHub** and enable Anypoint Monitoring for new applications that have been deployed to CloudHub. This means that any newly deployed application will have Anypoint Monitoring enabled.

For any existing application, you can simply enable/disable Anypoint Monitoring for individual applications by selecting the environment and application for which Anypoint Monitoring needs to be enabled or disabled. To do this, check or uncheck the checkbox for each application:

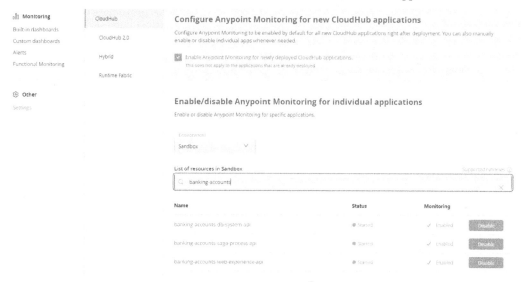

Figure 14.12 - Enabling Anypoint Monitoring (CloudHub)

Enabling Anypoint Monitoring in CloudHub's settings

Anypoint Monitoring can be enabled by adding the `anypoint.platform.config.analytics.agent.enabled=true` property in the application settings of Runtime Manager in CloudHub. To disable Anypoint Monitoring, change this property's value to `false`. Enabling Anypoint Monitoring can increase the CPU utilization of the application. However, note that utilization variation depends on the application's behavior, such as the inbound and outbound call rate:

Figure 14.13 - Enabling Anypoint Monitoring from Runtime Manager (CloudHub)

Anypoint Monitoring can be disabled for an application that's been deployed to CloudHub by setting `anypoint.platform.config.analytics.agent.enabled` to `false`.

Enabling Anypoint Monitoring for applications deployed to CloudHub 2.0

Applications deployed to CloudHub 2.0 have Anypoint Monitoring enabled by default. You don't have to do any additional configuration to enable Anypoint Monitoring for applications deployed to CloudHub 2.0:

Figure 14.14 - Enabling Anypoint Monitoring (CloudHub 2.0)

To disable Anypoint Monitoring for applications deployed to CloudHub 2.0, add the `anypoint.platform.config.analytics.agent.enabled=false` property to the application's settings in the Runtime Manager console:

Figure 14.15 - Disabling Anypoint Monitoring from Runtime Manager (CloudHub 2.0)

Enabling Anypoint Monitoring for applications deployed to Runtime Fabric

Anypoint Monitoring is enabled for applications that are deployed to Runtime Fabric by default:

Figure 14.16 - Enabling Anypoint Monitoring (Runtime Fabric)

To disable Anypoint Monitoring for applications that are deployed to Runtime Fabric, add the `anypoint.platform.config.analytics.agent.enabled=false` property to the application settings in the Runtime Fabric console.

Enabling Anypoint Monitoring for applications deployed in hybrid environments

A hybrid environment in this context means that the runtime plane is in your data center and the control plane is in Anypoint Platform. To enable Anypoint Monitoring for applications deployed in a hybrid environment, an Anypoint Monitoring agent needs to be set up on the runtime plane so that it can send monitoring data to the Anypoint Monitoring API endpoints.

To enable Anypoint Monitoring, download the am.zip file from the Anypoint Monitoring console by selecting the environment and server, server group, or cluster, and follow the instructions given on the console to set up the Anypoint Monitoring agent on the runtime plane:

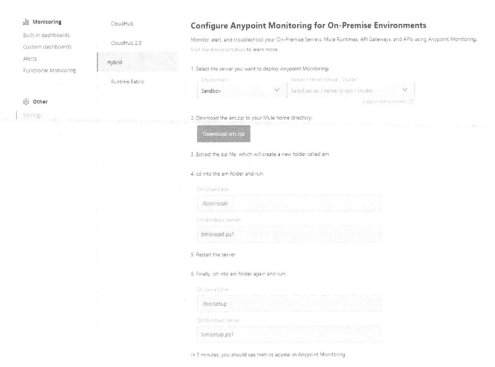

Figure 14.17 - Enabling Anypoint Monitoring (hybrid environments)

Once the agent has been set up, restart the Mule runtime. Within 5-10 minutes, application metrics will start appearing on Anypoint Monitoring's built-in dashboards:

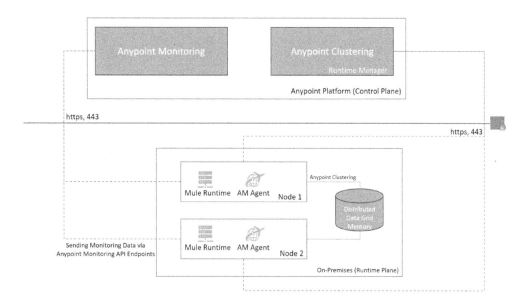

Figure 14.18 - Anypoint Monitoring architecture (hybrid environments)

Enabling Anypoint Monitoring can increase the CPU utilization of the application, but any variation in utilization depends on the application's behavior, such as inbound and outbound call rates.

Typically, CPU utilization impact will be less than 5% for the application. However, to come to an accurate figure, impact analysis must be done by performing application testing on different environments. You can do this by enabling and disabling Anypoint Monitoring.

Data retention policy and limits

The following table describes the data retention policy and limits for Anypoint Monitoring:

Gold and Platinum Subscriptions	Limit
Logs	30 days or 100 MB.
Application Metrics	30 days.
Enhanced API Metrics	30 days. The limit for data in client applications is 30 days.
Basic Alerts for Mule Apps and Servers	50 alerts.
Basic Alerts for APIs	Six basic alerts per instance.

Titanium Subscriptions	Limit
Logs	In raw format, your logs can occupy as much space as you receive with your Titanium subscription.
Application Metrics	365 days.
Searchable logs	Additional storage that is 10% of the size of purchased storage for indexes for searchable logs.
Enhanced API Metrics	30 days. The limit for data in client applications is 30 days.
Custom Metrics	365 days.
Advanced Alerts	20 per parent organization.
Basic Alerts for Mule Apps and Servers	50 times the number of productions vCores in your organization plus 100.
Basic Alerts for APIs	10 basic alerts per instance.

Table 14.1 - Anypoint Monitoring data retention policy and limits

Monitoring connectors

Anypoint provides a built-in dashboard for Anypoint connectors and includes databases, Salesforce, Anypoint MQ, JMS, SMTP, HTTP, and all other Anypoint connectors. Three metrics are provided for each connector:

- **Requests:** The average number of requests for the connector, grouped by automatic time intervals

- **Response Time:** The average response time for the connector, grouped by automatic time intervals

- **Failures:** The average number of request failures for the connector, grouped by automatic time intervals:

Figure 14.19 - Anypoint Monitoring connectors metrics

Figure 14.19 shows the metrics for the database and salesforce connectors.

Server information for hybrid environments

When we register a server in Anypoint Platform (on the control plane), it provides **CPU Utilization (%)** and **Heap Memory (MB)** metrics for that server, as well as the statuses of applications that are running on the server, alongside the number of Mule messages, response time, and errors for each application:

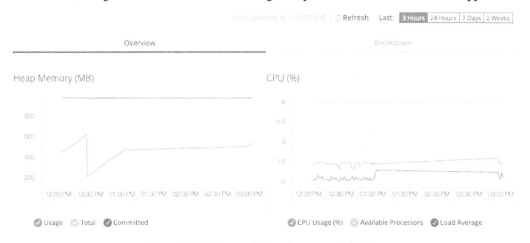

Figure 14.20 - Server CPU and memory utilization

Figure 14.20 shows the CPU and memory utilization for specific time intervals. You have the option to choose **3 Hours**, **24 Hours**, **7 Days**, or **2 Weeks**.

Enabling alerts for hybrid environments with Runtime Manager

MuleSoft provides out-of-the-box alerts that can be configured on servers, server groups, and clusters. Alerts can be configured in the Runtime Manager **Alerts** console. There is no rate limit on API manager alerts.

A variety of alerts can easily be configured.

The following alerts can be configured for servers:

- **Agent version changed**
- **Runtime version changed**
- **Server CPU usage**
- **Server load average**
- **Server memory usage**
- **Server thread count**

- **Server connected**
- **Server deleted**
- **Server disconnected**

The following alerts can be configured for server groups:

- **Server group connected**
- **Server group deleted**
- **Server group disconnected**
- **Server group's node CPU Usage**
- **Server group's node Load average**
- **Server group's node Memory Usage**
- **Server group's node Thread count**
- **Server group's node connected**
- **Server group's node disconnected**
- **Server added to server group**
- **Server removed from server group**

The following alerts can be configured for clusters:

- **Cluster connected**
- **Cluster deleted**
- **Cluster disconnected**
- **Cluster presents visibility issues**
- **Cluster's node CPU usage**
- **Cluster's node load average**
- **Cluster's node memory usage**
- **Cluster's node thread count**
- **Cluster's node connected**
- **Cluster's node disconnected**
- **Server added to cluster**
- **Server removed from cluster**

The following alerts can be configured on applications that have been deployed to hybrid environments:

- **Application undeployed**
- **Deployment failure**
- **Deployment success**
- **Number of Mule messages**
- **Number of errors**
- **Response time**

Enabling alerts for CloudHub with Runtime Manager

MuleSoft provides out-of-the-box alerts that can be configured on CloudHub. Alerts can be configured in the Runtime Manager **Alerts** console. There is no rate limit on API manager alerts.

The following alerts can be configured for applications deployed to CloudHub:

- CPU usage
- Custom application notification
- Deployment failed
- Deployment success
- Exceeds event traffic threshold
- Memory usage – Cloudhub
- Secure data gateway connected
- Secure data gateway disconnected
- Worker not responding

Enabling alerts for CloudHub 2.0 with Runtime Manager

MuleSoft provides out-of-the-box alerts that can be configured on CloudHub 2.0. Alerts can be configured in the Runtime Manager **Alerts** console. There is no rate limit on API Manager alerts.

The following alerts can be configured for applications deployed to CloudHub 2.0:

- Deployment failed
- Deployment success

The severity levels for alerts are **Critical**, **Warning**, and **Info**. Alerts can be configured on servers and applications. There are no out-of-the-box alerts available for applications that are deployed to Runtime Fabric.

Functional Monitoring

Functional Monitoring enables you to monitor the availability and reliability of the public APIs and private APIs that are part of your application networks. With Functional Monitoring enabled, you can continuously test APIs to measure their performance and functional behavior in production and non-production environments.

You can set up Functional Monitoring in the Functional Monitoring console in Anypoint Monitoring.

There are two ways to create a monitor in Functional Monitoring:

- Using the Anypoint Monitoring GUI
- Using the BAT CLI

Using the Anypoint Monitoring GUI on the Functional Monitoring console, you can create a monitor. Follow these steps:

1. **Set up the monitor**: Provide the monitor's name, select the location where you want to create the monitor, and schedule the monitor:

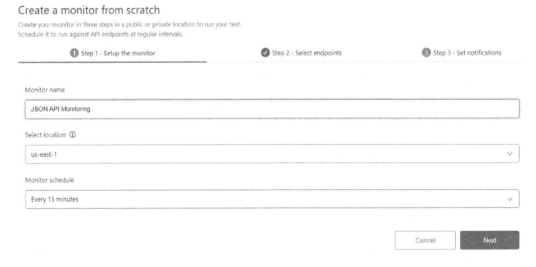

Figure 14.21 - Step 1 (Set up the monitor)

Next, we will select the endpoints that need to be monitored.

2. **Select endpoints**: Add one or more endpoints that need to be monitored. You can provide the API endpoint that needs to be monitored and, optionally, any headers. You can add one or more assertions to validate the HTTP status code, response body, or response header:

Figure 14.22 - Step 2 (Select endpoints)

In the next step, we will set the notifications. These can be email, slack, PagerDuty, and so on.

3. **Set notifications**: Functional Monitoring supports five types of **Notifier – Slack**, **PagerDuty**, **NewRelic**, **SumoLogic**, and **Email**:

Figure 14.23 - Step 3 (Select notifications)

Select which notifier you wish to use and click **Create Monitor**. This will create a monitor, which will continuously monitor and test the APIs. Once the monitor has been created, it will monitor the API endpoints continuously according to the schedule. You can add more schedules to the same monitor:

Figure 14.24 - API Functional Monitoring Dashboard

The following information is provided by the monitor:

- Average response times in milliseconds

- Status of the last execution

- Summary of the last few executions, such as **Assertions Status**

- Schedule information such as next run, schedule, execution location, and location status

- The option to add more schedules

- Duration of the test for the monitor

Monitoring the endpoints of public APIs

Functional Monitoring allows you to monitor public APIs in public locations. Public APIs have endpoints that are available publicly over the internet. Public locations are the regions that have been shared with other MuleSoft customers. Public locations can be associated with one or more schedules for than one monitor.

The following diagram depicts how to monitor public endpoints, which can have relationships with APIs, schedules, public locations, and environments:

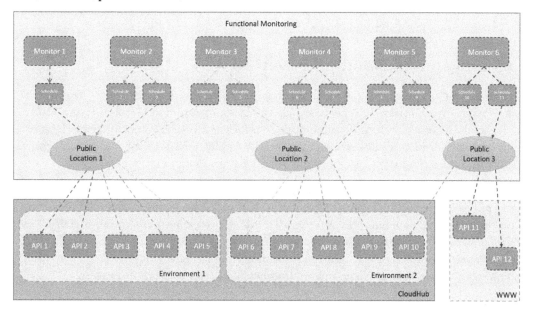

Figure 14.25 - Monitoring the endpoints of public APIs

The following monitors have been created in public locations for monitoring public endpoints:

- **Monitor 1 (single schedule, single public location, and single environment)**: Monitor 1 runs on a single schedule (**Schedule 1**), which is associated with **Public Location 1**. Monitor 1 is set up to test public **API 1** and public **API 2** in a single environment.

- **Monitor 2 (multiple schedules, single public location, and single environment)**: Monitor 2 runs on multiple schedules (**Schedule 2** and **Schedule 3**), and they are associated with **Public Location 1**. Monitor 2 is set up to test public **API 3** and public **API 4** in a single environment.

- **Monitor 3 (multiple schedules, multiple public locations, and multiple environments)**: Monitor 3 runs on multiple schedules (**Schedule 4** and **Schedule 5**), and they are associated with multiple public locations (**Public Location 1** and **Public Location 2**). Monitor 3 is set up to test **public API 5** and public **API 6** in multiple environments.

- **Monitor 4 (multiple schedules, single location, and single environment)**: Monitor 4 runs on multiple schedules (**Schedule 6** and **Schedule 7**), and they are associated with **Public Location 2**. Monitor 4 is set up to test public **API 7** and public **API 8** in a single environment.

- **Monitor 5 (multiple schedules, multiple locations, and single environment)**: Monitor 5 runs on multiple schedules (**Schedule 8** and **Schedule 9**), and they are associated with multiple public locations (**Public Location 2** and **Public Location 3**). Monitor 5 is set up to test public **API 9** and public **API 10** in a single environment.

- **Monitor 6 (multiple schedules, single location, and the World Wide Web): Monitor 6** runs on multiple schedules (**Schedule 10** and **Schedule 11**), and they are associated with a single public location (**Public Location 3**). **Monitor 6** is set up to test **API 11** and **API 12**, which are available over the World Wide Web.

Monitoring the endpoints of private APIs

Functional Monitoring allows you to monitor private endpoints that are accessible to the Anypoint Virtual Private Cloud. Private APIs are accessible within your network inside an Anypoint Virtual Private Cloud. Tests can only be run against private APIs that are accessible within the private location. Multiple private locations can be created in a single Anypoint Virtual Private Cloud and private locations that are associated with the Anypoint Virtual Private Cloud.

To set up a monitor for private endpoints running within Anypoint Virtual Private Cloud, we need to create a private location within Functional Monitoring that will create the application within Anypoint Virtual Private Cloud to monitor the private APIs. This will consume **0.2 vCores** by default. This configuration can be changed according to your requirements, such as more workers and worker size. To create a private location, select **Create new location** from the **Select location** dropdown while creating your monitor. Provide **Name** and **Environment** details for your private location:

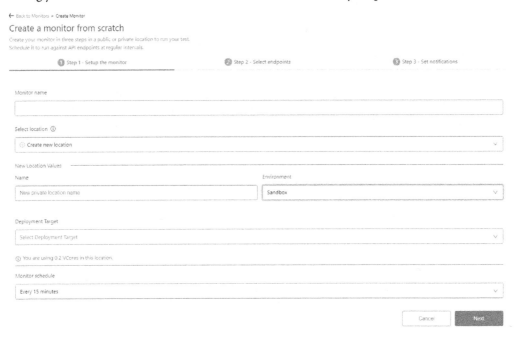

Figure 14.26 - Creating a private location and monitor in Functional Monitoring

Once the private location has been created, it will deploy the application in CloudHub within Anypoint Virtual Private Cloud so that you can monitor your private endpoints:

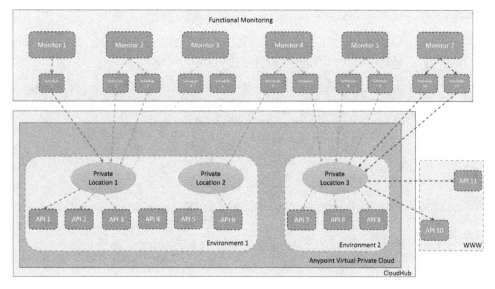

Figure 14.27 - Private location application deployed to CloudHub

In *Figure 14.27*, we can see that the application was deployed to CloudHub within Anypoint Virtual Private Cloud so that we can monitor private endpoints. It is also capable of monitoring public endpoints.

The following diagram shows how to monitor private endpoints that have relationships with APIs, schedules, private locations, and environments:

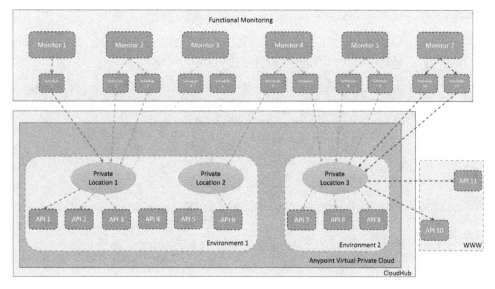

Figure 14.28 - Monitoring the endpoints of private APIs

The following monitors have been created in public locations for monitoring private endpoints:

- **Monitor 1 (single schedule, single private location, and single environment)**: **Monitor 1** runs on a single schedule (**Schedule 1**), which is associated with **Private Location 1**. **Monitor 1** is set up to test private **API 1** in a single environment.

- **Monitor 2 (multiple schedules, single private location, and single environment)**: **Monitor 2** runs on multiple schedules (**Schedule 2** and **Schedule 3**), which is associated with **Private Location 1**. **Monitor 2** is set up to test private **API 2** and private **API 3** in a single environment.

- **Monitor 3 (multiple schedules, multiple private locations, and single environment)**: **Monitor 3** runs on multiple schedules (**Schedule 4** and **Schedule 5**), which are associated with multiple private locations (**Private Location 1** and **Private Location 2**). Monitor 3 is set up to test public **API 5** and public **API 6** in multiple environments.

- **Monitor 4 (multiple schedules, multiple private locations, and multiple environments)**: **Monitor 4** runs on multiple schedules (**Schedule 6** and **Schedule 7**), which are associated with multiple private locations (**Public Location 1** and **Private Location 2**). **Monitor 4** is set up to test public **API 6** and public **API 7** in multiple environments.

- **Monitor 5 (multiple schedules, single private location, and single environment)**: **Monitor 5** runs on multiple schedules (**Schedule 8** and **Schedule 9**), which are associated with a single private location (**Private Location 3**). **Monitor 5** is set up to test public **API 8** and public **API 9** in a single environment.

- **Monitor 6 (multiple schedules, single private location, and the World Wide Web)**: **Monitor 6** runs on multiple schedules (**Schedule 10** and **Schedule 11**), which are associated with a single private location (**Public Location 3**). **Monitor 6** is set up to test **API 10** and **API 11**, which are available over the World Wide Web.

MuleSoft provides options so that you can monitor private endpoints from public locations. This can be easily achieved by adding a firewall rule to Anypoint Virtual Private Cloud.

In the Anypoint Virtual Private Cloud firewall rule, **Type** must be set to `https.port`, **Source** can be customized, and **Port Range** must be **8082**. For the custom source, add one of the following IP addresses shown in *Table 14.2*, depending on your public location:

Type	Source	Port Range	
https.port ⌄	3.82.89.58/32 ⌄	8082	⋯

Figure 14.29 - Anypoint Virtual Private Cloud firewall rules for monitoring private endpoints

With this approach, you don't have to create a private location to monitor private endpoints. This will result in you saving the vCores that are required for running the application so that you can monitor private endpoints from private locations:

Public Location	IP Address
us-east-1	3.82.89.58
us-east-2	3.128.151.139
eu-central-1	18.156.106.167

Table 14.2 - IP addresses (Public Location)

Table 14.2 shows various IP addresses for public locations.

Why is logging important?

Logging is important for any application for event and message tracing, troubleshooting, measuring application performance, and identifying errors that occur in an application. Logging is crucial for any developer and operational person to identify and troubleshoot issues quickly.

MuleSoft provides application and runtime logs to troubleshoot issues related to the application and the Mule runtime. The logger component can be used in your applications for monitoring and troubleshooting. It logs error information, payloads, and any other information. This component can be used anywhere in the flow to log strings or dataweave expressions, or a combination of strings and dataweave expressions.

Logs in Anypoint Monitoring

To enable logs in Anypoint Monitoring, you require a Titanium subscription. Anypoint Monitoring aggregates the log files, which you can then manage, search, filter, or analyze. Logs can be filtered by application, environment, log level, environment type, class, timestamp, worker, and so on. Anypoint Monitoring allows you to see logs in tabular or JSON format, and you can use advanced search queries to search the logs.

Understanding logging with MuleSoft applications deployed to CloudHub

Whenever an application is deployed to CloudHub, it will provide deployment logs, including system and worker logs for that application. The logs will be retained for 30 days (about 4 and a half weeks) or 100 MB of data, whichever limit comes first:

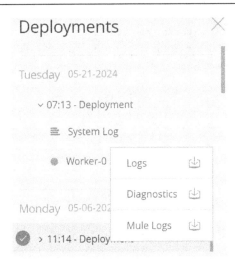

Figure 14.30 - CloudHub deployment logs

As shown in the preceding figure, CloudHub provides the option to download **Logs**, **Diagnostics**, and **Mule Logs**:

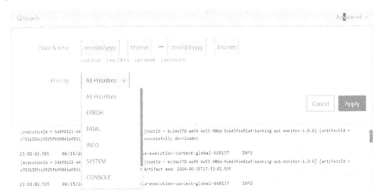

Figure 14.31 - CloudHub logs search

Figure 14.31 shows that logs can be searched based on their period and priority.

Sending CloudHub application logs to an external system

Applications that are deployed to CloudHub can be integrated with external logging systems such as ELK or Splunk using `log4j2.xml`. We need to disable the CloudHub logs settings if we want to send logs to an external system. By default, you will not see the option for disabling CloudHub Logs. To make it visible in the application settings of CloudHub, you need to contact the MuleSoft support team:

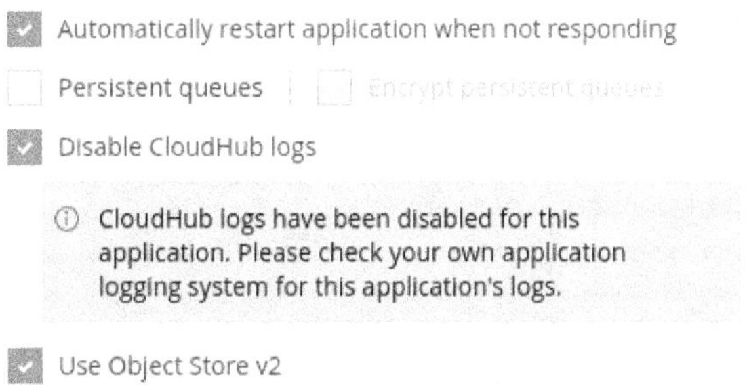

Figure 14.32 - Disabling CloudHub logs on CloudHub

Once the option is visible, as shown in *Figure 14.32*, you can check **Disable CloudHub logs** to send logs to external systems such as Splunk and ELK. Note that you also need to add an appender to the `log4j2.xml` file to send logs to an external system.

To send logs to Splunk, you can add a Splunk or HTTP appender to the `log4j2.xml` file of the application that's being deployed to CloudHub:

Here's the Splunk appender:

```
<SplunkHttp name="SPLUNK-CLOUD" source="mule-cloudhub-app"
url="http://localhost:8088/"
        token="b3a34eabd-b5f4-471431-97d2-e5b234af5bae9e"
        index="main"
        disableCertificateValidation="true">
        <PatternLayout pattern="[%d{MM-dd HH:mm:ss}] %-5p %c{1}
        [%t]: %m%n" />
</SplunkHttp>
```

Here's the HTTP appender:

```
<Http name="Splunk" url="http://localhost:8088/services/
collector/raw">
    <Property name="Authorization" value="Splunk eert8e102-5f55-40ad-
    a047-b55a82245419"></Property>
    <PatternLayout pattern="%-5p %d [%t] [event: %X{correlationId}] %c:
    %m%n"></PatternLayout>
</Http>
```

To send logs to ELK, you can add a socket appender to the `log4j2.xml` file of the application that's being deployed to CloudHub.

Here's the socket appender:

```
<Socket name="socket" host="${sys:elk.host}" port="${sys:elk.port}"
protocol="TCP">
    <PatternLayout pattern="%-5p %d [%t] [event: %X{correlationId}] %c:
    %m%n"></PatternLayout>
</Socket>
```

If you disable CloudHub logs but can still send logs to CloudHub, use Log4J2CloudhubLogAppender in log4j2.xml. Log4J2CloudhubLogAppender sends log data to CloudHub. Here's the log4j2 CloudHub appender:

```
<Log4J2CloudhubLogAppender name="CLOUDHUB"
            addressProvider="com.mulesoft.ch.logging.
            DefaultAggregatorAddressProvider"
            applicationContext="com.mulesoft.ch.logging.
            DefaultApplicationContext"
            appendRetryIntervalMs="${sys:logging.appendRetryInterval}"
            appendMaxAttempts="${sys:logging.appendMaxAttempts}"
            batchSendIntervalMs="${sys:logging.batchSendInterval}"
            batchMaxRecords="${sys:logging.batchMaxRecords}"
            memBufferMaxSize="${sys:logging.memBufferMaxSize}"
            journalMaxWriteBatchSize="${sys:logging.
            journalMaxBatchSize}"
            journalMaxFileSize="${sys:logging.journalMaxFileSize}"
            clientMaxPacketSize="${sys:logging.clientMaxPacketSize}"
            clientConnectTimeoutMs="${sys:logging.
            clientConnectTimeout}"
            clientSocketTimeoutMs="${sys:logging.clientSocketTimeout}"
            serverAddressPollIntervalMs="${sys:logging.
            serverAddressPollInterval}"
            serverHeartbeatSendIntervalMs="${sys:logging.
            serverHeartbeatSendIntervalMs}"
            statisticsPrintIntervalMs="${sys:logging.
            statisticsPrintIntervalMs}">
            <PatternLayout pattern="%-5p %d [%t] [event:
            %X{correlationId}] %c: %m%n"/>
</Log4J2CloudhubLogAppender>
```

Understanding logging with MuleSoft applications deployed to CloudHub 2.0

Whenever an application is deployed to CloudHub 2.0, it will provide runtime and application logs. In CloudHub 2.0, application and runtime logs are merged. They can be downloaded from the Runtime Manager GUI.

These logs are retained for 30 days (about 4 and a half weeks) or 200 MB of data, whichever limit comes first.

If **Enable application logs** is unchecked in the settings of the application, logs will not be forwarded to Anypoint Monitoring and Anypoint Runtime Manager:

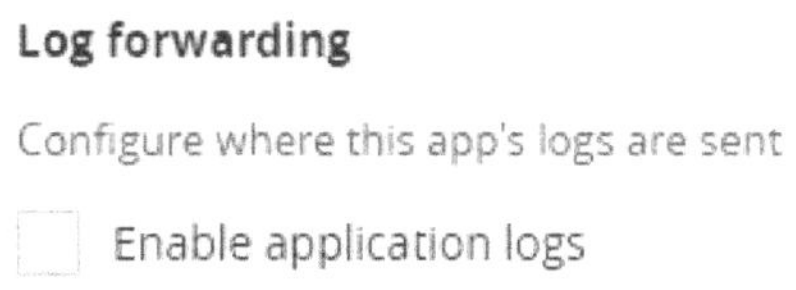

Log forwarding

Configure where this app's logs are sent

☐ Enable application logs

Figure 14.33 - Enable application logs in CloudHub 2.0

Applications that are deployed to CloudHub 2.0 can be integrated with an external logging system by configuring the relevant appender in the `log4j2.xml` file of the application, as discussed earlier in this chapter.

Understanding logging with MuleSoft applications deployed to on-premises/hybrid environments

Logs for applications that are deployed to an on-premises Mule runtime can be found in the `$MULE_HOME/logs` folder, where you can find application-specific logs and runtime logs. It is also possible to send logs to external systems by adding the appropriate appender to the `log4j2.xml` file.

As we have already discussed, we can use Splunk and an HTTP appender to send logs to Splunk, and a socket appender for sending logs to ELK.

Whenever an application is deployed in a hybrid environment, it is possible to configure Splunk or ELK to send event tracking or API analytics to Splunk or ELK. This can be enabled in the Server Plugin console in Runtime Manager:

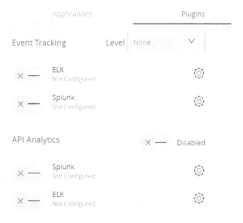

Figure 14.34 - Enabling logging for an application that's been
deployed on-premises in a hybrid environment

Figure 14.34 shows API analytics and event tracking, which can be enabled for Splunk and ELK for the hybrid environment:

Figure 14.35 - Configuring Splunk event tracking for a hybrid environment

Figure 14.35 shows how to configure Splunk event tracking for a hybrid environment.

Understanding logging with MuleSoft applications deployed to Runtime Fabric on bare-metal systems/VMs

Applications deployed to Runtime Fabric generate logs for applications, Runtime Fabric services, API proxies, and Kubernetes services. Logs for Runtime Fabric hosted on bare-metal servers or VMs are visible in OpsCenter.

You can configure Runtime Fabric to forward logs to an external logging system such as Splunk, ELK, CloudWatch, Data Dog, or Syslog, and it can be configured to forward logs to Anypoint Monitoring. To forward logs to Anypoint Monitoring, you require a Titanium subscription.

Logs can be forwarded to external systems such as Splunk or ELK by configuring an appender in the `log4j2.xml` file of the application that's deployed to Runtime Fabric. We discussed how to configure the appender in the `log4j2.xml` file earlier in this chapter.

OpsCenter is a web-based tool that can be used to monitor Runtime Fabric for bare-metal servers or VMs. OpsCenter allows us to forward logs to external systems and Anypoint Monitoring, provides SSO integration, and provides health reporting for Runtime Fabric. It also provides dashboards to view the CPU core usage, pod metrics, ingress metrics, and so on.

Runtime Fabric comes with various built-in alerts and custom alerts can be configured using Kapacitor.

JSON logging with a Mule application

MuleSoft provides an out-of-the-box logger component that can be used in an application to log information, errors, payloads, and status notifications. This can be useful while you're debugging and troubleshooting any problems or issues. The logger component can be used anywhere in the Mule flow, and it allows you to log the string data, the output of a DataWeave expression, or a combination of string data and an expression.

There is another component available for logging called JSON Logger, an open source custom connector that allows you to log in JSON format. It is not officially supported or managed by MuleSoft as it is a custom connector. This component provides the following features:

- Logs are in JSON format.
- Masks sensitive data before logging it.
- Hides fields that shouldn't be logged.
- Sends logs to external systems such as JMS, Anypoint MQ, AMQP, and others.
- The scope logger allows you to calculate the elapsed time for one or more components. It can be used to measure the performance of one or more components in the Mule flow.
- A DataWeave function to accommodate the desired log formatting.
- JSON Logger can be customized according to your requirements and needs.
- Log location information.
- JSON Logger can be added anywhere in the Mule flow, where it logs asynchronously.

Anypoint Visualizer

Anypoint Visualizer provides a real-time graphical representation of running and discovering APIs and Mule applications. It also shows third-party systems that are called by the Mule API, a proxy, or an application in your application network.

Anypoint Visualizer gathers data about Mule applications, APIs, and proxies that are deployed on CloudHub, independently of Mule runtime engines (Mule instances), or in Runtime Fabric to locate all incoming and outgoing connections. The application, API, or proxy will be found with all dependencies if it is operating on a Mule instance that's supported:

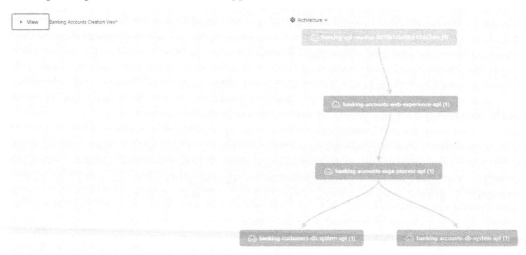

Figure 14.36 - Anypoint Visualizer

Summary

Anypoint Monitoring provides built-in dashboards and supports custom dashboards. It also allows you to configure alerts for various conditions, such as exceeding CPU usage or memory usage.

Functional Monitoring can be configured to monitor and test public and private endpoints. Runtime Manager supports out-of-the-box alerts for applications that have been deployed to CloudHub or hybrid environments.

Applications that have been deployed to CloudHub, hybrid environments, and Runtime Fabric can forward logs to external systems such as Splunk, ELK, Data Dog, and Syslog. API Manager provides information about API analytics and allows you to configure custom dashboards and set up API alerts.

In the next chapter, we will learn how to control API sprawl via Universal API Management.

Further reading

To learn more about the topics that were covered in this chapter, take a look at the following resources:

- *MuleSoft documentation*: CloudHub Architecture | MuleSoft Documentation
- *A few tables in this chapter that were referenced were from MuleSoft's official documentation*: `https://docs.mulesoft.com/`
- *Anypoint Monitoring*: `https://docs.mulesoft.com/monitoring/`
- *Logs*: `https://docs.mulesoft.com/monitoring/logs`
- *JSON Logger*: `https://blogs.mulesoft.com/dev-guides/how-to-tutorials/json-logging-mule-4/`

15

Controlling API Sprawl with Universal API Management

This chapter will demonstrate how to use API Manager to manage the life cycles of both MuleSoft and non-MuleSoft APIs. This chapter will address the causes of API sprawl and provide an overview of using universal API management to control API sprawl.

In this chapter, we will cover the following topics:

- API sprawl
- Universal API management
- API gateways
- Governing and securing APIs
- Enabling API policies on APIs
- Managing API alerts and analytics
- API governance and security

API sprawl

API sprawl is the concept that is used to characterize the unchecked growth of APIs inside an enterprise. When teams or departments within an organization develop their own APIs to suit their purposes without enough monitoring or control, API sprawl may result. This may lead to a high volume of improperly maintained, undocumented, or unsecured APIs. API sprawl presents serious security vulnerabilities from an API security standpoint, which must be addressed.

The following reasons can lead to API sprawl:

- **Absence of centralized governance**: Duplicate, overlapping, or incompatible APIs may result from several teams or departments within a company creating their own APIs without a centralized governance framework.

- **Unplanned growth**: New APIs are developed to enable the adoption of new technologies and changes in an organization's demands. This might result in an impossible-to-manage proliferation of APIs if sufficient preparation isn't done.

- **Vendor lock-in**: An organization may develop a proliferation of vendor-specific APIs that are incompatible with other systems if it depends too much on a single vendor for its technological requirements.

- **Acquisitions and mergers**: Companies that buy out or merge with other businesses may take over a range of APIs developed by the acquired business. There might be an incompatibility between these APIs and the organization's current APIs, which could result in API sprawl.

- **Lack of standards and documentation**: It might be challenging for developers to comprehend how to utilize APIs efficiently when they are not well documented or do not adhere to industry standards. This may result in the development of additional, redundant APIs, which would then add to API sprawl.

How to prevent API sprawl

It is critical for organizations to prevent API sprawl by adopting API best practices and implementing a clear API governance strategy. The first step in preventing API sprawl is to take inventory of the APIs within the organization, determine which APIs are critical for the business, and retire the APIs that are not in use or required anymore.

Once an inventory of APIs that are essential for the business has been created, you can start defining strategies for preventing API sprawl. The following are strategies that can prevent API sprawl:

- **Use a single source for API discovery**: It is difficult for developers to locate APIs and work out their functionality without a single source of truth. For example, multiple lines of business may create APIs that other teams are unaware of. This will create redundant APIs within the organization, which will reduce the APIs' reusability within the organization. A centralized platform where all APIs can be stored in a single place will allow developers to discover the APIs within the organization. A developer portal can be used to discover the APIs and would be a central place for developers to understand and discover the APIs within the organization.

- **Establish API governance**: Organizations should establish strong API governance to control or prevent API sprawl. This will ensure that APIs are designed for reuse and can be scaled easily. API governance is the process of defining API best practice guidelines and standards within the organization to foster API reusability and promote API consistency and security. API governance is key for adopting an API First strategy, wherein APIs are the basis for product creation. In an API First strategy, all the stakeholders, developers, designers, architects, and product managers are aware of APIs even before they are created. To achieve this, API governance strategies are important to establish.

- **Use proper API versioning**: API versioning is very crucial because most APIs outgrow their original scope, or require bug fixes, so this means that there are likely to be changes in API functionalities. API versioning will ensure the backward compatibility of APIs, so changes will not impact existing API consumers and they can gradually move to the latest version of the APIs.

- **Limit the number of APIs created**: Restricting the number of APIs created is one strategy to prevent API sprawl. This can be achieved by establishing stringent guidelines for when a new API is required and making sure that all relevant parties concur on its necessity. In addition, this should be communicated to the developer and CISO teams so that tasks are coordinated across all development teams.

- **Implement universal API management**: The use of APIs will only grow over time. Therefore, it's best to deal with API sprawl now rather than waiting for it to get out of hand. Stopping API sprawl in its tracks and resolving a host of other problems can be achieved by developing a universalized solution that guarantees that all your APIs are discoverable and capable of interacting with one another. We will discuss universal API management more in this chapter.

- **Design API specs**: API specifications are a valuable tool in preventing API sprawl. Developers can see the API and all its parts with the help of API specs. It is a type of automatically generated documentation that is easily readable by humans and that explains the functionality of APIs, the format of the requests and responses from the API, and other parameters, such as headers, that the API requires. API specs can be written in **Rest API Modeling Language** (**RAML**), **Open API Specification** (**OAS**), or others.

The topic of API sprawl and its prevention was covered in this section. The idea of universal API management, which can help to stop API sprawl, will be covered in the next section.

Universal API management

The ability to provide APIs with complete lifecycle management capabilities irrespective of their design, hosting environment, or place of development is known as universal API management.

With the help of universal API management, you can control, regulate, and secure multiple APIs from a single control plane. This can be accomplished in the following areas, regardless of whether the APIs are Mule or non-Mule, or where they are hosted (on-site, in the cloud, or somewhere else).

The advantages of universal API management that businesses can take advantage of are as follows:

- **Work in any architecture**: Enterprises are embracing or implementing a range of architectural styles, from microservices architecture to monolithic architecture. Through platform-based security and management, universal API management allows enterprises to work with any architecture style or pattern.

- **Work with APIs of any origin**: Businesses are incorporating new protocols such as AsyncAPI and GraphQL into their RESTful technology stacks because of the adoption of microservice architectures. Organizations can work with any API, regardless of where it was developed or the protocol it uses, thanks to universal API management.

- **Work in any environment**: You can discover, manage, secure, and interact with APIs running in any kind of environment – on-premises, cloud, hybrid, or otherwise – with the help of universal API management.

- **Work with any technology**: Universal API management enables businesses to handle the API life cycle from a single pane of glass, independent of the technology platform used to implement the API.

- **Engage any audience**: A central repository for all of an organization's APIs is provided by universal API management, enabling engagement and value addition from internal and external audiences in a variety of roles. This entails developing new alliances, enhancing end user experiences, and creating fresh business strategies.

Let's discuss each of the components provided by MuleSoft to achieve universal API management:

- **Design Center**: Design Center is part of the Anypoint Platform that allows developers to write API specifications in OAS, RAML, and AsyncAPI.

- **Anypoint CLI**: Anypoint CLI allows developers to automatically catalog, discover, or reuse the APIs in Anypoint Exchange.

- **API Manager**: API Manager will manage the entire life cycle of an API. It is a single unified platform that allows you to manage all your APIs. API Manager enables you to apply security policies such as an IP allowlist, an IP blocklist, a client ID enforcement policy, and a JWT validation policy to secure the APIs.

- **Flex Gateway**: This is an ultrafast API Gateway that enables you to manage and secure the APIs with quicker responses and low footprints.

- **Anypoint Exchange**: Anypoint Exchange is a repository of reusable assets. Anypoint Exchange allows you to store connectors, templates, APIs, fragments, custom assets, and so on within your enterprise. You can catalog (publish), share, search, discover, and reuse assets to promote standards, increase productivity, and foster collaboration.

- **Anypoint Community Manager** (**ACM**): You can create and manage communities around your APIs using Anypoint API Community Manager for partners and developers, both inside and outside of your company. It creates apps that utilize your APIs. With the help of Salesforce Experience Cloud, API Community Manager can be customized, branded, promoted, and engaged to meet the various demands of your developer audiences. Use API Community Manager to manage client apps, API access credentials, and consumption analytics in addition to providing rich API presentations for APIs cataloged in Anypoint Exchange.

- **API Experience Hub**: You can build dynamic ecosystems and increase engagement for your API products with the help of Anypoint API Experience Hub. Using off-the-shelf templates, you can quickly and simply create customized API portals to productize and publish APIs developed on any platform or technology.

We have talked about the benefits of universal API management and how to prevent API sprawl. We will now examine the API management capabilities and components provided by MuleSoft to oversee the full API life cycle in detail.

API management

The process of creating, designing, testing, monitoring, securing, and analyzing APIs for businesses is known as API management. API management platforms offer a comprehensive set of software solutions and procedures that can be hosted in a hybrid environment, in the cloud, or on-premises. With API management, enterprises can guarantee that APIs exposed internally or publicly are secure, consumable, and scalable.

The full API management life cycle

The process of managing an API for its entire life, from creation to retirement, is known as full API life cycle management. This covers every aspect of creating, disseminating, recording, safeguarding, and evaluating APIs. An API management system that facilitates API discovery and reuse while guaranteeing appropriate governance and security is an essential component of any successful API strategy.

MuleSoft's Anypoint Platform provides a robust solution for end-to-end API life cycle management. Having a clear understanding of each stage can help you enhance API effectiveness and resolve potential issues faster. Each stage of the API life cycle is as follows:

1. **Design**: Using API Designer, you can specify the API's functionalities. For instance, you would specify endpoints to obtain account information, create accounts and customers, and so on if you were developing an API for a banking website. Creating functional tests and documentation, as well as designing RAML or OAS specifications for REST APIs and AsyncAPI for event-driven architecture, is all part of this phase. The design phase is the first and one of the most important phases of the API life cycle. Prior to development and implementation, the API structure must be planned and designed during this phase:

    I.   **Create the API specification**: This includes defining what the API will do, the data it will handle, and the business logic it will execute. The specification is created using a language such as RAML or OAS.

    II.   **Define endpoints and methods**: Design the API resource URIs and the HTTP methods (GET, POST, PUT, DELETE, etc.) that will operate on these resources.

    III. **Design the data model**: Define what data will be sent and received by the API. This involves planning the JSON or XML message structure, data types, and data elements.

    IV.   **Create a mocking service**: MuleSoft allows you to create a mock service in the design phase. This lets API consumers interact with the API before it's fully implemented.

    V.   **Documentation**: Generate API documentation automatically from the API specification. The documentation explains in detail how to use the API and provides examples.

    VI.   **Collaboration and review**: Share the design with stakeholders and API consumers for review and feedback. This can be done directly through the Anypoint Platform via Anypoint Exchange.

    Recall that the success of APIs ultimately depends on how well they are designed for users. Making sure that the API is simple to use and understandable, as well as ensuring that it accurately meets the business needs and objectives it was designed to accomplish, is crucial during the design phase.

2. **Develop**: Anypoint Studio allows you to convert your design into functional code. Mule apps are created by developers utilizing pre-made connectors and components. For example, in the banking scenario, you could define a flow that handles GET and POST requests for an account's information and creation, respectively, and use an HTTP listener as the source.

3. **Secure**: In this stage, you safeguard your APIs using policy-driven security models such as Oauth and JWT validation. For example, you could apply policies to API proxies to secure your banking API endpoints, including IP whitelisting or rate limiting.

4. **Deploy**: APIs can be deployed in the cloud, on-premises, or in hybrid environments using Anypoint Runtime Manager. For instance, your banking API could be deployed to CloudHub, ensuring availability and scalability during peak shopping times.

5. **Operate**: Anypoint Monitoring and Anypoint Visualizer manage, monitor, analyze, and visualize APIs. In the banking API example, Anypoint Monitoring monitors the API's response times and the number of requests. Also, Anypoint Visualizer can create a live view of all APIs and integrations to depict the application network in real time.

6. **Manage**: Anypoint Exchange and Anypoint API Manager provide an environment for managing, governing, and publishing APIs. Let's say that your banking has several APIs. API Manager will manage these APIs from a single place, set up SLAs and policies, and control access.

7. **Version and deprecate**: Anypoint Platform simplifies API versioning. Whenever changes are needed, you can introduce new versions and retire old ones. In our banking example, if the way in which orders are processed changes, a new version of the API can be introduced.

8. **Engage**: This is where API users can explore and try out APIs, provide feedback, and discover assets in Anypoint Exchange. In our banking example, third-party developers can access Anypoint Exchange, find your APIs' documentation, understand their functionality, and learn how to integrate them into their apps.

Through these stages, APIs constantly evolve. Life cycle management ensures that this evolution doesn't affect the services offered and that the transition between stages is smooth, enhancing overall API usefulness, reliability, and profitability.

The API management life cycle for setting up and maintaining APIs was shown in this section. We will discuss MuleSoft's API gateways for managing and safeguarding APIs in the next section.

API gateway

An API gateway is a typical element that aids in routing API calls, aggregating API answers, and enforcing SLAs via functionalities such as rate limiting. It serves as an entry point for incoming messages and requests, making it a crucial component or tool of API administration systems.

An organization's APIs are safeguarded by an API gateway, which also serves as a secure access point. They put industry-standard encryption and access control into practice, providing API developers with the ability to grant access and point users in the appropriate direction. Gateways isolate the backend services and APIs that you build into a layer that can be controlled by your API management solution.

Why are API gateways needed?

API gateways play an important role in securing and controlling API traffic. API gateways hide the actual implementation of the APIs and provide insulation between the API consumers and the API implementation.

The following are the functionalities provided by the API gateway:

- **Traffic control**: Traffic can be throttled by applying rate-limiting policies, and this will help in reducing **Distributed Denial of Service (DDoS)** and **Denial of Service (DoS)** attacks. For example, an API can be called 20 times per minute per client.

- **API analytics**: Businesses that rely on APIs must invest in API analytics because it offers comprehensive insights on customer behavior and API performance, which has a direct bearing on the effectiveness of digital strategy.

- **API alerts**: API alerts can be enabled for response time, request count, policy violation, and response code alerts.

- **Authentication and authorization**: APIs can be authorized and authenticated by applying security policies such as basic authentication, JWT validation policies, and OAuth policies.

- **Productive and efficient API development**: Run several API versions to facilitate the rapid iteration, testing, and delivery of new versions. Convert protocols to support various clients with a single API.

MuleSoft supports three types of API gateway that can serve different purposes for managing APIs:

- Mule Gateway
- Service Mesh
- Flex Gateway

Mule Gateway

Mule Runtime includes an embedded API gateway, which allows you to secure APIs by applying security API policies on top of the API, enriching incoming and outgoing API messages and dropping requests coming from untrusted sources using IP allowlist or blocklist policies. Mule Gateway allows you to add an orchestration layer on top of your backend API or services, which will isolate the orchestration layer with an implementation layer.

Mule Gateway is the component of Anypoint Platform API Manager that controls API traffic and API access, enforces usage policies, and collects and collates API analytics. It serves as a gatekeeper for all your APIs, limiting access to only those users or applications that have been authorized and verified. Enforcing SLAs, authentication, and authorization, as well as request routing, composition, and protocol translation, is all handled by the API gateway. It provides security between user apps and your API or microservices, as well as on your network.

Now, we will discuss the two key concepts of leveraging API Autodiscovery and an API proxy to provide API management features on MuleSoft and non-MuleSoft APIs.

API proxies

A Mulesoft functionality called an API proxy serves as a bridge between an application and a backend API. MuleSoft's API proxies make it possible for you to manage your APIs more efficiently, ensuring that they are scalable, secure, and able to handle traffic.

The following are the benefits of API proxies:

- **Security**: It is possible to set up an API proxy to provide security features such as permission and authentication, shielding the backend API from unwanted access.

- **Throttling**: API proxies allow us to control the number of requests that can be sent to the backend APIs or services. In simpler words, API proxies can limit the number of requests sent to backend APIs or services, preventing backend APIs from being overwhelmed by too many requests at once.

- **Monitoring and analytics**: For monitoring and debugging purposes, an API proxy can keep track of requests and responses and provide valuable data.

- **Caching**: The proxy can save responses from the backend API that are used to reply to identical requests, reducing the load on the backend and speeding up response times.

- **Hiding API implementation**: API proxy hides the backend API implementation by not directly exposing the backend API's URL.

A MuleSoft API proxy can be deployed on CloudHub 1.0, CloudHub 2.0, the on-premises Mule Runtime, and Anypoint Runtime Fabric. Whenever you create an API proxy using API Manager, it will create a proxy application on the chosen platform. For example, creating an API proxy on CloudHub 1.0 will require a minimum of 0.1 vCores and one worker.

When to use an API proxy

The following are the reasons for using an API proxy:

- When your API is a non-MuleSoft API and you are looking to enable MuleSoft API management capabilities for non-MuleSoft APIs

- When you are looking to validate APIs using RAML, OAS, or SOAP APIs

- When your Mule application is closed code and you don't have access to apply API auto-discovery

The following is a diagram of an API proxy:

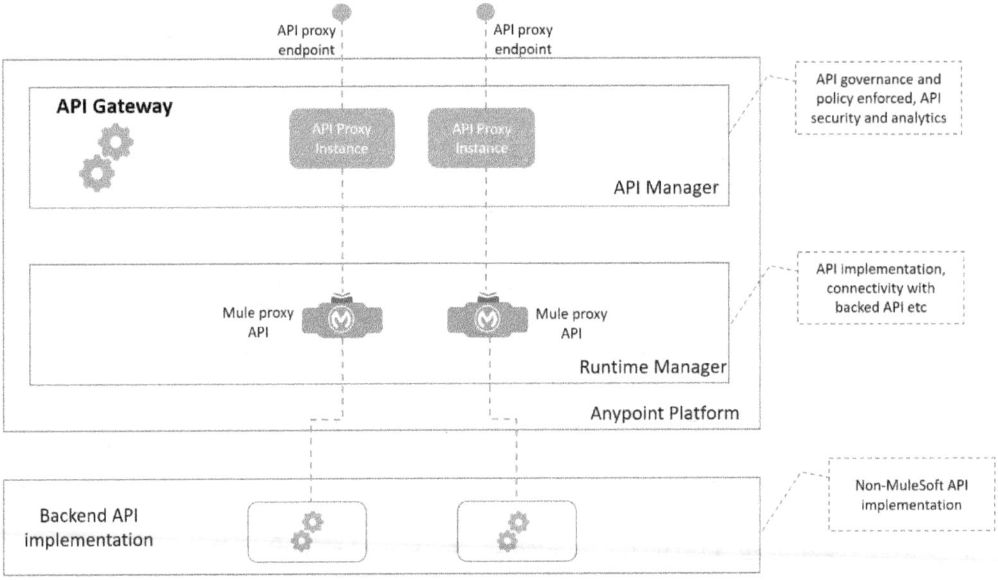

Figure 15.1: An API proxy

Figure 15.1 shows how to enable an API proxy for backend APIs and benefit from its API management capabilities to enable API policies, security, and analytics. Let's talk about how to manage non-MuleSoft APIs by implementing an API proxy in front of the backend APIs.

Managing non-MuleSoft APIs hosted in an on-premises data center

The APIs of J&J Music are housed in an on-site data center that is not directly reachable via the open internet. To manage, secure, govern, and engage with those APIs, they want to take advantage of API management capabilities. To put their API management into practice, they have selected the Anypoint Platform.

There are two ways to approach this scenario. To implement the API management capabilities on the backed APIs that are operating in the on-premises data center, we will require an API proxy. We will require a Mule Runtime, which can be CloudHub or an on-premises Mule Runtime, to configure and deploy the API proxy.

Solution 1 – deploying an API proxy in CloudHub to manage the non-MuleSoft APIs

To implement an API proxy on CloudHub to manage backend non-MuleSoft APIs, we will need to set up an Anypoint **Virtual Private Cloud** (**VPC**) and **Virtual Private Network** (**VPN**). Anypoint VPN allows API proxies deployed to CloudHub to communicate with the backend APIs hosted in an on-premises data center. The following is a diagram of implementing an API proxy on CloudHub for the backed APIs hosted in an on-premises data center:

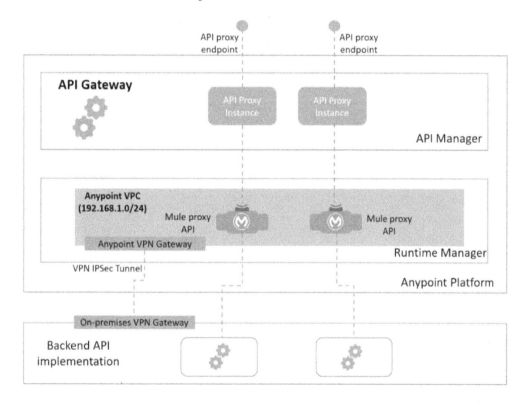

Figure 15.2: An API proxy on CloudHub for non-MuleSoft APIs hosted in an on-premises data center

Solution 2 – deploying an API proxy in an on-premises Mule Runtime to manage non-MuleSoft APIs

Deploying an API proxy to an on-premises Mule Runtime that can interface with the backend APIs is necessary to manage the backend APIs. In this instance, a VPN is not required because the backend APIs and Mule Runtime are in the same data center.

Here's an example of how to set up an API proxy for the backend APIs operating in an on-premises data center in the on-premises Mule Runtime.

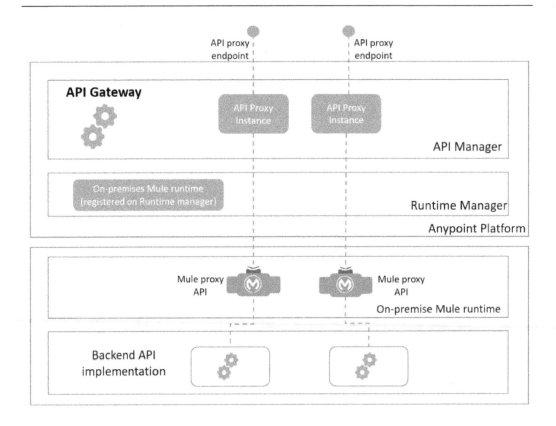

Figure 15.3: An API proxy for non-MuleSoft APIs hosted in an on-premises data center

It is important that an on-premises Mule Runtime must be registered in the runtime manager (Anypoint Platform control plane) as a server, server group, or cluster. This will allow us to deploy the API proxy in the on-premises Mule Runtime.

API autodiscovery

In MuleSoft, the process of connecting an API to its deployed Mule application instance is known as API autodiscovery. The API autodiscovery process links a Mule application that is deployed to the corresponding Anypoint Platform API, making the API visible within the platform and enabling version and status tracking. With the help of this procedure, you can now control, monitor, and track APIs in real time from Runtime Manager in the Anypoint Platform.

Some essential features of MuleSoft API Autodiscovery are as follows:

- Real-time binding of deployed instances of APIs to facilitate tracking and management

- Using Anypoint Platform to directly manage and keep an eye on a deployed API

- Improving version and status visibility for the API

Any organization that wants to keep visibility and control over its APIs should take advantage of this feature, especially those with intricate, high-volume API environments. It should be mentioned that an API-specific policy must be applied to use API autodiscovery.

API autodiscovery can be implemented for Mule APIs deployed to CloudHub 1.0, CloudHub 2.0, Runtime Fabric, and an on-premises Mule Runtime.

The following figure illustrates the API Autodiscovery for MuleSoft APIs deployed to the CloudHub, Runtime Fabric, or an on-premises Mule Runtime:

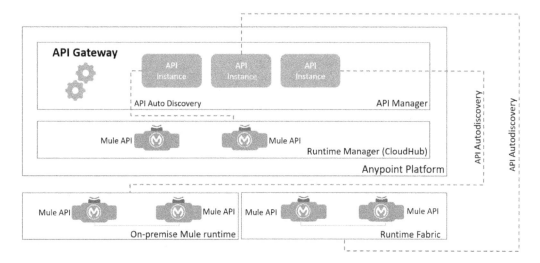

Figure 15.4: An API autodiscovery

API Autodiscovery can be implemented for MuleSoft APIs deployed to the on-premises Mule Runtime, Runtime Fabric, or CloudHub. To implement API autodiscovery, the first step is to create an API instance in API Manager that will generate an API ID. We can configure that API ID and the main Mule flow in the API autodiscovery component in the Mule code. During deployment, we need to pass two properties:

- `anypoint.platform.client_id`
- `anypoint.platform.client_secret`

The values of these two properties are different for each environment. For an on-premises Mule Runtime, these two properties can be set up in `wrapper.conf`.

API proxies versus API autodiscovery

The following are the differences between API proxies and API autodiscovery:

	API proxies	API autodiscovery
Definition	An interface known as an API proxy is used to conceal the backend service or API from client-side apps. It may be used in the development, testing, and production phases of API implementation. An API proxy's primary goals are traffic management and security. It provides features such as routing, adaptability, rate limitation, and security.	By essentially establishing a connection between the API and its deployed Mule application, MuleSoft's API Autodiscovery feature allows a deployed Mule application to be seen by the API Manager. This makes it possible to control the version and status of an API from the Anypoint Platform.
Purpose	It is able to hide and protect the backend API implementation.	It is able to link deployed MuleSoft APIs to API Manager instances to manage and secure the APIs.
Managing non-MuleSoft APIs	API proxies can be used to manage non-MuleSoft APIs as well as MuleSoft APIs.	API autodiscovery can only manage MuleSoft APIs.
Usage	It is utilized as a client-side application's interface for communicating with the backend service or API.	It is used to administer and keep an eye on the API after a Mule application has been deployed.
vCores requirements on CloudHub and Runtime Fabric	API proxies deploy a proxy application on the Runtime plane, which requires vCores.	No extra vCores are required.

Table 15.1: API proxies versus API autodiscovery

Anypoint Service Mesh

A software architecture pattern called a service mesh is used to deploy proxy servers as microservices and uses sidecars to facilitate secure, quick, and continuous communication between the services. Most service meshes, including Istio, are deployed using Kubernetes clusters. Despite the abundance of commercial offerings and open source service mesh projects, Istio has become the de facto industry standard.

To implement them, the sidecar's proxy pattern is typically utilized. A sidecar proxy goes along with every application that manages all service-to-service communication. It oversees east-west traffic discovery, route, security, and supervision. Every proxy instance is linked to a control plane that provides a way to control the mesh. Your inter-service interactions are governed by security and communication policies that are managed by a control plane. Authentication and authorization policies can now be applied at the control plane level, directing sidecars to respond appropriately during inter-service network calls.

Anypoint Service Mesh is a product provided by MuleSoft that simplifies the management and control of microservices. It's designed to provide the benefits of a service mesh while extending the capabilities of the Anypoint Platform to any microservice deployed in a non-Mule runtime engine.

The following are the features of the Anypoint Service Mesh:

- **Service discovery**: Automatically discover non-Mule applications and services across your distributed environment
- **Security and reliability**: Apply consistent, prebuilt policies for security and reliability in one click, with no need to update microservices code
- **Traffic management**: Control microservice traffic and prevent downtime with policies for retries, rate limiting, and circuit breaking
- **Performance monitoring**: Gain deep visibility into microservice performance and health by integrating with Anypoint Monitoring
- **Analytics and insights**: Understand and visualize the metadata of service performance and dependencies via API and integration analytics
- **Governance and control**: Extend Anypoint Platform governance and control capabilities to all deployed instances

Using Anypoint Service Mesh, organizations can ensure that their microservices – whether these are built with MuleSoft or another platform – can be discovered, managed, and secured in a standardized way.

The following is a diagram of the Anypoint Service Mesh architecture:

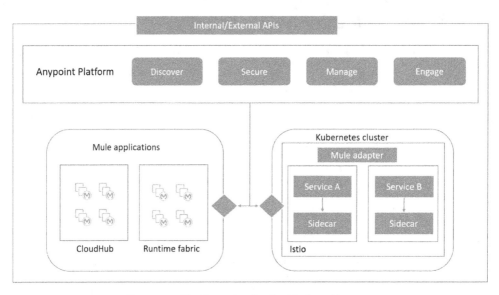

Figure 15.5: The Anypoint Service Mesh architecture

As shown in *Figure 15.5*, Anypoint Platform sits at the top of the architecture and provides full life cycle API management capabilities to microservices constructed with the Mule runtime engine. These Mule instances may be set up locally in Runtime Fabric or CloudHub. Istio installed on a Kubernetes cluster uses a sidecar proxy to use Envoy for service management. The sidecar lives in the same container as your service and oversees all communications with it. You can continue to use Istio's native policies for security and traffic control even with Anypoint Service Mesh enabled.

Components are connected to the Anypoint Platform via the MuleSoft adapter. The adapter works with a broker to allow all mesh-managed services to share metadata, which allows Anypoint Platform to identify your current microservices in the Kubernetes cluster as APIs. Anypoint Exchange uses metadata to automatically find and create APIs (HTTP, REST, or SOAP) for each service after the services are found. Then, API Manager can be used to manage these APIs. In a similar vein, Anypoint Monitoring obtains data from the sidecar proxy via metadata and provides it to API Analytics.

Flex Gateway

Anypoint Flex Gateway is incredibly quick and is designed to secure and administer APIs that are used anywhere. Anypoint Flex Gateway provides enterprise security and manageability in any environment, along with the performance needed for even the most demanding applications. It is designed to integrate seamlessly with DevOps and CI/CD workflows.

Flex Gateway is a lightweight, Envoy-based API gateway that can manage, secure, discover, and engage with APIs under a single umbrella. This gateway prevents API sprawl because it is capable of managing the APIs implemented in any technology (it is technology agnostic), following any architecture (monolithic to microservices architecture), and running anywhere (cloud, on-premises, hybrid, etc.).

Benefits of Flex Gateway

The following are the benefits of using Flex Gateway:

- Able to manage and secure APIs located anywhere

- Extend Anypoint Platform's capabilities to MuleSoft and non-MuleSoft APIs

- Achieve consistent security and governance across every API operating in any environment

- Adapt any architecture with a lightweight and flexible API gateway to manage and secure APIs

- Govern all APIs under a single umbrella

- Flex Gateway can be set up as a Linux service, in a Docker container, or as a Kubernetes Ingress controller

- Flex Gateway can be set up in connected and local mode

Flex Gateway in Connected Mode

In connected mode, Flex Gateway is registered in the Runtime Manager, and we can see API instances and policy configuration in API Manager. Connected mode gives you access to all the features of Anypoint Platform, including reusability through Exchange and monitoring via API Analytics, while allowing you to manage all your non-Mule APIs from a single, unified control plane. The following is a diagram of Flex Gateway in connected mode as a Kubernetes Ingress controller:

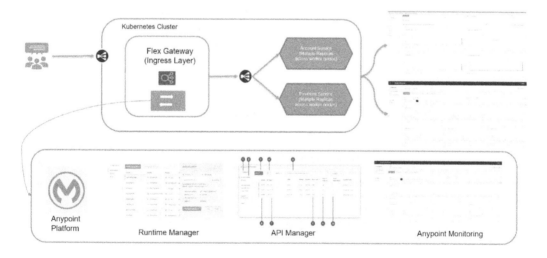

Figure 15.6: Flex Gateway in connected mode

In *Figure 15.6*, we can see that Flex Gateway in connected mode can use out-of-the-box components provided by MuleSoft such as API Manager, Anypoint Monitoring, and Runtime Manager to manage and secure APIs published to Flex Gateway.

Flex Gateway in Local Mode

In local mode, Flex Gateway is completely disconnected from the Anypoint Platform. The primary way that Flex Gateway is controlled in local mode is via a configuration file or YAML file. We can control API instances and related security policies by using this file. Non-Mule APIs can be managed by Flex Gateway in local mode without requiring assistance from the Anypoint control plane (declarative configuration files that are locally saved are used to handle all configuration and policy applications in local mode).

The following is a diagram of Flex Gateway in local mode as a Kubernetes Ingress controller:

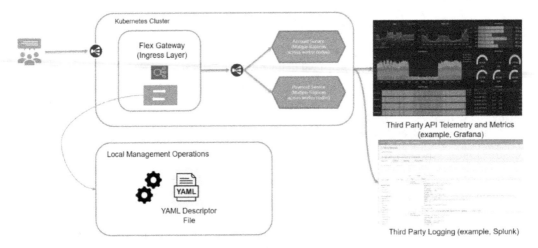

Figure 15.7: Flex Gateway in local mode

In *Figure 15.7*, we can see that Flex Gateway in local mode is managed by YAML descriptor files, and that it requires third-party tools such as Splunk and the ELK stack for monitoring and logging. Flex Gateway can be set up in local mode whenever enterprises have strict policies that API traffic should not leave the internal network or when there are any compliance or security requirements.

Flex Gateway deployment models

Flex Gateway supports multiple deployment models that can be implemented in connected mode and local mode. The following deployments can be implemented to set up Flex Gateway.

Standalone deployment model

In a standalone deployment model, Flex Gateway acts as a standalone service to protect one or more APIs within the enterprise. The following is a diagram of a Flex Gateway standalone deployment:

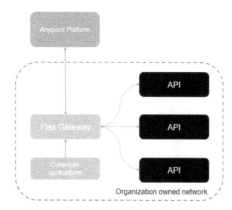

Figure 15.8: A Flex Gateway standalone deployment

In *Figure 15.8*, we can see that all traffic is inside the organization's network. Internal traffic is routed through Flex Gateway to the consumer applications.

Ingress deployment model

The Ingress deployment model acts as a standalone service that protects one or more APIs. In this model, Flex Gateway manages the external traffic entering the internal network via a load balancer. It is one of the widely used deployment models that can act as an ingress gateway and an egress gateway. The following is a diagram of a Flex Gateway ingress deployment:

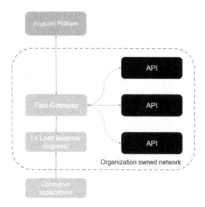

Figure 15.9: A Flex Gateway ingress deployment

In *Figure 15.9*, we can see all external traffic entering the internal network via a load balancer. All traffic passes through Flex Gateway to consumer applications.

Egress deployment model

An egress deployment is the opposite of ingress deployment model and acts as a standalone service that protects one or more APIs. In the egress deployment model, Flex Gateway manages the internal traffic leaving the organization to connect to non-organization-owned APIs. The following is a diagram of a Flex Gateway egress deployment:

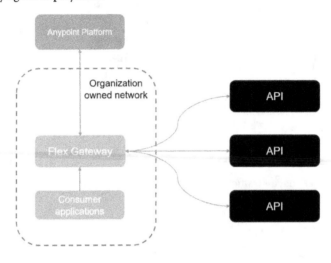

Figure 15.10: A Flex Gateway egress deployment

In *Figure 15.10*, we can see Flex Gateway managing internal traffic that is leaving the organization to connect external APIs, and this model acts as an ingress and egress gateway.

Sidecar deployment model

Each Flex Gateway deployment in a sidecar deployment solely safeguards the APIs that are made accessible by its protected service. Every time a protected service is added, a new replica of Flex Gateway is added.

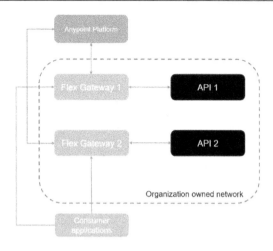

Figure 15.11: Flex Gateway sidecar deployment

In *Figure 15.11*, traffic in a sidecar deployment is routed to the appropriate consumer API. Either an external network or the same network as Flex Gateway may host a consumer application.

High availability and scalability with Flex Gateway

High availability can be achieved by running multiple instances of Flex Gateway and by configuring the load balancer in the front of the Flex Gateway instances to distribute the traffic and ensure high availability and business continuity if one or more Flex Gateway instances fail.

With Flex Gateway running in a Kubernetes cluster, high availability can be achieved by deploying more than one replica in the Kubernetes cluster. Using a Helm chart installed in the Kubernetes namespace, you can run the following command to add more replicas to Flex Gateway:

```
helm -n gateway upgrade \
ingress flex-gateway/flex-gateway \
--reuse-values \
--set replicaCount=4
```

By adding additional replicas, Flex Gateway can be scaled horizontally. Autoscaling is also supported by Flex Gateway, although it is turned off by default.

Helm charts can be used to enable autoscaling; by default, two replicas are supported as the minimum and 11 replicas as the maximum.

Flex Gateway's autoscaling feature can be enabled using the following Helm attributes:

Parameter	Description	Default value
`autoscaling.enabled`	This is a boolean indicating whether the **Horizontal Pod Autoscaler (HPA)** is active; it is set to `false` by default.	false
`autoscaling.minReplicas`	This shows the minimum number of replicas that can be produced by the HPA scaler.	2
`autoscaling.maxReplicas`	This shows the maximum number of replicas that can be produced by the HPA scaler.	11
`autoscaling.targetCPUUtilizationPercentage`	This is a resource metric that determines the proportion of each deployed Pod's average CPU usage.	50
`autoscaling.targetMemoryUtilizationPercentage`	This is a string that shows the percentage of all deployed Pods' average memory usage.	nil
`autoscaling.behavior`	This is a Kubernetes configuration that enables the `HorizontalPodAutoscaler` object. The HPA settings govern the autoscaling behavior, which includes adjusting the number of application resources in accordance with the workload's rate of change.	

Parameter	Description	Default value

`autoscaling.behavior.scaleUp,`
 	
`autoscaling.behavior.scaleDown`
	These are the configurations for the autoscaling behavior that occurs when the number of replicas is increased (`scaleUp`) or decreased (`scaleDown`) by the HPA scaler. We can describe the behavior of scaling using nested parameters:
	
	selectPolicy: This setting controls when to scale Pods if a metric of configured resources indicates that scaling is necessary. Since Pods can have varying numbers of replicas, this setting is required. `Min`, `Max`, and `Disabled` are acceptable values. It is set to `Max` by default.
	
	stabilizationWindowSeconds: This gives the minimum number of seconds that must pass before rescaling an application in response to a workload modification. The intention is to stop HPA from responding in an excessively aggressive or erratic manner when scaling too frequently.
	
	policies: A catalog of policies governing scaling behavior:
	
	type: Percent or Pods, depending on the value type for a particular policy
	
	value: The type's value for a particular policy
	
	periodSeconds: The time interval in seconds for a specific policy's scaling operations	

Table 15.2: Flex Gateway Helm chart settings

Routing in Flex Gateway

Request traffic is managed by Flex Gateway through a variety of routes, each of which can route traffic to several upstream services. Utilizing both the route order and the specific rules for each route, Flex Gateway routes traffic to destinations. To control the percentage of requests sent to the upstream service, you can also assign a weighted percentage to each upstream service inside a route. Up to 50 routes can be supported by each API instance, and up to 10 upstream services can be supported by each route. Multiple API instances that expose different upstream services through a single consumer endpoint can be supported by Flex Gateway version 1.5.x or higher.

In the following diagram, different routes manage requests to the banking information databases. Route 1 has been configured with two upstream services, which direct 80% of the traffic to the primary API, and that is then connected to the stable database. 20% of the traffic is directed to the secondary API, which is connected to the beta version of the database.

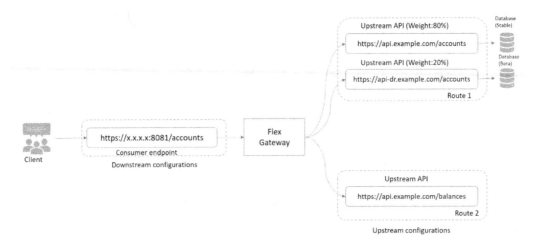

Figure 15.12: Flex Gateway routing

Requests can be routed to comparable services by utilizing many upstream services in a single route. For instance, you can route half of the traffic to a stable upstream service and the other half to the new upstream service to test the functionality of a new beta upstream service without sending all the traffic to the new service. Flex Gateway also uses the order of the routes' appearance on the page, from top to bottom, to route requests to various routes. If a request satisfies the route rules, Flex Gateway routes it to the first route.

Flex Gateway allows you to route requests to an upstream API using the port or path.

Figure 15.13 shows Flex Gateway's port-based routing. Whenever a request comes to Flex Gateway on port **8081**, the request will be routed to **Employee API** and, in a similar way, if a request comes to Flex Gateway on port **8082**, it will be routed to **Order API**.

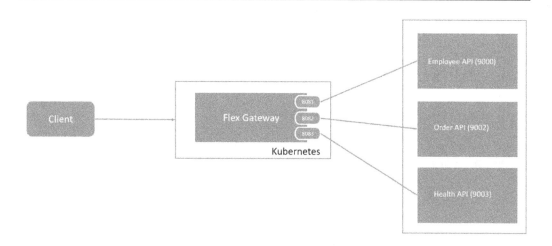

Figure 15.13: Flex Gateway's port-based routing

The limitation of this approach is that we need to use a unique port whenever we publish new APIs to Flex Gateway. When using Kubernetes as an ingress controller, ports must be also enabled on the ingress service. There is another approach, whereby we can route requests using the path and we can continue to use the same port for each API published to Flex Gateway. *Figure 15.14* shows Flex Gateway's path-based routing:

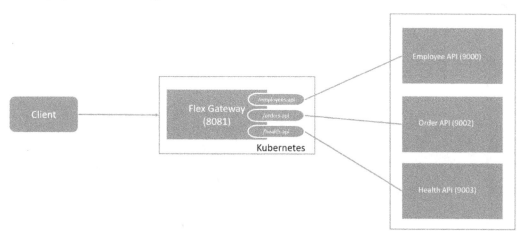

Figure 15.14: Flex Gateway's path-based routing

In *Figure 15.14*, the base path can be configured on the API instance created in the API manager, and that will be used to route requests to the upstream APIs. A unique base path is required for each API published to Flex Gateway on the same port.

As shown in *Figure 15.14*, requests coming to Flex Gateway with the **/employees-api** base path will be routed to **Employee API**. Similarly, requests coming to Flex Gateway with the **/orders-api** base path will be routed to **Order API**. In this approach, all the APIs are published to the Flex Gateway on the same port, **8081**.

Flex Gateway in Centralized Mode

In centralized mode, one Flex Gateway will manage all the APIs within the organization irrespective of technology, location, or architecture. The following figure shows Flex Gateway in centralized mode:

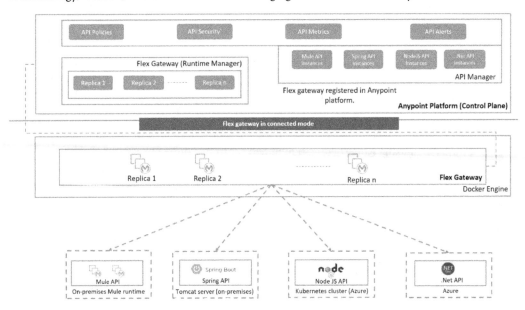

Figure 15.15: Flex Gateway in centralized mode

In *Figure 15.15*, we have a centralized Flex Gateway managing all APIs within the organization irrespective of technology, location, and architecture.

Flex Gateway in Decentralized Mode

In decentralized mode, multiple Flex Gateways will manage all the APIs within the organization. The following diagram illustrates Flex Gateway in decentralized mode:

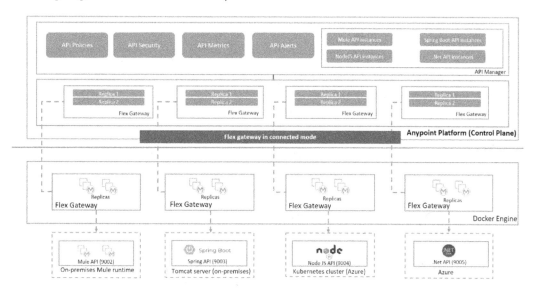

Figure 15.16: Flex Gateway in decentralized mode

In *Figure 15.16*, we can see that multiple Flex Gateways have been implemented to manage the APIs within the organization, and we can see that there is one Flex Gateway for one technology-specific API.

Figure 15.17 illustrates that one Flex Gateway will manage the APIs in one Kubernetes namespace. In simpler words, each namespace in the Kubernetes namespace will have its own Flex Gateway for managing the APIs in that namespace.

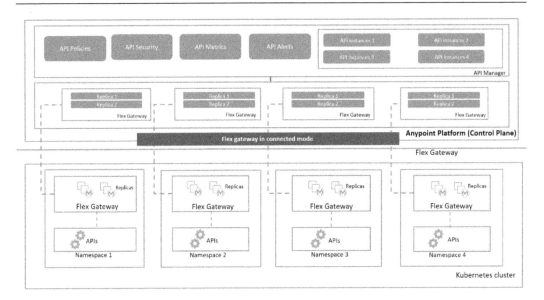

Figure 15.17: Flex Gateway in decentralized mode (one Flex Gateway in each namespace)

In *Figure 15.17*, one Flex Gateway is implemented in one namespace. This means that each namespace in Kubernetes will have its own Flex Gateway.

Figure 15.18 shows that one Flex Gateway will manage one API. This concept is known as the sidecar deployment model.

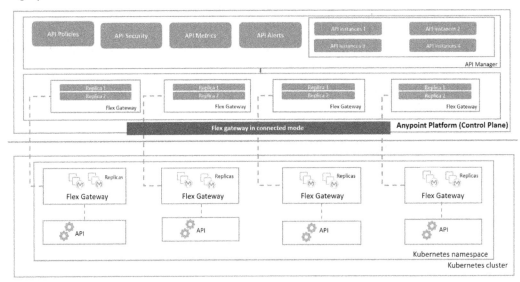

Figure 15.18: Flex Gateway in decentralized mode (one Flex Gateway for one API sidecar)

In *Figure 15.18*, each API has its own Flex Gateway for managing the API. The API and Flex Gateway will run on the same Pod in Kubernetes.

Flex Gateway API policies

MuleSoft offers declarative configuration files (Local Mode) or Anypoint Platform (Connected Mode,) allowing you to apply policies to your APIs. Rate limiting, caching, authorization, authentication, threat prevention, monitoring, and logging are among the policies that are offered.

Sometimes, though, those off-the-shelf policies fall short of our exact specifications. Thankfully, we can use the Rust programming language to create our own unique policies for those situations. Proxy-wasm ABI, an event-driven, Envoy-independent low-level proxy interface, serves as the foundation for custom policies. The interaction between a **WebAssembly (WASM)** extension and its host is defined by this interface.

Flex Gateway versus Mule Gateway

The following are the differences between Flex gateway and Mule gateway.

Mule Gateway	Flex Gateway
Mule Gateway can manage single APIs	Flex Gateway can manage MuleSoft as well as non-MuleSoft APIs
Java based API gateway embedded into mule for managing mule APIs using API Autodiscovery	Envoy-based API gateway that supports multiple deployment patterns and architecture
Works only in connected mode	Works in connected as well as local mode
Support custom policies development using Java and Mule DSL	Support custom policies using Rust WASM SDKs
An integrated Java Spring application within Mule	Foundational engine based on Envoy that uses FluentBit for logging
Ideal for handling (protecting, observing, and so on) Mule applications using a dedicated proxy or a basic endpoint (also accessible as a Mule proxy application installed in CloudHub)	Suitable for managing the Mule and non-Mule applications that are deployed anywhere and have high availability and performance

Table 15.3: Mule Gateway versus Flex Gateway

Share and discover APIs using Anypoint Platform

Sharing and discovering APIs in MuleSoft is done through Anypoint Exchange – a central hub for sharing, discovering, and reusing APIs, as well as other integration assets.

Anypoint Exchange is a component of Anypoint Platform that serves as a marketplace for integration assets. It allows developers to share, discover, and reuse APIs, connectors, templates, examples, and other resources created by MuleSoft or MuleSoft's user community.

Anypoint Exchange also serves as a repository that allows enterprises to publish custom assets, connectors, templates, APIs, policies, and common frameworks such as logging and error handling frameworks that can later be discovered and reused across the organization.

The following are the benefits of Anypoint Exchange:

- **API repository**: It provides a central location or directory where APIs can be published and discovered. Developers can also access detailed information on how to use these APIs, including documentation and examples.

- **Resource cataloging**: It stores and catalogs not just APIs but also connectors, templates, examples, and API fragments that can be reused across multiple applications within enterprises.

- **Developers collaboration**: Developers can rate, comment, and provide feedback on assets, fostering collaboration and continuous improvement.

- **Version control**: It provides version management for APIs and other assets, allowing developers to document changes and easily upgrade or roll back versions as required.

- **Dependency tracking**: It helps developers understand the dependencies between different assets, which is beneficial in managing complex integration scenarios.

Anypoint Exchange is essential to the advancement of reusable assets and API-led connections, which may drastically cut down on development time, boost output, and guarantee consistency throughout apps.

Developer portal

MuleSoft's developer portal is a component of Anypoint Exchange within the Anypoint Platform that serves as a marketplace for sharing, searching, and consuming reusable APIs. An API developer portal can play a significant role as a bridge between API providers and API consumers. It provides the tools required for API developers to design, implement, and test APIs and is where consumers can learn about, access, and use APIs in their applications.

The following are the features of the developer portal:

- **API documentation**: This contains detailed guides and references on how to use the API, usually generated from the API's specification. This is automatically generated documentation from an API specification.

- **API explorer**: This is an interactive interface where users can make test calls to the API and experiment with its endpoints. They can explore the functionality of the API before they consume the APIs.

- **Mocking service**: This is the developer portal allows us to test APIs with a mock service to understand an API's behavior and functionality.

- **Authentication and authorization**: Developer portals provide information about which authentication authorization mechanisms are needed to access the APIs.

- **Community**: Community forums helps the developers to interact with each other and developers can post any question on the forum.

- **Support**: Developer portal can have support forums to raise any queries or raise tickets for any issues or to get more information about the APIs.

There are other API developer portals provided by MuleSoft for sharing and discovering APIs. Those developer portals have rich features and allow the customization of the **Graphical User Interface** (**GUI**). We will discuss those API developer portals in the next section.

ACM

ACM is a product provided by MuleSoft that enables organizations to build and manage a developer portal and community for their APIs. ACM is a vital component in the API-led connectivity approach as it promotes the visibility and reuse of digital assets by setting up a central location for API consumers to self-serve and collaborate.

The following are the key features provided by ACM:

- **Customizable developer portal**: ACM allows organizations to create a fully customizable and branded developer portal where it's possible to publish and manage APIs, SDKs, templates, and other resources.

- **API documentation and testing**: It provides features to generate and publish interactive API documentation and enable API consumers to test the APIs directly from the portal.

- **Collaboration and engagement tools**: ACM promotes collaboration by providing tools for forum discussions, support case management, and consumption analytics. This improves engagement with API consumers.

- **Self-service API management**: It empowers API consumers with self-service capabilities for managing applications, obtaining credentials, and managing key/API tokens.
- **Simplified discovery of APIs**: It allows API consumers to easily discover and consume APIs and digital assets.

By using ACM, organizations can promote API adoption, elevate the consumer experience, and turn APIs into products that can be effectively shared and reused.

The following are the limitations of ACM:

- **Salesforce expertise is needed**: To set up and manage ACM, you need Salesforce expertise
- **Complex setup and new user onboarding**: Setting up and managing ACM is a complex task, and it requires Salesforce Experience Cloud and MuleSoft expertise
- **Poor performance and scalability**: The ACM portal is bulky, which leads to performance issues, and it is not easy to scale

API Experience Hub

Anypoint API Experience Hub is a tailored, enriched, and engaging API engagement experience for developers and partners. It serves as a developer portal where developers can discover, explore, and test APIs, and create applications.

The following are the key features provided by API Experience Hub:

- **Fully customizable interface**: With API Experience Hub, businesses can develop a branded and user-friendly API portal that meets their specific needs
- **API Catalog**: The portal provides a catalog of APIs, documentation, SDKs, and other reusable assets that developers can use in their API-led connectivity projects
- **API documentation and testing**: API Experience Hub delivers interactive API documentation and lets developers test APIs from the portal itself, promoting a greater understanding and effective utilization of the APIs
- **Collaborative environment**: It provides a space where developers can interact with each other, ask questions, share insights, and collaborate more effectively through community forums
- **Analytics**: It shows how APIs are used, measures engagement, and drives an API program with metrics

By centralizing the discovery, learning, testing, and development of APIs, API Experience Hub streamlines the process of API-led connectivity for developers.

API Experience Hub overcomes the limitations of ACM as follows:

- Designed to scale and provide high performance
- No need for Salesforce expertise to set up and manage API Experience Hub
- Simplified user onboarding management
- Improved and lightweight GUI

ACM versus API Experience Hub

API Experience Hub and ACM are both provided by MuleSoft as part of the Anypoint Platform. Let's compare them:

- **ACM**: This is a product provided by MuleSoft that enables businesses, both large and small, to build and manage a developer portal and community. It essentially acts as the umbrella under which all API community engagement activities fall. This includes hosting documentation for their APIs, allowing developers to test APIs, fostering collaboration through forums and discussions, and even providing usage analytics and metrics data stored in Salesforce, exposed via Salesforce objects.
- **API Experience Hub**: API Experience Hub, on the other hand, is a specific aspect or component of ACM. It essentially refers to the interactive and customizable portal where developers can discover, learn about, and use APIs. This includes features such as the API catalog, API documentation and testing, interactive forums, and API analytics data stored in the Anypoint Platform, which is exposed via consumable APIs.

In simpler terms, ACM is broader in scope – it involves all aspects of building and managing a developer community. In contrast, API Experience Hub is more focused on the aspect of the developer portal where APIs are discovered and consumed.

API Analytics

Mule API Analytics is a feature within the Anypoint Platform that provides visibility of the usage and performance metrics of APIs. It allows organizations to monitor and measure the effectiveness of their APIs, identify issues, and make data-driven decisions.

The following are the features of API Analytics:

- **Real-time insights**: It gives real-time visibility into API performance, tracking key API usage metrics, throughput, response time, and error rate.
- **Detailed reporting**: With API Analytics, you can drill down into individual API calls to diagnose issues or understand specific transactions.

- **Historical data analysis**: API Analytics provides historical data, enabling trend analysis, capacity planning, and identifying areas for optimization.

- **Customizable dashboards**: Users can create customizable dashboards to monitor the metrics that are most important to them and their business.

- **Proactive issue identification**: It identifies issues and anomalies in API behavior that can be used for early error detection and rectification.

- **Usage tracking**: It provides insights into who is using the APIs, how often, and in what ways. This can inform about API adoption patterns and trigger the development of features or fixes.

To access API Analytics, users must have an Anypoint Platform account and the necessary permissions to view analytics.

API policies

MuleSoft API policies are a set of capabilities within the Anypoint Platform that allow API developers to manage and control APIs. These policies enforce specific behaviors on APIs, such as security, compliance, operations, and quality of service.

The following are the API policies provided by MuleSoft:

API policies	Description
Security policies	These policies can help secure APIs by validating client credentials, filtering, limiting traffic, validating user roles, and more. Examples include OAuth 2.0 access token enforcement, client ID enforcement, JSON, and XML threat protections.
Rate limiting and throttling policies	These policies ensure resources are not overwhelmed by controlling the number of requests processed by an API at any one time. Examples include rate limiting and spike control.
Compliance policies	These policies can help meet regulations and standards, such as those regarding logging and data masking.
Operational policies	These include Cross-Origin Resource Sharing (CORS) policies to govern how resources are shared among different domains.
SLA-based policies	This policy tier manages the application's access to an API. Applying this type of policy enforces limits on the processing time and the number of messages, failure rate, and others. An example is rate limiting with SLAs.

API policies	Description
Quality of service policies	These make sure that services are performing at the standard expected by users. They can specify API availability, response time, error rates, and so on.
Custom policies	MuleSoft provides an Mule and Java DSL for writing custom policies, which can be used if you don't have an out-of-the-box policy to fulfill the business requirements.

Table 15.4: API policies

By applying these policies in API Manager, organizations can guard their APIs by ensuring that they remain functional, secure, and reliable throughout their life cycle.

API Governance

API Governance is the component of the Anypoint Platform that enables you to apply governance rules to your APIs to ensure API consistency. It provides several default rulesets, such as a top 10 OWASP API Security, Anypoint API Best Practices, and OpenAPI Best Practices governance rulesets that can be apply to the API specification during design time to ensure that API specification is compliant and consistent with organizational API standards and guidelines. API Governance will ensure that the API designs across the enterprise are consistent and designed with API best practices and guidelines in mind. This will ensure the security of the APIs and improve the quality of the APIs.

Implementing API Governance

The first step for implementing API governance is to create a profile in Anypoint Platform's API Governance component and select the rulesets that you need to enable for that profile. You can add filters and notifications. Filters will select the APIs that need to be scanned against the profile that we have created. Notifications will generate emails to the users in case the APIs haven't been designed according to the rulesets associated with the profile, and they will be marked as **non-conformant**.

There are three statuses maintained for your APIs as part of API Governance:

- **Not validated**: The API is not validated against the API Governance profile
- **Conformant**: The API has satisfied the rulesets that were associated with the profile
- **Non-conformant**: The API has not satisfied the rulesets that were associated with the profile

Developers or architects can apply API Governance during the API design phase in the Design Center by adding governance rulesets as dependencies directly to API specifications, so developers or architects can verify compliance with the specifications during the API design phase.

The following screenshot shows the API Governance interface:

Figure 15.19: The API Governance interface

The following details are visible in the API Governance interface:

- There is an overview of the selected draft profile's API conformance.
- Notice the APIs that the draft profile is aiming for. Although these APIs are subject to governance, unless they are also the subject of an active profile, their conformance information is only displayed within the draft profile view.
- Export a CSV conformance report for each API that this draft profile is intended to target.

The following out-of-the-box rulesets can be configured on API Governance profiles:

Figure 15.20: API Governance rulesets

Anypoint API Manager alerts

Anypoint API Manager alerts are notifications that you can set up in MuleSoft's Anypoint Platform to monitor specific activities or changes related to APIs. These alerts help businesses proactively identify and mitigate potential issues with their APIs.

The following API Manager alerts can be configured to send an alert based on different factors:

- **Response time**: If the response time of your API exceeds a certain threshold, an alert will be triggered to notify you

- **Request volume**: You can set an alert if the number of API requests exceeds a specific limit in a certain period

- **Failed requests**: Configure an alert if the rate of failed API requests surges beyond a certain percentage

- **Policy violation**: If there is a policy violation, you can receive a policy violation alert

You can set up these alerts in Anypoint Platform's Runtime Manager. The process involves specifying the alert type, setting conditions for the alert, and then designating the recipients of alert notifications. You can receive these alerts via various channels, such as emails, third-party applications (e.g., Slack), and webhooks, depending on how you set up the alert. By using API Manager alerts, businesses can take a proactive approach to API management, quickly and efficiently troubleshooting and resolving any issues that arise.

API security threats

API security threats refer to the potential risks or vulnerabilities that compromise the confidentiality, availability, and integrity of the data and services.

The following are some API security threats:

- **Injection attacks**: When malicious commands or data are entered into an API with the goal of accessing, compromising, or altering private data, it is referred to as injection.

- **Broken authentication**: Attackers may pose as authorized users and obtain unauthorized access if APIs fail to properly authenticate users.

- **Insecure Direct Object References (IDOR)**: A vulnerability known as Insecure Direct Object Reference (IDOR) occurs when an attacker manipulates IDs used in the URLs or parameters of a web application, allowing them to access or edit objects.

- **Security misconfiguration**: Attackers may be able to access sensitive data if the API's server or code has incorrect security settings.

- **Excessive data exposure**: Overly transparent APIs may be used to obtain sensitive data without authorization.

- **Lack of rate limiting**: APIs are susceptible to DoS and brute force attacks in the absence of appropriate rate limits.

- **Broken function-level authorization**: In this situation, unauthorized access results from APIs failing to correctly authorize functions that should only be available to specific roles.

- **Mass assignment**: Here, an attacker makes an educated guess about the composition of an API request to change an object's properties that they shouldn't be able to.

- **XML External Entity (XXE)**: If an attacker can upload XML or include hostile content in an XML document, they can take advantage of vulnerable XML processors, which can result in the disclosure of internal files, DoS, or remote code execution

- **Cross-site Scripting (XSS)**: An XSS attack may occur if an API sends user input back to a web browser without encoding or validating it, allowing the browser to run it as a script.

After having talked about the OWASP top 10 security threats, we will now address DoS attacks.

DoS

DoS is a kind of cyberattack that involves the attacker sending an excessive number of requests to the targeted computer system, network, or service to overload its resources and bandwidth. Consequently, the system stops being accessible to its intended users. A typical DoS attack involves saturating the network with traffic, breaking connections, or driving the system to use excessive amounts of resources, which can slow it down or even stop it from operating.

DDoS is a more potent and sophisticated DoS attack. A DDoS attack leverages several compromised or controlled sources, typically dispersed throughout the internet, to initiate an attack against the target. In a network of devices known as a **botnet**, every single device serves as a bot. These bots, which can number in the thousands or even millions, then flood the target network with requests at the same time, resulting in a DOS. It is difficult to stop the attack because it originates from so many different places and stopping one source doesn't stop the others.

The following figure shows a DDoS attack:

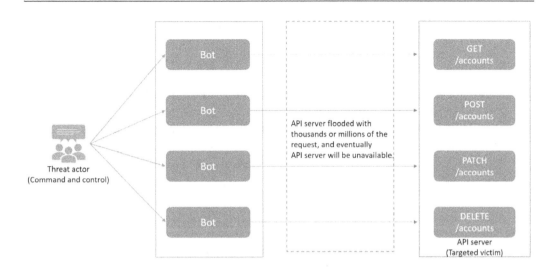

Figure 15.21: A DDoS attack

The following measures can be implemented to protect APIs against security threats or attacks:

- **API gateway**: OAuth 2.0, JWT, SAML, and other security protocols are just a few of the protocols that MuleSoft's API gateways can handle. By serving as a barrier between traffic management and API implementations, it offers centralized policy management.

- **Anypoint Security**: Anypoint Security from MuleSoft provides multiple levels of protection for APIs using cutting-edge security features such as tokenization, rate limitation, IP whitelisting, and blacklisting. Anypoint Security is only supported by Runtime Fabric.

- **Rate limiting and throttling**: This feature safeguards APIs from sudden spikes in traffic and guards against DoS attacks.

- **Tokenization**: When handling sensitive data, MuleSoft can substitute sensitive data for tokens, providing an additional degree of security. Tokenization is only supported by Runtime Fabric.

- **Security policies**: MuleSoft facilitates the implementation of pre-made or personalized security policies on APIs, such as the HTTP basic authentication policy and the OAuth 2.0 scope validation policy.

- **DataWeave**: To further reduce data exposure, MuleSoft's transformation language aids in the anonymization of sensitive data prior to logging activities.

- **Secure properties**: MuleSoft offers the ability to secure data at rest by encrypting sensitive information inside application properties. Use a safe algorithm such as AES256 or Blowfish to encrypt all of your security properties in the app.

- **Auditing and monitoring**: To identify irregularities, monitor API activity, and track any unauthorized access, MuleSoft comes with auditing and monitoring tools.

- **API security in transit**: Encryption protocols such as **Transport Layer Security** (**TLS**)are used to protect your data when it moves so that it can be protected from data manipulation and interception. The standard security technology that will keep online transactions and logins secure behind the scenes is TLS, also known as Secure Socket Layers. In all your Mule APIs, your organization can implement TLS security, which will ensure the confidentiality of messages on the network and the integrity of the data. Adding a TLS context using Anypoint Secrets Manager will allow you to configure TLS settings at the application or API proxy level. This is also supported by Flex Gateway. In particular, the implementation of TLS would minimize vulnerabilities in your API such as security errors and unsafe consumption.

- **Secure APIs during the design phase**: MuleSoft provides API governance rulesets that can be applied to APIs during the design phase. This ruleset will scan the APIs to ensure quality, compliance, security, and consistency. We have already discussed API governance in this chapter.

Recall that integrating these defensive measures into the design, implementation, and deployment phases – rather than merely adding them as an afterthought – is the optimal approach for securing MuleSoft APIs. Industry standards and best practices should also be adhered to by appropriate security measures.

Summary

In this chapter, we have studied how to use universal API management to stop API sprawl. To implement universal API management – which allows users to manage, administer, protect, and interact with APIs from a single pane of glass – we have spoken about several components, including Flex Gateway, API Governance, developer portals, and API Manager.

The non-functional requirements that must be addressed to provide a solid framework for building high-quality APIs will be covered in the upcoming chapter.

References

The following are rhe references for the Flex Gateway documentation:

- Custom API polices using Rust: `https://docs.mulesoft.com/gateway/latest/policies-custom-flex-implement-rust`

- Flex Gateway: `https://docs.mulesoft.com/gateway/latest/`

16

Addressing Non-Functional Requirements – from a Thought to an Operation

This chapter will show the reader about implementing Non-Functional requirements like HA, Fault Tolerance, Resilience, and allocating and optimizing the vCores to enhance the application performance.

In this chapter, we will cover the following topics:

- NFRs such as scalability, high availability, and fault tolerance
- **Disaster recovery** (**DR**) for the MuleSoft platform
- vCores allocation and optimization

Prerequisites

The following are the prerequisites for this chapter:

- Knowledge of the MuleSoft platform, such as CloudHub 1.0, CloudHub 2.0, Runtime Fabric, and the on-premises Mule runtime
- Knowledge of Kubernetes and its container-based application architecture
- A basic understanding of NFRs such as scalability, high availability, fault tolerance, and others

What are NFRs?

NFRs are a set of specifications that describe the operating capabilities and limitations of a system. They act as requirements that describe how well a feature will work, such as its high availability, scalability, security, reliability, and data integrity. Let's take a closer look at these terms:

- **High availability**: How well a system is available in the event of any system failures. This guarantees business continuity.

- **Scalability**: How well a system can handle an increase in the number of requests or workloads.

- **Performance**: How fast a system can respond to any requests.

- **Security**: How well a system is protected against any unauthorized request, malicious attacks, or data breaches.

- **Reliability**: How well a system is designed. Here, the percentage of failures should be small and the system should be reliable.

- **Data integrity**: How well a system is designed to minimize the risk of data breaches.

- **Fault tolerance**: How well a system is designed so that it can recover in the event of failures or system crashes.

- **DR**: DR involves applying IT technologies and best practices to mitigate the effects of catastrophic events, such as cyberattacks, natural disasters, civil emergencies, and equipment failures, on business operations and data loss

In this chapter, we will explore a few non-functional criteria, such as DR, scalability, fault tolerance, and high availability. A few of the non-functional needs, such as API security, reliability, and performance, were covered in the previous chapters.

High availability

High availability refers to the ability of an IT system, component, or application to function continuously and at a high level for extended periods, without the need for assistance. Infrastructure with high availability is set up to deliver excellent performance and manage different loads and breakdowns, with little to no downtime.

High availability and fault tolerance with CloudHub 1.0

CloudHub 1.0 provides several components, such as the Anypoint Platform API and services, shared load balancers, monitoring components, and many other components that are highly available by default within any AWS region. Mule applications running on CloudHub 1.0 can be deployed to more than one worker, ensuring high availability and improving overall application performance. If one worker fails, other workers are available to handle the request.

Deploying an application to multiple workers ensures that traffic is distributed among them using a load balancer. CloudHub 1.0 supports persistent queues to implement message reliability. Persistent queues are abundant in the region and may not be available when the AWS region is down. Here, data loss is possible, but communication is restored through the queues when the AWS region is back up.

Some CloudHub components, such as Object Store V1, application settings, and monitoring-related data, are stored in the US East region, regardless of the application deployed in any region. Object Store V2 is stored in the same AWS region as the CloudHub 1.0 application AWS region. Object Store V1 is not available if the US East region is not available, and Object Store V2 is not available in the AWS region where the application is deployed. The information in the object store is persisted and is available again when the area is used. The Anypoint **Virtual Private Cloud** (**VPC**) is configured on a region-by-region basis. If a region isn't available, the Anypoint VPC won't be available until a previous instance of Anypoint VPC has been configured for the other region.

CloudHub 1.0 availability within a region

CloudHub 1.0 uses AWS cloud infrastructure, and the availability of CloudHub 1.0 depends on the AWS availability. CloudHub 1.0 availability and deployments are divided into different regions, and each region refers to its corresponding Amazon region.

When an Amazon region goes down, applications in that region are unavailable and no longer automatically replicated to other regions.

For example, if the us-east-1 region is unavailable, the cloud management UI, as well as the various REST services that enable deployment, are unavailable until region availability is restored. No new application is deployed to the us-east-1 region.

CloudHub 1.0 availability within availability zones

Deploying an application to multiple workers ensures high availability as the application is deployed to separate Availability Zones.

If one availability zone fails, your application is available in another Availability Zone to service your requests. Meanwhile, applications running in the failed availability zone will attempt to recover or restart in another Availability Zone.

If the application is enabled for one worker and that worker fails due to availability zones going down, the worker will automatically try to recover and can restart in another availability zone. This may cause some brief downtime.

We will cover this topic in more detail in *Chapter 9*.

High availability and fault tolerance with CloudHub 2.0

CloudHub 2.0 is highly available and scalable and provides redundancy, intelligent remediation, and zero-downtime updates. You can run multiple replicas of the same application for load balancing and high availability purposes.

CloudHub 2.0 supports clustering, something that applications benefit from in terms of increased stability, workload distribution, and scalability. CloudHub's replica scale-out and scalable load balancing solutions power these features.

Clustering allows multiple replicas to communicate with each other and share data via the object store and VM queues across multiple replicas of the same application. A minimum of two replicas is required for an application's high availability and to enable clustering on the application.

CloudHub 2.0 monitors replicas for problems and provides a self-healing mechanism for recovery. If the underlying hardware fails, the platform automatically migrates applications to a new replica. There is a private ingress load balancer within a private space that auto-scales to accommodate traffic.

Anypoint VPN in CloudHub 2.0 is highly available by default. You can create a redundant VPN in CloudHub 2.0 to ensure high availability. Certain configuration parameters from the original VPN setup are automatically transferred to the redundant VPN.

High availability and fault tolerance with the on-premises Mule runtime

Clustering can be used to enable high availability for applications that are deployed to the on-premises Mule runtime. It provides a basic failover capability for Mule.

In the event of the primary node becoming unavailable, due to a **Java Virtual Machine** (**JVM**) failure, planned maintenance, or a hardware failure, one of the other nodes in the cluster will become the primary node and resume processing where the failed instance left off.

The following figure shows how a node transitions to the primary node from the secondary node in the event of a primary node failure:

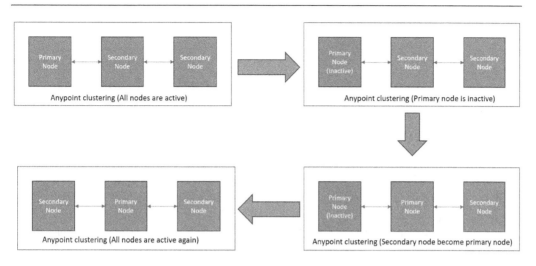

Figure 16.1: Anypoint clustering node transition (from the secondary node to the primary node)

For HTTP workloads, you should configure a third-party load balancer in front of the nodes to distribute traffic across multiple nodes, as well as to ensure that it goes to active nodes.

The following figure shows how to use a load balancer in front of nodes in a cluster to distribute HTTP workloads:

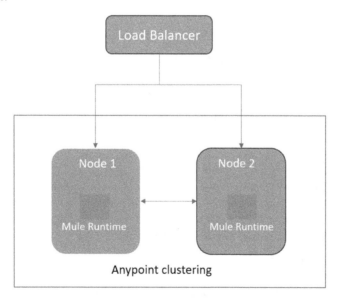

Figure 16.2: An HTTP load balancer with Anypoint clustering

We discussed Anypoint server groups in *Chapter 12*. A server group can be also configured with a third-party load balancer so that it can distribute traffic across multiple nodes in the server group.

Note that the customer is responsible for configuring and managing the load balancer, as well as setting up and managing the infrastructure required to run the on-premises Mule runtime.

High availability and fault tolerance with Runtime Fabric (bare-metal servers/VMs)

High availability on Runtime Fabric can be achieved at the infrastructure level and the application level. Infrastructure-level high availability can be achieved by setting up multiple master and worker nodes, as discussed in *Chapter 11*.

In *Chapter 11*, we discussed Quorum management and how to use it to ensure high availability and a fault tolerance infrastructure for Runtime Fabric. We discussed the minimum master and control nodes required for production and non-production environments to ensure the infrastructure's high availability.

High availability and fault tolerance with Runtime Fabric (self-managed Kubernetes)

Both the application and infrastructure layers of Runtime Fabric can achieve high availability. Setting up multiple worker nodes can help you achieve infrastructure-level high availability. Self-managed Kubernetes provides managed Kubernetes master nodes, which eliminates the need to manage master nodes. AWS oversees the EKS master nodes. Once again, managing the availability of the master nodes is the responsibility of the cloud providers (AWS, in the case of EKS) and is not the duty of MuleSoft.

To achieve application-level high availability for Runtime Fabric on self-managed Kubernetes and VMs/bare-metal servers, you can deploy multiple replicas for your application. You can cluster multiple replicas to ensure that data and information are distributed among the replicas. Just like an on-premises cluster, Runtime Fabric supports the cluster.

We discussed Anypoint clustering in detail in *Chapter 11*.

Scalability

The capacity of a system to adapt its performance and cost to changes in application and system processing demands is known as scalability. Examples include the way an operating system functions on various hardware classes, the way a database handles an increasing volume of queries, or the way a hardware system handles an increase in user count.

There are two types of scaling:

- **Horizontal scaling**: Horizontal scaling means adding more machines to your pool of resources. Horizontal scaling is divided into two types:

  - **Scaling up**: Adding more machines to your pool of resources

  - **Scaling down**: Removing a machine from your pool of resources

- **Vertical scaling**: Vertical scaling means adding more power or compute resources, such as memory and CPU, to existing servers:

  - **Scaling out**: Adding more power to your existing machines
  - **Scaling in**: Reducing the power of your existing machines

Now, let's consider scalability in terms of CloudHub 1.0.

Scalability with CloudHub 1.0

CloudHub 1.0 is a managed service where we don't have to oversee its infrastructure, and it is completely managed by MuleSoft. We are only responsible for choosing the correct worker and worker size required to run the Mule applications or proxies.

MuleSoft will automatically configure infrastructure, depending on the worker and worker size we have selected for the application. An application can be horizontally scaled by increasing or decreasing the number of workers and vertically scaled by increasing or decreasing the worker size.

CloudHub 1.0 supports auto-scaling features, as discussed in *Chapter 9*, which allows an application to auto-scale depending on an increase or decrease of its traffic.

Scalability with CloudHub 2.0

Like CloudHub 1.0, CloudHub 2.0 is a managed service that doesn't have to oversee its infrastructure, and it is completely managed by MuleSoft. We are only responsible for choosing the correct replica and replica size required to run the Mule applications or proxies.

MuleSoft will automatically configure infrastructure, depending on the replica and replica size we have selected for the application. An application can be horizontally scaled by increasing or decreasing the number of replicas and vertically scaled by increasing or decreasing the replica size. CloudHub 2.0 doesn't support the auto-scaling feature.

We discussed scalability with CloudHub 2.0 in detail in *Chapter 10*.

Scalability with Runtime Fabric (bare-metal servers/VMs)

The Runtime Fabric infrastructure can be scaled horizontally by adding more worker or master nodes to the cluster and scaled vertically by increasing or decreasing computing resources, such as CPU and memory. It is the customer's responsibility to perform the changes for implementing scalability at the infrastructure level.

An application can be scaled horizontally by adding more replicas of the application and vertically scaled by increasing the replica size (the reserved CPU, CPU limit, or memory).

Runtime Fabric is a service provided by MuleSoft on top of Kubernetes for running Mule applications. This abstracts away the complexities of administering and managing the Kubernetes cluster, allowing developers to focus on application development and deployments.

However, Runtime Fabric doesn't directly provide capabilities for scaling applications. In such cases, Kubernetes comes into play to provide robust scaling.

Kubernetes is an open source platform for automating containerized application deployment, scaling, and administration.

Kubernetes provides two different ways of auto-scaling application instances:

- A **Horizontal Pod Autoscaler (HPA)**

- A **Vertical Pod Autoscaler (VPA)**

The HPA adds more Pods in the event of more traffic. In the event of load decreases, the number of Pods will scale down to a minimum.

The HPA is used as a controller and resource for the Kubernetes API. The controller's behavior is dictated by the resource. The horizontal directory autoscaling controller, which is housed in the Kubernetes control plane, uses observed metrics, such as average CPU usage, average memory usage, or any other custom metric you specify, to determine the appropriate scale of its object (such as a deployment) regularly.

The HPA works on the principle of targets. It adjusts the number of Pods in a deployment or replica that have been set to match a predefined target usage level for a given resource (such as CPU or memory).

To create an HPA, you need to use the `kubectl autoscale` command:

```
kubectl autoscale deployment mule-test-app --cpu-percent=80 --min=2
--max=6
```

Let's break down the preceding `kubectl` command:

- Here, `mule-test-app` is the name of the application.

- Then, we have `--cpu-percent=80`, which means Kubernetes will add more replicas when the average CPU utilization of all Pods goes above 80%

- Finally, `--min=2` is the minimum number of replicas that will always run, and `--max=6` is the maximum number of replicas that Kubernetes can create if there is high CPU utilization

The `kubectl autoscale` command is a simple command that activates the HPA. However, defining the HPA with a manifest file is more flexible as it allows multiple metrics to enable scaling.

The following manifest file allows you to scale horizontally if the average CPU utilization of a node reaches 80% or higher. Create a `mulesoft-test-app-hpa.yaml` manifest file. Then, execute the `kubectl apply` command to enable the HPA:

```
kubectl apply -f mulesoft-test-app-hpa.yaml
```

Here's the output:

```
apiVersion: autoscaling/v2
kind: HorizontalPodAutoscaler
metadata:
  name: mulesoft-test-app
spec:
  scaleTargetRef:
    apiVersion: apps/v1
    kind: Deployment
    name: mule-test-app
  minReplicas: 2
  maxReplicas: 6
  metrics:
  - type: Resource
    resource:
      name: cpu
      target:
        type: Utilization
        averageUtilization: 80
```

Let's take a closer look at the attributes that have been defined in this YAML file:

- Here, `scaleTargetRef` is the MuleSoft deployment that this HPA will manage.

- Then, we have `minReplicas`, which specifies the minimum number of replicas that will always run, and `maxReplicas`, which specifies the maximum number of replicas that Kubernetes can scale in the event of CPU or memory utilization exceeding that defined utilization threshold.

- `metrics` specifies the attributes that the HPA will use to determine when to scale. In this case, we have used CPU utilization as an attribute for the HPA.

The following figure shows how a Pod scales horizontally when the average CPU utilization reaches 80% or higher:

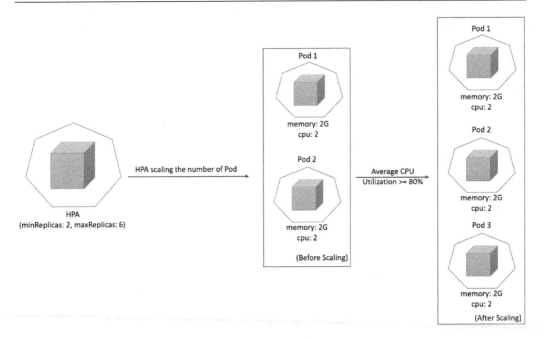

Figure 16.3: Kubernetes' HPA

The VPA automatically adjusts the CPU and memory required for a Pod to run an application at its correct size. This will ensure the effective utilization of resources in the cluster. There are two types of configurations needed for the VPA:

- Requests
- Limits

Requests are the minimum number of resources allocated to a Pod, and this guarantees the resources that the Pod will be allocated. Limits are the maximum number of resources that the Pod can consume in the event of more traffic. However, this is not guaranteed, and they can only be allocated if there are extra resources available to accommodate more traffic.

The following figure shows how a Pod vertically scales in the event of more resources being required:

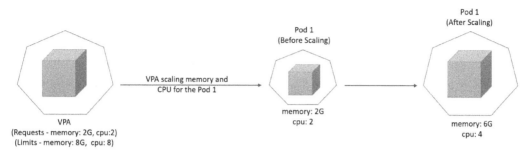

Figure 16.4: Kubernetes' VPA

The following table shows what can be done if more resources are required:

Capacity Adjustment Required	HPA	VPA
More resources	Add more Pods	Increase the memory or CPU of the existing Pod
Fewer resources	Remove Pods	Decrease the memory or CPU that's been allocated to the existing Pod

Table 16.1: HPA and VPA resource allocation

We have talked about how to allocate resources to the application deployed to Runtime Fabric allocates. We'll now discuss the scalability of Runtime fabric.

Scalability with Runtime Fabric (self-managed Kubernetes)

Self-managed Kubernetes is a managed service provided by a cloud provider (**Elastic Kubernetes Service (EKS)** by AWS, **Azure Kubernetes Service (AKS)** by Azure, and **Google Kubernetes Engine (GKE)** by Google). Users can concentrate on their applications and workloads as the cloud provider, using self-managed Kubernetes, manages the API server and the Kubernetes control plane, which includes master nodes, storage, and other components. This means that cloud providers maintain and ensure that essential components are scalable and highly available.

Self-managed Kubernetes can easily be scaled to meet your applications' requirements. It facilitates worker node provisioning and management automatically, which makes scaling your cluster easier when an application demands change. The etcd persistence layer and Kubernetes API servers' scalability and availability are automatically managed by cloud providers.

An application can be scaled horizontally by adding more replicas of the application and vertically scaled by increasing the replica size (the reserved CPU, CPU limit, or memory), such as the Runtime Fabric component of bare-metal servers/VMs.

DR

DR is a critical consideration for any organization to ensure business continuity and resume critical business functions as quickly as possible after unexpected disruptions, such as natural disasters, regional failure, and cyberattacks. You need to define a DR strategy to ensure business continuity; otherwise, you may incur revenue loss or reputational damage, and businesses can fold as a result.

DR for CloudHub 1.0 (multi-region)

CloudHub 1.0 provides automatic DR across availability zones in the same region. We discussed this option in *Chapter 9*. It is possible to set up DR across multiple regions so that if an entire region goes down, we have other regions to ensure business continuity.

Here are some important points about DR for CloudHub 1.0:

- Multi-region DR can be set up by creating two Anypoint VPCs in two different regions. One of the regions is the primary region, and the other is the DR region.

- Two separate Anypoint dedicated load balancers can be set up for each region. Each dedicated load balancer can be mapped with CNAME records on the DNS server.

- A global load balancer is the customer's responsibility, and it is not provided by MuleSoft. It will route traffic between the primary and DR regions. The customer can use Route 53 or any DNS router to route traffic between primary and DR regions.

- The application name, Anypoint VPC name, and Anypoint dedicated load balancer name must be unique across regions.

- The object store is a regional service and cannot be accessed across regions. We need to define a strategy to use the object store or any persistent storage across regions.

- Separate VPN tunnel, VPC peering, or AWS Transit Gateway connectivity must be established between the primary and DR regions.

- In an active/active DR mechanism, switching from the primary region to the DR region will be faster than active/passive DR as the load balancer will identify that the primary region isn't healthy and automatically route all traffic to the DR region.

- In an active/passive DR mechanism, switching from the primary region to the DR region will be manual. You might need to deploy the application to the DR region, and it will take additional time to activate it. This can lead to a high **recovery time objective** (**RTO**).

The RTO is the amount of downtime that businesses can accept during a region failure. For example, if a business can accept 1 hour of downtime, the RTO will be 1 hour.

The **recovery point objective (RPO)** is the amount of data loss that is acceptable by the business after system recovery. For example, if the system fails at 2 P.M. and a maximum of 2 hours of data loss can be accepted, the RPO will be 4 P.M.:

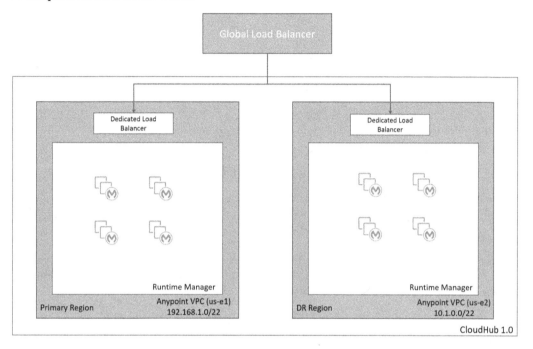

Figure 16.5: CloudHub 1.0 DR

Figure 16.5 shows how to set up DR across multiple regions in CloudHub 1.0, ensuring that an application is available even if one region completely goes down. We can set up two Anypoint VPCs in two different regions, and each region will have a dedicated load balancer to route traffic to the application that's been deployed within the Anypoint VPC. The global load balancer is responsible for load balancing traffic between two regions. If one of the regions goes down, the global load balancer will detect that, and all traffic will be routed to the other region.

DR for CloudHub 2.0 (multi-region)

CloudHub 2.0 provides automatic DR across availability zones in the same region. We discussed this option in *Chapter 10*. It is possible to set up DR across multiple regions so that if an entire region goes down, we have other regions to ensure business continuity.

Here are some important points about DR for CloudHub 2.0:

- Multi-region DR can be set up by creating two private spaces in two different regions. One of the regions is the primary region, and the other is the DR region.

- Separate private and public endpoints will be created for the private space in different regions.

- A global load balancer is the customer's responsibility, and it is not provided by MuleSoft. It will route traffic between the primary and DR regions. The customer can use Route 53 or any DNS router to route traffic between primary and DR regions.

- The object store is regional and cannot be accessed across the region. We need to define a strategy to use the object store or any persistent storage across the regions.

- A separate VPN tunnel or AWS Transit Gateway connectivity must be established between the primary and DR regions. VPN in CloudHub 2.0 is highly available by default in all regions.

- In an active/active DR mechanism, switching from the primary region to the DR region will be faster than active/passive DR as the load balancer will identify that the primary region isn't healthy and automatically route all traffic to the DR region.

- In an active/passive DR mechanism, switching from the primary region to the DR region will be manual. You might need to deploy the application to the DR region, and it will take additional time to activate it. This can lead to a high RTO:

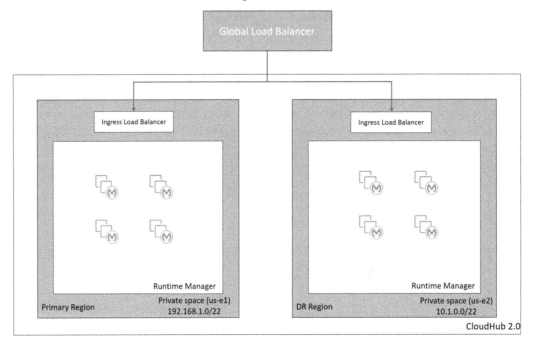

Figure 16.6: CloudHub 2.0 DR

Figure 16.6 shows how to set up DR across multiple regions in CloudHub 2.0 to ensure that an application is available even if one region completely goes down. We can set up two private spaces in two different regions, and each region has an ingress load balancer to route traffic to the application that's been deployed within the private space. The global load balancer is responsible for load balancing traffic between two regions. If one of the regions goes down, the global load balancer will detect that, and all traffic will be routed to the other region.

DR for the on-premises Mule runtime

DR for the on-premises Mule runtime was discussed in *Chapter 12*. We explored various options to implement it.

The following are the options we discussed in *Chapter 12* for implementing high availability and DR for the on-premises Mule runtime:

- Cold standby
- Warm standby
- Hot standby – active-passive
- Active-active

You can use the on-premises Mule runtime (or backend applications) to provide enhanced dependability and prompt failover in the event of a main connection failure. Clients frequently adhere to the on-premises MuleSoft runtime DR plan that complements their entire data center DR plan.

The following figure shows the architecture of the on-premises DR plan:

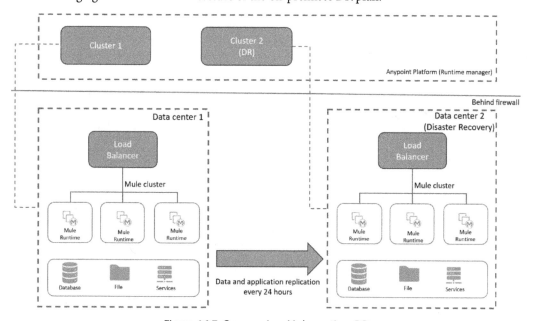

Figure 16.7: On-premises Mule runtime DR

We've spoken about the NFRs that must be met for Mule apps to operate. In addition to these non-functional criteria, other requirements must be considered for the application to operate reliably and efficiently. We will address vCores allocation and optimization in the upcoming portion of this chapter as they are essential to achieving this.

vCores allocation and optimization

vCores refer to the number of CPU and computing resources required to run an application. A vCore is an abbreviation of the term virtual core. An application that's deployed to CloudHub or Runtime Fabric is measured in terms of vCores. In previous *chapters*, we discussed what different vCore sizes are available for different platforms.

It is necessary to allocate the right vCores to an application so that it can perform consistently and stably. It is possible to end up under or over-allocating vCores to an application. If vCores are under-allocated, the application may not perform well and drop incoming traffic. If vCores are over-allocated, we may end up wasting the vCores that have been allocated to applications.

An application may be given additional resources for the following reasons:

- An application is restarting frequently.
- Errors in logs related to performance problems.
- An application is timing out frequently, with high resource usage recorded in the runtime dashboard. A slow response time may take up more resources.

Other factors need to be considered while allocating vCores to an application:

- The number of requests per second
- The payload size
- The number of errors in the application
- The response time of the application
- Throughput
- The number of Mule flows
- Data transformation complexity
- Flow complexity
- Object storage usage in the application

Multiple levels need to be considered when you're deciding on the number of vCores to allocate:

- Flow level:

  - Flow complexity

  - Data transformation complexity

  - The object store

- Application level:

  - The number of flows

  - The type of integration/flow (batch/API/integration/async)

- Worker level:

  - Memory requirements

  - Computational requirements

  - Performance requirements

  - The number of workers

  - Application availability

Real-time integration can be scaled horizontally or vertically. In most cases, real-time time integration will be scaled horizontally to accommodate more traffic. Batch integration cannot scale horizontally, but it may require additional memory or CPU to accept or process bigger payloads or files.

Another approach can be used to determine the exact resources required for an application – that is, testing the performance of an application in the sandbox environment before deploying it to production. This can help you determine the near-exact amount of vCores required for the application.

vCores optimization and allocation with CloudHub 1.0 and CloudHub 2.0

Workers or replicas that have the capacity for fewer than 1 vCores (0.1 vCores and 0.2 vCores) offer limited CPU and I/O for smaller workloads. It is recommended to allocate more vCores to an application that requires high performance.

There is no golden rule that says how many vCores should be allocated to an application to achieve x performance. An application that's deployed to CloudHub 1.0 and CloudHub 2.0 and allocated the same amount of vCores may not perform similarly.

One of the benefits of deploying an application to CloudHub (1.0 and 2.0) is that each application is run in a separate isolated container. Each application is allocated its own CPU and memory, so performance issues with one application will not impact the other application. Each application can scale horizontally or vertically separately.

An application that's been deployed to more than one worker or replica will allow traffic to be distributed across multiple replicas or workers via a load balancer.

For example, an application that's been deployed to CloudHub 1.0 with two workers and a worker size of 0.2 vCores means a total of 0.4 vCores will be consumed by the application, and there will be a 0.2-0.2 vCores split between both workers. The load balancer will ensure that traffic is distributed among the workers. The same logic applies to CloudHub 2.0.

Performance testing is important to allocate the right worker or replica size to an application.

vCores optimization and allocation with the on-premises Mule runtime

Applications running on the same on-premises Mule runtime don't allow you to allocate vCores to individual applications. It is always recommended that batch application processing on the on-premises Mule runtime is run during off-peak hours. This will ensure that a real-time API can get more resources to process the requests.

When we deploy an application to the on-premises Mule runtime, there is no restriction on how many applications we can deploy to it, but it is necessary to make sure we don't end up deploying more applications than the amount of resources available on the server. This will degrade the performance of the Mule application and can impact other applications running on the on-premises Mule runtime.

vCores optimization and allocation with Runtime Fabric

With Runtime Fabric, we allocate the CPU that's been reserved and the CPU limit to the application during deployment; this means an application will get the guaranteed CPU reserved value, and it can burst to CPU limit value. An application will only burst up to the CPU limit value if a spare CPU is available; otherwise, the CPU limit value is not guaranteed.

The following strategies can be used when an application is deployed to Runtime Fabric, ensuring that extra CPU is available for other applications to use if there is high traffic:

- Always deploy a nightly batch job for applications that have high traffic during the day. This way, an application can get extra CPU during the day, and a nightly batch job can get extra CPU during the night.

- To optimize the surface area for unallocated CPU, distribute multiple replicas of an application among worker nodes.

Regardless of whatever strategies you use, it is recommended to do performance testing and validate the resources that have been allocated to an application. Applications allocated with more vCores take less time to deploy compared to applications deployed with fewer vCores.

Summary

In this chapter, we covered NFRs, which include DR, fault tolerance, high availability, and vCores allocation and optimization. Ensuring business continuity by implementing NFRs is crucial for API implementation.

The foundation of application performance is application sizing. Low application performance can result from allocating less memory or CPU than an application needs.

In the next chapter, we will discuss how to get ready for the MuleSoft Certified Platform Architect exam.

17

Prepare for Success

In this chapter, we will discuss how to prepare for the **MuleSoft Certified Platform Architect** (**MCPA**) – Level 1 examination and the eligibility criteria for it. We will also cover the important topics that you need to know for the exam and recommendations for the exam.

In this chapter, we will cover the following topics:

- The format and validity of examinations
- How to prepare for the exam
- Who can take the MCPA – Level 1 exam?
- Important topics that need to be understood
- System requirements for the exam
- Practice questions

MCPA – Level 1 certification

MCPA – Level 1 certification validates that the architect has the knowledge and skills to build a robust and secure platform for running the MuleSoft application network.

It also ensures that the architect can do the following activities:

- Select the right platform for your organization's requirements and ensure the organization's compliance, security, and policies
- Provide guidance for creating API standards, security best practices, reusable components, templates, and accelerators
- Enable a robust platform application monitoring and alert mechanism

Format of the examination

The examination is in English. It is an online, closed-book exam, meaning that you can't have any notes or books with you, and it is proctored, which means that special software will monitor your computer screen and your actions while taking the exam.

The duration of the exam is 120 minutes, and there are 60 multiple-choice questions in total. To pass the exam, you need a score of at least 70%, which means that a minimum of 42 questions should be answered correctly. There is no negative marking, meaning you won't lose marks for incorrect answers.

Validity

The certification will be valid for two years from the date of passing. You can have five attempts at the exam, with a 24-hour waiting period between each attempt. After five unsuccessful attempts, you need to purchase and register for the certification again.

MCPA – Level 1 Maintenance exam

To extend the certification's validity, you can take the MCPA – Level 1 MAINTENANCE exam. The duration of this exam is 45 minutes, with 25 multiple-choice questions in total. You need a score of at least 70% to pass this exam. Again, there is no negative marking. You can have two attempts at this exam, with a 24-hour waiting period between each attempt.

How to prepare for MCPA – Level 1

The best way to prepare for the examination is to gain some experience in setting up and building the MuleSoft platform. Most of the questions on the exam are scenario-based, so hands-on experience will be critical to help you pass.

Go for instructor-led training such as *Anypoint Platform Architecture: Application Networks*, which is officially provided by MuleSoft. This training comes with two free attempts at the MCPA – Level 1 exam.

Reading this book will also prepare you for the examination. It explores the architecture and capabilities provided by the Anypoint Platform and covers hosting options supported by MuleSoft, such as CloudHub, CloudHub 2.0, Runtime Fabric Manager, and on-premises Mule Runtime. After reading this book, you will have mastered the MuleSoft platform architecture and components.

MuleSoft provides a practice exam that is of a similar format to the real one. The questions are of the same style with a similar difficulty level. You can attempt the practice exam multiple times to gain confidence before the real examination.

Why take the MCPA – Level 1 exam?

This certification will validate your skills and knowledge of the MuleSoft platform.

Its credentials will set you apart in the marketplace, placing you in a higher position than others, and it is one of the recognized certifications in the industry.

Who should take the MCPA – Level 1 exam?

The following are the ideal candidates for this exam:

- **Senior developers**, ideally with MuleSoft Certified Developer – Level 1 certification, who have a strong understanding of MuleSoft and are looking to gain expertise in developing an architecture for an application network by combining integration solutions in an optimized, sustainable, scalable, and reusable way

- **Technical architects** who have knowledge of integration and APIs and are looking to understand how to implement these solutions with the MuleSoft Anypoint Platform

- **MuleSoft senior developers** who want to take on MuleSoft platform architect roles and want to understand the platform's capabilities in depth

- **Infrastructure architects** who need to understand and define MuleSoft hosting options and who are responsible for their organization's Anypoint Platform strategy

What topics are covered in the examination?

MCPA is one of the most reputed exams for architects. It validates the architect's skill and in-depth knowledge of the MuleSoft platform. The following is a list of topics that are critical and need to be understood for the examination:

- Architecting and implementing CloudHub 1.0:

  - Setting up Anypoint Virtual Private Cloud, the Anypoint dedicated load balancer, and network connectivity options such as Anypoint Virtual Private Network, VPC peering, AWS Direct Connect, and AWS Transit Gateway

  - Application deployment to CloudHub and choosing the right number of workers and the worker size

  - Non-functional requirements such as scalability, high availability, and fault tolerance

  - Concepts of static IP addresses and shared load balancers

- Architecting and implementing CloudHub 2.0:

  - Setting up a private space and network connectivity options such as Anypoint Virtual Private Network and AWS Transit Gateway

  - Ingress load balancer, private and public endpoints, and inbound and outbound firewall rules

  - Understanding the shared space

  - Non-functional requirements such as scalability, high availability, and fault tolerance

  - Application deployment options

- Architecting and implementing the customer-hosted Mule Runtime:

  - Setting up Mule Runtime on-premises

  - Anypoint clustering, server group, and HTTP load balancer

  - Anypoint Platform **Private Cloud Edition (PCE)**

  - Scalability, fault tolerance, disaster recovery, and high availability

  - Application deployment options

- Architecting and implementing Runtime Fabric Manager:

  - Setting up Runtime Fabric Manager on the self-managed Kubernetes and bare-metal server/VMs

  - The concept of CPU bursting

  - Replicas, replica size, and replica clustering

  - Application deployment options

  - High availability, fault tolerance, and scalability

- Enabling Anypoint Monitoring:

  - Anypoint Monitoring metrics, custom dashboards, reports, and so on

  - Functional monitoring for private and public endpoints

  - Anypoint Monitoring logging options

  - Monitoring on-premises Mule Runtime

  - Alerts on high CPU and memory usage

- Governing the APIs:

  - Enabling API Manager for applications deployed to Runtime Fabric Manager, CloudHub (1.0 and 2.0), on-premises, and so on

  - Applying API policies such as rate limiting, spike control, and basic authentication – LDAP, JWT validation, IP allowlist and blocklist, and so on

  - Enabling API Manager analytics, alerts, custom dashboards, and so on

  - API auto-discovery and API proxies

  - Configuring the identity and client providers in the Anypoint Platform

  - Securing the APIs at the edge via Anypoint Security

- API architecture:

  - API-led connectivity and event-driven architecture

  - Microservices with domain-driven design and bounded context

  - Circuit breaker pattern

A complete list of topics that you will need to understand to prepare for the examination can be found on the MuleSoft training site.

Strategies for answering multiple-choice questions

Read the question completely and carefully and focus on the keywords in the question. After reading the question, try to think what the answer will be without reading the options.

Use the eliminator technique. Eliminate the wrong options that might not be related to the question or might be completely off. In this way, you will reduce the options and you may end up with just one option left at the end, which will be the correct one. But there might be a question where more than one option remains. In this case, read the question again and try to select the right answer from the remaining ones.

Answer all the questions as there is no negative marking. Make sure you don't waste time on a question for which you don't know the correct answer; instead, mark it for review so you can revisit that question later. If you have answered a question and you are not 100% sure about the answer you have selected, you can also mark that question to review at the end.

Time is very important and so you need to manage it well during the exam. You will get 120 minutes to answer 60 questions, which gives you 2 minutes for each question. Try to spend 1.5 minutes on each question instead; this will mean it will take 90 minutes to answer all the questions, and the remaining 30 minutes can be used to check or answer the questions that have been marked for review.

System requirements for the examination

The supported operating systems are Windows and macOS; Linux is not supported. Make sure you have Guardian Browser installed on your computer, as this is the only supported browser. A functioning microphone and high-resolution webcam are needed.

Multiple monitors or screens are not supported during the examination. Make sure you have a strong and stable internet connection on the day of the exam as it is online proctored, and it will require screen sharing and installed proctoring software on your machine.

These are the minimum bandwidth speeds needed for the examination:

- **Download**: 1.5 MBPS
- **Upload**: 1 MBPS

Test your internet speed using the following links:

- `www.speedcheck.org`
- `fast.com`

Hotspots and tethering are not supported.

Do not allow anyone else to use the internet connection while you are taking the exam as it will increase the bandwidth.

The following are not supported: Google Chromebooks, tablets such as iPads and Nexus, Windows 10 S or Surface RT, and remote desktop software such as TeamViewer and Chrome Remote Desktop.

Make sure no other software is opened on your machine. All other software must be closed before the exam starts.

Exam day

Finally, the day has arrived and you are going to take the exam. Make sure you are well prepared for the exam and are feeling confident. Make sure that you have taken care of all the system requirements mentioned in the previous section. Keep one or two official proofs of identity near you as these will be checked during the examination to validate your identity.

After completing all the prechecks, you can start the examination, and you will get two hours to complete it. Use the strategies for answering multiple-choice questions that we discussed earlier. Once you have completed the exam, you need to submit it. After submitting, you will get your result immediately on the screen with a status of **Pass** or **Fail**. It will also show the section-wise percentages you have scored.

If you have passed the examination, you will receive an email confirmation soon after. The certificate can be downloaded from the MuleSoft training website, and it will be auto-generated after receiving the email confirmation. This certificate will be valid for two years from the date of the examination.

If you fail the examination, you can reattempt it 24 or more hours later. Make sure you prepare for the section(s) for which you scored the least before reattempting.

Summary

The MCPA – Level 1 exam is highly regarded in the industry and serves as a validation of architects' abilities to construct secure and resilient MuleSoft platforms. This chapter delves into the essential topics that must be comprehended to prepare for the exam, as well as the system requirements for the day of the test. Additionally, we explored effective and efficient strategies for answering multiple-choice questions and identified the ideal candidates for this examination. Finally, we concluded with a set of practice questions designed to familiarize you with the exam's format and level of complexity.

Questions

Have a go at answering the following questions:

1. An organization is looking to set up MuleSoft for deploying APIs. They have a requirement that data and metadata should not leave the corporate datacenter. What is one of the best options that is suitable for hosting the runtime and control plane?

    A. Customer-hosted Mule runtime plane and customer-hosted Anypoint Platform PCE control plane

    B. MuleSoft-hosted runtime plane and customer-hosted Anypoint Platform PCE control plane

    C. Customer-hosted Mule runtime plane and MuleSoft-hosted Anypoint Platform control plane

    D. MuleSoft-hosted runtime plane and MuleSoft-hosted Anypoint Platform control plane

2. An organization is using CloudHub 1.0 to run MuleSoft APIs. MuleSoft APIs deployed to CloudHub 1.0 require access to the services or databases that are located behind the corporate firewalls. What is one of the options that can be leveraged to connect the corporate data center securely from CloudHub?

    A. Services and databases located behind the corporate firewall are accessible with the default CloudHub 1.0 setup. No customization to the platform is required.

    B. Set up Anypoint Virtual Private Cloud in CloudHub 1.0 and create a VPN IPSec tunnel between Anypoint Virtual Private Cloud and the corporate data center.

    C. Use a static IP address on the application that needs to connect to services located behind the corporate firewall and whitelist the static IP address in the corporate data center firewall.

    D. It is not possible to connect the service located behind the corporate firewall from CloudHub 1.0. You need to set up Mule Runtime on-premises to connect resources behind the corporate firewall.

3. An organization has deployed an API that is using Object Store v2 on CloudHub. There is another API deployed on the on-premises Mule Runtime that wants to access the data from Object Store v2. What is the best way to access Object Store v2 on CloudHub from the application running on the on-premises Mule Runtime?

   A. Using the Anypoint CLI

   B. Using Object Store Connector

   C. Using the Object Store v2 REST API

   D. It is not possible to access Object Store v2 from on-premises Mule Runtime

4. Which API policy will be least applied at the Experience API?

   A. IP Blocklist

   B. IP Allowlist

   C. JSON Threat Protection policy

   D. Client ID Enforcement policy

5. An organization has Kubernetes running on the AWS cloud as a managed service by AWS. They are looking to set up Runtime Fabric Manager to deploy MuleSoft APIs. What is the best option to choose?

   • Runtime Fabric Manager on Elastic Kubernetes Service

   • Runtime Fabric Manager on bare-metal server/VMs

   • Runtime Fabric Manager on OpenShift

   • You cannot use your own Kubernetes running on AWS to run Runtime Fabric Manager

6. In which situation would you require a dedicated load balancer on the Anypoint Platform?

   A. To route traffic to the application running in Anypoint Virtual Private Cloud on the private port

   B. To load balance the traffic between applications running in multiple regions of CloudHub

   C. To route traffic to the application running on the on-premises Mule Runtime

   D. To route traffic to the application running in Anypoint Virtual Private Cloud on the public port

7. An organization is running MuleSoft APIs on the on-premises-hosted runtime plane with multiple nodes. APIs deployed to the runtime plane are facing concurrency issues due to using file connectors, topics, and so on. How can you resolve the concurrency issue for the application running on the runtime plane?

   A. Add all the nodes into the server group to resolve the concurrency issues

   B. Add all the nodes into the cluster to resolve the concurrency issues

C. Add an HTTP load balancer in front of all the nodes to resolve the concurrency issues

D. Do not use the connectors that cause concurrency issues

8. An organization has non-MuleSoft APIs, and they are looking to manage them using Anypoint Platform API Manager. What is the most cost-effective and highly performant solution for managing the non-MuleSoft APIs?

A. Create API proxies for all the non-MuleSoft APIs to manage them using API Manager

B. Set up Flex Gateway to manage the non-MuleSoft APIs using API Manager

C. Create MuleSoft APIs in front of each non-MuleSoft API, peer MuleSoft APIs with API Manager using API auto-discovery, and manage the non-MuleSoft APIs using API Manager

D. There is no way to manage non-MuleSoft APIs from Anypoint Platform API Manager

9. An organization has a backend system that can handle a certain number of requests within a certain time frame. If more requests arrive than the backend system cannot handle, those requests need to be queued and retried, but they should not be rejected until the time limit or retry limit is exceeded. Which API policy can handle this scenario to protect the API and backend system?

A. Spike control policy

B. Rate limiting

C. Rate limiting with SLA tiers

D. IP allowlist

10. An organization is using Runtime Fabric Manager on Elastic Kubernetes Service. They have a few APIs deployed with multiple replicas sharing the object store, and replicas are clustered. They are facing challenges with data in the object store being lost during application redeployment or restart. As a platform architect, how will you fulfill this requirement?

A. Enable the tokenization service and use the persistent object store in the MuleSoft application

B. Enable Persistence Gateway and use the transient object store in the MuleSoft application

C. Enable the tokenization service and use the transient object store in the MuleSoft application

D. Enable Persistence Gateway and use the persistent object store in the MuleSoft application

11. What are the different metrics that can be configured while creating a custom dashboard in Anypoint API Manager?

A. Request size, CPU usage, response size, memory usage

B. Request size, CPU usage, response size, HTTP status code

C. Request size, requests, response size, responses

D. Request size, requests, response size, response time

12. An organization has private endpoints and they are looking to test and monitor the private endpoints without consuming extra vCores to create private locations. Is it possible, and if so, how can it be achieved?

    A. Yes, it is possible. Create a public location for monitoring private endpoints. You need to allow IP addresses in the Anypoint Virtual Private Cloud firewall rules for public locations.

    B. No, it is not possible. You will always need a private location for monitoring private endpoints.

    C. Yes, it is possible. Create a public location for monitoring private endpoints. There is no other configuration required.

    D. No, it is not possible to monitor the private endpoints from functional monitoring.

13. An organization has deployed the MuleSoft API on CloudHub. This API started facing the performance issue that it is not able to process more requests at a time and there has been latency added to the response time. As an architect, what solution would you suggest to resolve the performance issue?

    A. Implement vertical scaling by increasing the worker size or enable an autoscaling policy for memory usage

    B. Implement horizontal scaling by increasing the number of workers for the application or enable an autoscaling policy for memory usage

    C. Implement horizontal scaling by increasing the number of workers for the application or enable an autoscaling policy for CPU usage

    D. Implement vertical scaling by increasing the worker size or enable an autoscaling policy for CPU usage

> **Note**
> The autoscaling feature is not enabled on CloudHub by default. Contact your MuleSoft account representative.

14. What cannot be enforced using the API policy for applications deployed to CloudHub?

    A. Logging the HTTP requests and responses

    B. Allowing and blocking requests from certain IP addresses or IP address ranges

    C. Tokenizing and detokenizing the data in the request and response payload

    D. Controlling the number of requests to avoid overloading the backend systems

15. An organization is looking to deploy an application on Runtime Fabric Manager with zero downtime. Which is the best solution to use for zero-downtime deployments?

    A. Use the Recreate deployment model with more than one replica

    B. Use the Rolling Update deployment model with more than one replica

C. Use the Recreate deployment model with a minimum of one replica

D. Use the Rolling Update deployment model with a minimum of one replica

16. An organization is using CloudHub 2.0, and they have APIs deployed using the API-led connectivity architecture. They don't want System and Process APIs to be publicly accessible. Only Experience APIs can be publicly accessible. What is the best solution to implement this in CloudHub 2.0?

A. Use shared space in CloudHub 2.0 and remove public endpoints from the System and Process APIs

B. Use shared space in CloudHub 2.0 and define firewall rules for not allowing traffic from external services for System and Process APIs

C. Use private space and remove public endpoints from the System and Process APIs

D. Use private space and define firewall rules for not allowing traffic from external services for System and Process APIs

17. What are the different alerts that can be configured from Anypoint API Manager for the API instance?

A. Request count, Response code, policy violation, response time

B. Request count, CPU usage, policy violation, response time

C. Request count, CPU usage, policy violation, memory usage

D. Request count, CPU usage, HTTP status code, memory usage

18. An organization has assets in Anypoint Exchange. Some of the versions of those assets are of no use as new versions have been published in Anypoint Exchange. What should happen to the old asset versions so that users are aware that they are not in use?

A. Decommission the asset version

B. Retire the asset version

C. Deprecate the asset version

D. Remove the asset version

19. How does a fine-grained microservices architecture benefit the application network?

A. The number of discoverable and reusable assets will increase in the application networks

B. The number of API connections will decrease in the application networks

C. Resource usage will decrease as fine-grained microservices require fewer resources

D. Response time will improve for end consumers as microservices are smaller

20. An organization is looking to set up Anypoint Virtual Private Cloud. To do that, they need to decide on the CIDR mask. They have the following requirements:

- 100 applications are to be deployed on the production

- Each application will be deployed to two workers for high availability

  What will be a suitable CIDR mask for these requirements?

  A. 0/24

  B. 0/23

  C. 0/22

  D. 0/21

21. What cannot be effectively enforced with Anypoint Security?

  A. Guarding the API against denial-of-service attacks

  B. Limiting the size of the payload

  C. Validating the OAuth token

  D. Allowing a request from certain IP addresses or IP ranges

22. An organization has implemented a dedicated load balancer and they want to allow public traffic from certain IP addresses and need to restrict all other traffic on the dedicated load balancer. What is the best solution to implement this requirement?

  A. Apply the IP blocklist policy on the API instance

  B. Remove 0.0.0.0/0 from allowed CIDRs and add the required IP addresses or IP ranges to the allowlist CIDRs on the dedicated load balancer to allow traffic from those IP addresses and restrict all other traffic

  C. Apply the IP allowlist policy on the API instance

  D. Apply the IP allowlist policy on the API security to allow traffic from certain IP addresses or IP ranges

23. An organization hosts APIs on the customer-hosted Mule Runtime, and they have configured Active Directory as an identity provider in the Anypoint Platform. They don't have the budget to go for any other external identity provider. Which API policy can be used to authenticate users within the organization when accessing the APIs?

    A. Basic authentication – LDAP

    B. Basic authentication

    C. JWT validation

    D. IP allowlist

24. An organization has permanently moved API implementation to a new location. What is the best approach to tell the client that the requested resources have been permanently moved to a new location?

    A. Respond with status code 500 and the message "Error while processing request"

    B. Respond with status code 404 and the message "Requested resource not found"

    C. Respond with status code 301 and the message "Requested resource has been moved permanently to a new location"

    D. Respond with status code 302 and the message "Requested resource has been moved permanently to a new location"

25. An organization has an API that connects to the backend system, which intermittently goes down or is under maintenance two to three times a week. The client is looking to avoid overloading the backend system during maintenance, which is likely to fail all the requests. Which API policy can be used to implement this situation?

    A. Canary deployment

    B. Spike control

    C. Rate limiting

    D. Circuit breaker

Note

The canary deployment and circuit breaker policies are available in the MuleSoft Catalyst GitHub.

Further reading

- `https://training.mulesoft.com/certification/architect-platform-level1`

- `https://training.mulesoft.com/course/architecture-application-networks`

Answers

Question	Answer
1	A
2	B
3	C
4	B
5	A
6	A
7	B
8	B
9	A
10	D
11	D
12	A
13	C
14	C
15	D
16	C
17	A
18	C
19	A
20	B
21	C
22	B
23	A
24	C
25	D

18

Tackling Tricky Topics

We explored MuleSoft's range of hosting options in earlier chapters, including CloudHub, on-premises, hybrid, Runtime Fabric manager on VMs/bare-metal machines, and Self-Managed Kubernetes.

The following topics will be covered in this chapter:

- Considerations for choosing the right deployment model
- Resilient API techniques
- Anypoint CLI
- Idempotent and cache scope
- Core components
- Use cases for implementing the platform architecture

Considerations for choosing the right deployment model

MuleSoft is a very adaptable platform that offers a variety of deployment choices to host your network of apps. To ensure that your enterprise's digital transition is smooth and error-free, you must assess the best deployment model.

For businesses looking to host their network of apps, MuleSoft provides the following deployment options:

- CloudHub 1.0
- CloudHub 2.0
- On-premises Mule Runtime (standalone and hybrid)
- Runtime Fabric manager on VMs/bare-metal machines, OpenShift, and Self-Managed Kubernetes

Selecting a MuleSoft deployment strategy is based on several considerations, including data security, control over data, scalability, and particular business requirements. The following instances will show you when to choose each model. *Table 18.1* illustrates the differences and similarities across deployment choices with respect to platform capabilities, data and metadata storage, and platform maintenance and upgrades.

Factors	Fully cloud-hosted (control plane and runtime plane in the cloud)	Fully customer-hosted (control plane and runtime plane in on-premises or customer-hosted)	Hybrid (control plane in the cloud and runtime plane on-premises)
Platform	Anypoint Platform (control plane) CloudHub 1.0 and CloudHub 2.0 (runtime plane)	Anypoint **Private Cloud Edition** (PCE) (control plane) On-premises Mule Runtime (runtime plane)	Anypoint Platform (control plane) On-premises Mule runtime (runtime plane) or Runtime Fabric on Self-Managed Kubernetes, VMs/bare-metal, and OpenShift
Data and metadata	Data and metadata will be in the vendor's infrastructure	Data and metadata will be in the customer's infrastructure	Only metadata will be in the vendor's infrastructure
Platform and upgrade management	Platform maintenance and upgrades will be managed by the vendor (MuleSoft)	The customer is responsible for upgrades, patches, and platform maintenance for Mule runtime and Anypoint PCE.	The customer is responsible for upgrades, patches, and platform maintenance for Mule runtime and Anypoint Platform, and upgrades will be managed by MuleSoft

Table 18.1: MuleSoft deployment considerations (platform, data and metadata, and upgrade management)

Table 18.2 illustrates the differences and similarities across deployment choices with respect to network connectivity.

Factors	Fully cloud-hosted (control plane and runtime plane in the cloud)	Fully customer-hosted (control plane and runtime plane in on-premises or customer-hosted)	Hybrid (control plane in the cloud and runtime plane on-premises)
Network connectivity options	CloudHub 1.0 supports Anypoint Virtual Private Cloud, which can connect to an on-premises data center or any cloud using VPN IPSec tunneling, VPC peering, AWS Direct Connect, or Transit Gateway.\n\nCloudHub 2.0 supports a private space that can connect to an on-premises data center or any cloud using VPN IPSec tunneling and Transit Gateway.	Customers must manage the network connectivity between the Mule application and other systems.\n\nCustomers must control the inbound and outbound traffic using a firewall or by implementing a VPN or any other connectivity options to connect to other data centers or private clouds.	Customers must manage the network connectivity between the Mule application and other systems.\n\nCustomers must control the inbound and outbound traffic using a firewall or by implementing a VPN or any other connectivity options to connect to other data centers or private clouds.

Table 18.2: MuleSoft deployment considerations (network connectivity)

Table 18.3 illustrates the differences and similarities across deployment choices with respect to business continuity.

Factors	Fully cloud-hosted (control plane and runtime plane in the cloud)	Fully customer-hosted (control plane and runtime plane in on-premises or customer-hosted)	Hybrid (control plane in the cloud and runtime plane on-premises)
Business continuity	Features such as high availability, fault tolerance, and intelligent healing are provided and managed by MuleSoft. Applications can be horizontally or vertically scaled by adding more instances (workers or replicas) or increasing the vCores or replica size. The scalability and high availability of Anypoint Platform are managed by MuleSoft. The customer is not responsible for managing any infrastructure for running the Mule applications or proxies.	The customer is responsible for high availability, fault tolerance, scalability, and so on. The customer is responsible for managing the infrastructure and networks for running the MuleSoft application and implementing the Anypoint PCE. MuleSoft will only provide Mule runtime for running the MuleSoft application and the setup for Anypoint PCE on the customer's infrastructure.	The customer is responsible for managing the underlying infrastructure for running the Mule applications or proxies. Customers need to ensure the high availability and scalability of the nodes or servers. Applications can be scaled easily by increasing the number of replicas and the replica size on Runtime Fabric with zero downtime. Runtime Fabric provides the mechanism for intelligent healing and fault tolerance at the application level. Mule Runtime running on-premises must be deployed on multiple nodes in a cluster or group to ensure high availability. The scaling of nodes can only be done by adding extra nodes to the group and server. The customer is responsible for managing the underlying infrastructure and networks. Anypoint platform will be completely managed by MuleSoft. MuleSoft will ensure the availability and scalability of the Anypoint platform. It supports Anypoint clustering at the application level to ensure the availability of the application.

Table 18.3: MuleSoft deployment considerations (business continuity)

Table 18.4 illustrates the differences and similarities across deployment choices with respect to the load balancer.

Factors	Fully cloud-hosted (control plane and runtime plane in the cloud)	Fully customer-hosted (control plane and runtime plane in on-premises or customer-hosted)	Hybrid (control plane in the cloud and runtime plane on-premises)
Business continuity	Features such as high availability, fault tolerance, and intelligent healing are provided and managed by MuleSoft. Applications can be horizontally or vertically scaled by adding more instances (workers or replicas) or increasing the vCores or replica size. The scalability and high availability of Anypoint Platform are managed by MuleSoft. The customer is not responsible for managing any infrastructure for running the Mule applications or proxies.	The customer is responsible for high availability, fault tolerance, scalability, and so on. The customer is responsible for managing the infrastructure and networks for running the MuleSoft application and implementing the Anypoint PCE. MuleSoft will only provide Mule runtime for running the MuleSoft application and the setup for Anypoint PCE on the customer's infrastructure.	The customer is responsible for managing the underlying infrastructure for running the Mule applications or proxies. Customers need to ensure the high availability and scalability of the nodes or servers. Applications can be scaled easily by increasing the number of replicas and the replica size on Runtime Fabric with zero downtime. Runtime Fabric provides the mechanism for intelligent healing and fault tolerance at the application level. Mule Runtime running on-premises must be deployed on multiple nodes in a cluster or group to ensure high availability. The scaling of nodes can only be done by adding extra nodes to the group and server. The customer is responsible for managing the underlying infrastructure and networks. Anypoint platform will be completely managed by MuleSoft. MuleSoft will ensure the availability and scalability of the Anypoint platform. It supports Anypoint clustering at the application level to ensure the availability of the application.

Table 18.4: MuleSoft deployment considerations (load balancer)

Table 18.5 illustrates the differences and similarities across deployment choices with respect to the time to value.

Factors	Fully cloud-hosted (control plane and runtime plane in the cloud)	Fully customer-hosted (control plane and runtime plane in on-premises or customer-hosted)	Hybrid (control plane in the cloud and runtime plane on-premises)
Time to value	Requires a small amount of setup time and most things are readily available. You may have to configure the Anypoint VPC, VPN, and dedicated load balancer.	Requires a lot of setup time. The infrastructure needs to be configured to run the Mule application and Anypoint PCE.	Requires setting up the infrastructure for the runtime plane

Table 18.5: MuleSoft deployment considerations (Time to value)

Table 18.6 illustrates the differences and similarities across deployment choices with respect to monitoring and logging.

Factors	Fully cloud-hosted (control plane and runtime plane in the cloud)	Fully customer-hosted (control plane and runtime plane in on-premises or customer-hosted)	Hybrid (control plane in the cloud and runtime plane on-premises)
Monitoring and logging	MuleSoft provides out-of-the-box monitoring that can be used to monitor Mule applications deployed to CloudHub 1.0 and CloudHub 2.0. CloudHub 1.0 also supports functional monitoring and allows you to set up alerts on the applications. Application logging is supported by CloudHub 1.0 and CloudHub 2.0. This is an out-of-the-box capability provided by MuleSoft. The Titanium license required or the Advance logging features like aggregates log files so you can manage, search for, filter, and analyze your logs.	Third-party monitoring and logging tools are required to monitor applications deployed in the customer environment. Can be integrated with Splunk or ELK for logging and monitoring.	MuleSoft provides out-of-the-box monitoring that can be used to monitor the Mule applications and nodes running in hybrid environments. Third-party monitoring is required to monitor the infrastructure and networks. Third-party logging tools can be integrated into the hybrid environment. Can be integrated with Splunk or ELK for logging and monitoring.

Table 18.6: MuleSoft deployment considerations (monitoring and logging)

Table 18.7 illustrates the differences and similarities across deployment choices with respect to use cases.

Factors	Fully cloud-hosted (control plane and runtime plane in the cloud)	Fully customer-hosted (control plane and runtime plane in on-premises or customer-hosted)	Hybrid (control plane in the cloud and runtime plane on-premises)
Use cases	Small or medium-sized organizations that don't have a team that manages the infrastructure. Your company is brand new and has never used cloud service management before. You have few applications and do not want to invest in a standalone cloud infrastructure. There are no laws or government regulations that apply to data.	You have a team that manages the entire infrastructure and has an obligation to move into the cloud. Your data/metadata should not leave your organization.	You're going to deploy more applications and you're thinking it's going to be expensive to use the full cloud. You plan to keep your existing infrastructure and gradually move toward a cloud environment. You're thinking that a hybrid solution will cut costs and time to build infrastructure.

Table 18.7: MuleSoft deployment considerations (use cases)

We have discussed the many factors to consider when selecting the best deployment option for your company. Depending on your organization's needs and capabilities, CloudHub 1.0, 2.0, **Runtime Fabric (RTF)**, or a hybrid implementation may be the best option. To fully understand the benefits and drawbacks of each deployment model, it may be best to speak with MuleSoft or a reliable partner. The following are the deployment options provided by MuleSoft for hosting the applications and proxies.

CloudHub 1.0

MuleSoft's cloud-based **integration platform as a service (iPaaS)** is called CloudHub 1.0. It is helpful in cases where the company lacks the infrastructure required for on-premises deployment or doesn't want to. It has integrated load balancing, easy scalability, automatic updates, and instant deployment options. It does away with the need for hardware and software maintenance, but MuleSoft handles most of the data control.

Assume that a retail company has just begun to increase its online presence. They want to seamlessly integrate the new e-commerce platform with their current systems (such as order management, inventory, and **customer relationship management** (**CRM**)) without having to deal with a lot of infrastructure management hassles. CloudHub 1.0 would be advantageous to this company. They wouldn't need to spend money on new hardware or worry about software updates and maintenance with the CloudHub 1.0 model because the platform would take care of these things. Additionally, they would benefit from smooth scaling and integrated load balancing to adapt to changing demands, particularly during busy times of the year.

CloudHub 2.0

CloudHub 2.0 adds more operational features to CloudHub 1.0, such as providing options for granular vCores size, improved load balancer strategies, and improved private space for hosting the application in the isolated and virtual network.

Let's take the example of an online media streaming provider that needs to continue providing fast and highly available services even when it grows and updates its software. Additionally, they want the ability to customize some operational settings to meet their own needs and the flexibility to do so. The service doesn't want any lag or outage to occur because this can cause users to become dissatisfied and result in a loss of subscribers.

CloudHub 2.0 would be advantageous to such a business. The scalability and zero-downtime updates of CloudHub 2.0 allow media services to manage their operations more effectively without compromising user experience. Additionally, the platform gives the business more control over data, enabling it to guarantee the security of sensitive user information.

Runtime Fabric

Anypoint RTF is a container service. This is advantageous for businesses that need the freedom to integrate Mule apps and APIs into their own cloud-based managed infrastructure (such as AWS, Azure, or GCP) or on-site data center. Although it can be more infrastructure-demanding than other options, it has benefits such as more control over data and system resources.

Imagine a financial institution that needs to integrate various services, such as CRM, payment systems, and account management. Given the delicate nature of its operations, it is required to abide by stringent privacy and data protection regulations. Furthermore, this bank must adhere to local regulatory requirements because it operates in multiple geographic regions. These specifications might dictate that the data must be located within a certain geographic region as opposed to internationally.

The bank can take advantage of Anypoint RTF in this challenging scenario. A banking institution can benefit from a hybrid application model by using RTF. It can use on-premises and different cloud deployment solutions to meet geo-compliant requirements and deploy applications and APIs within regulatory bounds. Furthermore, bank integration workflows processing financial data depend on high application performance and usability. RTF offers high availability, redundancy, and fault tolerance, ideal for these scenarios. Regardless of the deployment locations, the bank can also continuously operate and monitor systems while maintaining a high degree of security and infrastructure management. Anypoint RTF is therefore the best option in this kind of setting.

On-premises Mule runtime

On-premises Mule Runtime is ideal for companies that need to tightly control their data, adhere to strict data regulations, or invest heavily in their data centers.

Let us consider a healthcare organization that needs to integrate its medical billing systems, **laboratory information management systems (LIMS)**, and **electronic medical records (EMR)**. Strict laws such as HIPAA, which demand stringent data security and privacy, govern this healthcare organization. Furthermore, due to security or technological constraints, an organization may have legacy systems that are essential to daily operations but can only be accessed through the private network of the organization.

In this scenario, Mule Runtime can be installed locally by the organization. They can securely integrate with their legacy systems and keep strict control over their data thanks to this implementation. Since data never leaves the company's physical locations, security regulations are always followed. Furthermore, the healthcare company might have made significant investments in a private data center with suitable hardware. They could take advantage of their current infrastructure without switching to a cloud-based solution by using an on-premises Mule Runtime, which would lower the risks and expenses associated with a possible migration.

We've talked about some essential building blocks that can be applied to the creation and deployment of Mule APIs. This chapter will take us through a walk-through of Anypoint MQ in the next section.

Anypoint CLI

MuleSoft's Anypoint Platform offers a tool called Anypoint **Command-Line Interface (CLI)** that lets users conduct different operations on the platform without utilizing the Anypoint Platform's user interface. Alternatively, you can use a terminal to manage your servers, apps, APIs, and other entities from the Anypoint Platform web interface.

This can be helpful for users who prefer CLIs over graphical ones, as well as for automating tasks, scripting, and integrating with CI/CD tools. It facilitates the creation, management, and deletion of different Anypoint Platform resources, including servers, applications, APIs, and so forth. This tool is written in Node.js and can be installed using **Node Package Manager** (**npm**). It allows users to perform tasks such as creating and managing applications, deploying APIs, manipulating environments, applying policies, and more.

The following are the key features of the Anypoint CLI:

- **Manage Mule applications**: You can enable, modify, or disable Mule applications in different environments
- **API management**: Create and manage APIs, policies, and proxies
- **VPN management**: You can edit or create Anypoint VPNs
- **Hybrid management**: You can manage your hybrid servers directly from the CLI
- **Manage users and roles**: You can manage users, roles, and access rights associated with Anypoint Platform
- **Integration with CI/CD tools**: You can create scripts to integrate with various CI/CD tools for seamless deployment and upgrades

The Anypoint CLI tool is especially useful when you want to automate specific tasks or for developers who want to integrate Anypoint Platform features into their existing development workflows. Therefore, it offers an alternative to the more traditional interaction with the platform through a browser and expands the options available to interact with the platform.

Resilient API techniques

Resilient APIs are designed to cope gracefully with failures, whether they originate in the API itself, from dependent services, or due to external factors such as network problems or latency, API version mismatches, or other problems that may arise because of changes in the environment or unexpected user behavior.

The following are the reasons that APIs must be resilient and continue to operate.

- **Availability**: APIs must be highly available and continue to operate in the event of any hardware or infrastructure failure. It is important for APIs to ensure business continuity.
- **Performance**: By reducing the number of errors and interruptions, resilient APIs can help improve your applications' performance. This will lead to improved user experience and higher productivity.

- **Scalability**: By making your applications more resilient to load spikes and failures, resilient APIs can help to improve your application's scalability. This may help you to handle more traffic and users without affecting performance.

- **Security**: APIs must be resilient against any security threats or attacks. This can include SQL or PHP injection, **Distributed Denial of Service (DDoS)**, and **Denial of Service (DoS)**. APIs must be protected against unauthorized access.

- **Fault tolerance**: APIs must be fault tolerant and be recovered automatically in the event of any failures or crashes. APIs must be able to heal automatically in case of any failures related to infrastructure, or JVM crashes.

The following are some techniques that ensure that APIs are resilient and continue to operate in the event of any failures:

- **Load balancing**: Traffic coming to an API must be load-balanced across the multiple instances of APIs running on multiple servers. This will ensure that a single server doesn't get overloaded, and it will improve API performance and availability.

- **Error handling and logging**: APIs must handle errors gracefully and respond with the right error codes to the client. In the event of any errors, APIs must continue to operate and process further requests. It is also possible to track and record errors occurring in your APIs, which will help you debug, diagnose, and improve the performance and quality of your APIs through error handling and logging.

- **Failover**: If the main server fails, resilient APIs can use a failover function to move to an alternative server. This should help to keep your applications up and running even if you are having trouble with one of the servers.

- **Designing robust API security**: APIs must be secure to ensure that they are only accessible to the authorized client. APIs must be protected by implementing SSL or TLS. This will allow secure communication between client and server. API policies such as IP allowlists, blocklists, and other security policies can be applied to the API to ensure that requests are coming from authorized clients.

- **Designing for scalability and reliability**: The ability of your APIs to handle increasing or varying loads and demands, and to recover from failures or interruptions, is the ability of your APIs to be resilient and reliable. If you are planning for scalability and reliability, it may be helpful to prevent errors such as interruptions, crashes, or data loss due to the lack of or instability of available resources.

- **Monitoring and alerts**: To detect problems early, resilient APIs can be monitored. Before problems lead to outages or other disturbances, this can help you take corrective action. Monitoring will troubleshoot issues early, and issues can be fixed soon before they become too big. To ensure that you receive alerts in case of any failure or increased CPU and memory usage, it is necessary to set them up on your APIs.

- **Implementing API governance:** The practice of defining, implementing, and managing standards, policies, or processes that ensure your APIs are standardized, reliable, and safe is called API governance. In principle, API governance is a key component of a mature API management system and plays an essential role in ensuring that great APIs are created. MuleSoft provides API governance components that can be used to ensure the API specification is consistent and improve the overall quality of the APIs within your organization.

In this section, we saw a variety of techniques for API responsiveness. We will now examine a few use cases related to selecting a deployment model.

Idempotent scope

Idempotence is a design pattern that detects and eliminates the processing of duplicate messages. Let's look at an example that shows why the idempotent design pattern is necessary.

When clients send requests to servers, they may not receive a response. Clients cannot tell whether the response has been lost or whether the server crashed before it could process the request. To ensure that their request is processed, clients must send the request again. If the server processes the request and then crashes, servers will receive duplicate requests from clients when they try again.

To uniquely identify a client, each client is assigned a unique ID. Upon receiving a request, the server checks whether the request with that request number is already being handled by the same client. If the server finds a stored response, it sends the response to the client without reprocessing the request.

MuleSoft provides an idempotent filter for handling this situation and preventing the processing of duplicate messages. An idempotent filter checks the unique ID of an incoming message. This ID can be any message attribute or can be calculated using a DataWeave expression. The filter then checks whether that ID has already been processed. If so, the message is discarded. Otherwise, the message may continue through the Mule flow.

Processed message IDs can be stored in several object pools by configuring an idempotent filter. This enables you to select the object storage option—such as a distributed cache, local database, or even cloud-based object store—that best meets your requirements.

Figure 18.1 illustrates how idempotent filters work in the Mule flow.

Figure 18.1: Idempotent filter

The order with the order ID 1001 in the preceding figure was received in the Mule flow and will be validated by an idempotent message validator to make sure that no duplicate orders are processed for a specific amount of time. The order ID will also be stored in the local database, distributed cache, or object store so that future incoming orders can be validated against the stored order ID.

Order Id 1001 entered the Mule flow for the first time, and it will pass the idempotent message validator before being processed further. In this instance, no duplicates were found.

Figure 18.2: Idempotent filter (with a duplicate detected)

An idempotent message validator will verify the order with order ID 1001 in the preceding figure, which was received in the Mule flow, to ensure that no duplicate orders are processed for a certain period. Order ID 1001 has already been received in this instance, and an error message (MULE:DUPLICATE_ MESSAGE) will be thrown.

Cache scope

Cache scope is another valuable component provided by MuleSoft that needs to be configured inside a Mule flow to store and reuse data that is regularly referred to. This will enhance the general overall performance of the software by decreasing the number of times operations are executed.

The following figure illustrates how caching works in a Mule flow.

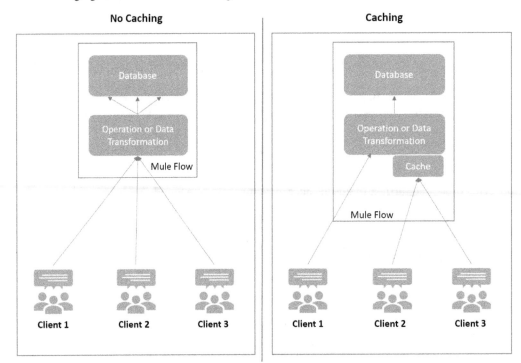

Figure 18.3: Caching versus no caching

In *Figure 18.3*, we have one Mule flow without caching and one with caching. The Mule flow without caching will always connect to the database to retrieve the data for every request, whereas the Mule flow with caching will only connect to the database once during the first request and retrieve the data, which it will store in the cache and respond to the client. Any subsequent requests will receive a copy of the data from the cache instead of connecting the database again and again.

Caching is good for static data and data that changes infrequently, but it may be not suitable when data changes frequently and is dynamic.

Let's look at the benefits of caching:

- Using a cache reduces the network overhead by caching the data near the consumer, and it reduces the number of connections with the end systems such as databases and web services.

- Overall application response time will be improved as caching reduces the number of operations performed in the Mule flow and stores the operation and data transformation data in the cache to be retrieved for future requests.

- The processing load on the Mule instance will be reduced, the overall application performance will be improved, and the speed of message processing within the Mule flow will be improved as well.

- Data will be available in the cache during network crashes. Your application may be unable to connect end systems to retrieve data; in such cases, caching can be used for storing and retrieving the data.

Core components

MuleSoft provides out-of-the-box components that can be used for routing, transforming, and processing incoming messages, and these components can be configured in the Mule flow.

Table 18.8 illustrates the core component groups provided by MuleSoft.

Core component group	Core components	Description
Batch	Batch Job, Batch Step, Batch Aggregator	Batch components are used to process large volumes of data by automatically splitting the data sources and stores in persistent queues and ensuring reliability.
Endpoints	Scheduler	Scheduler is a Mule source event that triggers the execution of a Mule flow based on the scheduler frequency or cron expression defined.
Error Handling	On Error Propagate, On Error Continue, Error Handler, Raise Error	Error handling components allow you to handle errors during message processing in Mule flows.
Flow Control	Choice, Scatter-Gather, First Successful, Round Robin	Flow control components are used to route messages to one or multiple targets depending on certain conditions. This helps you to implement enterprise integration patterns such as content-based routing, scatter-gather, and multicasting.

Core component group	Core components	Description
Transformers	Set Variable, Remove Variable, Set Payload	A transformer modifies or enhances a message payload or message header to get it ready for processing through a Mule flow.
Scopes	All, Any, Async, Cache, Flow, For Each, Parallel For Each, Sub Flow, Try, Until Successful	The message processors known as scopes—sometimes called "wrappers"—appear as processing blocks when you first place them on the message flow canvas.
Other Components	Custom Business Events, Dynamic Evaluate, Flow Reference, Idempotent Message Validator, Invalidate Cache, Invalidate Key, Logger, Parse Template, Set Transaction Id, Transform Message	Other valuable core components are used to transform messages, call other flows, validate data, and cache data.

Table 18.8: Core components

We have discussed a few core components. Now, we will discuss some more important core components that we frequently use in Mule flows.

Choice router

Messages are dynamically routed through a flow by the Choice router based on a set of DataWeave expressions that assess message content. Every expression has a distinct routing option attached to it. This is similar to `if/then/else` code blocks that exist in most programming languages.

The Choice router only has one route that runs (that is, only the first expression that evaluates to `true` causes that route to run); the other routes are not checked. The default route is used if none of the expressions are true.

Figure 18.4 illustrates how the Choice router works in a Mule flow.

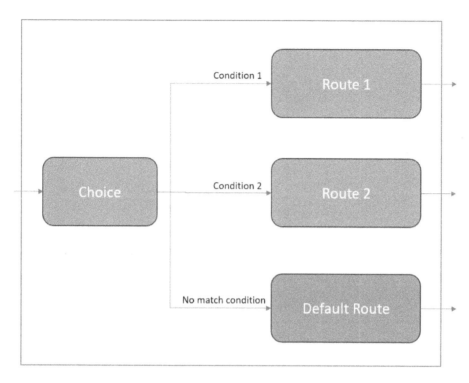

Figure 18.4: Choice router

The Choice router has a default route that runs when none of the expressions in the existing routes are true, and one route option that runs when the configured DataWeave expression evaluates to `true`. When you need to evaluate multiple conditions and then perform different actions based on which condition is met, add more routes.

Scatter-Gather router

Mule events are handled by a routing event processor known as the Scatter-Gather component. Mule events are routed via multiple parallel processing routes composed of different event processors. Each route executes a sequence of event processors upon receiving a reference to the Mule event.

Each of these routes has a separate thread for its event processors, and the resulting Mule event might be the same as the input one, or it could be a different one with different payloads, attributes, and variables. The Scatter-Gather component then combines the Mule events returned by each processing route to create a new Mule event, which is only passed to the next event processor after every route is successfully completed.

Figure 18.5 illustrates how Scatter-Gather works in a Mule flow.

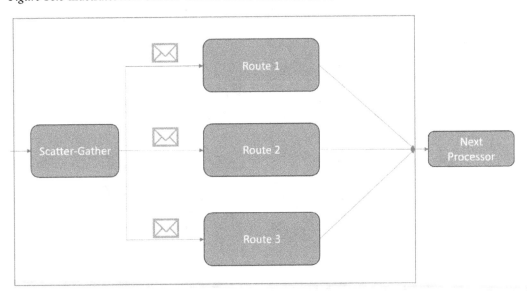

Figure 18.5: Scatter-Gather router

The Scatter-Gather component routes a copy of the message to all the routes in parallel, which will improve the overall performance of the Mule application. Scatter-Gather components work with repeatable streams, but they don't process non-repeatable streams.

Any errors that a route's event processors may produce can be handled by using a `Try` scope in each route of a Scatter-Gather component. The Scatter-Gather component throws an error of the `MULE:COMPOSITE_ROUTING` type after each route is executed, if any have failed with an error. Event processing stops at the Scatter-Gather component in the flow. Rather, the flow diverges to your event processors that handle errors.

We may have a situation where we want the output from a successful route even if other routes in Scatter-Gather components fail. In this case, you can place the individual route with a `try-catch` block with `on error continue` to ensure that we can get the aggregated output from the successful route and an error response from the failed route.

Error handling

MuleSoft provides out-of-the-box error-handling components to handle any kind of exception that occurs while executing the messages in a Mule flow. MuleSoft generates two types of errors, which are described here.

System errors

System errors are errors that occur at the system level or when a Mule event is not involved. System errors occur during application startup or when listeners cannot connect with the end systems. Such errors are not configurable or handled in the Mule flow.

Messaging errors

Messaging errors are errors that occur in the Mule flow during Mule events or message processing. Mule provides error components that can be configured in the Mule flow to handle any type of error, or we can rely on the default error-handling mechanism.

It is recommended to use error components (On Error components such as On Error Propagate and On Error Continue) instead of relying on the default error-handling mechanism:

- On Error Propagate: Within the On Error Propagate block, On Error Propagate intercepts the error, processes the Mule flow, and returns the error response (status code 500). The following figure illustrates how On Error Propagate works in a Mule flow.

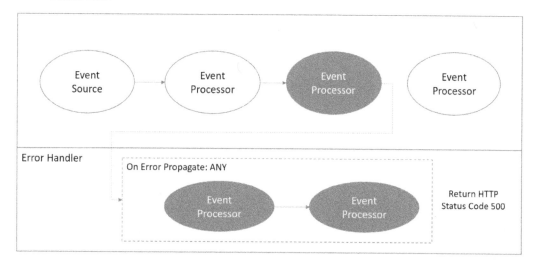

Figure 18.6: On Error Propagate

- On Error Continue: In On Error Continue, the error is caught, the Mule flow is processed, and the success response (status code 200) is returned. The following figure illustrates how On Error Continue works in a Mule flow.

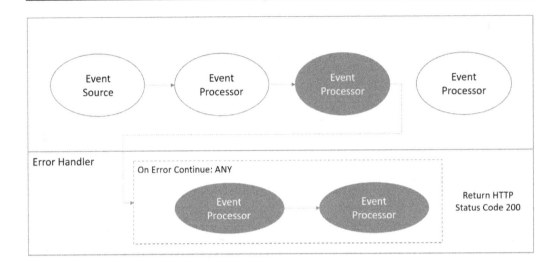

Figure 18.7: On Error Continue

- `Raise Error` is a core component that is used to raise errors with a custom description and a custom type in a Mule flow. This component can be used to raise the following errors:

- Core runtime errors, such as `MULE:SECURITY` and `MULE:CONNECTIVITY`

- Custom error types

Figure 18.8 illustrates how the `Raise Error` component can be configured and works in a Mule flow.

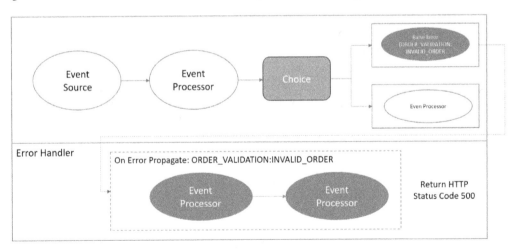

Figure 18.8: The Raise Error component

The process of managing exceptions and errors that arise during the execution of a Mule application at a central location is known as **global error handling** in MuleSoft. It offers a method for reliably capturing and managing errors across various integration flows and components.

Error handlers, which are unique MuleSoft components that can be set to handle kinds of errors or exceptions, are commonly used to implement global error handling. These error handlers are called whenever an error arises inside the application and are defined at the application level.

Please visit `https://docs.mulesoft.com/mule-runtime/latest/error-handling` for further information on global error handling.

As we've seen, MuleSoft offers several components to help handle errors in an efficient manner. As a best practice, we should always create a common error-handling framework using components provided by MuleSoft, and this common error-handling framework can be published to Anypoint Exchange and can be reused across multiple Mule applications.

Transform Message

The `Transform Message` component allows you to transform received input data. You can save the transformation explicitly in the DataWeave language or create it through the UI by dragging and dropping elements.

We have seen MuleSoft's basic building blocks and error-handling framework for building APIs and integrations. We will examine a few use cases for putting the platform architecture into practice in the following section.

Use case 1

J&J Music aims to enhance its online visibility by providing users with access to albums, songs, and additional information about the songs, such as song reviews and singers, among other things. Without having to worry about maintaining the infrastructure, they wish to integrate the current music management system on public clouds with CRM programs such as Salesforce. They intend to grow their business in the future, which means there's a good chance that traffic will rise. As a result, they need a platform that is both highly available and scalable.

The preceding requirements make it clear that J&J Music is searching for vendor-managed deployment options that guarantee scalability and business continuity. They also want to seamlessly integrate with their publicly accessible music management system and Salesforce CRM for customer management. We can use either CloudHub 1.0 or CloudHub 2.0 to accomplish this. What has been added to or improved in CloudHub 2.0 over CloudHub 1.0 has already been covered in an earlier section and in *Chapter 10*.

We will use CloudHub 1.0 as a MuleSoft application deployment option to carry out the requirement. CloudHub 2.0 can even meet this requirement.

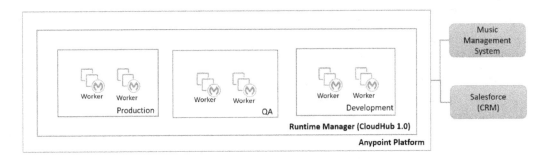

Figure 18.9: CloudHub 1.0 implementation

In *Figure 18.9*, we can leverage the vanilla CloudHub 1.0 platform features provided by MuleSoft. We don't need to configure any other extra components and are able to satisfy all the customer requirements.

J&J Music is extending the business and now they want to host all the APIs under a single domain and need to connect some of the resources located in the corporate data center or resources that are not accessible publicly.

To achieve the new requirement, we need to configure Anypoint VPC and an Anypoint **Dedicated Load Balancer** (**DLB**) to host all the APIs under a single domain. There is a need for Anypoint **Virtual Private Network** (**VPN**) to connect resources located in the corporate data center, so they can be accessed from the application running on CloudHub 1.0. The following figure illustrates how we can leverage the Anypoint VPC, DLB, and VPN with CloudHub 1.0.

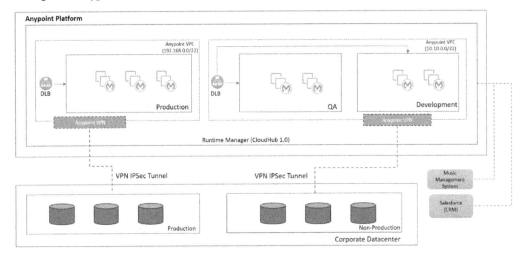

Figure 18.10: CloudHub 1.0 implementation with Anypoint VPC and VPN

As shown in *Figure 18.10*, we have configured Anypoint VPC, DLB, and VPN. The DLB will allow the hosting of all the APIs under a single domain and Anypoint VPN will allow connection to the resources located in the corporate data center.

J&J Music can enable API management capabilities for the APIs running on CloudHub 1.0 as shown in *Figure 18.11*.

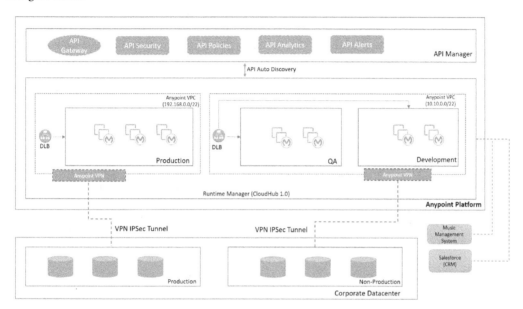

Figure 18.11: CloudHub 1.0 with API management

As shown in *Figure 18.11*, the API manager can be peered with APIs deployed to CloudHub 1.0 using API Autodiscovery. This will allow us to manage and secure the APIs.

Use case 2

Java is used to write J&J Music's APIs, which are hosted on-premises. To protect, manage, discover, and engage with the APIs, they are currently trying to activate API management features on the APIs. Additionally, they intend to gradually move every API to the cloud. MuleSoft is already the platform of choice for them to manage and implement the APIs.

From the use case, J&J Music wants to use Anypoint Platform to manage non-MuleSoft APIs. They also need to gradually migrate everything to CloudHub.

There are multiple solutions that can be used to implement this use case.

Hybrid implementation is an option (the control plane in Anypoint Platform and the runtime plane in the customer data center).

We must set up an API proxy that will peer with Java APIs to enable API management to manage Java APIs. Although the on-premises Mule runtime will enable this API proxy to operate closer to customer Java APIs, it does not fully satisfy the client's requirements as the client intends to migrate to the cloud soon. According to J&J Music's plan to migrate to the cloud, this solution will not be practical in the long run.

To fully meet J&J Music's requirements, we have selected CloudHub 2.0 as our hosting solution. To connect the Java APIs running on-premises via an API proxy running on CloudHub 2.0, we will also need to configure the private space on CloudHub 2.0 and the Anypoint VPN. More information regarding CloudHub 2.0 was covered in *Chapter 10*. This option will be more adaptable and fit the needs and long-term goals of the client.

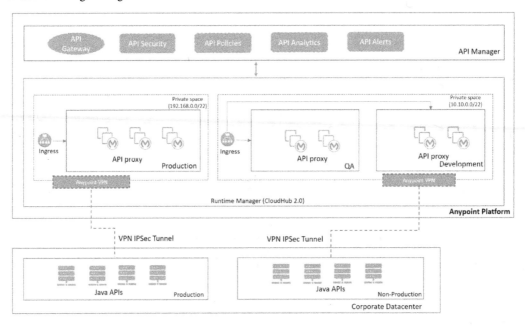

Figure 18.12: CloudHub 2.0 with API proxy

Figure 18.12 shows what J&J Music's architecture will look like for managing the Java APIs using Anypoint Platform.

> **Note**
>
> Like CloudHub 2.0, CloudHub 1.0 can also be utilized in a similar manner.
>
> Flex Gateway can be used to manage Java APIs; *Chapter 15* has more information on Flex Gateway. AWS, Azure, Google, and other cloud platforms can be used to set up Flex Gateway.

Use case 3

J&J Music desires to expand its business in a country with stricter laws and compliance requirements. The government of that country made cybersecurity, data protection, and privacy its top priorities through several laws and regulations. The rules of the country state that if you want to do business online, you must host your infrastructure there or use a cloud provider that gives you the option to host infrastructure there. Additionally, your data and metadata are not allowed to leave the country.

Although MuleSoft's control plane is situated in the US or the EU, it is not accessible in the country where we wish to grow our business and make our online presence possible. We are unable to manage the API life cycle in this scenario using Anypoint Platform. We must put into practice Anypoint PCE, which can be hosted in that country in a cloud computing environment or in the corporate data center.

Customer-hosted Anypoint PCE will be used to manage the APIs, and customer-hosted Mule runtime will be used to execute Mule applications.

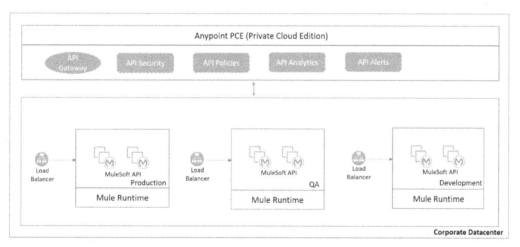

Figure 18.13: Anypoint PCE and customer-hosted Mule runtime

Figure 18.13 shows that the runtime plane and control plane are hosted in customer infrastructure. This will allow J&J Music to be compliant with the laws and regulations defined by the country.

> **Note**
>
> On-premises Mule runtime can be implemented instead of RTF.
>
> If the cloud provider permits hosting the necessary infrastructure in that country, the control plane and runtime plane may be hosted there.

Summary

In this chapter, we talked about the main components provided by MuleSoft. We have also seen flexible API techniques in the design and development of resilient APIs. Anypoint CLI for managing the MuleSoft platform and APIs was also discussed, including how Anypoint CLI can be integrated with CI/CD for application deployment and automation. We also discussed things to consider when choosing the right deployment option to run a MuleSoft application.

Thanks for taking the time to read this book. Your attention to this means a lot to me and is very much appreciated. Thank you.

Index

packtpub.com

Subscribe to our online digital library for full access to over 7,000 books and videos, as well as industry leading tools to help you plan your personal development and advance your career. For more information, please visit our website.

Why subscribe?

- Spend less time learning and more time coding with practical eBooks and Videos from over 4,000 industry professionals

- Improve your learning with Skill Plans built especially for you

- Get a free eBook or video every month

- Fully searchable for easy access to vital information

- Copy and paste, print, and bookmark content

Did you know that Packt offers eBook versions of every book published, with PDF and ePub files available? You can upgrade to the eBook version at packtpub.com and as a print book customer, you are entitled to a discount on the eBook copy. Get in touch with us at customercare@packtpub.com for more details.

At www.packtpub.com, you can also read a collection of free technical articles, sign up for a range of free newsletters, and receive exclusive discounts and offers on Packt books and eBooks.

Other Books You May Enjoy

If you enjoyed this book, you may be interested in these other books by Packt:

MuleSoft for Salesforce Developers

Arul Christhuraj Alphonse, Alexandra Martinez, Akshata Sawant

ISBN: 978-1-80107-960-0

- Understand how to use MuleSoft to achieve API-led connectivity
- Design and create documentation for your API
- Develop Mule applications and run them in Anypoint Studio
- Monitor your applications from Anypoint Platform
- Transform your data using DataWeave
- Use the CI/CD and Mule Maven plugins
- Run tests using MUnit and generate a code coverage report
- Use best practices to maintain coding standards

Salesforce Platform Enterprise Architecture

Andrew Fawcett

ISBN: 978-1-80461-977-3

- Create and deploy packaged apps for your own business or for AppExchange

- Understand Enterprise Application Architecture patterns

- Customize the mobile and desktop user experience with Lightning Web Components

- Manage large data volumes with asynchronous processing and big data strategies

- Learn how to go beyond the Apex language, and utilize Java and Node.js to scale your skills and code with Heroku and Salesforce Functions

- Test and optimize Salesforce Lightning UIs

- Use Connected Apps, External Services, and Objects along with AWS integration tools to access off platform code and data with your application

Packt is searching for authors like you

If you're interested in becoming an author for Packt, please visit `authors.packtpub.com` and apply today. We have worked with thousands of developers and tech professionals, just like you, to help them share their insight with the global tech community. You can make a general application, apply for a specific hot topic that we are recruiting an author for, or submit your own idea.

Share Your Thoughts

Now you've finished *MuleSoft Platform Architect's Guide*, we'd love to hear your thoughts! Scan the QR code below to go straight to the Amazon review page for this book and share your feedback or leave a review on the site that you purchased it from.

`https://packt.link/r/1805126180`

Your review is important to us and the tech community and will help us make sure we're delivering excellent quality content.

Download a free PDF copy of this book

Thanks for purchasing this book!

Do you like to read on the go but are unable to carry your print books everywhere?

Is your eBook purchase not compatible with the device of your choice?

Don't worry, now with every Packt book you get a DRM-free PDF version of that book at no cost.

Read anywhere, any place, on any device. Search, copy, and paste code from your favorite technical books directly into your application.

The perks don't stop there, you can get exclusive access to discounts, newsletters, and great free content in your inbox daily

Follow these simple steps to get the benefits:

1. Scan the QR code or visit the link below

https://packt.link/free-ebook/9781805126188

2. Submit your proof of purchase
3. That's it! We'll send your free PDF and other benefits to your email directly